STROKES *of* GENIUS

THE BEST OF DRAWING LIGHT AND SHADOW

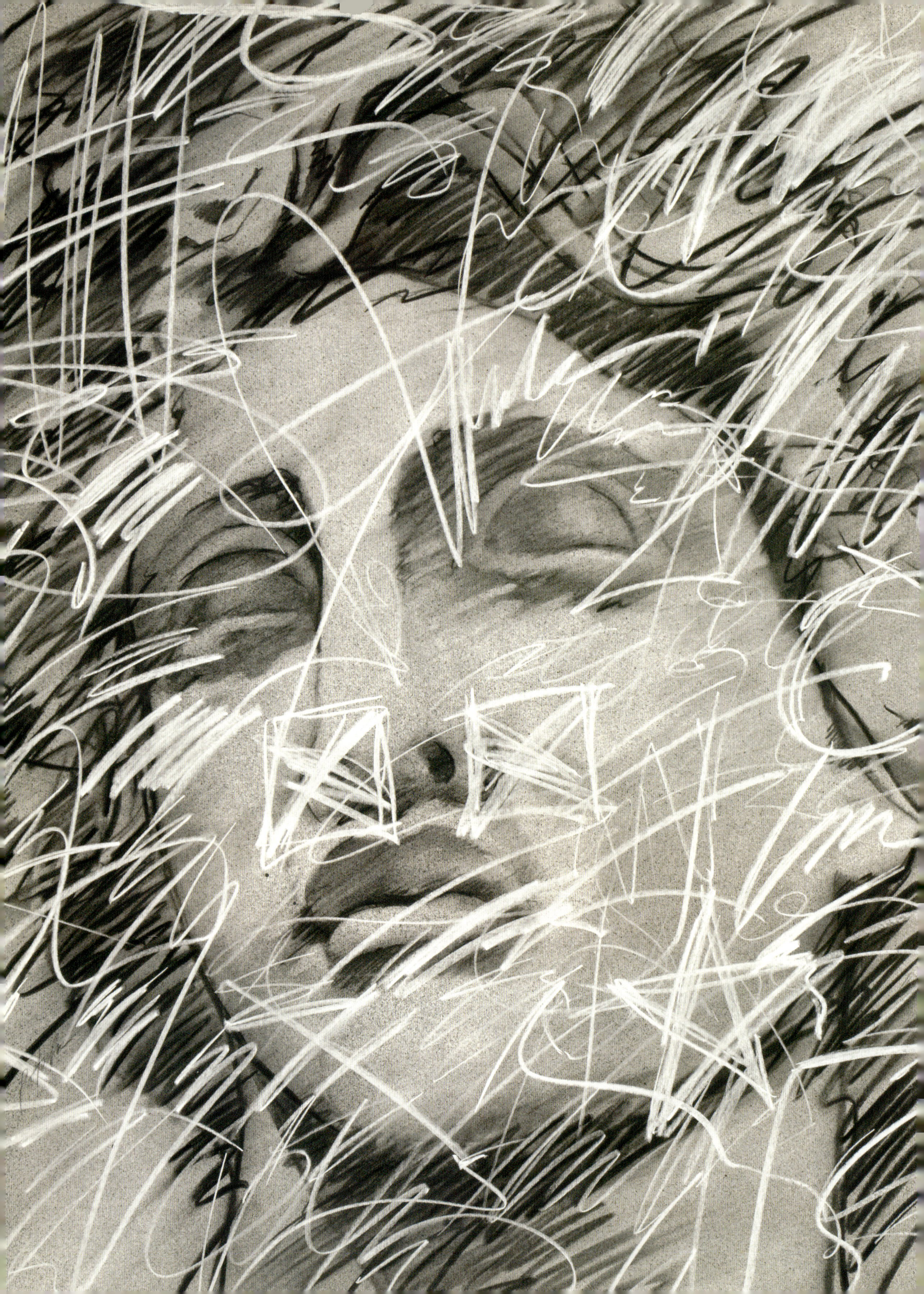

STROKES of GENIUS

2

THE BEST OF DRAWING LIGHT AND SHADOW

Edited by Rachel Rubin Wolf

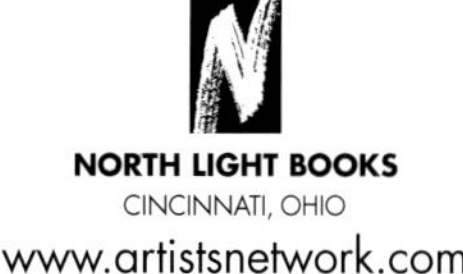

NORTH LIGHT BOOKS
CINCINNATI, OHIO
www.artistsnetwork.com

Strokes of Genius 2: The Best of Drawing Light and Shadow.

Copyright © 2009 by North Light Books. Manufactured in China. All rights reserved. No part of this book may be reproduced in any form or by any electronic or mechanical means including information storage and retrieval systems without permission in writing from the publisher, except by a reviewer who may quote brief passages in a review.

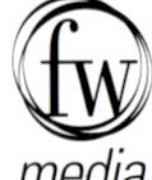 Published by North Light Books, an imprint of F+W Media, Inc., 4700 East Galbraith Road, Cincinnati, Ohio, 45236. (800) 289-0963. First Edition.

Other fine North Light Books are available from your local bookstore, art supply store or visit us at our website www.fwmedia.com.

13   12   11   10   09   5   4   3   2   1

DISTRIBUTED IN CANADA BY FRASER DIRECT
100 Armstrong Avenue
Georgetown, ON, Canada L7G 5S4
Tel: (905) 877-4411

DISTRIBUTED IN THE U.K. AND EUROPE BY DAVID & CHARLES
Brunel House, Newton Abbot, Devon, TQ12 4PU, England
Tel: (+44) 1626 323200, Fax: (+44) 1626 323319
Email: postmaster@davidandcharles.co.uk

DISTRIBUTED IN AUSTRALIA BY CAPRICORN LINK
P.O. Box 704, S. Windsor NSW, 2756 Australia
Tel: (02) 4577-3555

Library of Congress Cataloging-in-Publication Data

Strokes of genius 2 : the best of drawing : light and shadow / edited by Rachel Rubin Wolf. -- 1st ed.
p. cm.
Includes bibliographical references and index.
ISBN-13: 978-1-60061-158-2 (hardcover w/ jacket : alk. paper)
ISBN-10: 1-60061-158-3 (hardcover w/ jacket : alk. paper)
1. Drawing--20th century--Themes, motives. 2. Drawing--21st century--Themes, motives. I. Rubin Wolf, Rachel. II. Title: Strokes of genius two. III. Title: Best of drawing. IV. Title: Light and shadow.
NC95.S772 2009
741.9'243--dc22   2009009464

Edited by **Erika O'Connell** and **Jennifer Lepore Brune**
Designed by **Doug Mayfield**
Production coordinated by **Matthew Wagner**

Art on opposite page:
Bonnie · Donna Krizek · Charcoal on laid paper · 14" × 11" (36cm × 28cm)

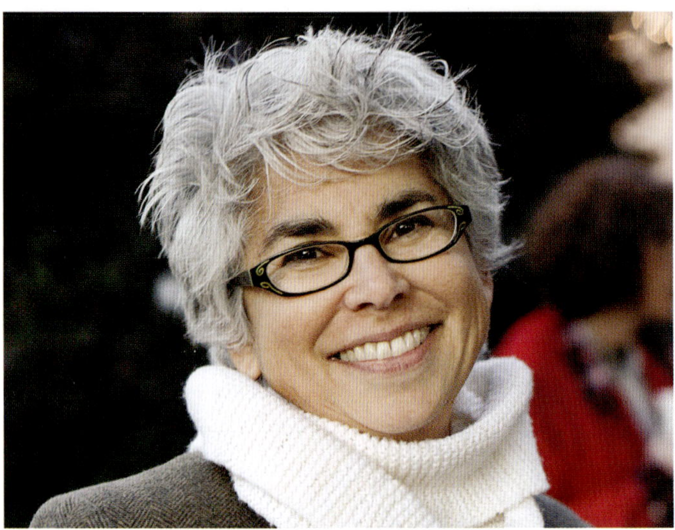

Photo by Don Lambert

About the Editor

Rachel Rubin Wolf is a freelance editor and artist. She edits and writes fine art books for North Light Books, including *Watercolor Secrets*, the *Splash* series (Best of Watercolor); *The Best of Wildlife Art* (editions 1 and 2); *The Best of Portrait Painting*; *The Best of Flower Painting 2*; *The Acrylic Painter's Book of Styles and Techniques*; *Painting Ships, Shores and the Sea*; and *Painting the Many Moods of Light*. She also has acquired numerous new fine art book projects and authors for North Light Books and has contributed to magazines such as *Fine Art Connoisseur* and *Wildlife Art*.

Acknowledgments

Thanks must always go to the editors, designers and staff at North Light Books who have made this into the beautiful final product it is, including Pamela Wissman, Vanessa Lyman, Erika O'Connell, Doug Mayfield and Matthew Wagner. A special thanks to editor Jennifer Lepore Brune, a longtime colleague and friend, back after doing a terrific job at North Light Book Club—it has been my pleasure to work with you again.

The biggest thanks of all belongs to the contributing artists. As always, it was near-impossible to narrow the selections down to those that would fit in a book this size. Thank you all for being so generous and attentive to detail, tackling the discomfort of new technology, as we all try to learn the ins and outs of digital photography. Mostly, thank you for sharing artwork that so obviously comes from your heart.

Metric Conversion Chart		
To convert	to	multiply by
Inches	Centimeters	2.54
Centimeters	Inches	0.4
Feet	Centimeters	30.5
Centimeters	Feet	0.03
Yards	Meters	0.9
Meters	Yards	1.1

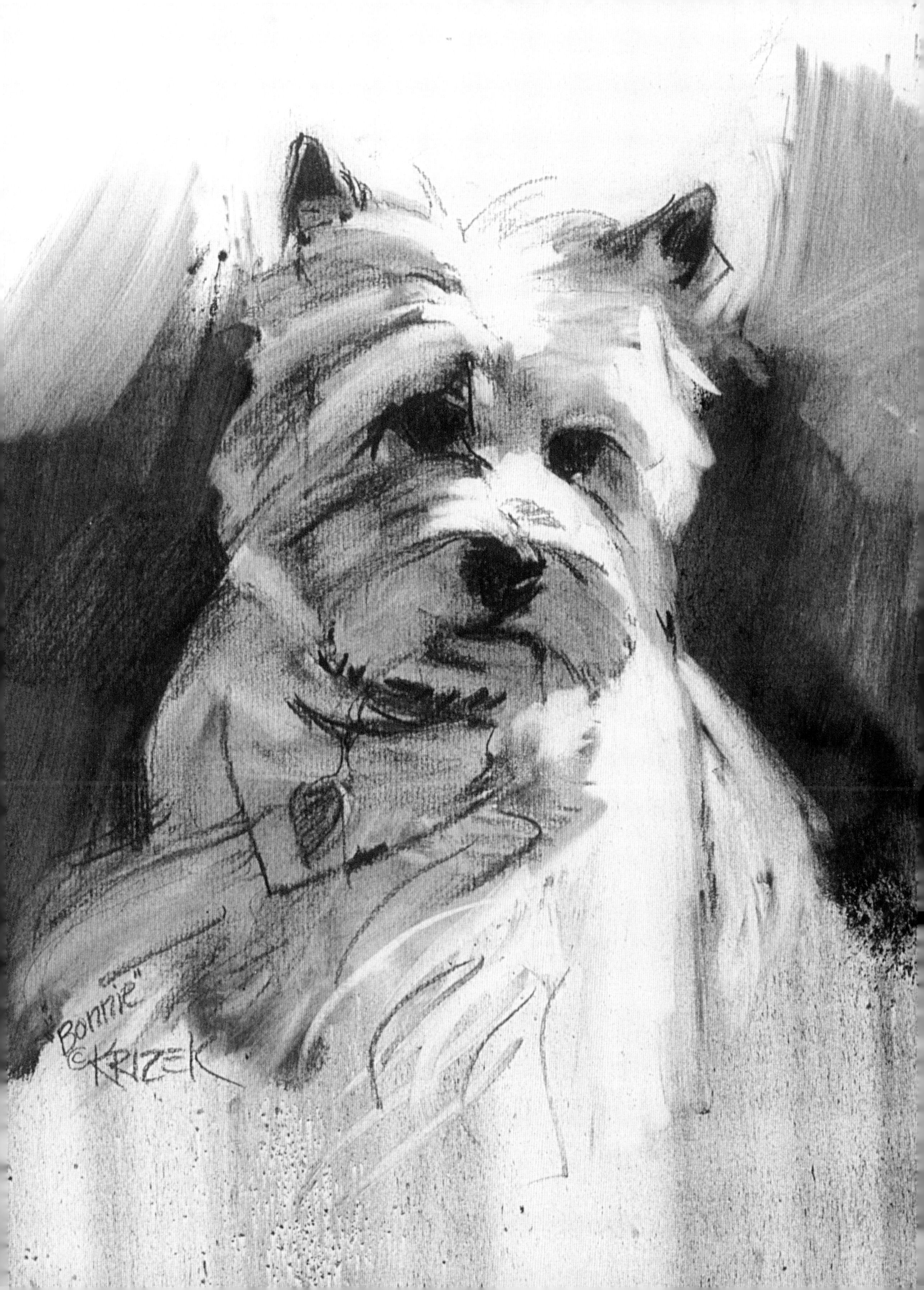

"Bonnie"
©KRIZEK

TABLE OF CONTENTS

INTRODUCTION

I am thrilled that you, our readers, voted a resounding YES for *Strokes of Genius*, the first volume in this series. Because of that, I now get to offer you volume two! I have always been drawn to the direct nature of drawing and greatly appreciate the range of nuance one can achieve in black and white, though there are also a number of creative color drawings here too. This book takes us a bit out of the box for North Light, showcasing a few styles and subjects not often seen in North Light books.

But that is as it should be. The great thing about drawing is that it gives you the freedom to experiment, to test, even to play. Hey, it's only a drawing. Have fun. Express yourself. Don't worry about the results. But that's the great paradox of life. As soon as we let go our "inner judge," we can go further and achieve more. So we have here a collection of masterful drawings in almost any medium, or combination thereof, you could think of, each one unique to the artist who created it.

We subtitled this volume "The Best of Drawing Light and Shadow," and we meant this in a very straightforward way. However, after living with these stunning works of art for many months, the subtitle has come to take on a more dynamic, personal meaning. Many of these works express the light and shadow of the human soul—the seasons that we all pass through on this journey we call life.

From Janvier Rollande's very tender portrait of her mother on her deathbed, to Marina Dieul's caring drawing of a sleeping toddler, to Steve Mihal's introspective self-portrait, to Elizabeth Patterson's almost ironic views of rainy streets through her windshield, to Donna Levinstone's romantic vision of clouds and water at sunset, to name just a few among many, these drawings represent tiny glimpses into the soul of the artist, and even into the human drama.

I selected the pieces in this book because they each had a voice—each had something individual to say to me. Because I want to let the drawings speak, I have limited my words here. I have enjoyed the process of putting these works together into this book. I hope you find that they each speak to you also.

Rachel Rubin Wolf

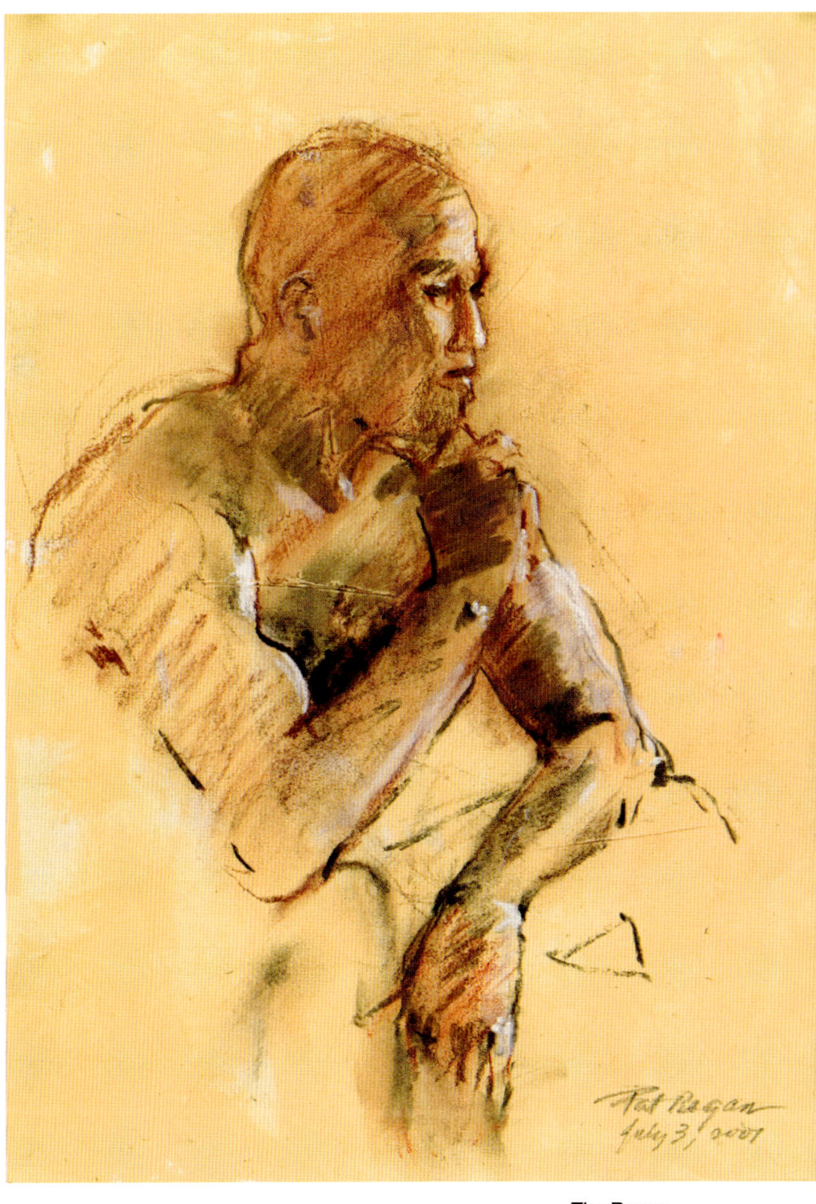

The Boxer
Pat Regan · Conté on toned paper · 11" × 9" (28cm × 22cm)

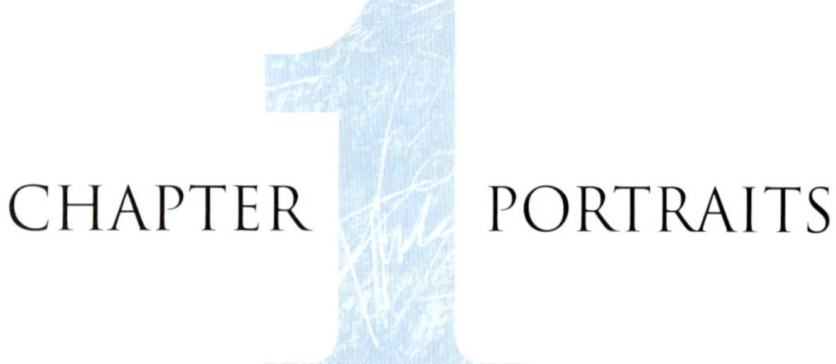

CHAPTER 1 PORTRAITS

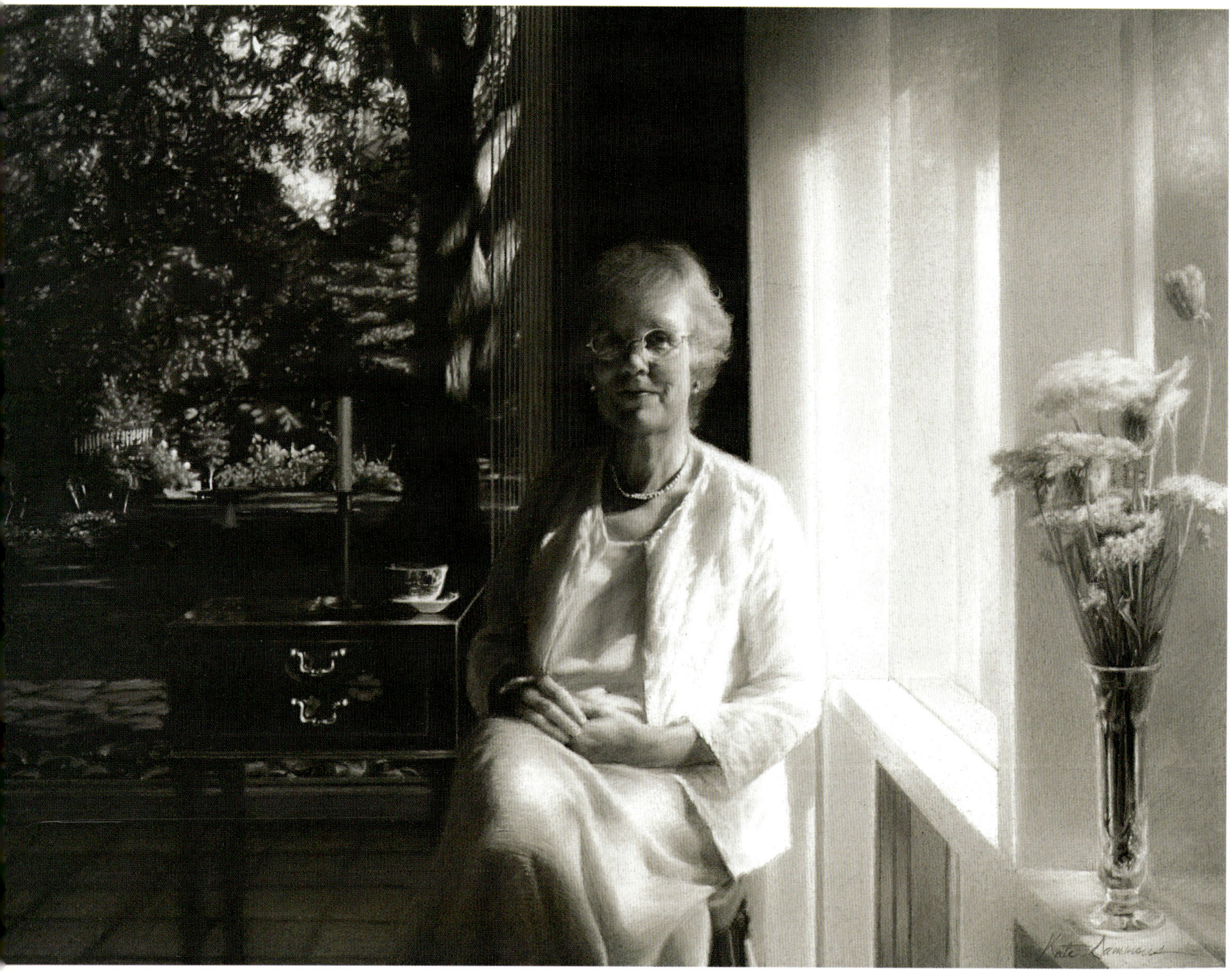

My Mother
Kate Sammons · Black and white charcoal on blue-toned paper · 14" × 18" (36cm × 46cm)

EXPRESS INTERACTION WITH YOUR SUBJECT

These works were both created in my studio over a period of weeks. For finished portraits, I let my interaction with the person solidify my psychological and emotional impressions, as well as use sketches and photos. When drawing from a photo or sketch, I get my best results if I have a fantastic reference to start with, observe it as I would a life reference and thoroughly understand the forms I am drawing. To help keep my decisions organized, I do the line drawing, value block-in and texture in separate stages.

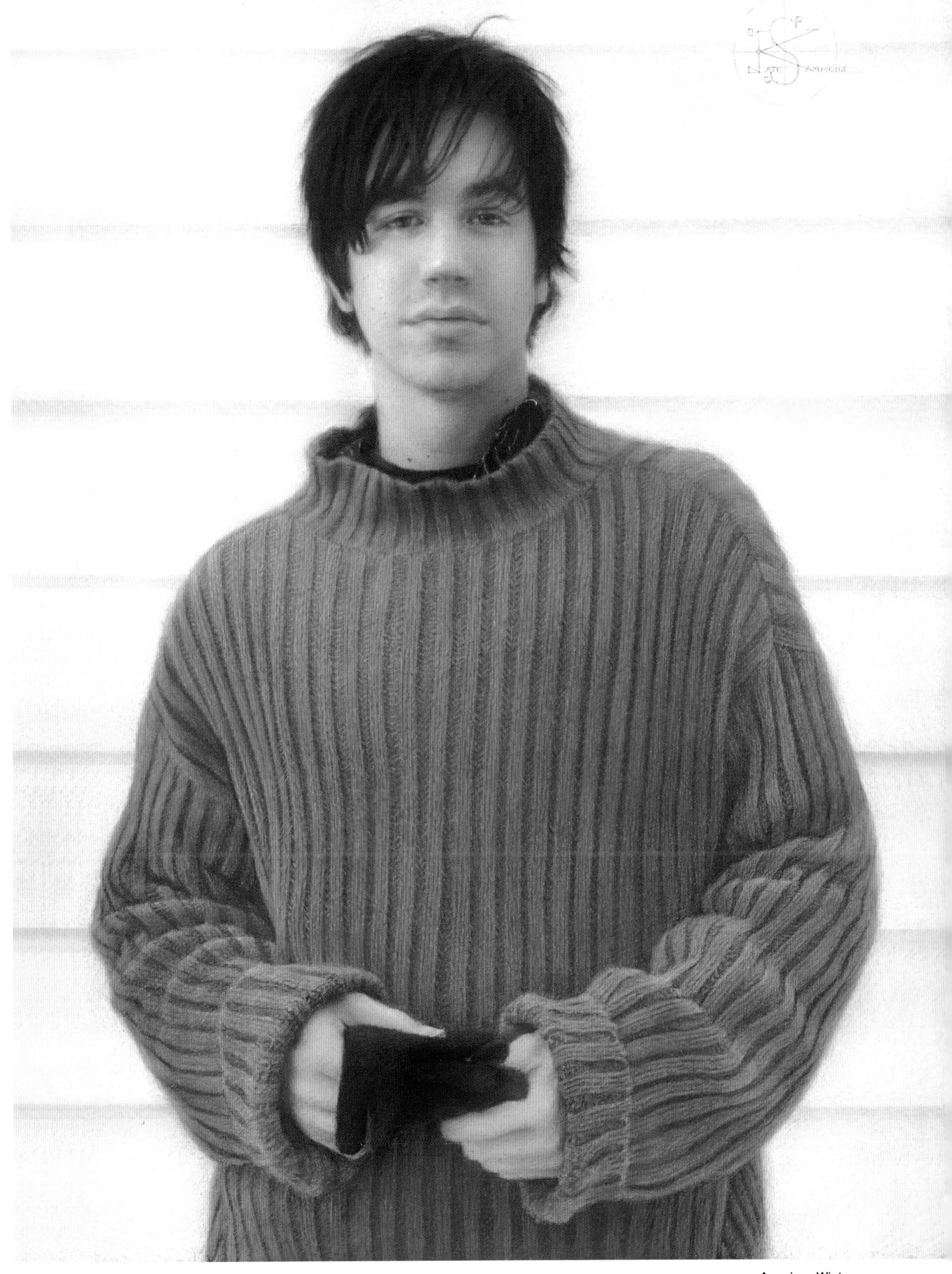

American Winter
Kate Sammons · Black and white charcoal on blue-toned paper · 25" × 20" (64cm × 51cm)

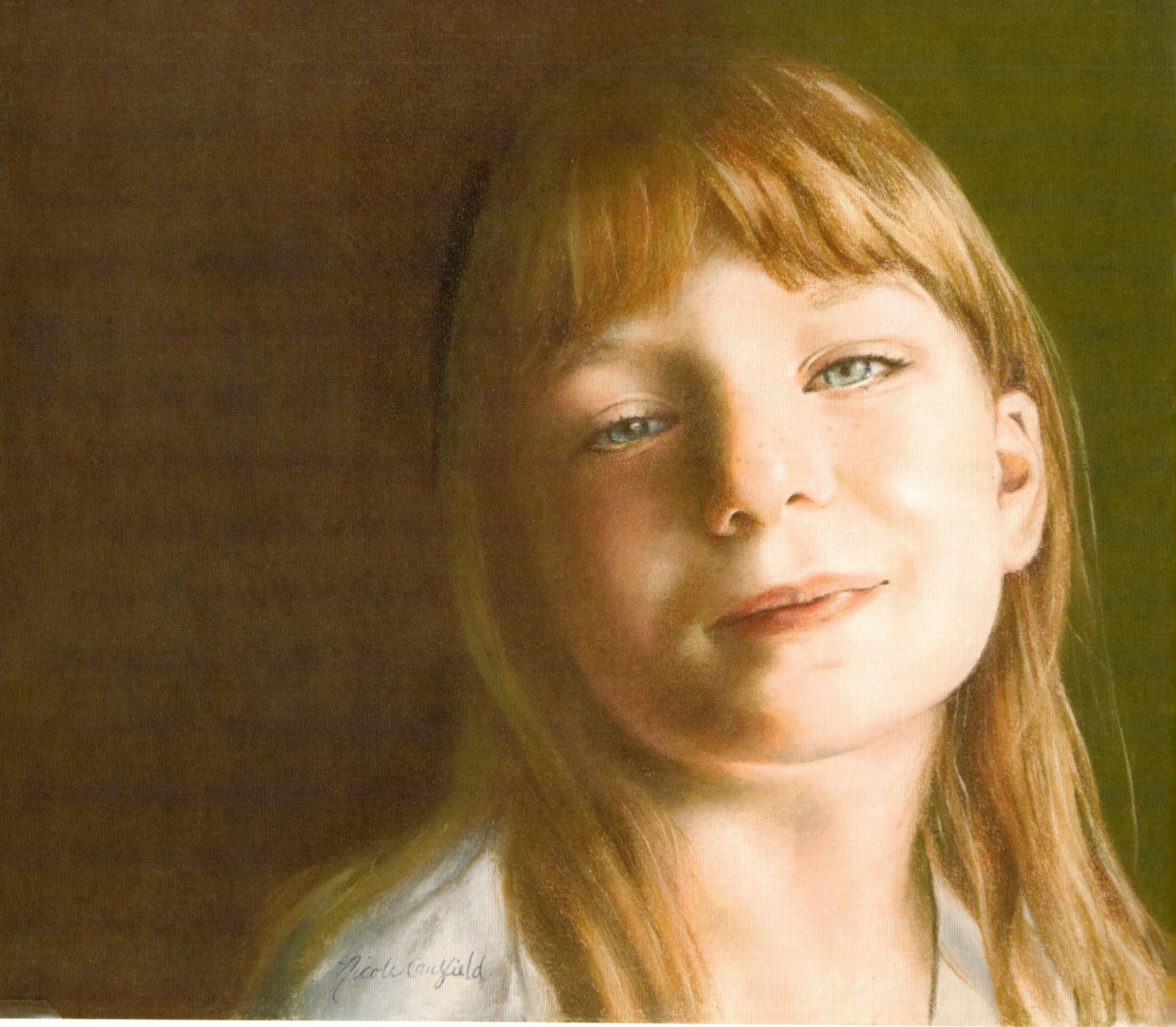

Katie: Defiance
Nicole Caulfield · Colored pencil on sanded pastel paper · 12" × 14" (30cm × 36cm)

ALLOW YOUR SUBJECT TO RELAX INTO THE POSE

This portrait was done with Faber-Castell Polychromos pencils on Fisher 400 paper, a sanded pastel paper, not unlike sandpaper. The sanded paper allows the pencil to go on thicker and brighter with fewer layers, and makes it possible to add light colors over dark. To me, the most important things in a portrait are lighting and a relaxed pose. In *Defiance,* I allowed the natural light from a window to light the subject, making sure the light lit up both eyes. I then made some color swatches from life to assure correct skin tone and eye color, and took literally hundreds of reference photos. I find that posing the sitter initially, and then allowing her to relax into a more natural position, achieves the best pose.

LIGHT AND SHADOW or "values" and "tones"
form the backbone of any good art.
PAY ATTENTION TO VALUES
and worry less about getting exactly the right color.

-Nicole Caulfield

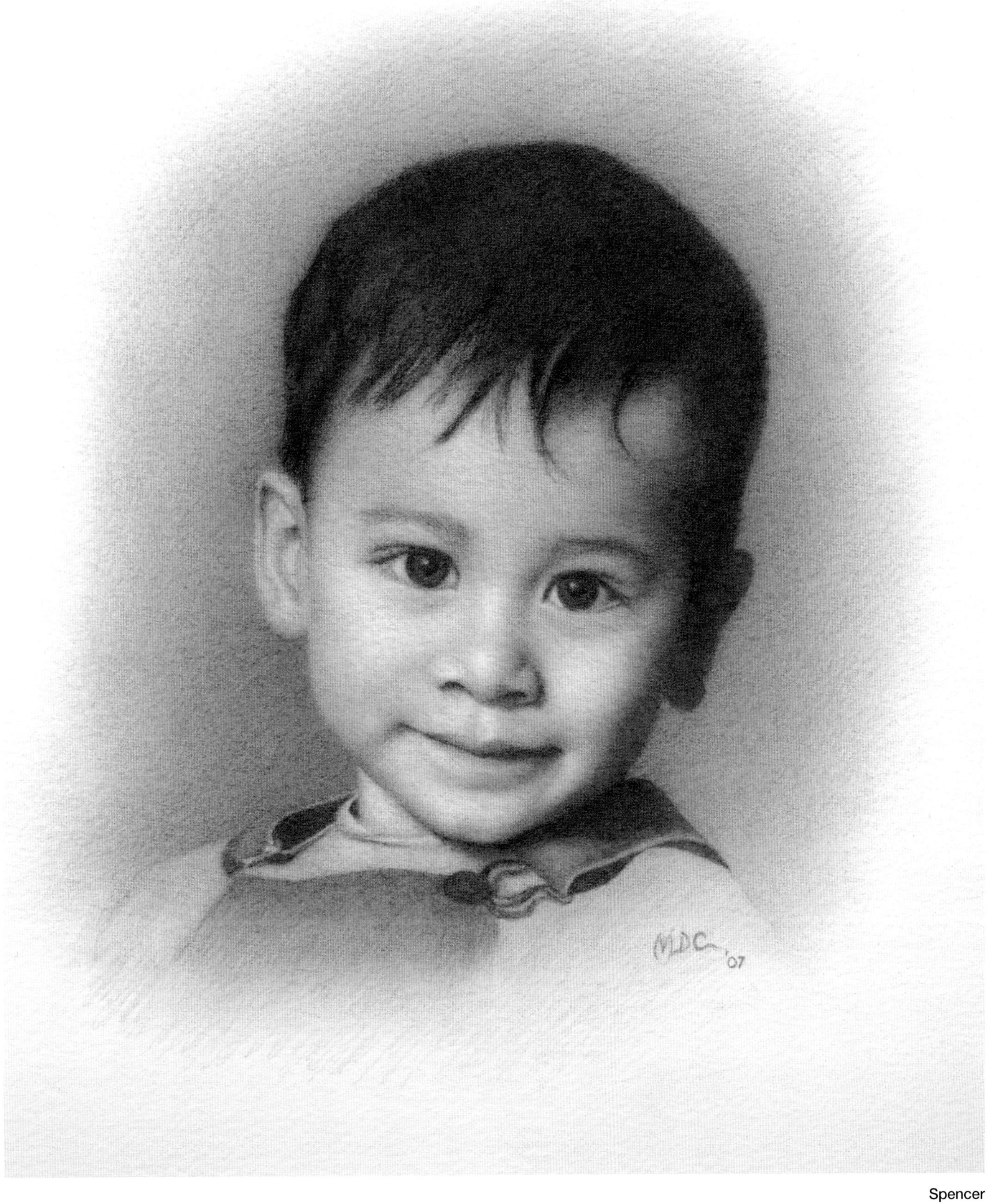

Spencer
Mina dela Cruz · Graphite on paper · 6½" × 4½" (17cm × 11cm)

START WITH A GESTURE DRAWING FROM A PHOTO

It is almost impossible to create a detailed drawing of children from life, so I use photographs. However, a portrait drawn from a photograph can look flat and lifeless. To avoid this, I use three main steps. First, create a gesture drawing: block in the major shapes of the head to ensure correct proportion and alignment. Second, accurately draw and evenly shade the shadow shapes. This improves the accuracy and helps establish likeness. The last step is using gradated tonal values to turn the form. Using halftones that go from dark to light creates the small shapes that establish the unique character of the individual.

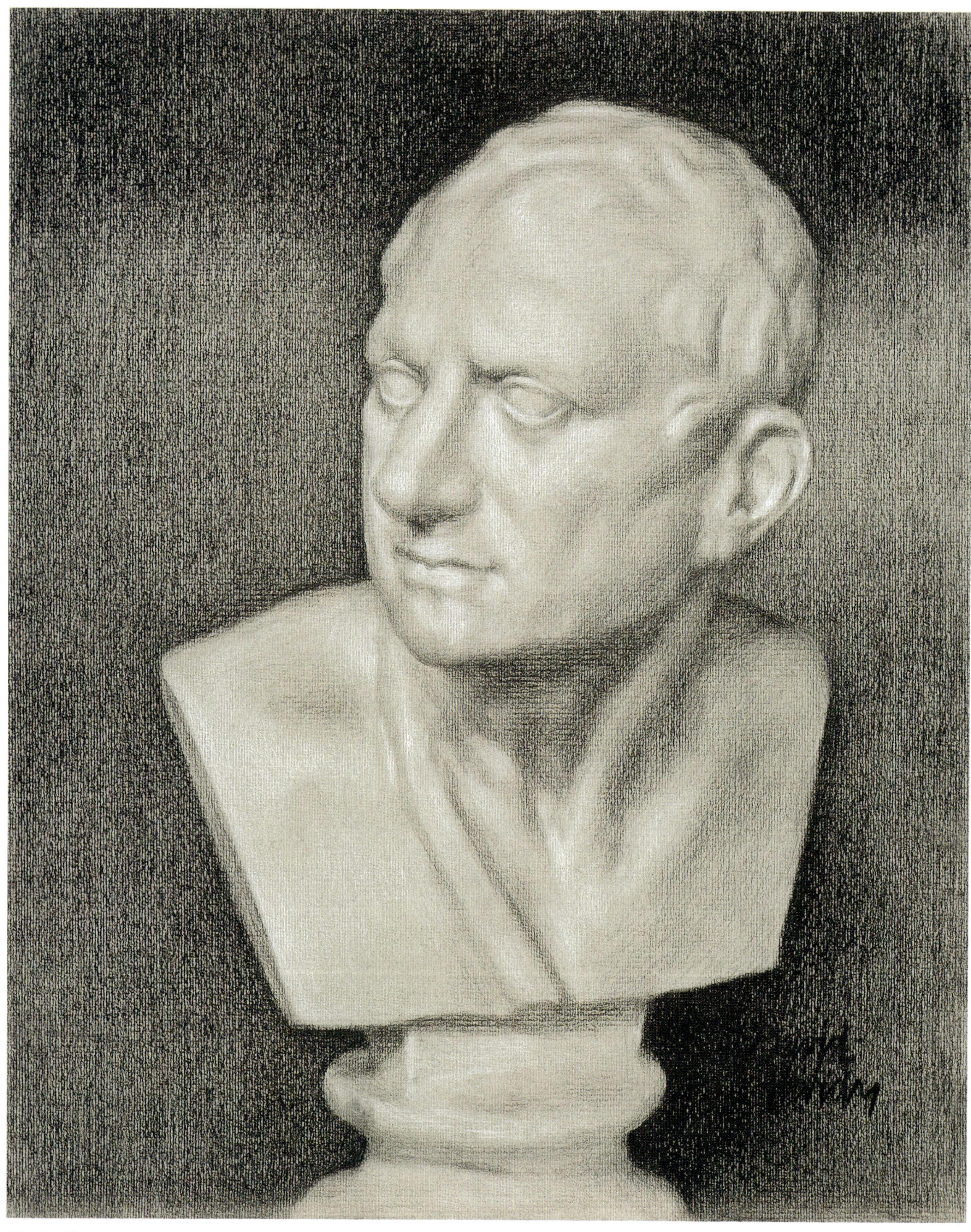

Classical Bust
David Hardy · Chalk and charcoal on toned paper · 16" × 13" (41cm × 33cm)

CLASSICAL TECHNIQUE CAN EXPRESS PERSONALITY

Classical Bust (above) and *Head of Arturo* (opposite, top) were constructed in four main steps. First, I do a simple line lay-in. I then develop tone with three values—understated light, middle and understated dark—leaving the paper for the middle value. Next, I strengthen subdivisions of both the light and shadow patterns into stronger contrast, taking care to evolve appropriate edges. Last, dynamic accents bring the drawings into finish. *Classical Bust* was refined into a more painterly feeling, while in *Head of Arturo,* drawing elements dominate. But beyond the technical, my goal in each was to develop a sense of individual personality.

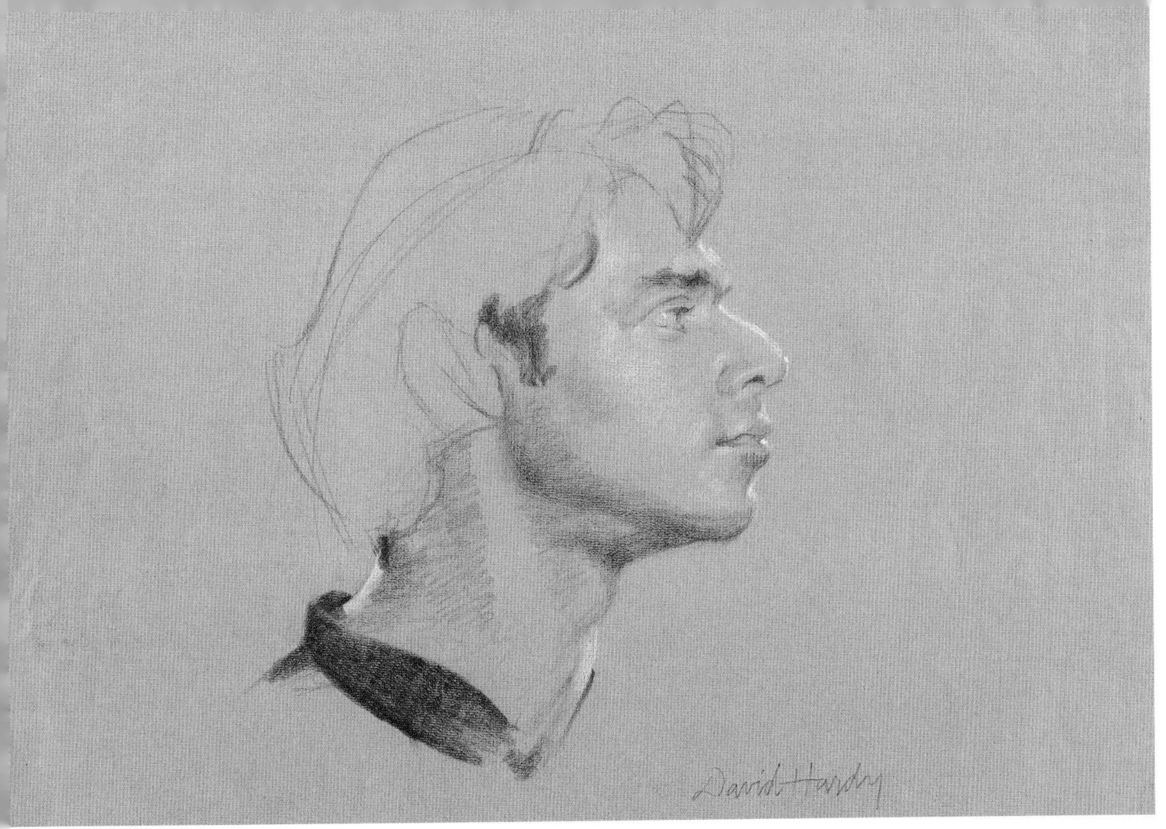

Head of Arturo
David Hardy · Chalk and charcoal on toned paper · 19" × 25" (48cm × 64cm)

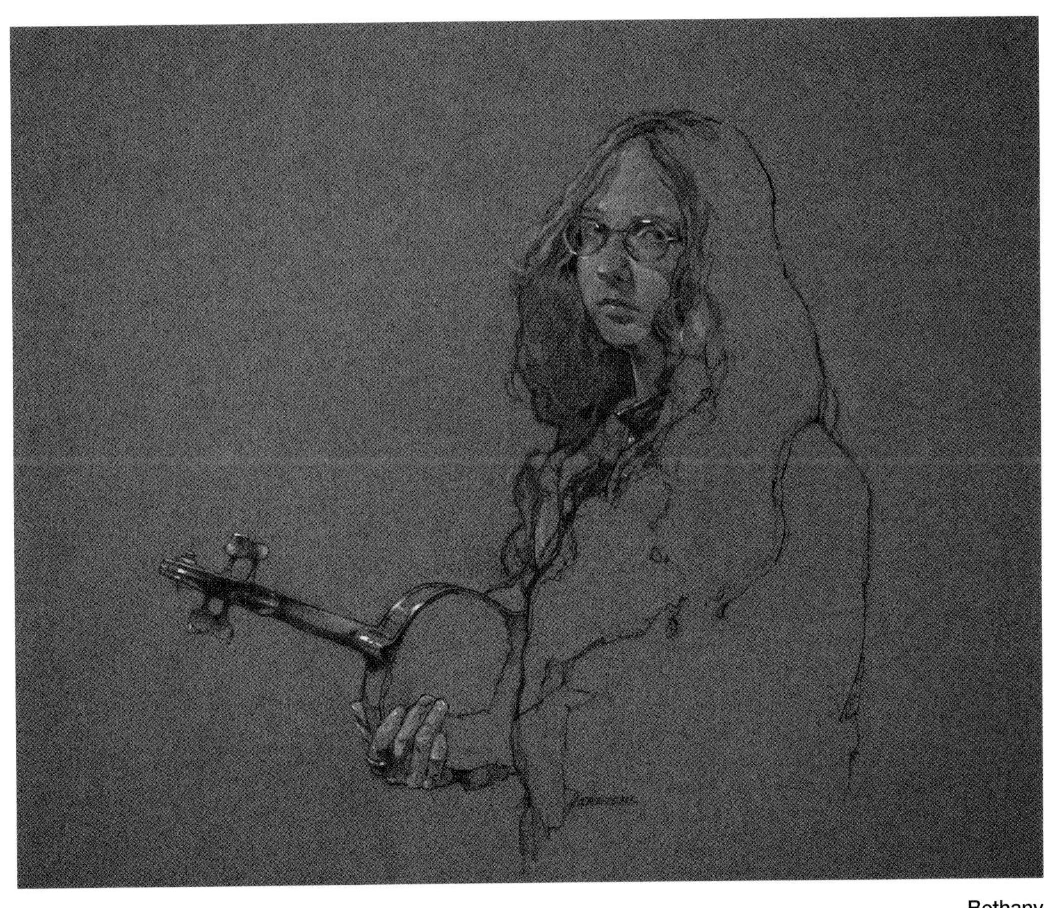

Bethany
Dennis Albetski · Charcoal, white pencil and gouache · 12" × 15" (30cm × 38cm)

FOCUS ON EXPRESSIVE AREAS

In this portrait, I tried to restrict the focus to the most expressive areas of the body—the face and hands—leaving the remaining areas as simple lines. Capturing a glimpse of that off-hand look from my favorite model, my daughter, was an important part of this drawing. Keeping the light areas soft and unobtrusive made it very rewarding.

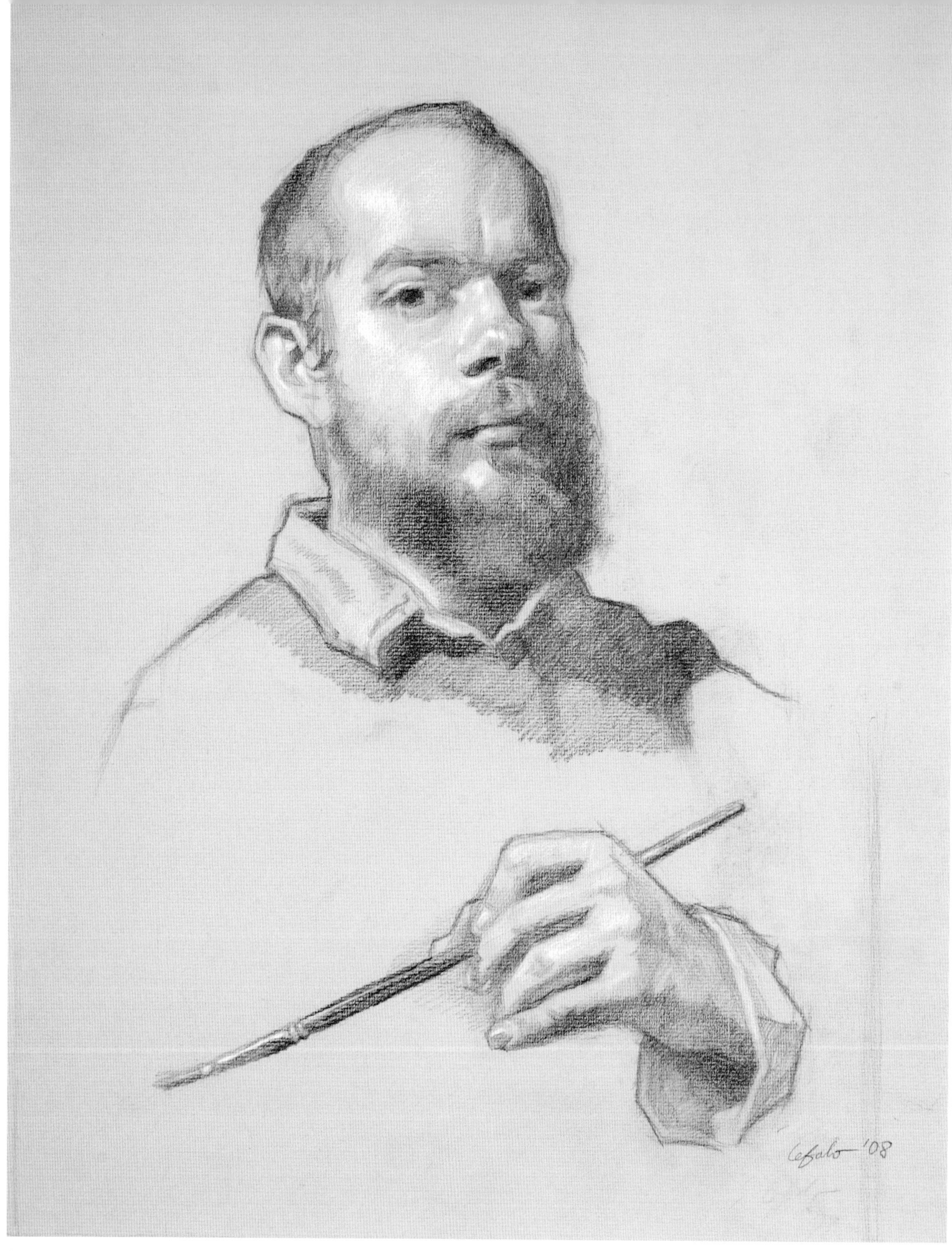

Self-Portrait With Paintbrush
Stephen Cefalo · Graphite and chalk on paper · 15½" × 11½" (39cm × 29cm)

CREATIVE CHALLENGES OF DRAWING FROM A MIRROR

A drawing comes to life by translating a living experience to paper. This drawing, from direct observation, is a study for a painting. After an initial composition sketch in charcoal, I completed the drawing in pencil to work out details in the head and hands. To achieve my desired composition, I had to place the easel in an awkward position and frequently turn my head from the mirror to the paper. I was forced to make each observation and then place it down from memory. For instance, to portray my right hand (appearing as the left hand in the mirror-image), instead of attempting to draw it with my left hand, I held the brush in the mirror, observing one angle relationship at a time, then placed it down from memory. I kept the shadows simple and pulled highlights out of the toned paper with white chalk.

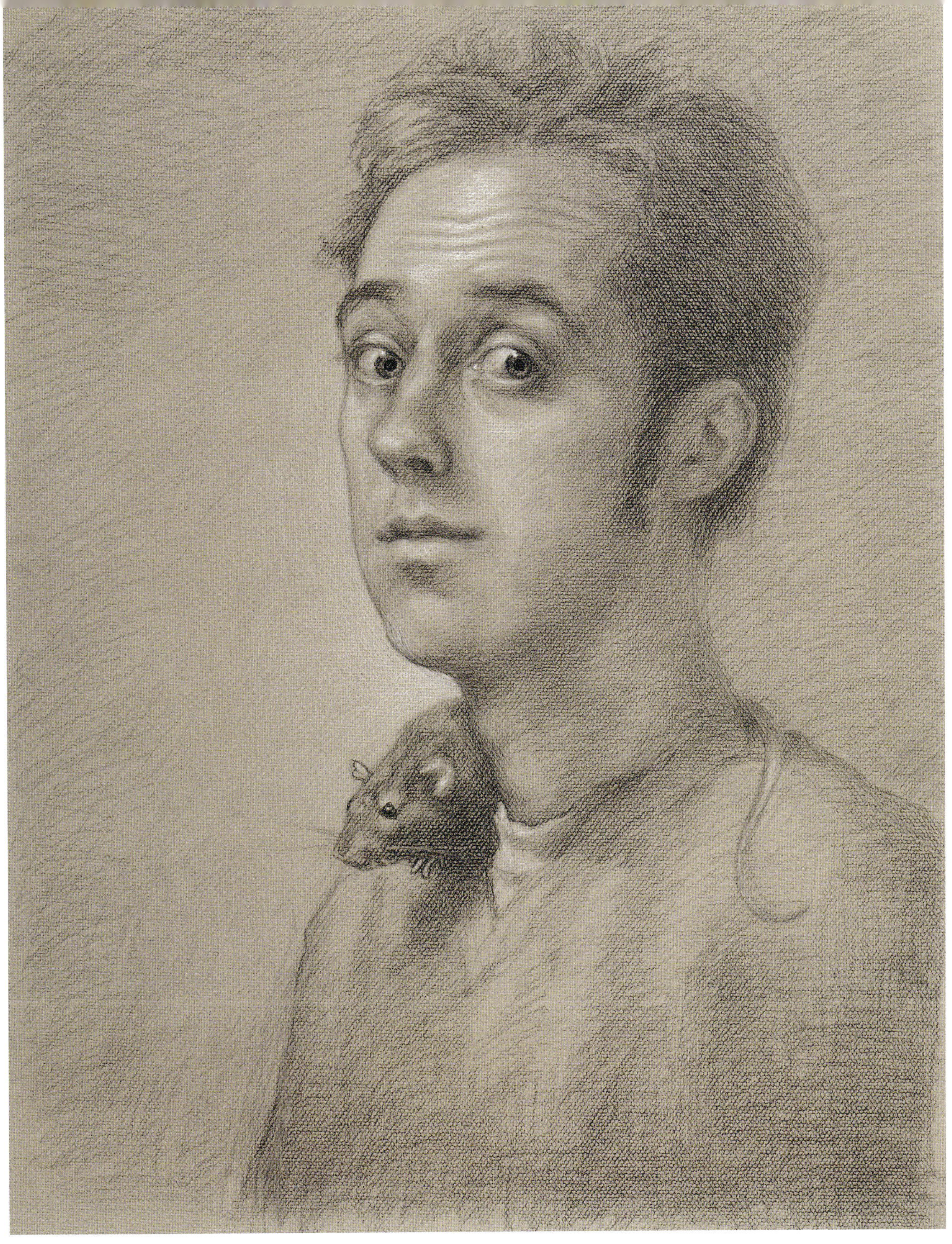

Preliminary Drawing for Self-Portrait With Django
Devin Cecil-Wishing · Charcoal and chalk on toned paper · 25½" × 19½" (65cm × 50cm)

GET ABSORBED IN THE DRAWING PROCESS

I did this drawing in the studio as a preliminary study before doing a painting of the same subject. Django was my pet rat who often rode around the house perched on my shoulder. I've always enjoyed drawing and painting animals, so I set up a mirror on a spare easel one day and sat down to do a portrait of the two of us together. I actually had intended to keep this drawing quick and just get the basic shapes down to guide me once I started the painting, but after I got started, I sort of got absorbed in it and just kept going.

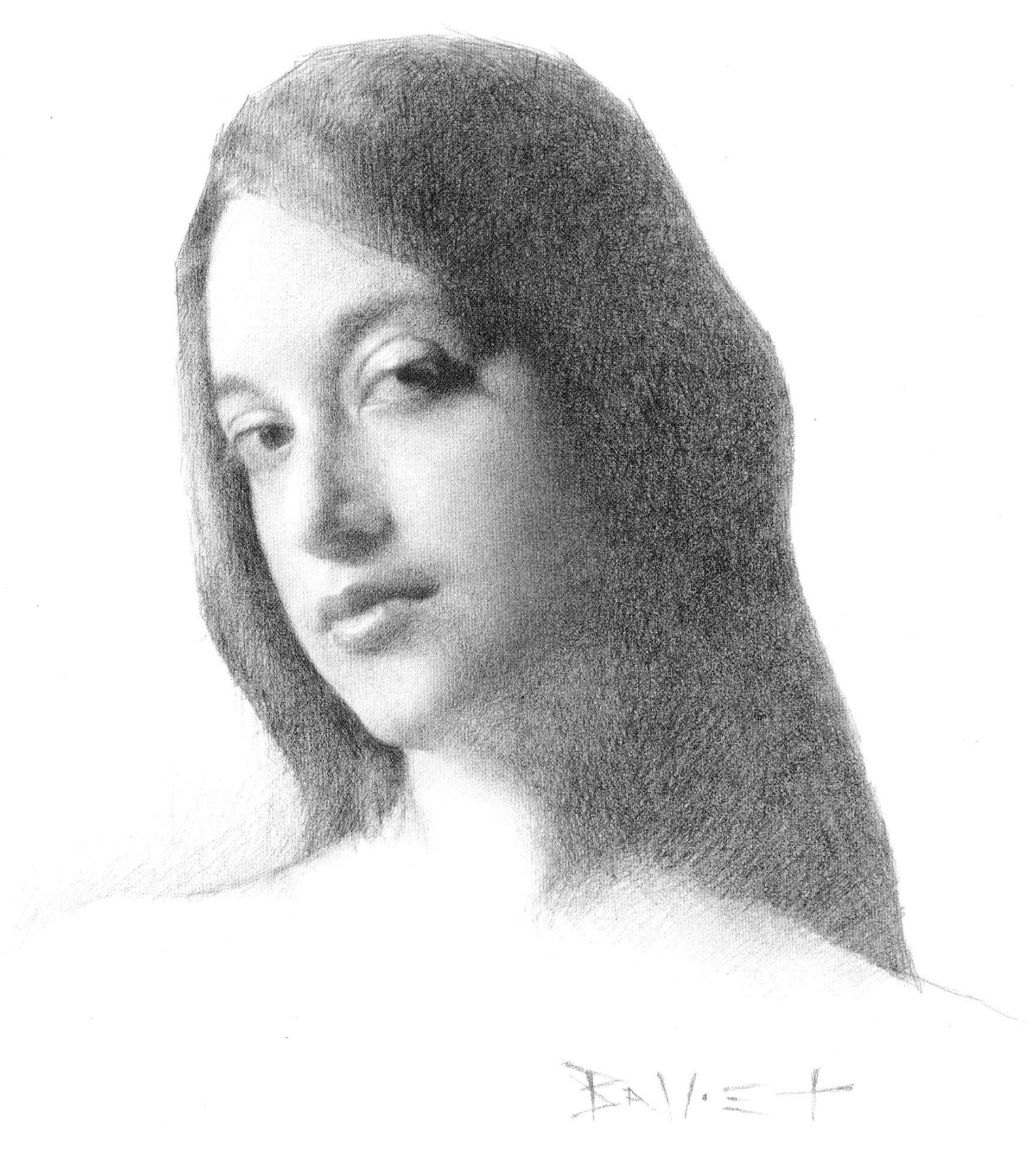

Paulina
Justin Balliet · Graphite on paper · 8" × 10" (20cm × 25cm)

SIMPLE TOOLS SUFFICE

Paulina was part of a series of graphite sketches done from my collection of portrait and figure references. Not having nearly enough time to render all of them, I started sketching them in graphite, spending roughly six hours on each. My only tools were a mechanical graphite pencil and a kneaded eraser. I began with a light contour drawing, separating the large shadow patterns from the light. I then worked on each feature of the face separately, slowly building up the values, working from dark to light. I then looked for areas that I could accent, or soften to enhance the form. My final step was to pull out a few small highlights with my kneaded eraser.

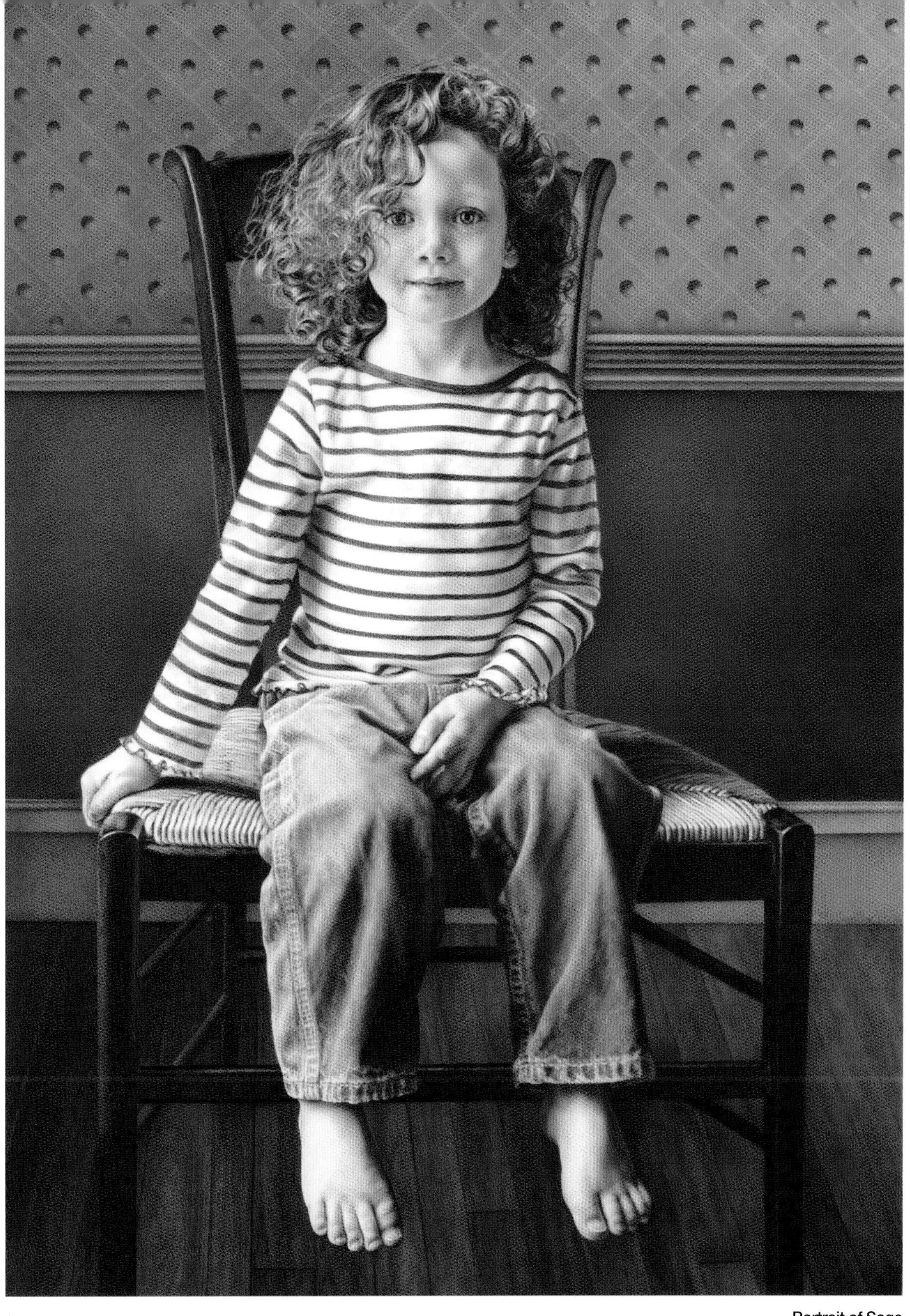

Portrait of Sage
Janvier Rollande · Graphite on paper · 17¼" × 12¼" (44cm × 31cm)

CAREFUL LAYERING LETS THE LIGHT BREATHE THROUGH

My drawings are tonal works that take about a year to complete. For this reason, I work primarily from photographs, which I take myself. I work with a very sharp HB lead and create tones by grouping and layering one-directional diagonal lines; the more layers, the darker the tone. I never press deep into the paper, nor do I smudge to create tone. By carefully layering the graphite, the light of the paper is able to breathe through, keeping a feeling of freshness and life in the work. It's a tedious process, but the soft and airy result is worth it.

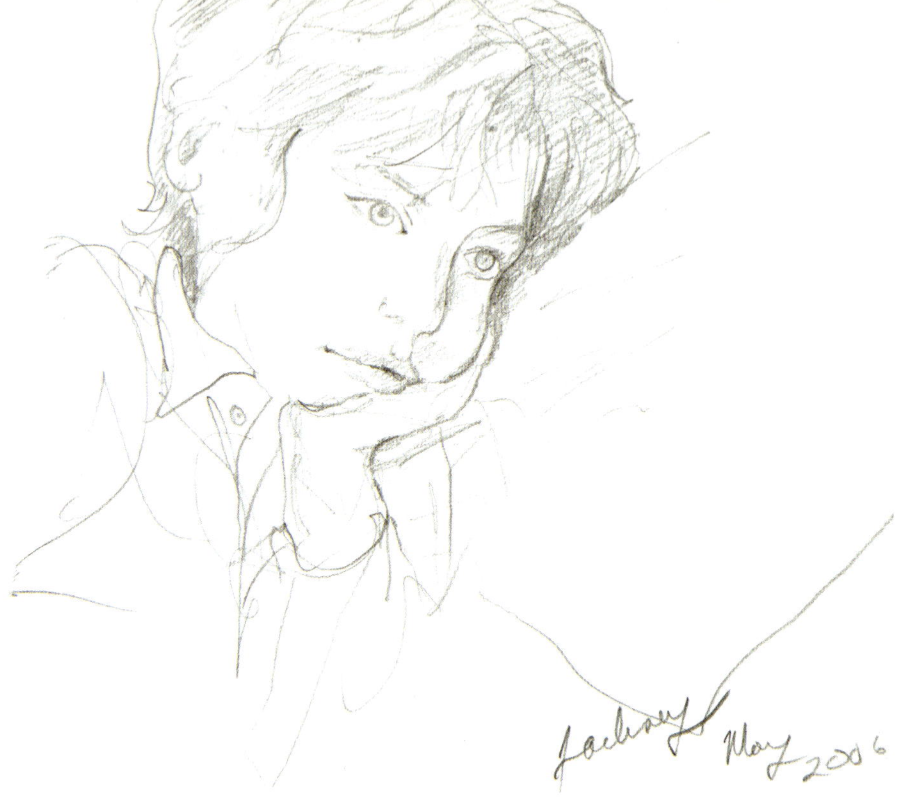

Jack
Susan Muranty · Graphite pencil on paper · 5" × 6" (13cm × 15cm)

Catch a Moment With Fast Contours

Using rapidly flowing contours to capture the inner light of a character is a favorite way of sketching the moment. As seven-year-old Jack lay on the sofa watching a much-loved Harry Potter movie, I worked quick and loose with a 4B pencil, barely looking at the paper, to frame the lightness of his clear eyes, fresh cheeks and tousled hair. Leaving white spaces to suggest skin tone, hair and eye color, I was able to say more about Jack's relaxed inner radiance than any amount of detailed pencil work could have in the same brief ten minutes.

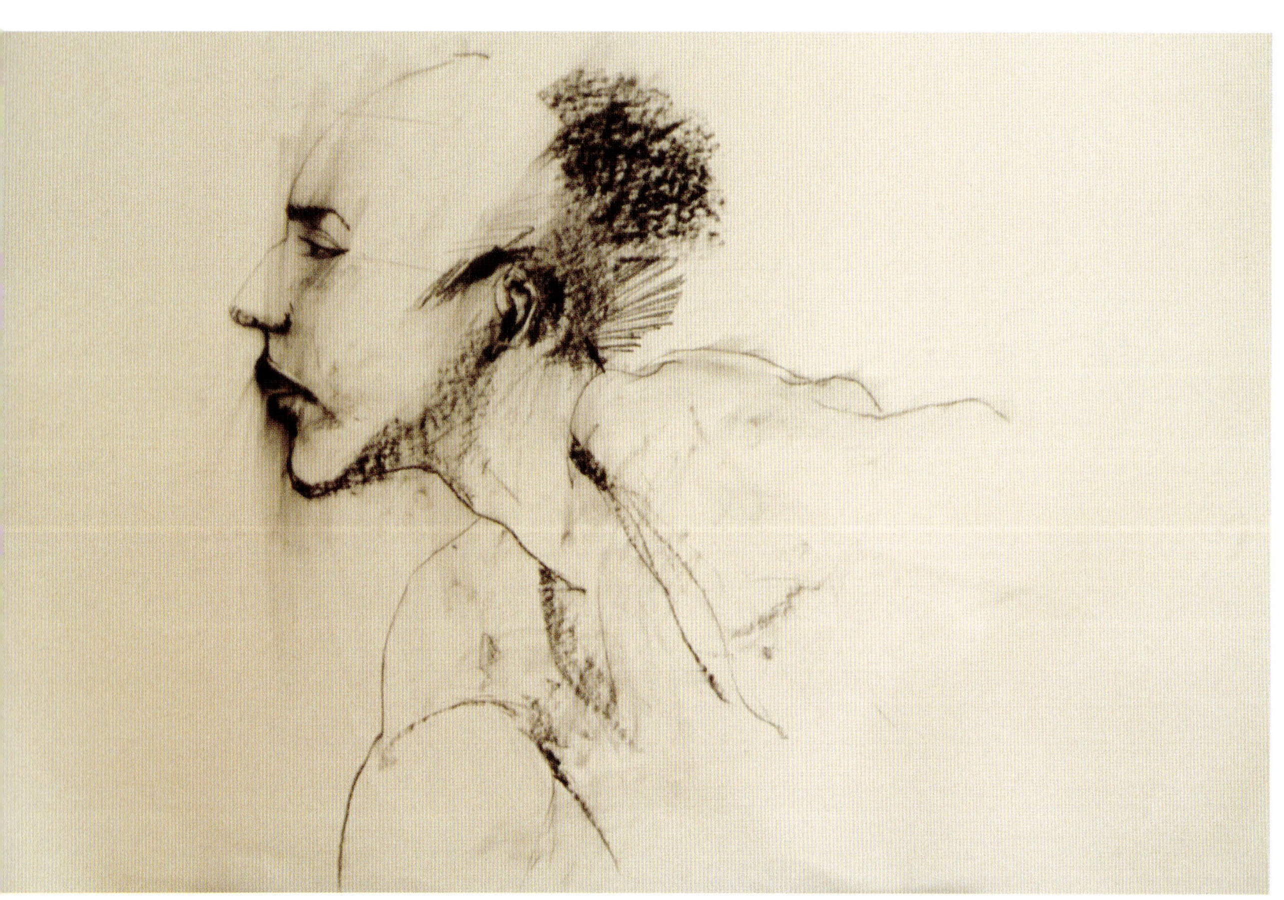

Cirque
Donald Sayers · Compressed chalk on paper · 18" × 24" (46cm × 61cm)

Recognize an Interesting Subject

This live studio model was Haitian. The drawing is predominately contour, using chalk and thumb and side-of-hand smudging. The model's high forehead and head thrust made for an intriguing profile rendering. I work on slick surface paper or synthetics such as Yupo.

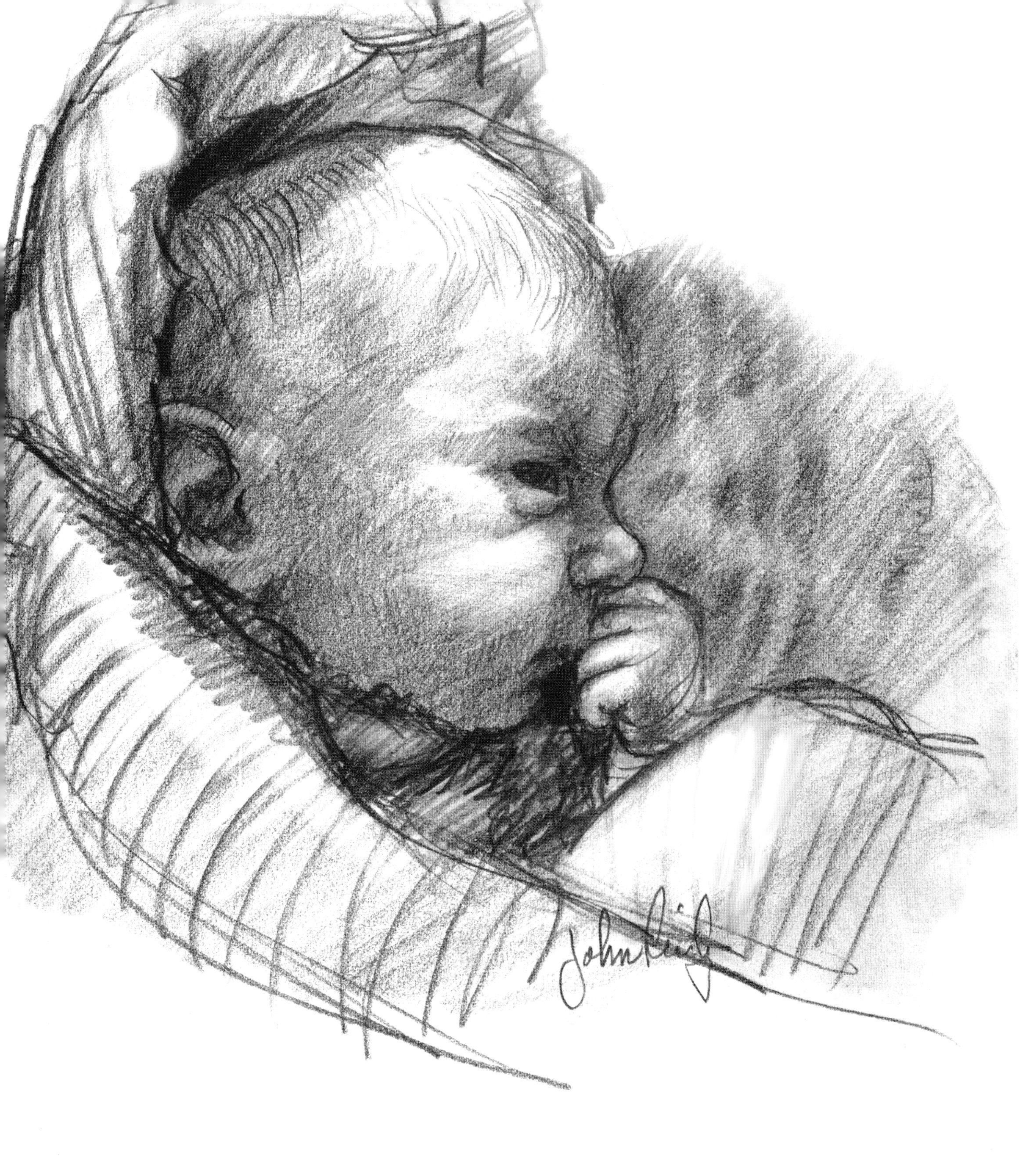

Karen
John Reidy · Graphite pencil on paper · 9½" × 8⅞" (24cm × 22cm)

ASK YOURSELF, "WHAT IS IT DOING?"

This is a sketch of my newborn daughter, Karen. She had been home only a few days when I drew this from life. Using a Sanford Design Ebony jet black extra smooth pencil, I started with a quick gesture, plotting the main features and keeping in mind the question, "What is it doing?"—what is closer, how does this compare to the rest of the subject, etc. After the overall shapes are established, I lay in values very quickly, progressing from larger shapes to smaller. I worked quickly and used every part of my pencil—the point and the side—as well as a kneaded eraser when necessary. This sketch took about ten minutes.

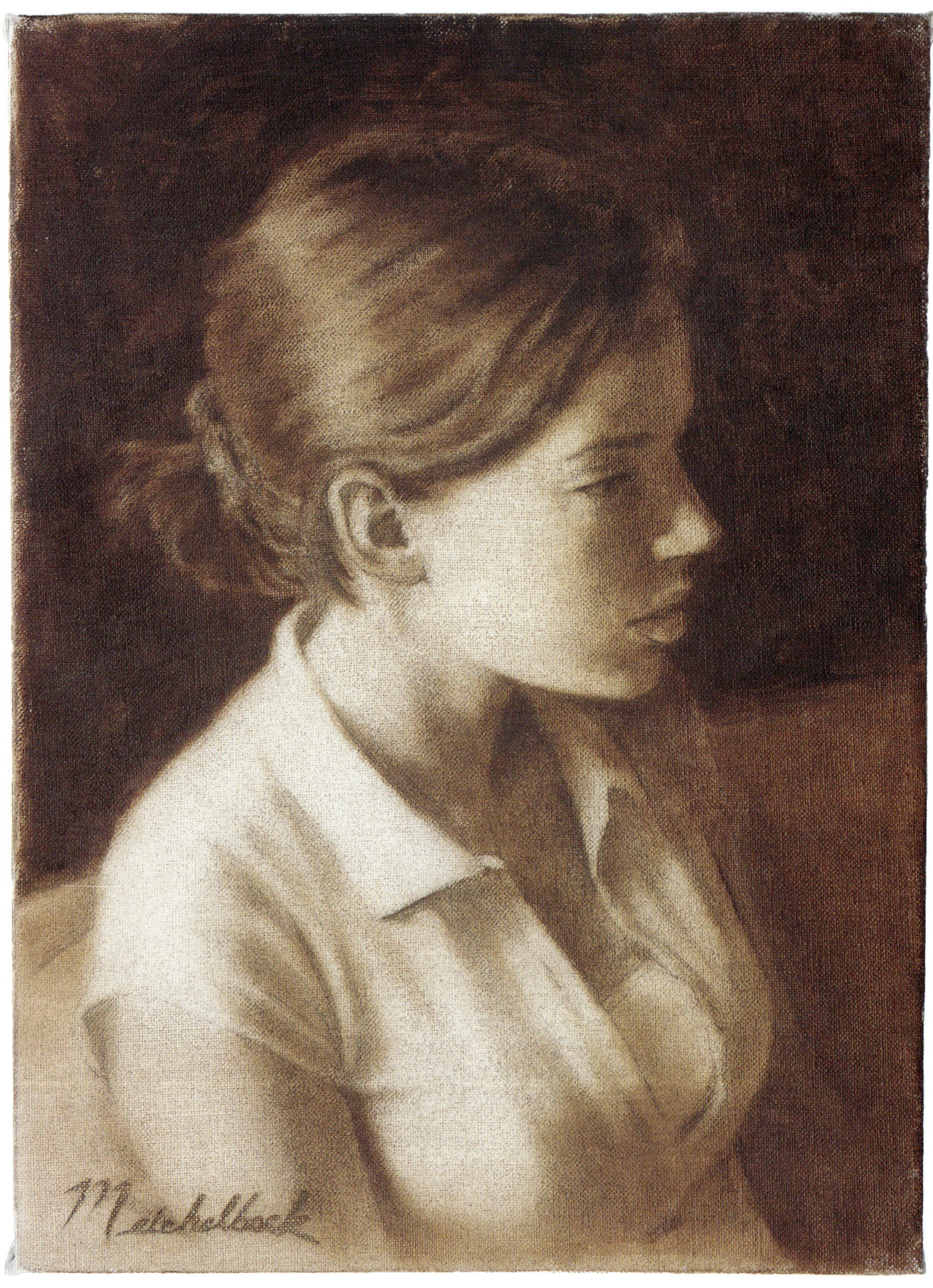

Window Light
Mark Meichelbock · Oil on linen · 12" × 16" (30cm × 41cm)

SCULPT LIGHT WITH A BRUSH

This is an oil underpainting achieved with a mixture of Burnt Umber and Venetian Red on a stretched Belgium linen canvas. The sitter is a friend of mine. From an initial toned canvas, I proceeded to sculpt the light with the brush, painting the planes like carving stone. I incorporated lost and found edges—some hard and others so soft they blur into the background. It is the softness of edges and planes that gives the illusion of reality, as well as enhancing the mood.

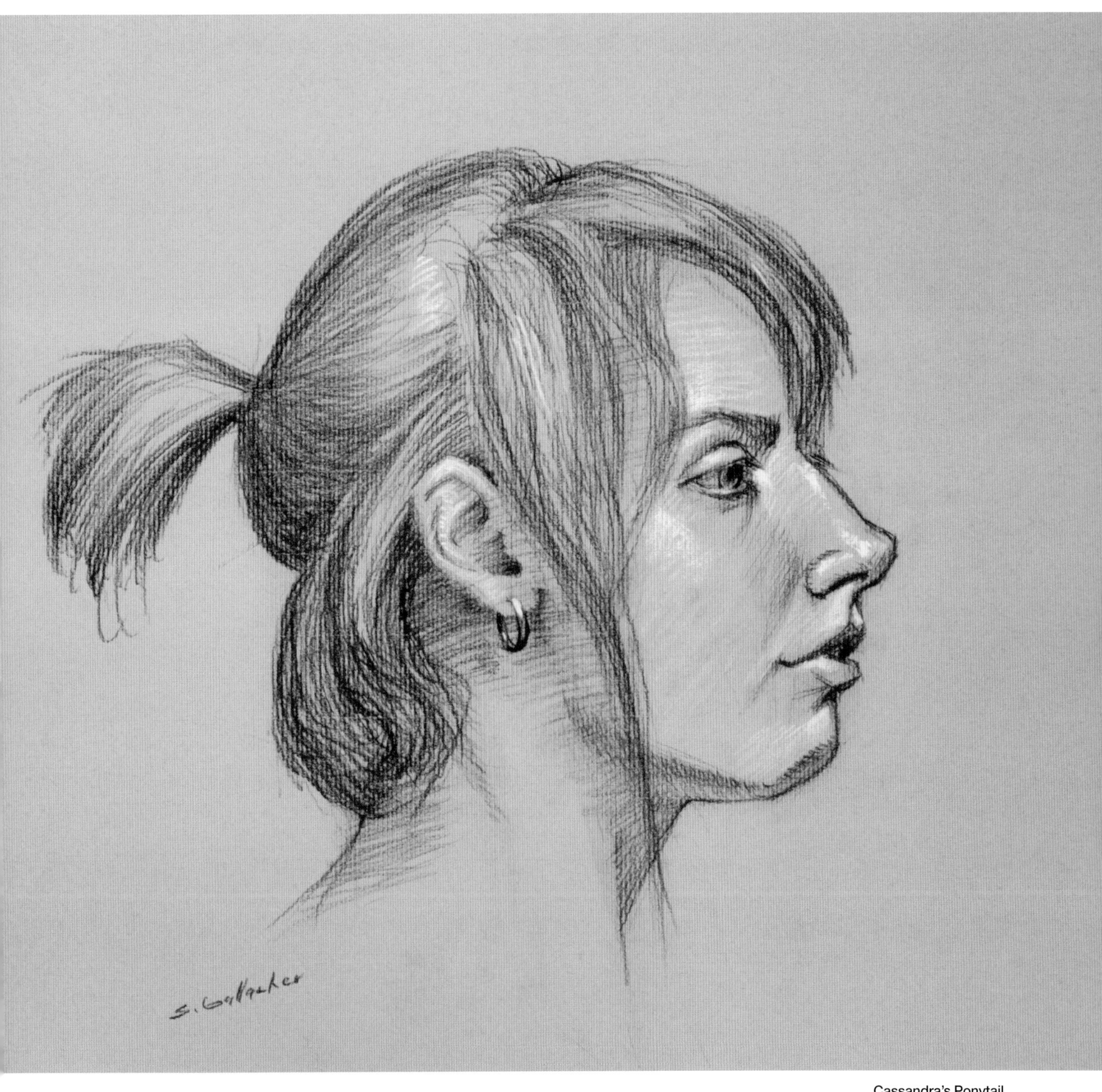

Cassandra's Ponytail
Susan Gallacher · Charcoal pencil and White Conté sketching crayon on pastel drawing paper · 18" × 16" (46cm × 41cm)

Create Dimension With White

This studio portrait is of my favorite model, Cassandra. When drawing portraits, I like to use single sheets of light gray pastel paper, because darker paper makes it difficult to see the charcoal lines. I prefer a smooth surface so the lines remain crisp. I use a soft charcoal pencil to draw the eyes, nose and a basic outline of the head, thinking "flat shape," not detail. I then begin to create the illusion of dimension by adding highlights with White Conté. I then draw surface contour lines with the white to create dimension, working back and forth between the light and dark areas until the drawing is completed.

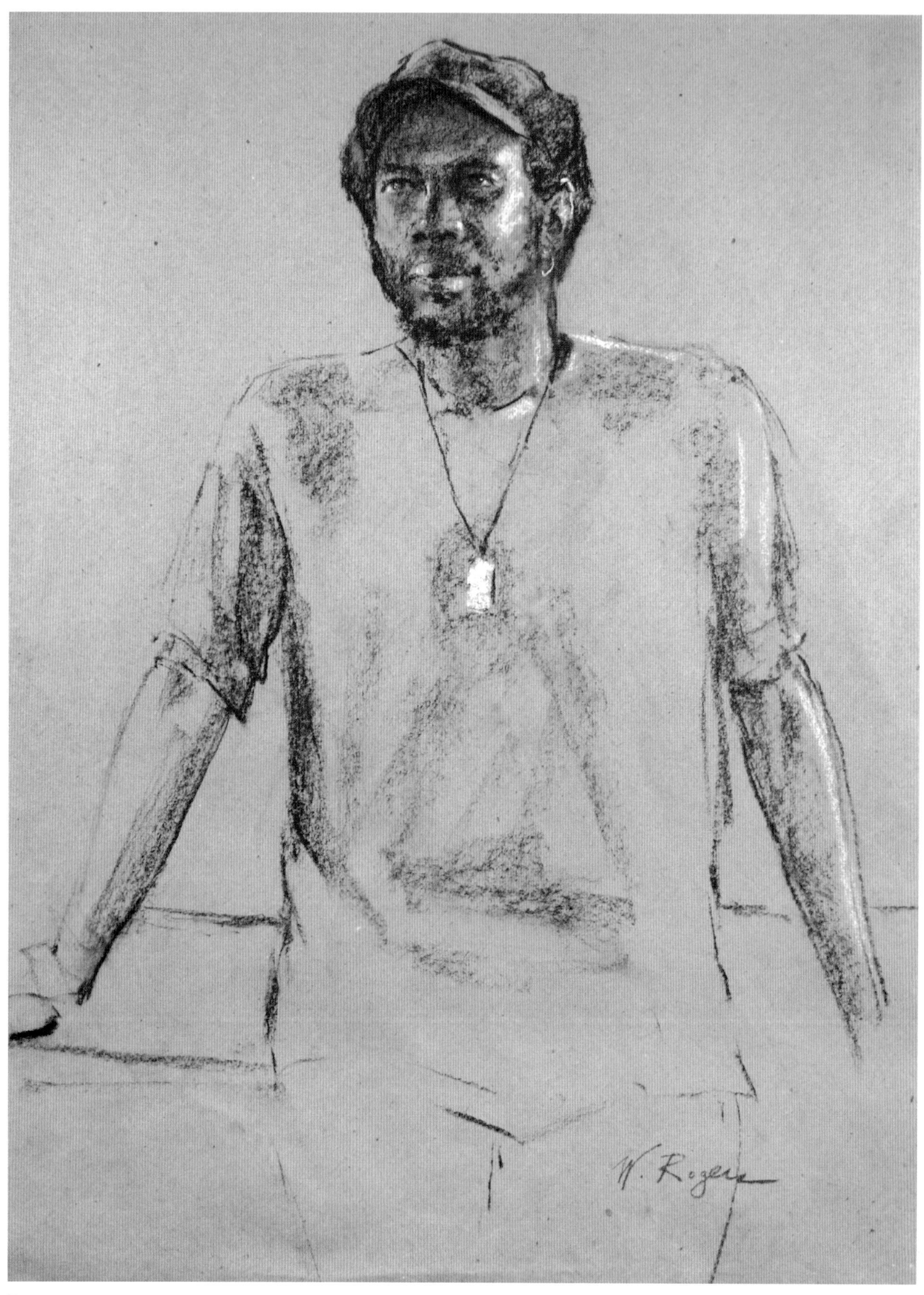

Damon
William Rogers · Sepia and white chalks on brown-gray wrapping paper · 22" × 16" (56cm × 41cm)

CHEAP PAPER CAN BE LIBERATING

This drawing of Damon, a frequently-used model, was completed from life in the studio. My familiarity with him allowed me to complete this short, ten-minute sketch quickly and accurately without much hesitation. I used Yarka Dark Sepia and White chalks on a unifying midtone brown-gray, heavy wrapping paper. The low cost of the paper liberated the process from being too cautious. The ten-minute pose necessitated an understated approach with intuitive placement and emphasis.

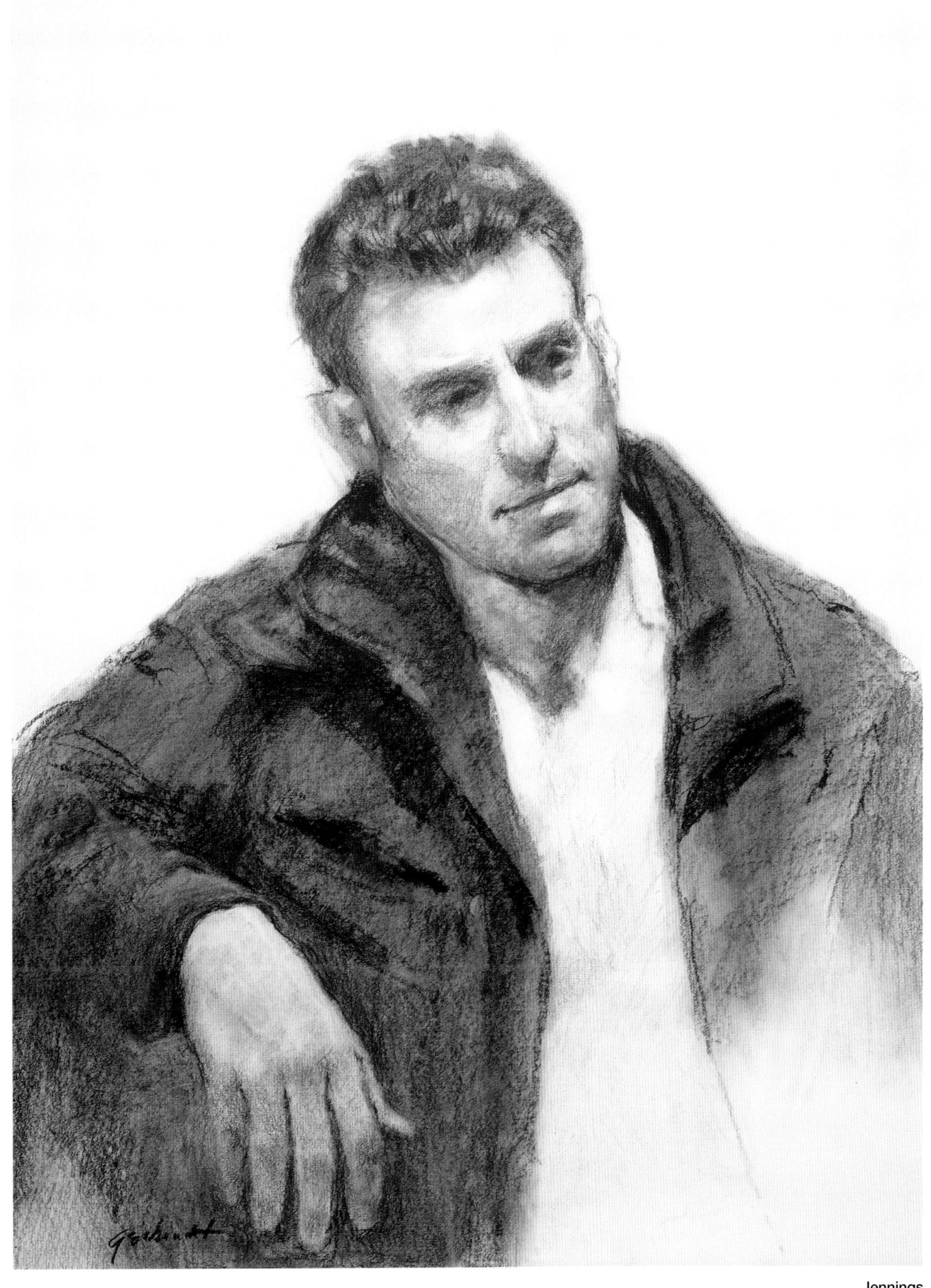

Jennings
Bob Gerbracht · Charcoal on paper · 24" × 18" (61cm × 46cm)

LEAVE PARTS UNFINISHED FOR INTEREST

As Jennings posed, I gave all of my mental attention to the attitude, the expression in the eyes, the angle and structure of Jennings's head, and the light and shadow pattern. I roughed in everything lightly before committing myself to further development until I felt it was right. I finished the head and then the body as I progressed down the paper, leaving parts unfinished to make an interesting composition. I like charcoal for light and shadow and getting black blacks.

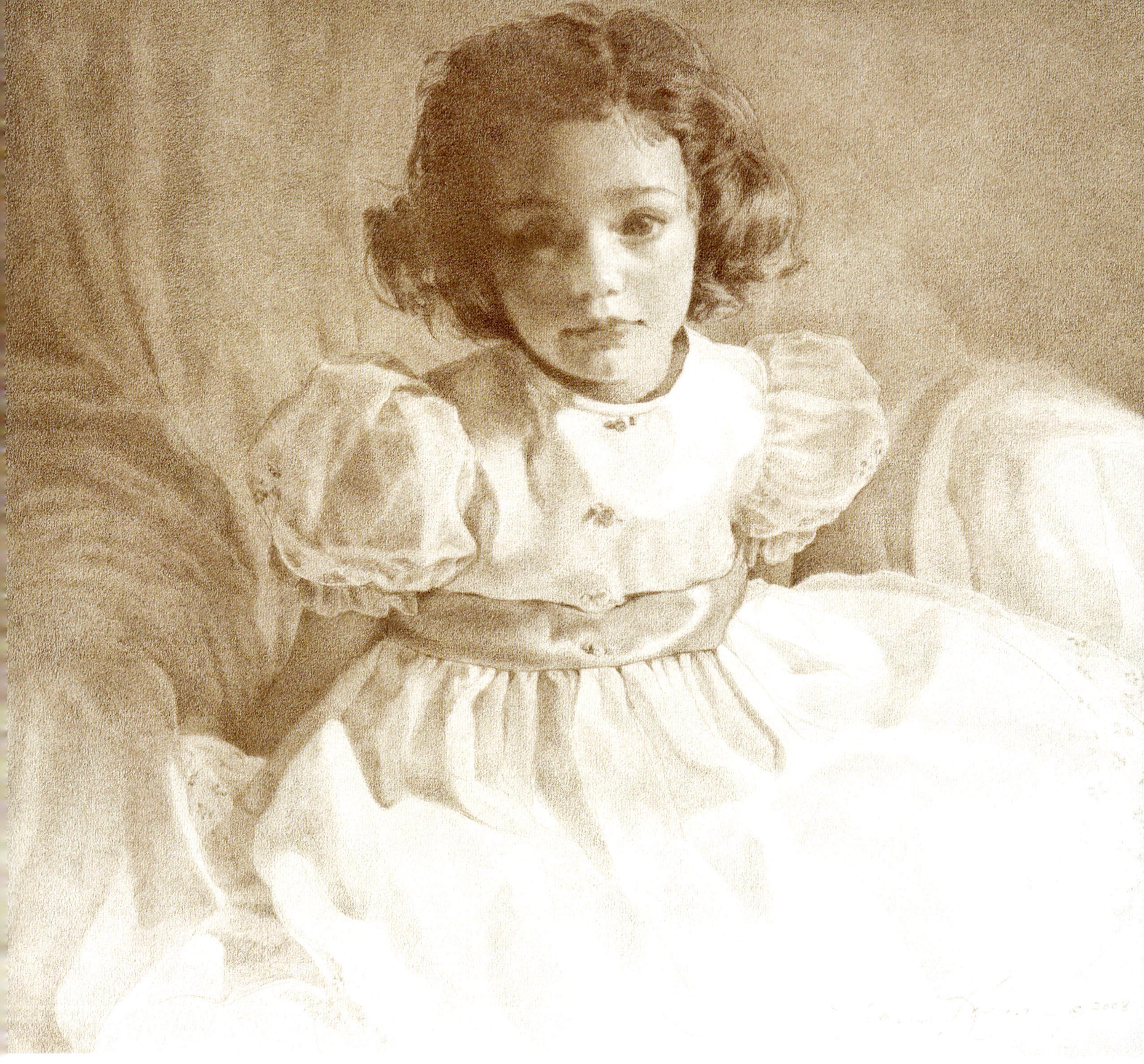

All Dressed Up
Yvonne Kozlina · Colored pencil on drawing paper · 13" × 14½" (33cm × 37cm)

GRAINY PAPER SURFACE SETS MOOD

This child posed in my studio where I took several photos and made quick sketches. I loved the strong light coming in from the window and her wistful expression. My drawing was done on Strathmore 80-lb. (170gsm) drawing paper with a Derwent Copper Beech colored pencil. I started with a very loose sketch and built up the details and the dark areas with many layers of small, delicate strokes, carefully leaving the light areas. I used an eraser to lift out the brightest spots. The combination of pencil strokes and the surface of the paper create a grainy effect that sets the mood of the piece.

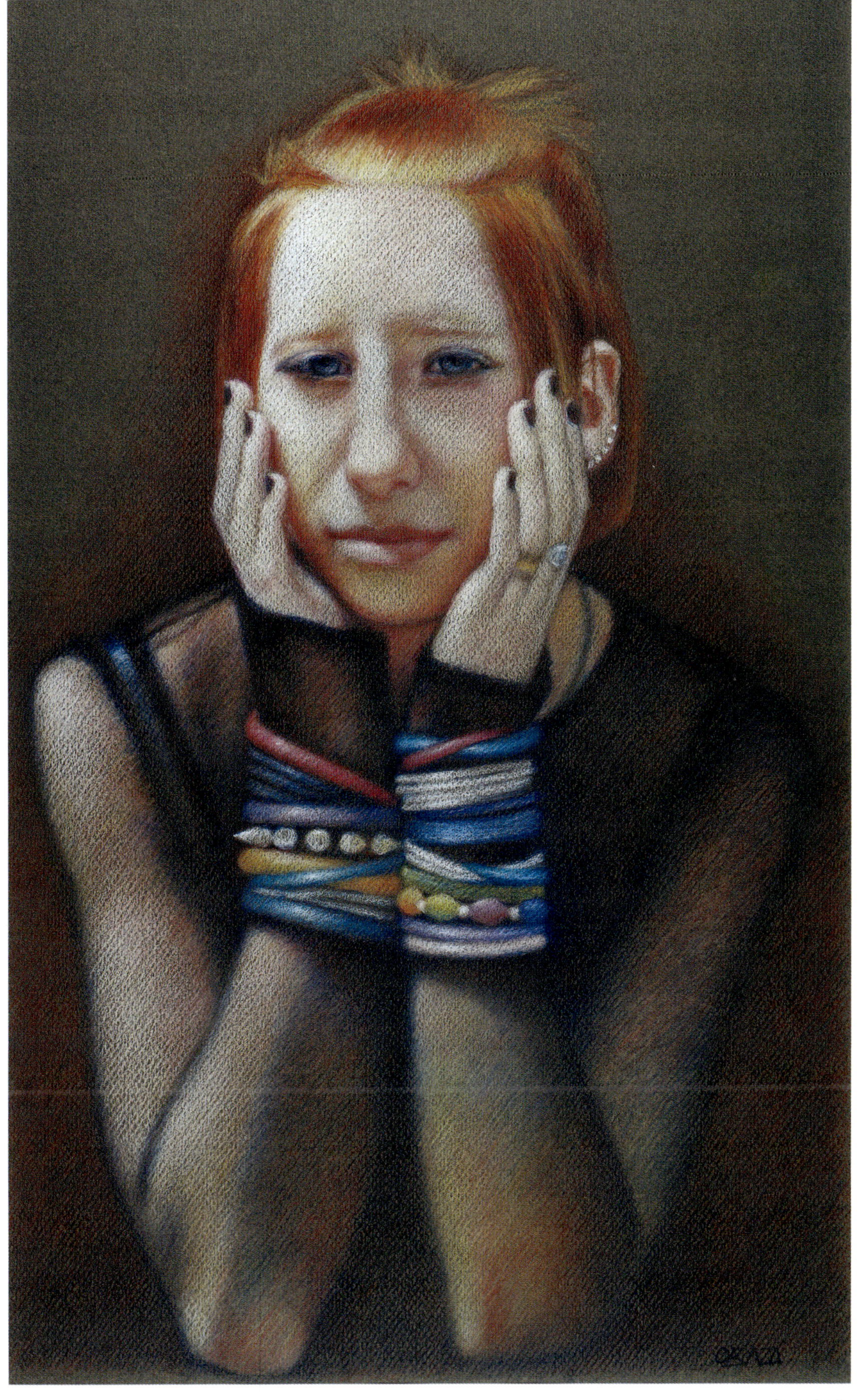

Sara, Smile
Susan Obaza · Colored pencil on Canson colored paper · 27" × 19" (69cm × 48cm)

USE AN OLD MASTER TECHNIQUE FOR A CURRENT SUBJECT

Sara, Smile was created from a cropped photograph. My inspiration came from the many Old Master paintings of a girl in a window. I tried to capture that feeling, even though the original photo was a seated, full-body shot taken outdoors. Colored pencils are translucent like watercolor, and so my technique incorporates the color of the paper as a design and harmonizing element. I heightened the light on the face and hands, and used a Mannerist sense of proportion to emphasize the facial expression and highlight Sara's wonderful bracelets and long arms.

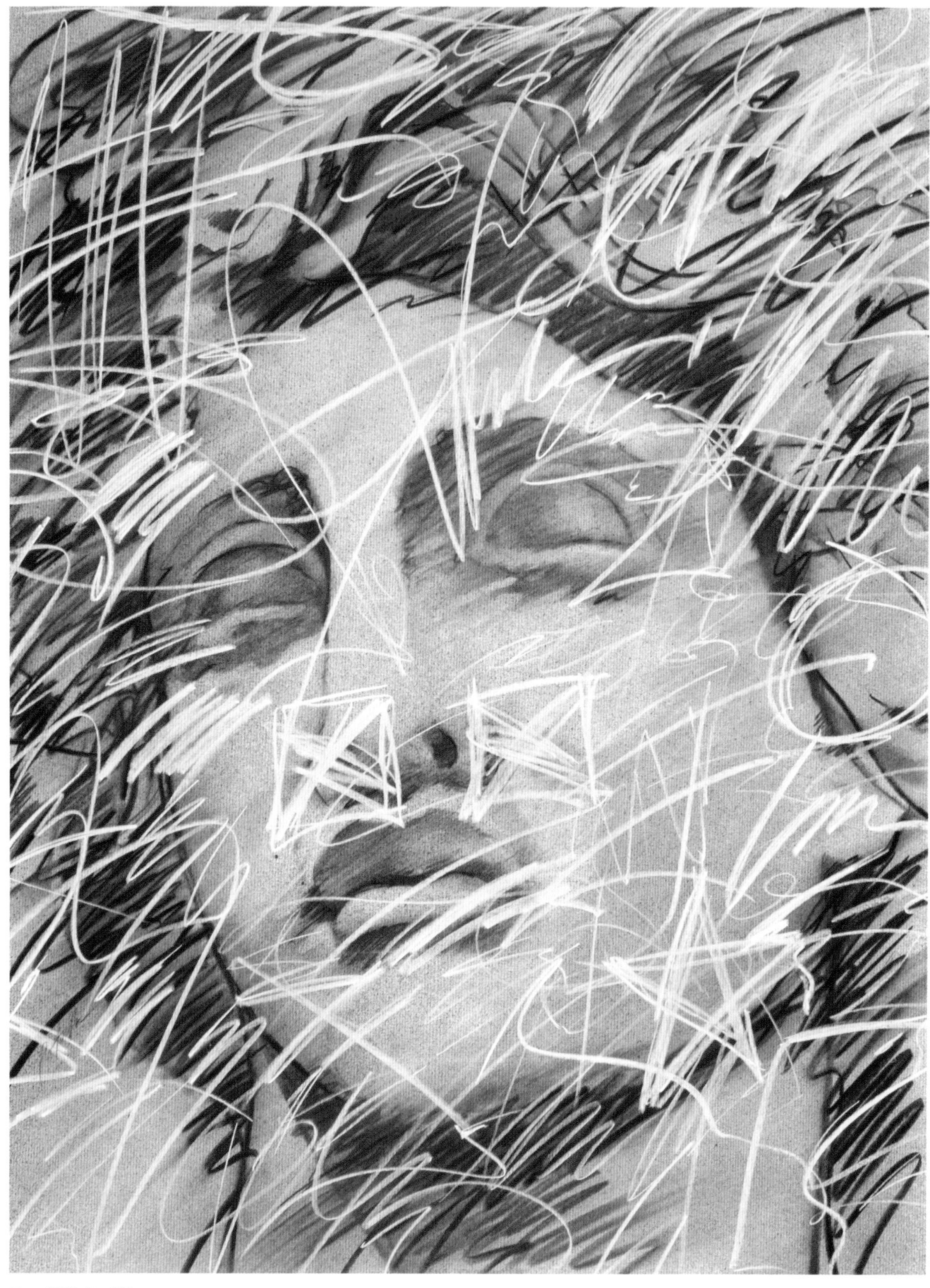

Face With Graffiti
Tom Potocki · Charcoal and Conté on illustration board · 40" × 30" (102cm × 76cm)

A DARING MOVE ADDS INTERESTING TENSION

The idea for this drawing came about while teaching a class in photography. To show the students how to use acetate to make negatives, I scribbled on clear acetate with ink, placed the acetate on photo paper and exposed it to produce a photogram of white scribbles. I wondered how this linear pattern would look superimposed over a drawing, so I printed a photo of a drawing through the acetate lines to produce a layered image. The result gave me the idea for *Face With Graffiti*. This was drawn without the use of photography. After rendering a drawing in charcoal, I used white Conté and vine charcoal to superimpose graffiti lines over the drawing. This creates a visual interplay and tension between the precision of the formal drawing and the chaos of the graffiti lines.

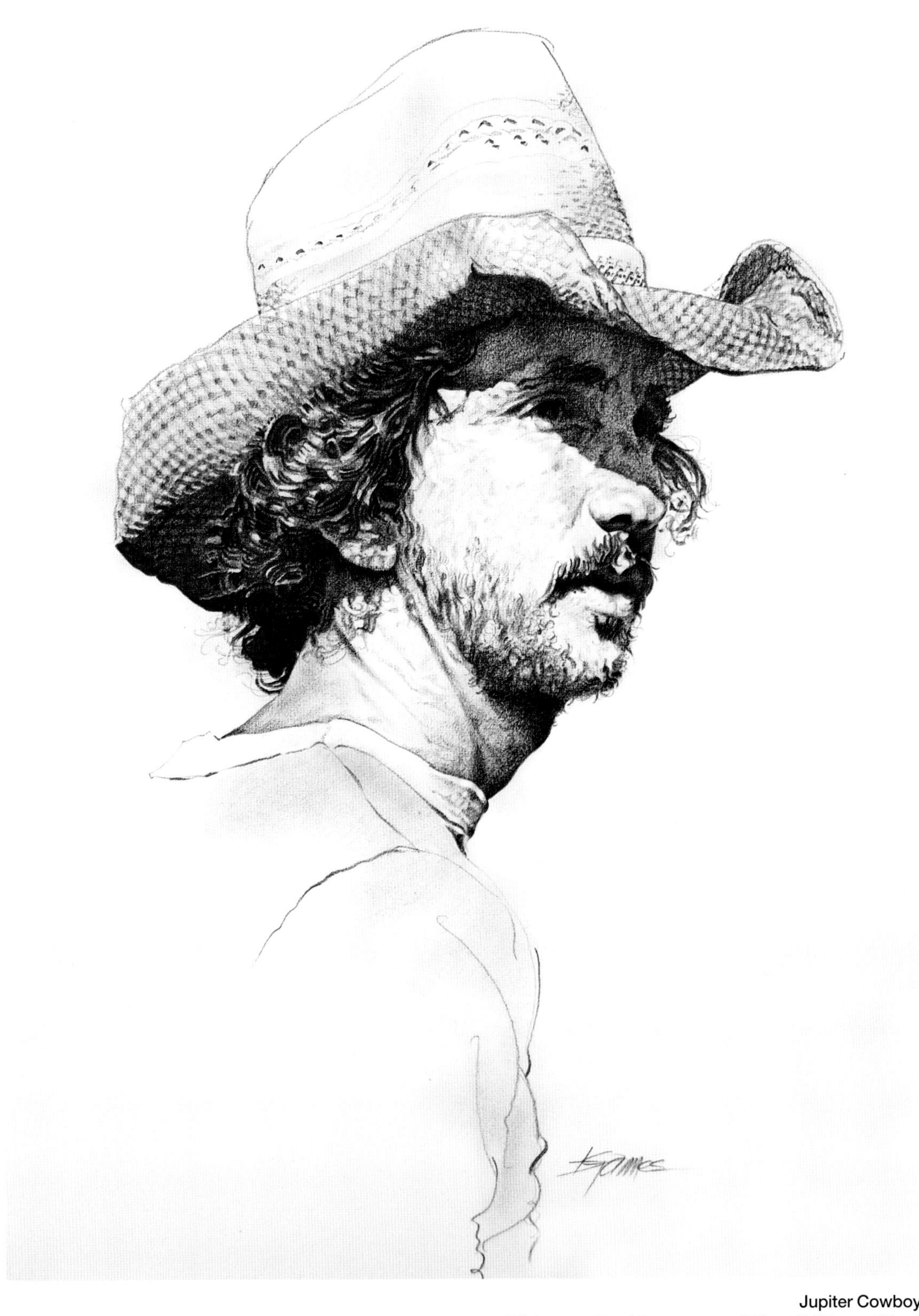

Jupiter Cowboy
Bill James · Graphite on paper · 20" × 14" (51cm × 36cm)

BE ON THE LOOKOUT FOR GREAT DRAWING SUBJECTS

My wife is a well-known breeder/handler of Doberman pinschers. I used to go with her to dog shows to take photos of the interesting people. I was with her in Jupiter, Florida, and noticed this guy watching the show. His look, with his beard and cowboy hat, was unique. I am always on the lookout for subjects to take back to my studio for painting and drawing.

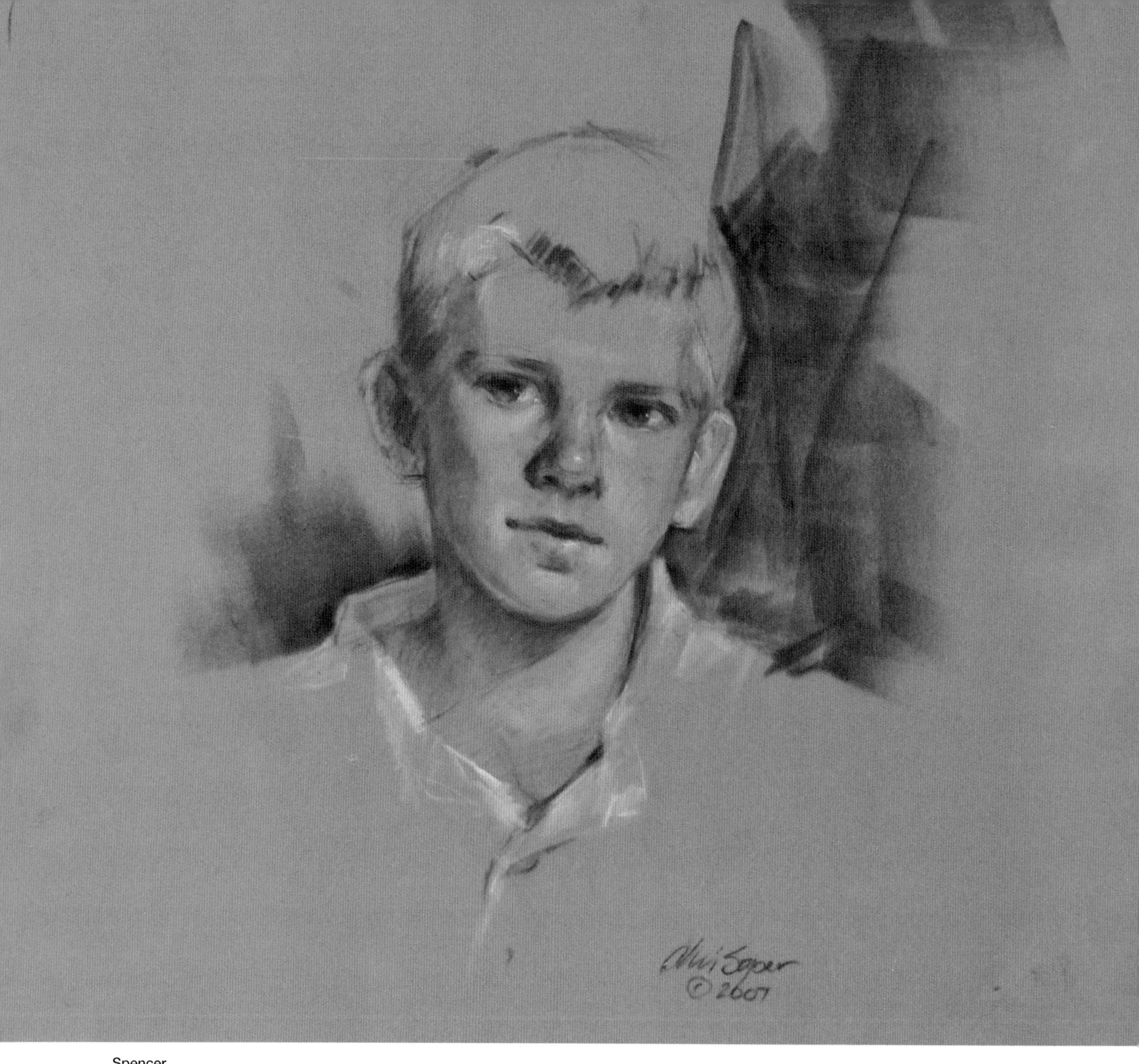

Spencer
Chris Saper · Nupastel/charcoal on Hahnemuehle Gray velour board · 20" × 16" (51cm × 41cm)

STIFFER SURFACE TAKES ABUSE

Spencer was drawn from life at the Mountain Artists Guild in Prescott, Arizona, in an open studio group. It was my first time using this velour-type paper, which is mounted to a cardboard-like surface and quite stiff; the surface can take a fair amount of abuse. Lighter charcoal and Nupastel marks can be lifted rather well with a kneaded eraser. I used some pencil/charcoal pencil and a little vine charcoal to make my first marks and then modeled using a deep reddish brown Nupastel, white charcoal pencil and White Nupastel.

A Limited Palette Helps Convey Innocence

I hoped to capture the innocence and vulnerability of this child in my drawing. It was done with a limited palette of soft pastels on Canson paper. I applied the colors loosely and then used a kneaded eraser to pull off the chalk to the underlying brown paper, adding pastel and subtracting with the eraser where needed.

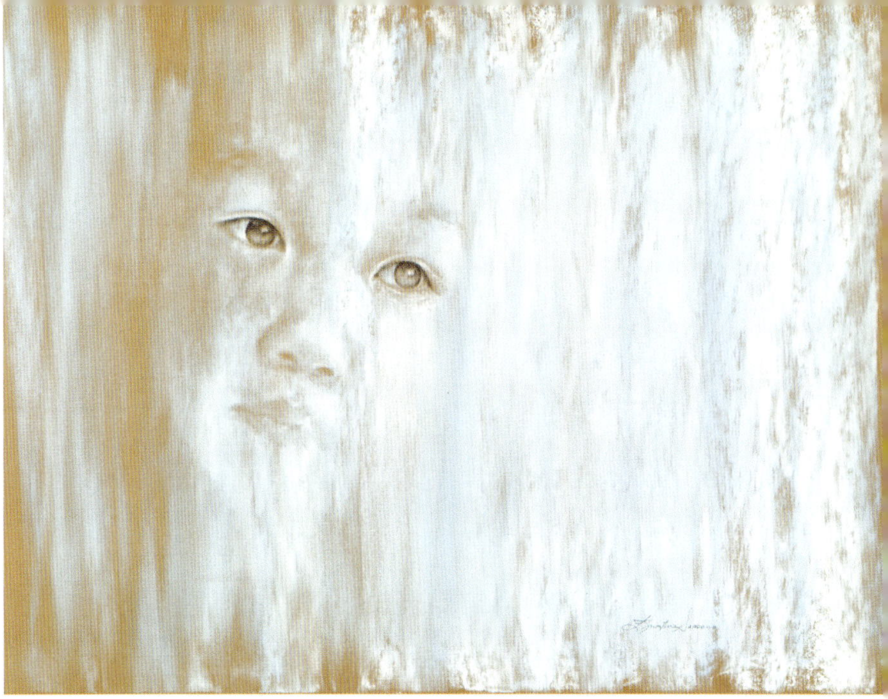

What I See
Kristine Sarsons · Pastel on Canson paper · 23" × 18" (58cm × 46cm)

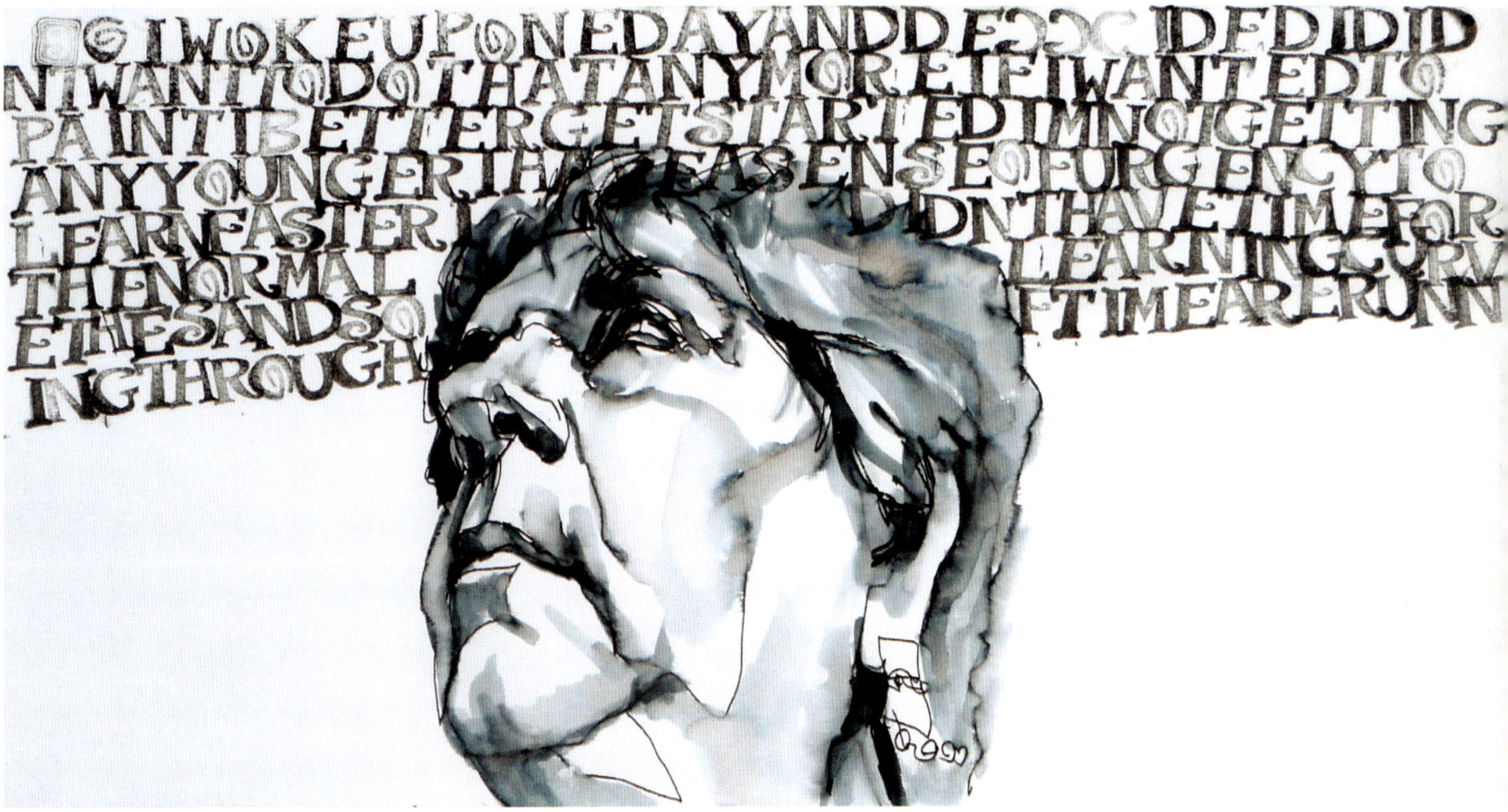

Self-Portrait With Dialogue
Myrna Wacknov · Elegant Writer calligraphy pen and wet brush on Aquabee sketchbook paper with rubber stamping · 6" × 12" (15cm × 30cm)

Add Verbal Content to Your Portrait

This drawing was from a photograph I took of myself as part of a series reflecting on the emotions of aging. I drew directly with the pen in modified contour style and then used a water brush to bleed out the ink line for shading. The ink in this pen turns blue and pink, creating interesting variations. I stamped in stream-of-conscious style with a small alphabet rubber-stamp set.

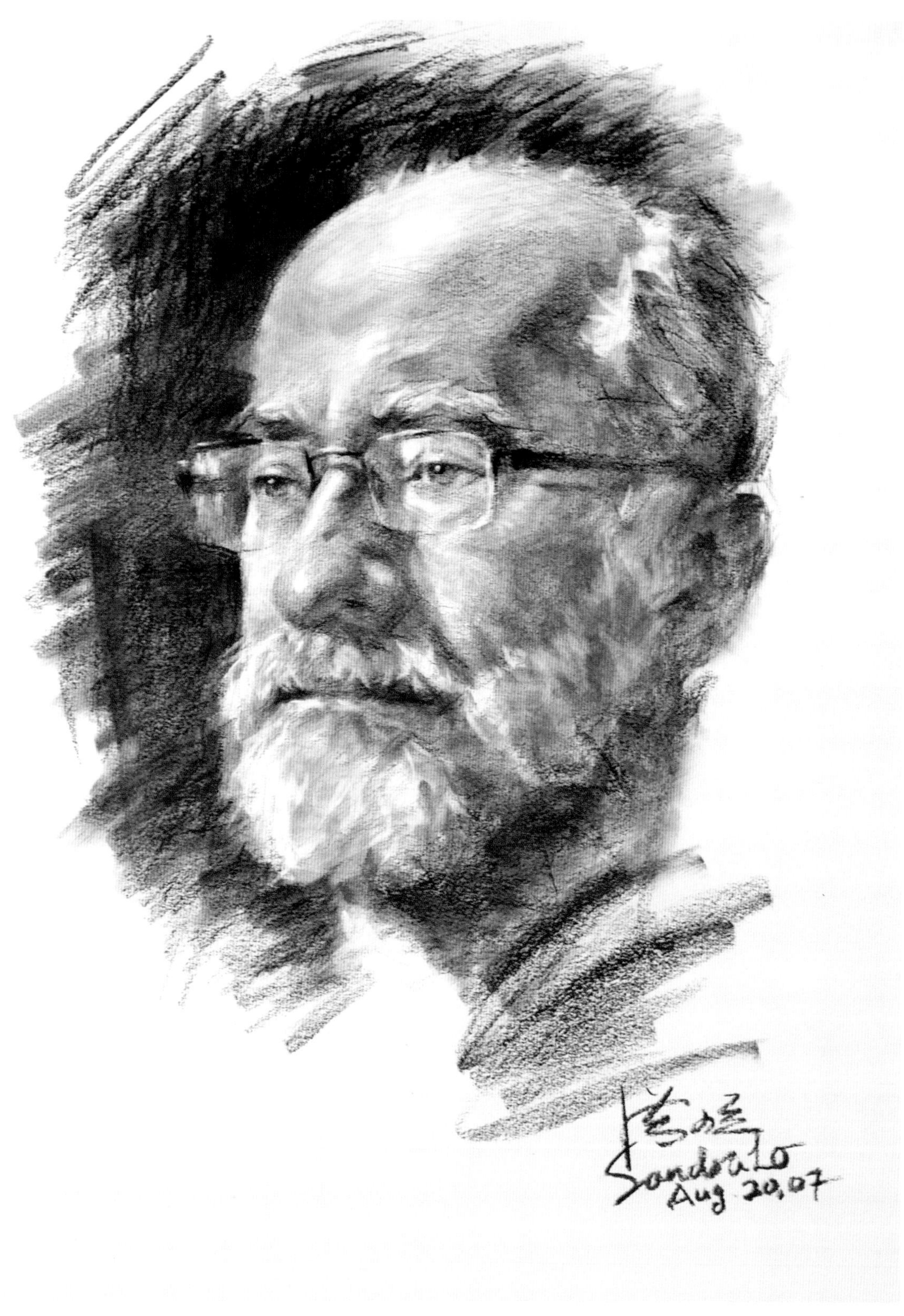

Thinking
Sandra Lo · Charcoal on Canson drawing paper · 19½" × 15" (50cm × 38cm)

OFFICE SERVES AS PORTRAIT STUDIO

Gary Deluhery, a friend from work, was the model. I turned my desk light on him to light his face.
First I drew a few lines to define the size of the head and the location of eyes, nose and mouth.
Then I held my charcoal flat to quickly apply values for the whole face. I only left the highlight portion
untouched. I used a blending stump to soften some areas and a rubber eraser to correct the tone.
I did about 50 percent of the drawing in about half an hour and took a photograph to finish the
portrait in my studio.

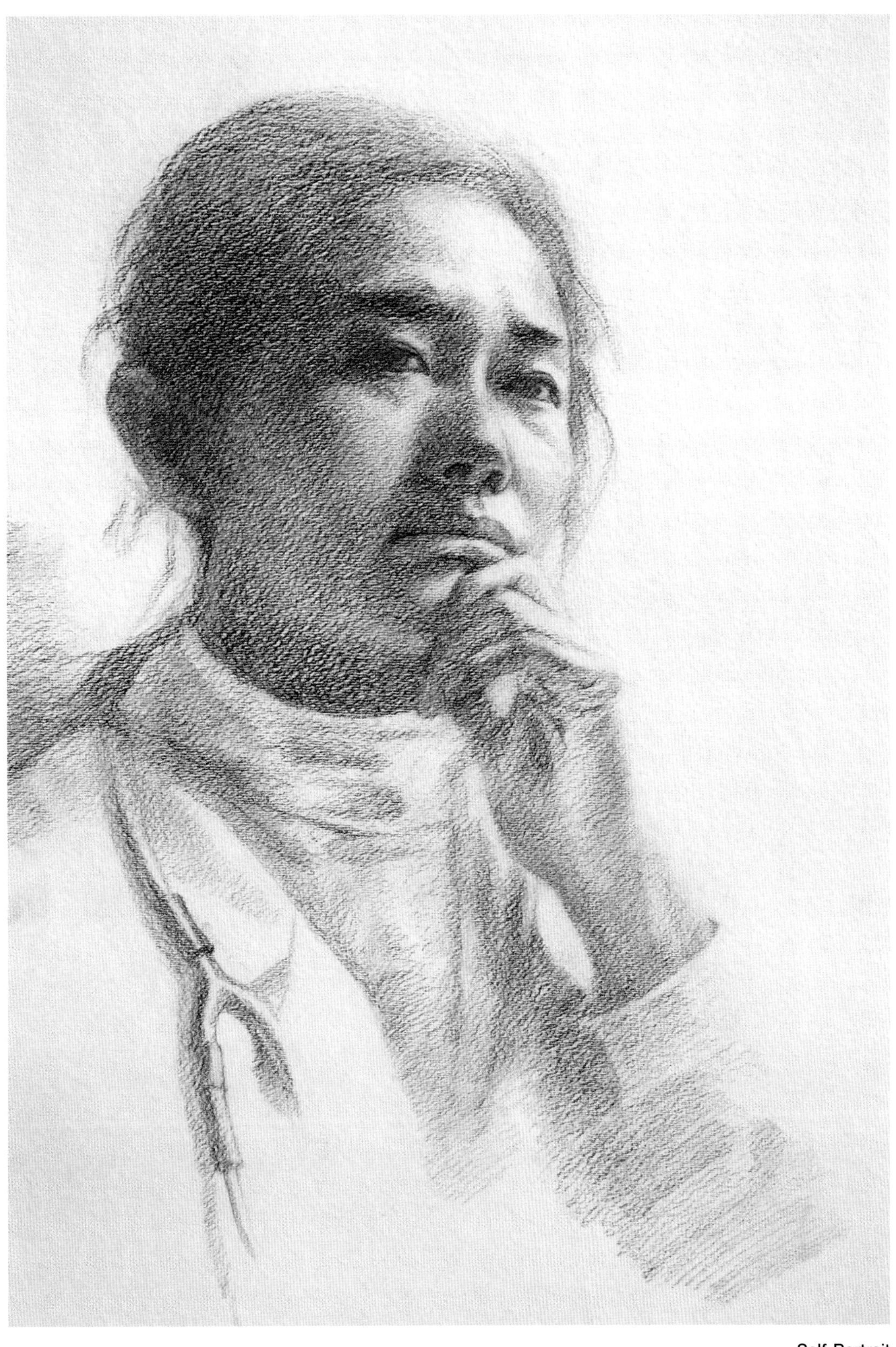

Self-Portrait
Wei Lu · Graphite on watercolor paper · 20½" × 14½" (52cm × 36cm)

A Moment of Retrospection Captured

I always aim to capture a portrait subject's personality. This self-portrait found me during a cloudy afternoon. I caught a glimpse of myself in the mirror; my reflection was so clear and bright that it contrasted deeply with the rest of the dimly lit room. Suddenly a lot of memories flooded back to me. I decided to capture this moment, caught in retrospection. I chose to use watercolor paper; its rough surface adds a more natural texture to the portrait. To keep this texture intact, I rubbed the paper lightly with the side of a soft pencil and built the sketch by shading directly, avoiding using an eraser.

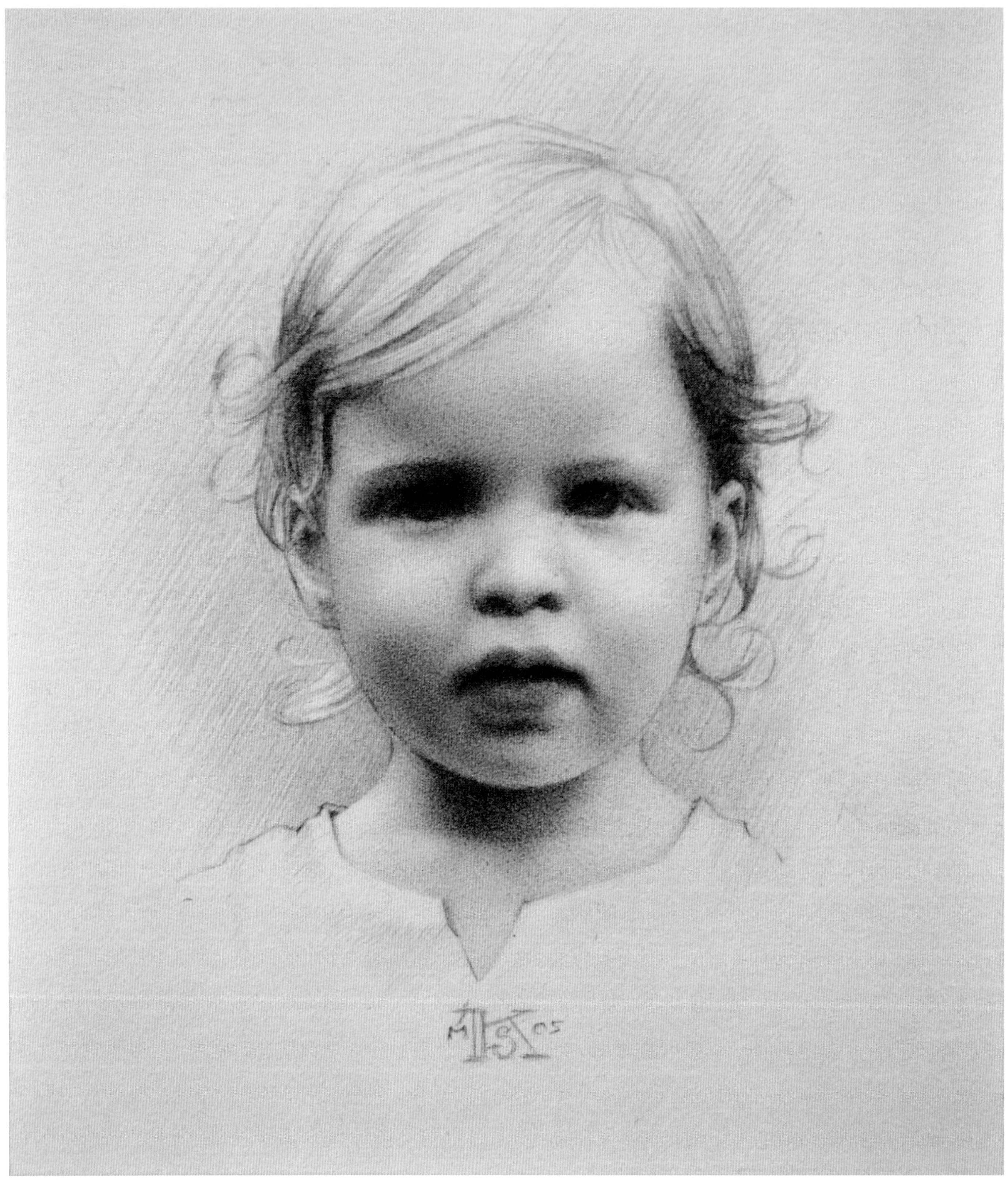

Maddy
Katherine Stone · Graphite pencil on gray paper · 4" × 3½" (10cm × 9cm)

GENTLE HATCHING STROKES FOR SMOOTH SKIN

This drawing was done from a photo. Who could expect a tot to hold still for more than a second? The smooth finish of the skin was not achieved through the use of a stomp or brush, but was the product of the gentlest of hatching strokes. The curls took less than five minutes to put in, but were the highlight of the process for me.

POWDERED GRAPHITE ESTABLISHES INITIAL VALUES

Julianna & Charlotte is a commissioned portrait that was done from a series of sketches and several different reference photos. Working on Strathmore 4-ply bristol plate, I begin with a fairly tight line drawing. Using powdered graphite, denatured alcohol and several round watercolor brushes, I establish my initial values. Using a no. 1 Nero pencil, my darkest darks are indicated, thus establishing my full value range early on. The portrait is then completed with a range of graphite pencils from 4H to 4B.

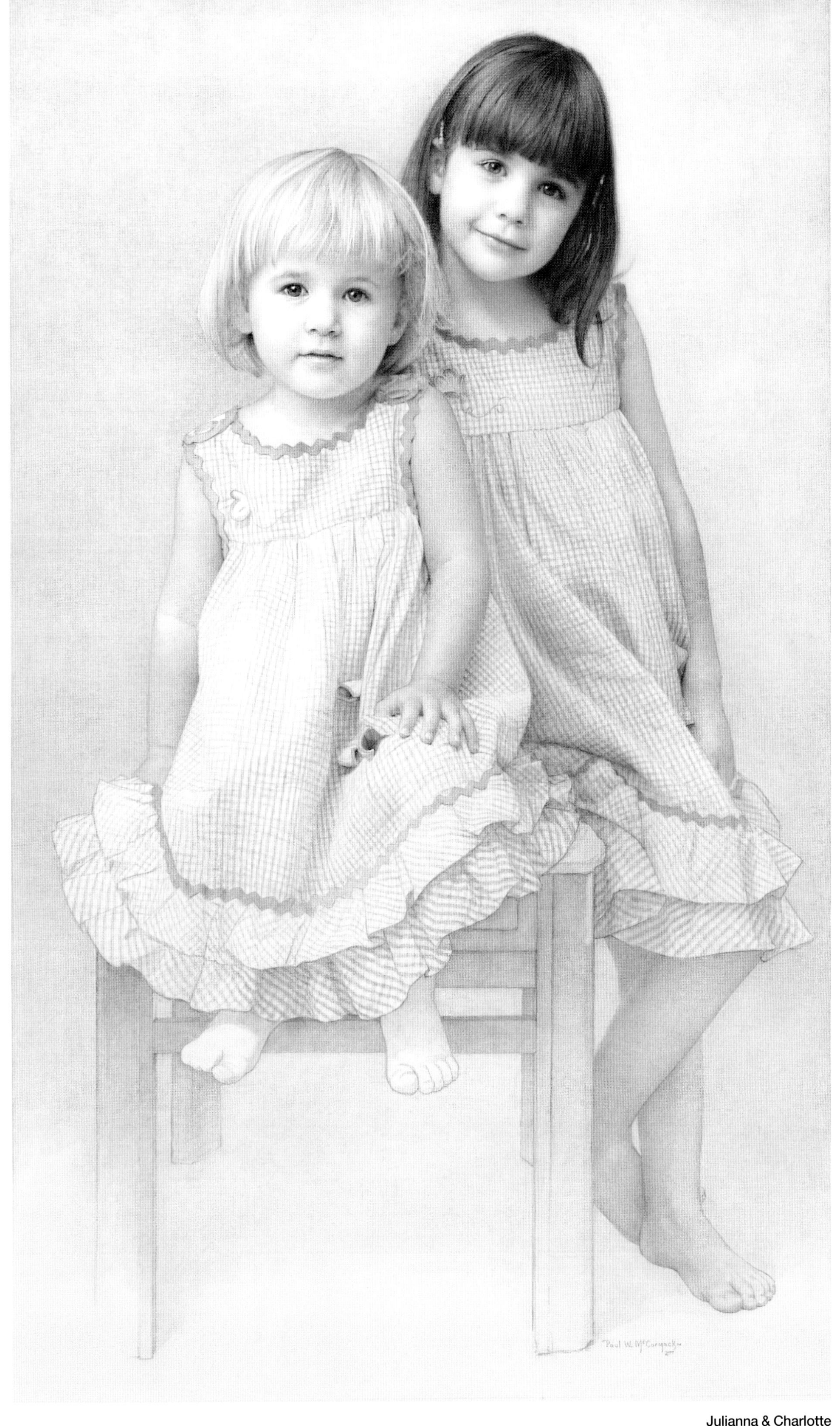

Julianna & Charlotte
Paul W. McCormack · Pencil and powdered graphite on bristol plate · 38¼" × 24¼" (97cm × 62cm)

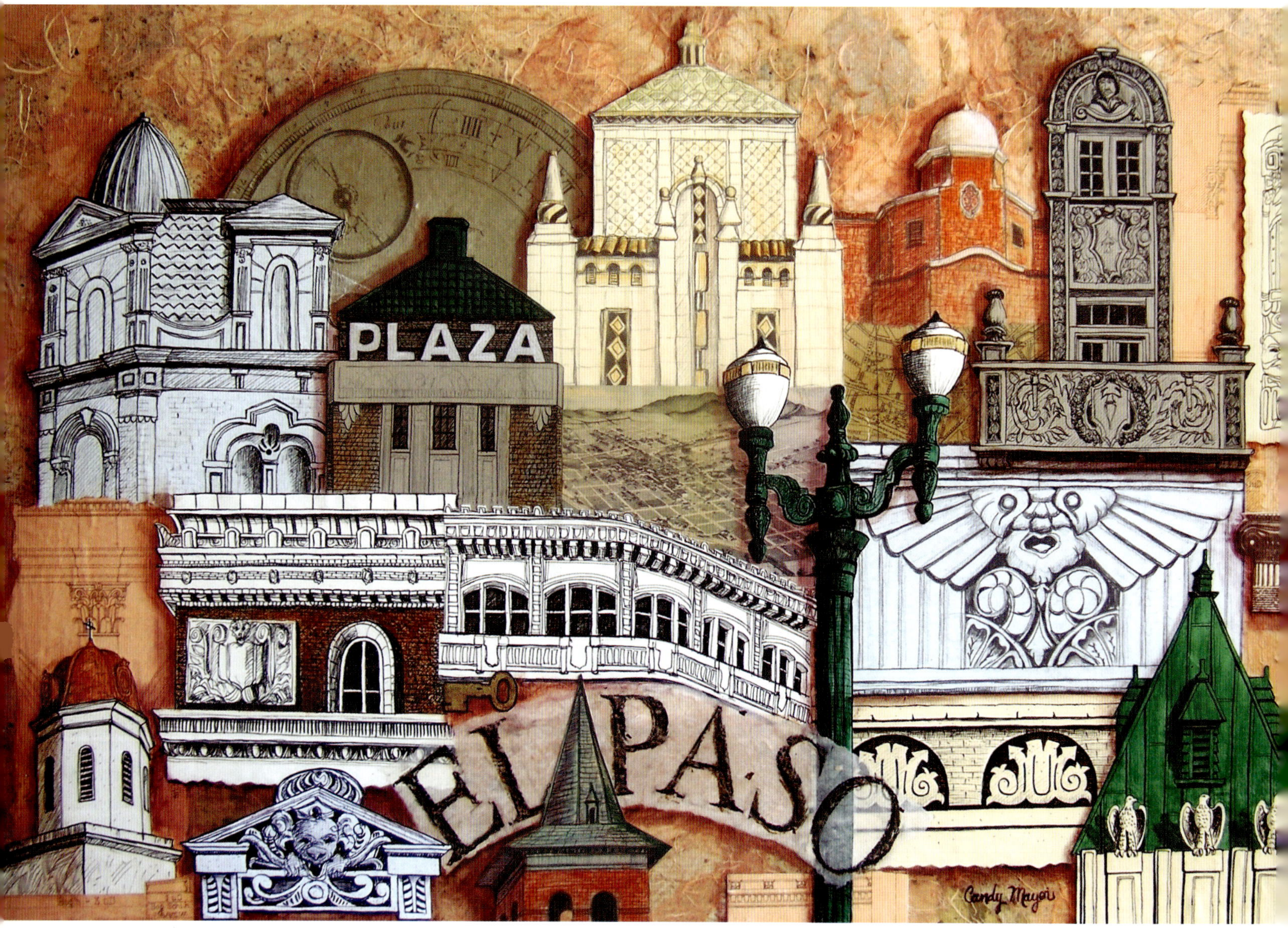

Downtown Architecture
Candy Mayer · Pen and ink and pencil drawings collaged with Oriental paper and acrylic on Masonite · 24" × 36" (61cm × 91cm)

COMBINE COLLAGE WITH DRAWING

In the *Downtown* collage, each drawing was done individually in pen and ink or pencil and then cut out. Using Masonite as a surface and Oriental papers as a background, the drawings were attached with acrylic matte medium. Then details and shadows were added with acrylic. The *Cathedral* drawing was done on Canson Mi-Teintes paper (smooth side). This toned paper gives more depth, as the mid-gray adds a third value to the usual black and white. A flexible quill pen captures the fine detail of the architecture. In both pieces, I concentrated on a smaller, more interesting part of the architecture instead of the whole building.

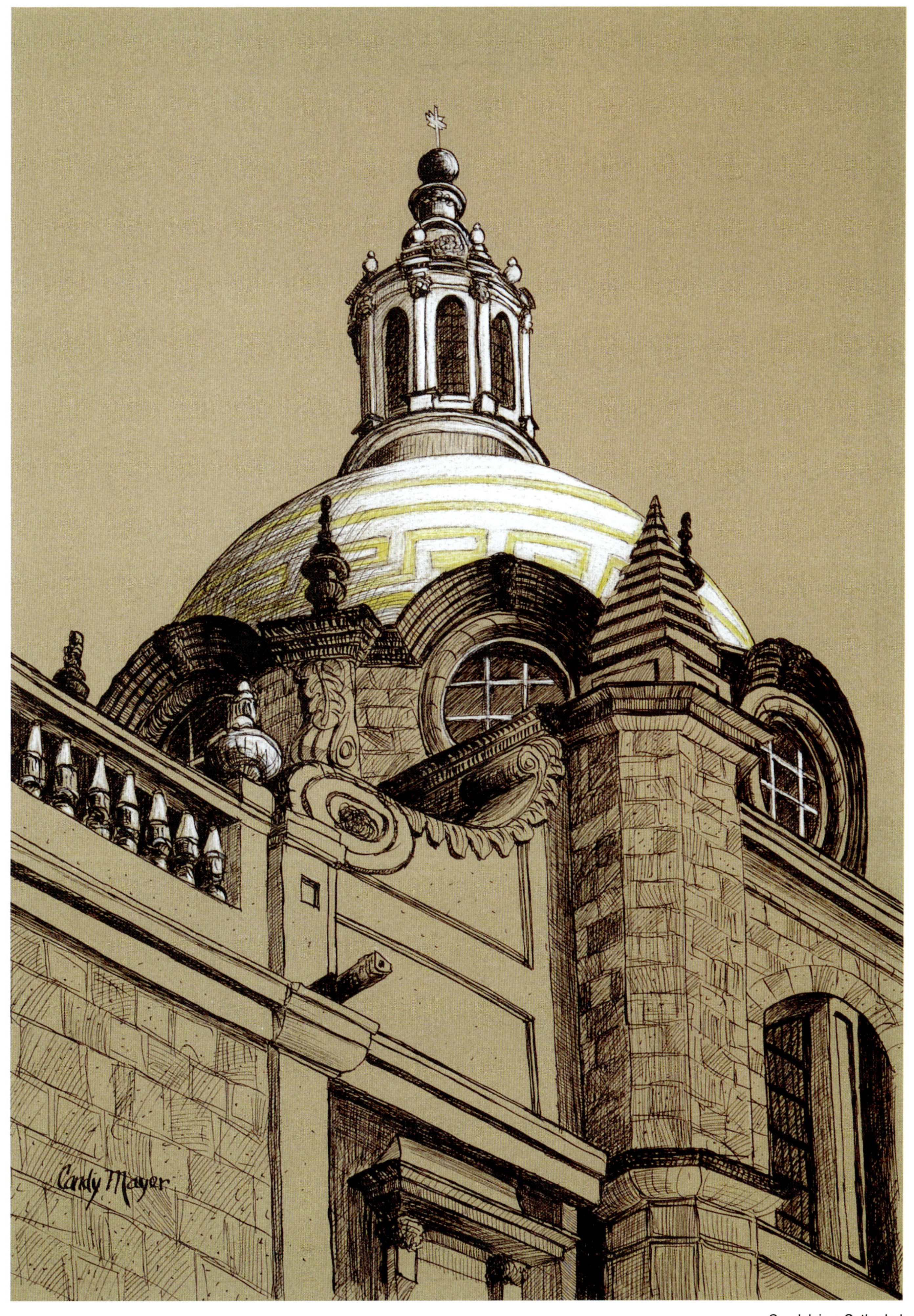

Guadalajara Cathedral
Candy Mayer · Pen and ink with colored pencil accents on toned paper · 16" × 12" (41cm × 30cm)

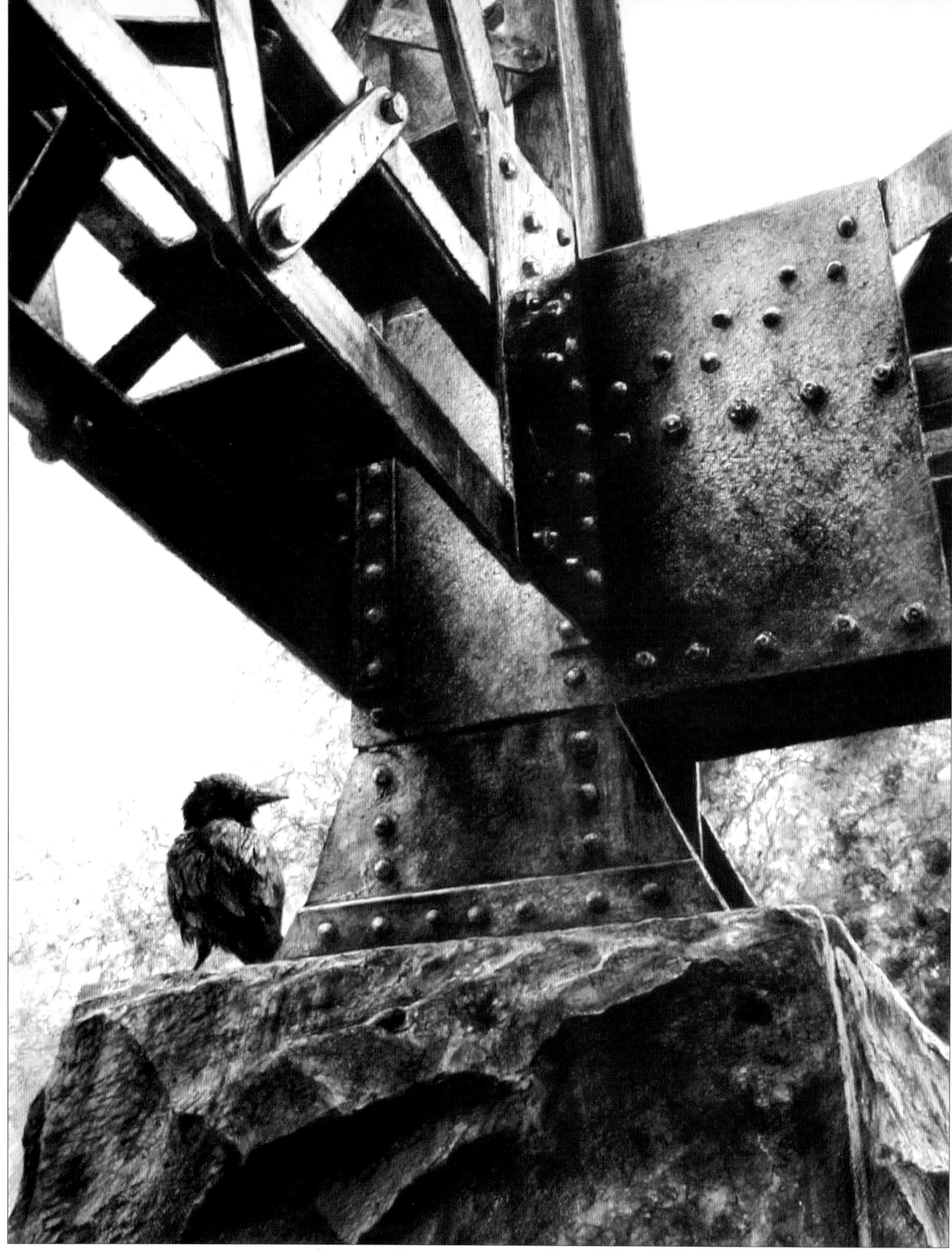

Bones
Terry Miller · Graphite on bristol board · 13" × 10" (33cm × 25cm)

CONTRAST ANIMAL LIFE WITH MAN-MADE ELEMENTS

In these works, both done in the studio, I set out to emphasize, specifically through light and shadow, the more abstract qualities of the main subjects. By adding the more animated, softer birds as secondary features, I hoped to make a distinct contrast between the man-made and natural elements. Dark areas were built up, layer upon layer as a painter might use glazes, with increasingly softer grades of graphite.

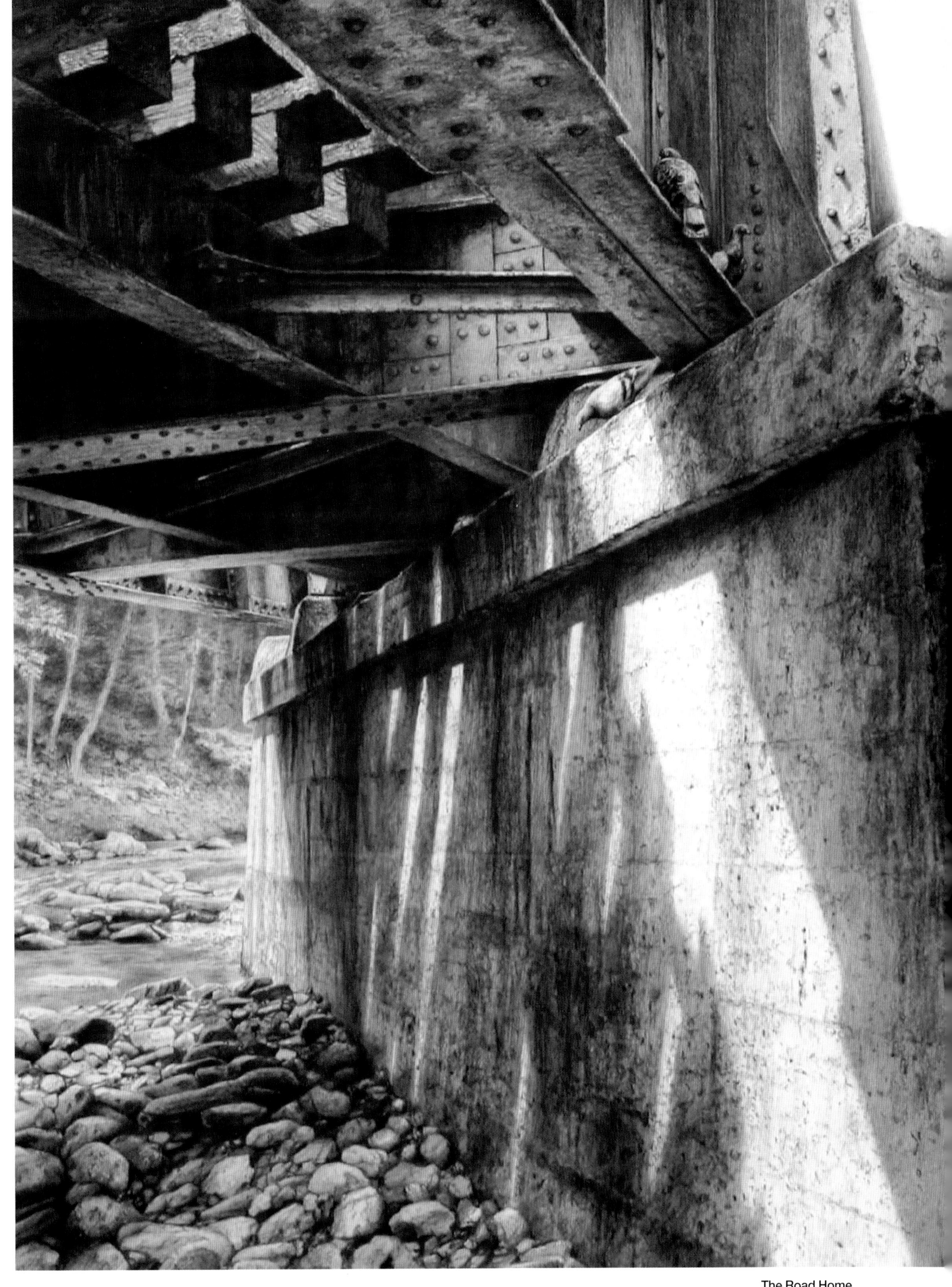

The Road Home
Terry Miller · Graphite on bristol board · 17" × 13" (43cm × 33cm)

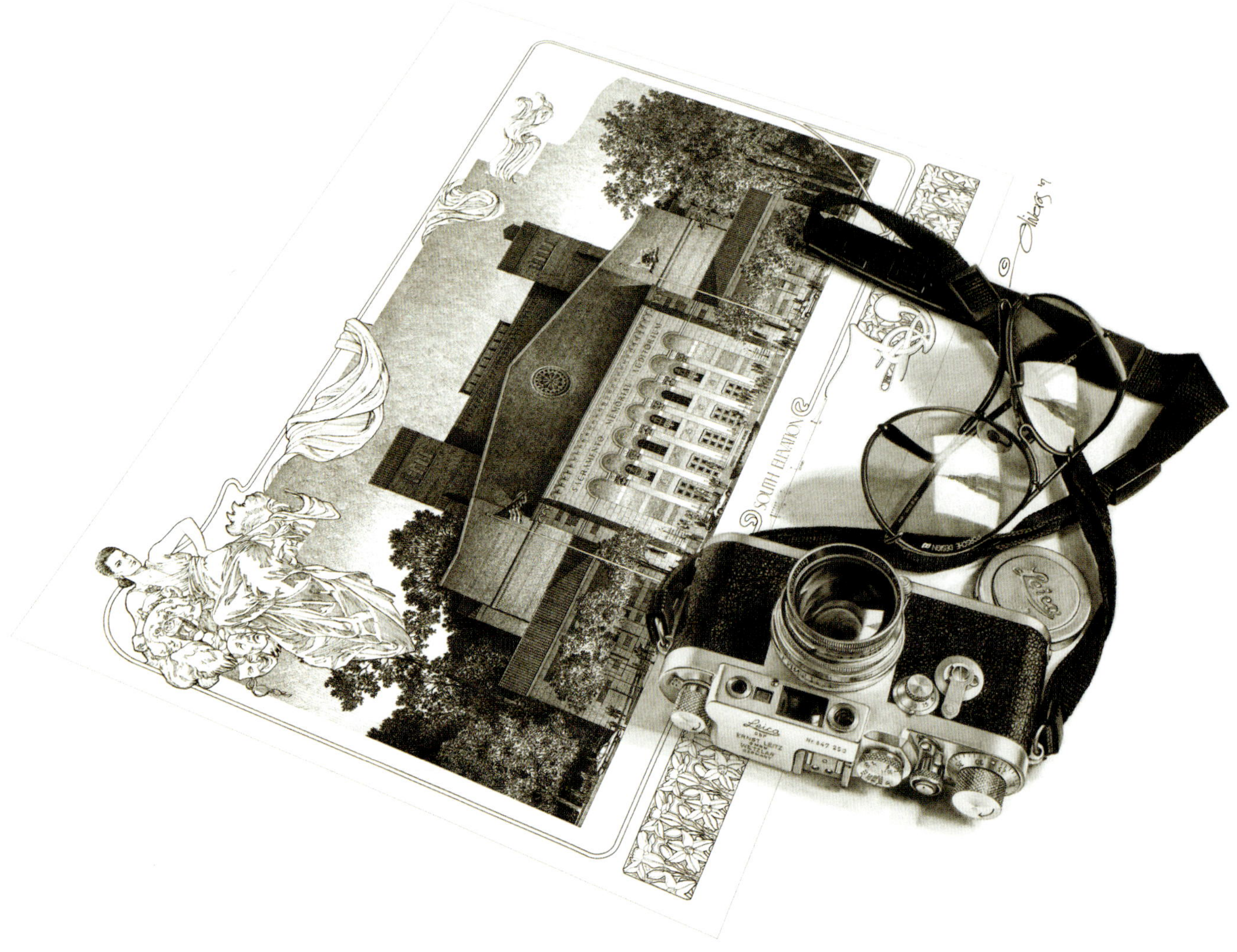

Self Promotion
Edmond S. Oliveros · Mixed media · 11" × 14" (28cm × 36cm)

A PHOTOSHOP COLLAGE OF DRAWINGS

This drawing, created in Adobe Photoshop®, is a collage of two original drawings. For the camera grouping, I drew my 1957 Leica camera in graphite on smooth illustration board and the rest of the drawing with a very sharp point without smudging. Because my business is architectural illustration, I added the reflection of the Empire State Building on the lens and glasses. Part of this original composition was a large logo of my business.

I later decided to use this composition for a brochure and scanned it, preserving the original character of the drawing. In place of the large logo, I decided to use a poster I had designed for the Sacramento Memorial Auditorium. This rendering was originally done in very fine, tight pen and ink on vellum, and measured 21" × 31" (53cm × 79cm). I used the Mucha style for the borders because the project was built during the Art Nouveau period. For impact, the building is not in perspective, but is a scaled elevation. I scanned the original drawing, reduced and manipulated it in Photoshop, and positioned it with the camera grouping to be part of this new composition.

Reflections (Grand Central Terminal, NYC)
Edmond S. Oliveros · Pen and ink on Mylar · 16" × 12" (41cm × 30cm)

MYLAR SURFACE MODERATES BLACKNESS OF INK

I love architectural details, especially neoclassical ones. My photo reference was taken from a window of one of the offices along 42nd Street, looking at the beautiful and ornate crown of the Grand Central Terminal. I was excited to see the building, with the rest of the cityscape, reflected on the glass curtain wall of the Grand Hyatt. I envisioned the finished art in black and white, so I drew it in tight pen and ink. I drew on Mylar to produce different shades of black; the ink appears lighter when you let the pen glide quickly, and darker when you press a little harder. This is a classic approach in ink drawing where the highlights are not delineated with any outline.

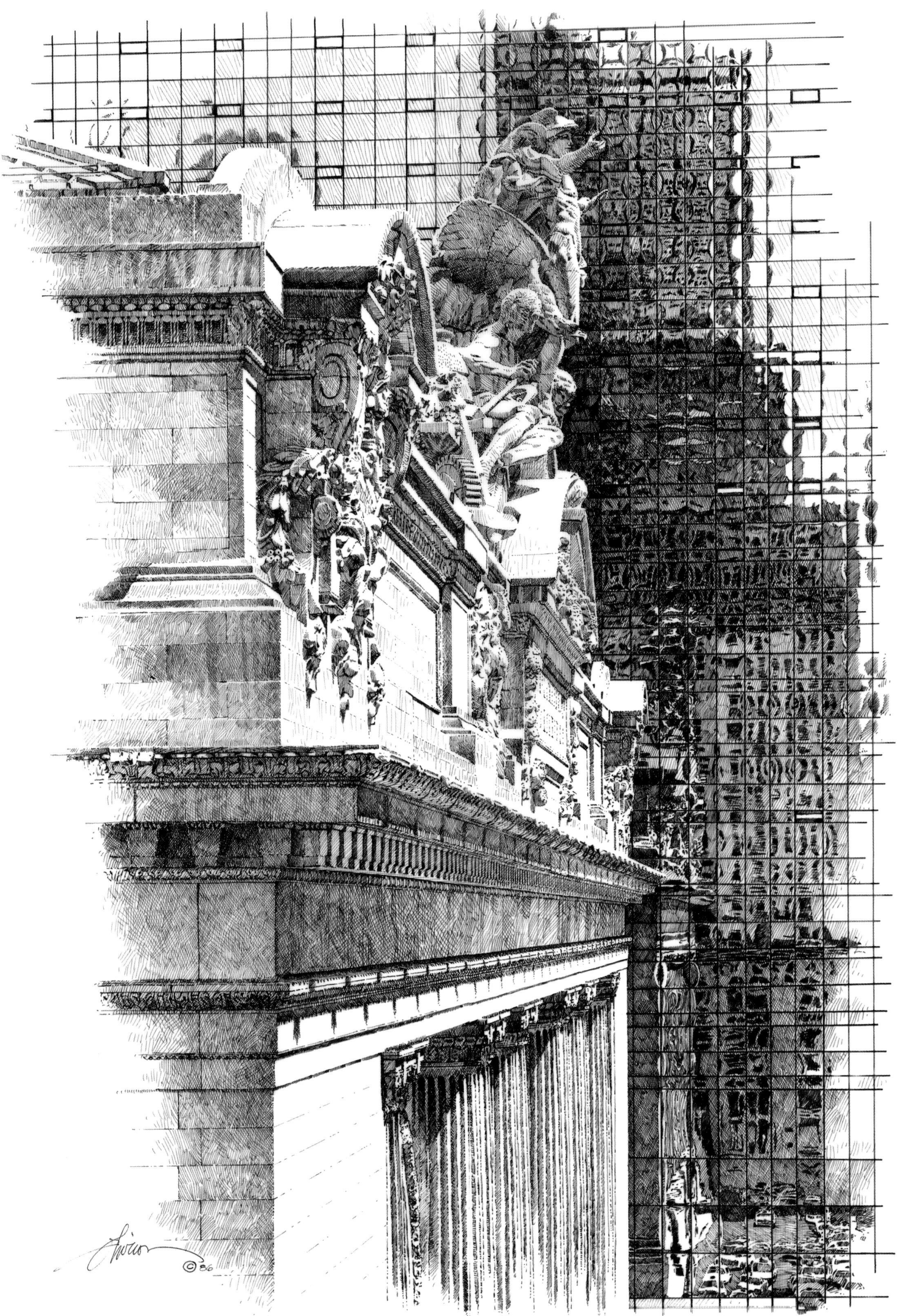

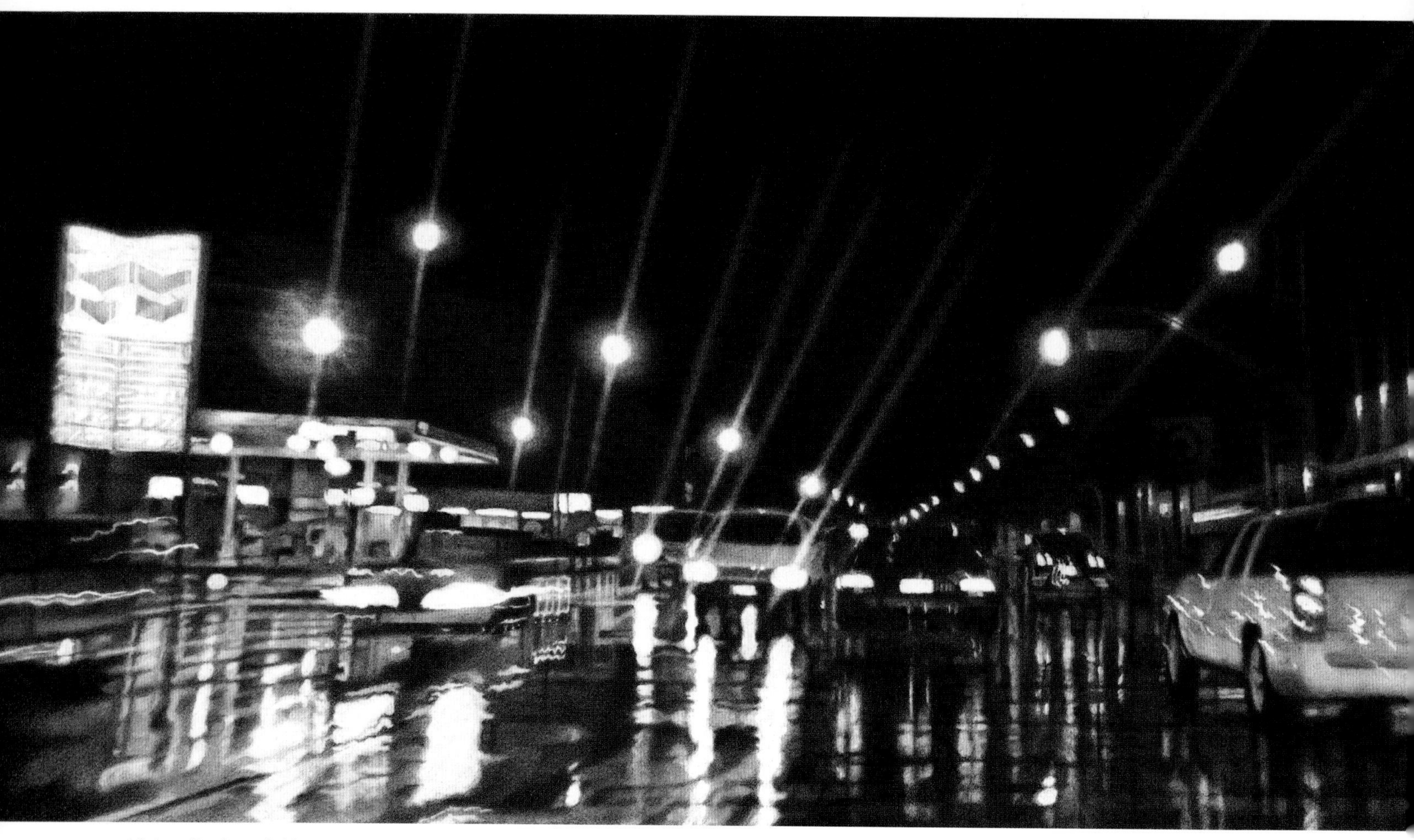

Victory Boulevard, 11pm
Elizabeth Patterson · Colored pencil, graphite and solvent on illustration board · 8" × 15" (20cm × 38cm)

A Drive in the Rain Launches Series

A chance experience while driving home in the rain launched this series. I found my attention drawn to observing the patterns on the windshield. *Victory Boulevard, 11pm* was developed in graphite, after which black colored pencil and solvent were added. The solvent melts the pigment into the surface of the paper and creates a dramatic effect with higher contrast. *Benedict Canyon, 5pm* is 100 percent graphite. These small format drawings are executed with a simple yet powerful set of tools: a few pencils, kneaded and electric erasers, and a handful of cotton swabs for blending. Having worked exclusively in colored pencil for many years, it is a joy to return to this wonderfully forgiving medium. (Both pieces are in private collections, courtesy Louis Stern Fine Arts.)

My current "RAINSCAPES" SERIES has shown me that interesting things happen to **LIGHTS AND DARKS** when one is in motion and it's wet outside.

-Elizabeth Patterson

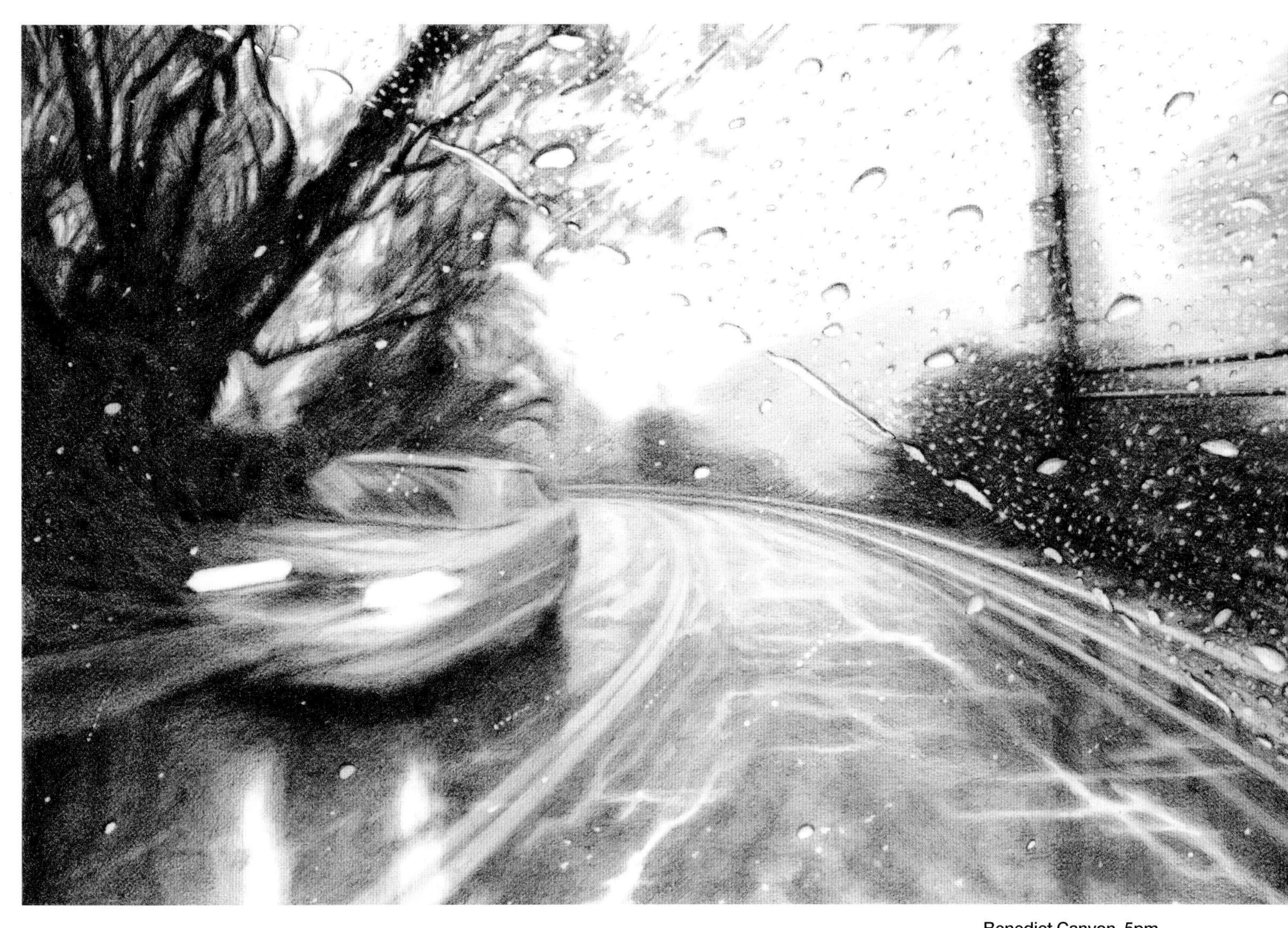

Benedict Canyon, 5pm
Elizabeth Patterson · Graphite on bristol paper with vellum finish · 6" × 9" (15cm × 23cm)

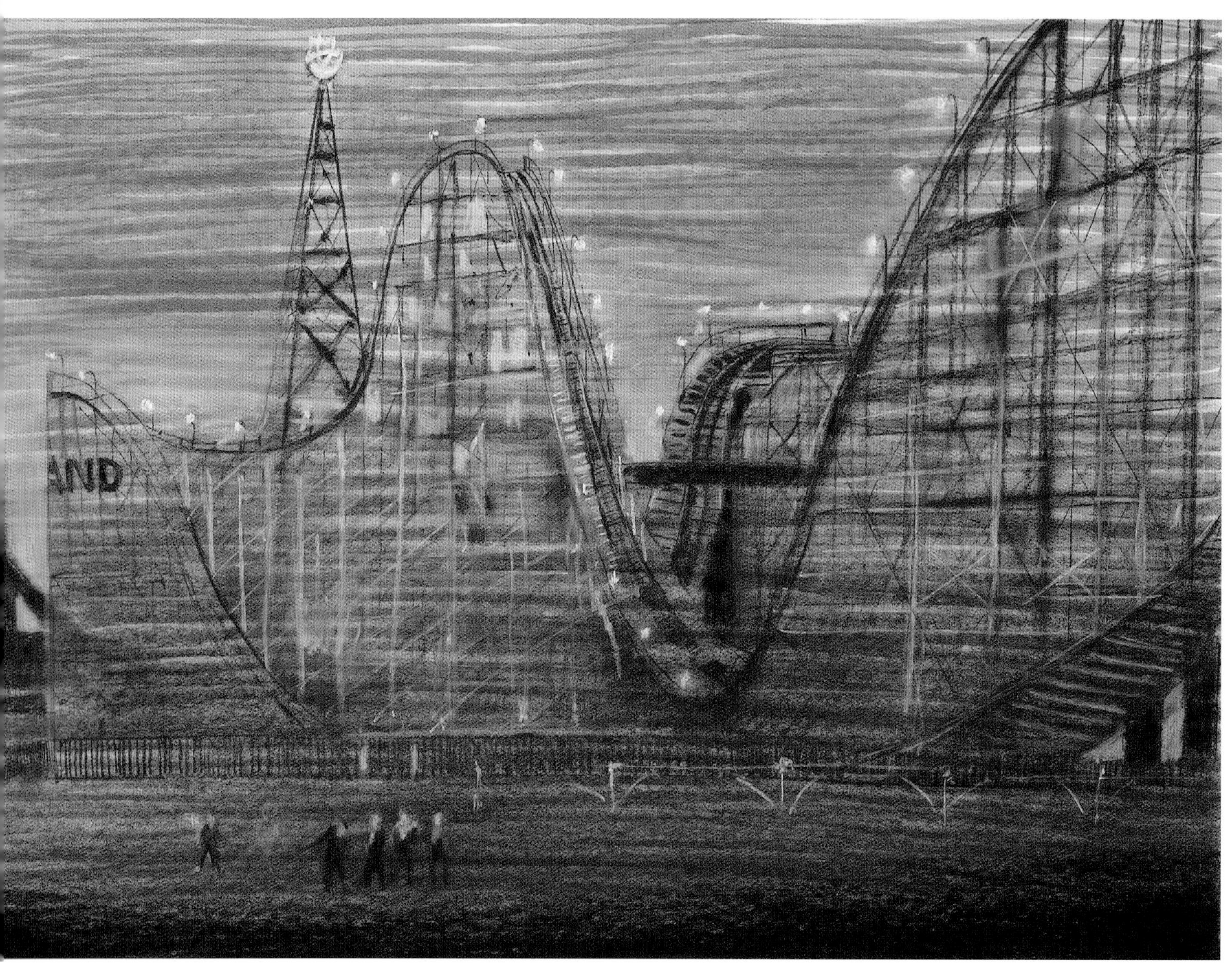

Playland
Lucille Rella · Felt pen and Conté pastel on paper · 18" × 24" (46cm × 61cm)

CREATING AN ATMOSPHERE OF DUSK

On a trip to New York, I drove out to Rockaway Beach and recorded the image of Playland in my sketchbook. This was the last time I saw this landmark; since then it has been demolished. To create an atmosphere of day turning into night, I used a Tomboy felt pen. Holding the brush end on its side, I drew horizontal stripes of gray color on the background. To further enhance the density of sky, I used a Gray Conté pastel pencil; this helped achieve a harmonious appearance. I brought out the structure of the roller coaster using a combination of charcoal and Conté along with color contrast to highlight the foreground.

Often artwork employs grays in gradation from
WHITE TO BLACK to create **SPACE AND FORM.**
However, *Playland* is a low-key drawing (mostly dark values)
in which the **ILLUSION OF SPACE** is nevertheless created,
along with a particular mood.

-Lucille Rella

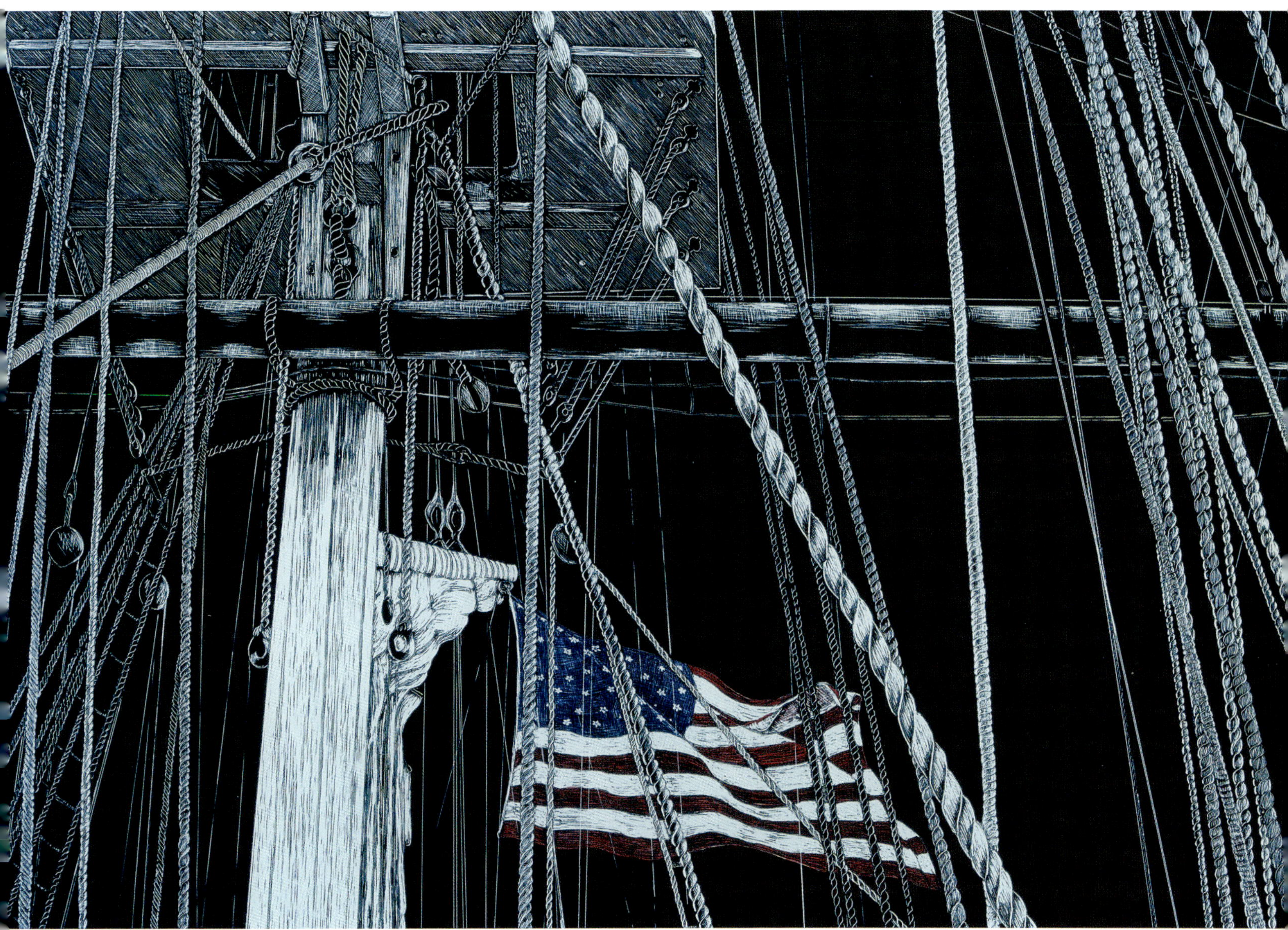

Old Ironsides
Lois I. Ryder · Scratchboard and acrylic · 21" × 25" (53cm × 64cm)

COMBINE ACRYLIC WITH SCRATCHBOARD

I am always looking for something unusual that catches my eye. On a trip to Boston with some artist friends, we visited *Old Ironsides*. The rigging, cannons, flags and wood carvings were all very inspiring. I drew the outline of the subject first on paper and then transferred it with white carbon to the scratchboard. I proceeded to scratch in the detail with a very fine-point metal pen. After the drawing was all finished, I added the color with acrylic paint.

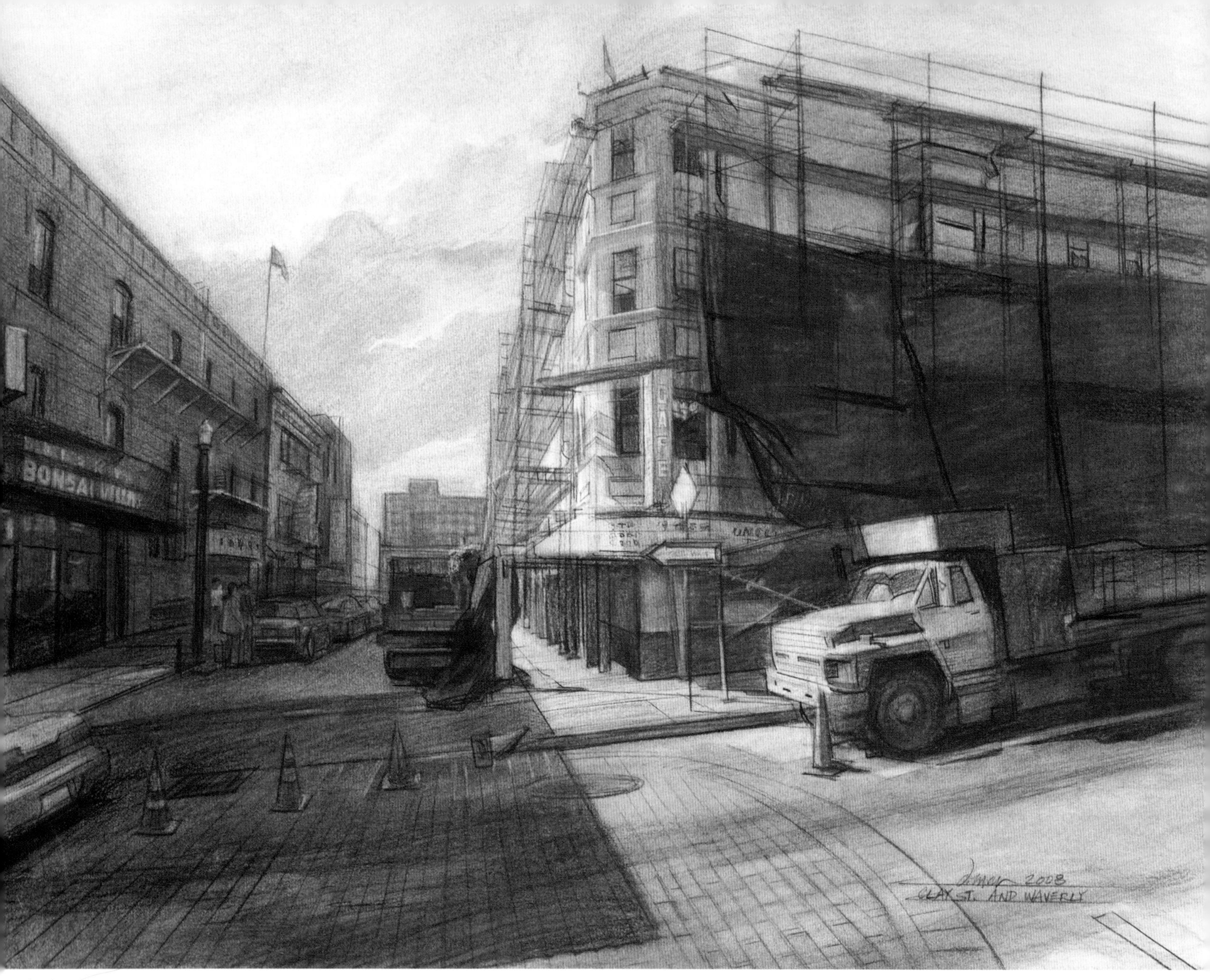

Clay St. and Waverly
David Mar · Charcoal and carbon pencil on paper · 18¼" × 24¼" (46cm × 62cm)

Drawing on Paper Brings Satisfaction

Although I do use photography and digital media for some art-related purposes, I find satisfaction primarily in drawing on paper because it has a level of performance to it that is not present in those other forms of expression. In drawing, as in life, one has to make decisions one way or another, and each choice leads to a different outcome, which isn't readily undone. It doesn't really matter how boldly or timidly the choices were made—the evidence of such decisions is what matters.

The carefully perceived transitory shapes of
SHADOWS can combine with what you know
about an object to create something
MORE REVEALING than either one alone.

-David Mar

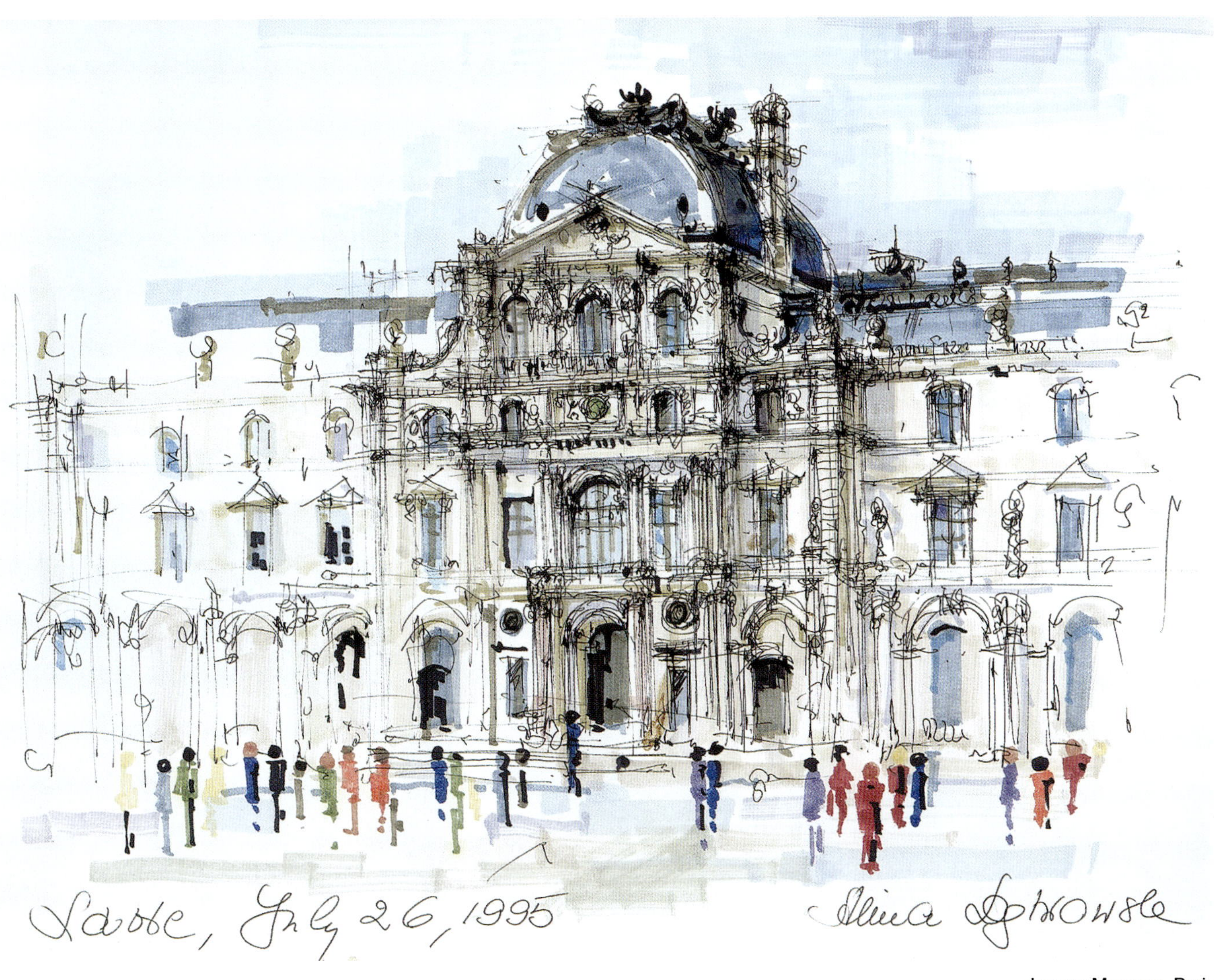

Louvre Museum, Paris
Alina Dabrowska · Pen and ink and markers on paper · 8½" × 11" (22cm × 28cm)

Draw Lightly and Then Add More Weight

As a trained architect I pay attention to perspective, proportion, line quality and weight, play of light, value changes, texture, and color relationships. For a sketch like this, I start with very light pen lines and then add some more weight to them. If it is going to be only pen and ink, I apply shadows with hatching and crosshatching, building darker values. If color is to be added, as here, I check line weights, think fore/background relationship to achieve depth of field, and apply markers starting with the lightest values.

As I travel around America and Europe, I keep my sketchbook, pens and markers in my backpack and am always on the lookout for interesting and original objects to draw.

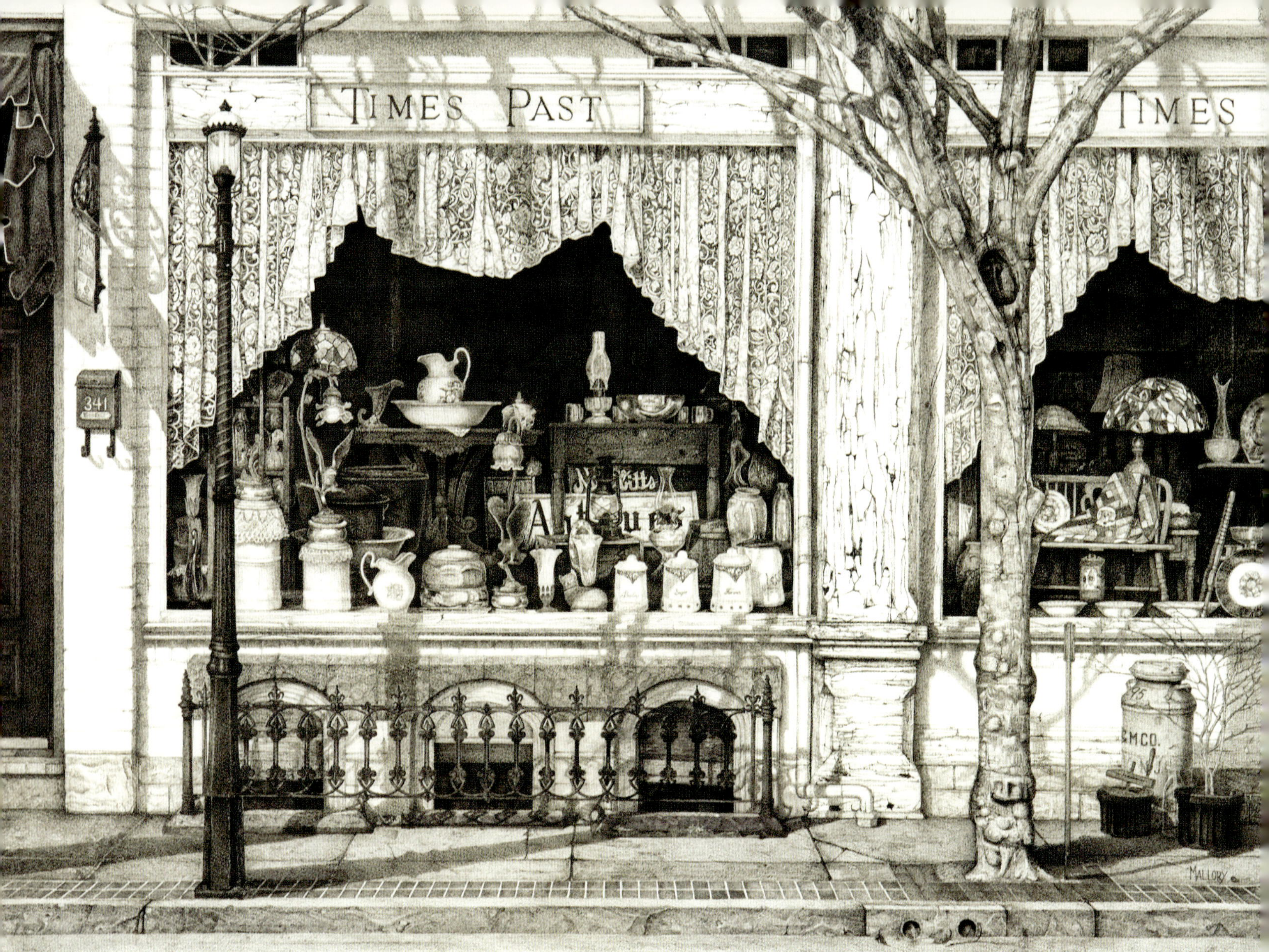

Times Past
Larry R. Mallory · Ink on watercolor paper · 20" × 28½" (51cm × 72cm)

APPLY INK WITH WATERCOLOR BRUSHES

This drawing was done in the studio using my photographs for reference. I combined several building fronts and rearranged various elements to complete the composition. I began by drawing the basic design on the reverse side of 140-lb. (300gsm) watercolor paper. Ink was then applied using round watercolor brushes, controlling light and dark values by the amount of ink and by the pressure and length of brushstroke. Dry-brush seemed well suited to the interplay of light and dark. I was especially drawn to the intricate lace curtains, the tree with burl and the vast array of antiques.

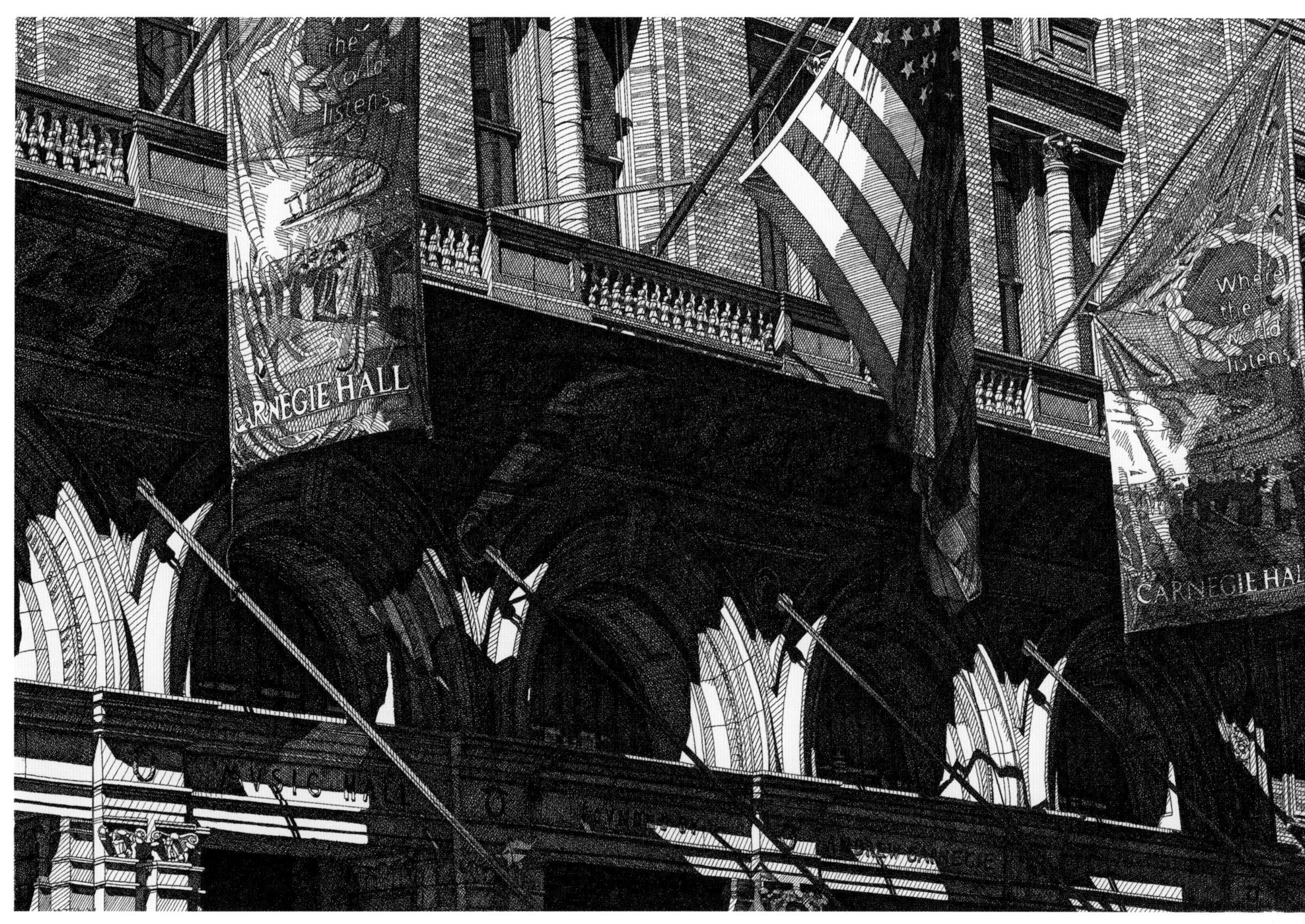

Carnegie Hall, NYC
Melissa B. Tubbs · Pen and ink on drawing paper · 10⅝" × 15½" (27cm × 39cm)

SHADOW PATTERNS TRANSFORM LANDMARK

When I first walked up to Carnegie Hall in New York City and saw the deep shadows and patterns of light on the arches above the marquee and on the flags, I knew I had to draw it. Working from the color photograph I took that day, I used Strathmore 400 Series drawing paper because of its warm off-white color. For this drawing, I used a Rotring Rapidoliner with a 0.18 point. A lot of detail goes into my drawings because it is all the little things that make the whole of what we see. I want people to see those details.

CHAPTER 3 ANIMALS

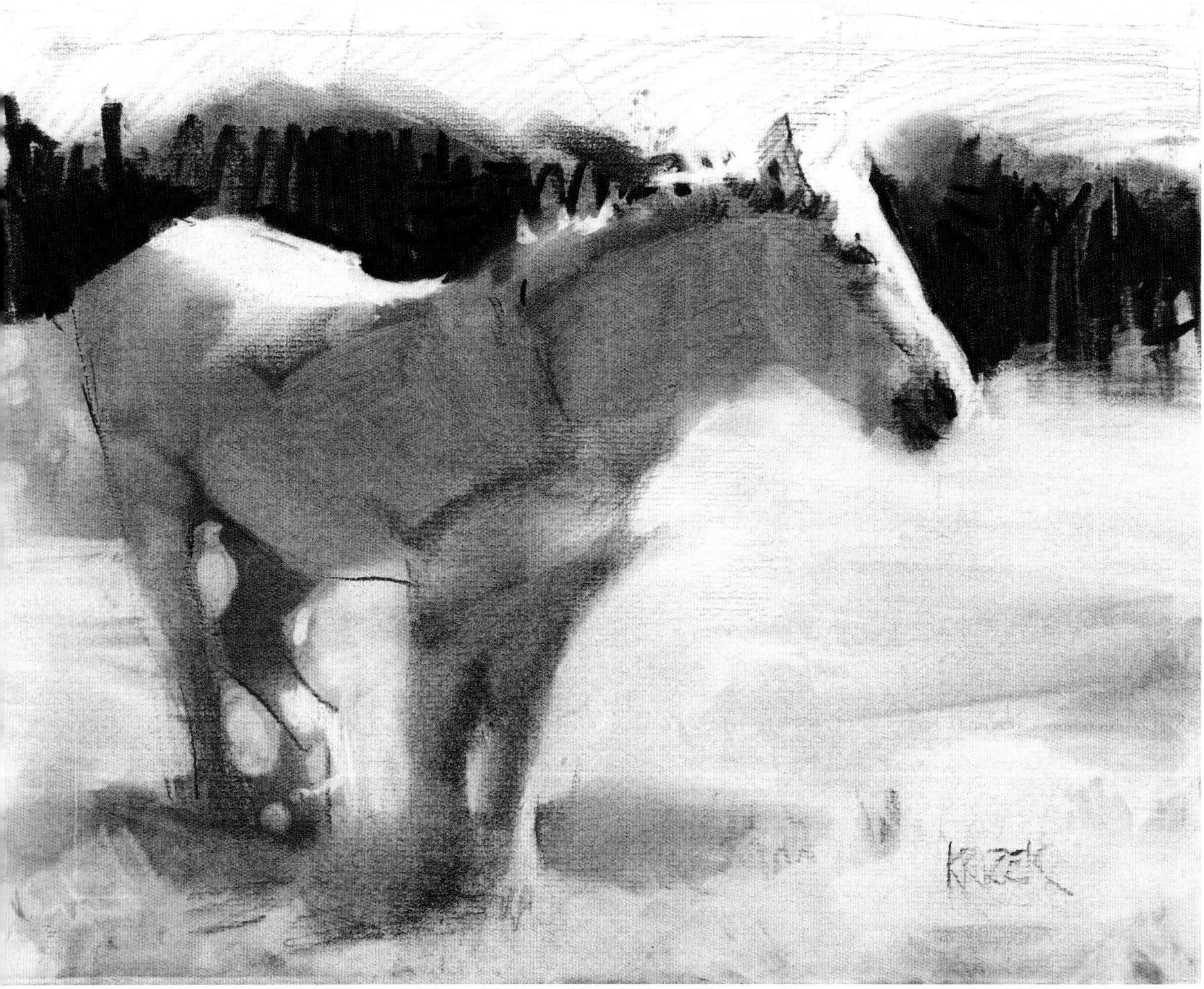

Spirit Guide
Donna Krizek · Charcoal on laid paper · 11" × 14" (28cm × 36cm)

DRAWING DISTILLED TO ITS SIMPLEST ELEMENTS

The pieces on these two pages are representational drawings distilled to their simplest forms. They were drawn from life and rendered in minutes. The big shapes were captured at the speed of thought, simultaneous with observation. I am attracted to contrast and seek to capture its drama. Contrast is most noticeable where the edge of the shape of the light touches the shape of the shadow. The drawings began with a quick gesture layout in vine charcoal to get something on the page; the light is already there in the white of the paper. A dash of charcoal powder is moved around with a sponge, chamois and kneaded eraser for the shapes of the shadow.

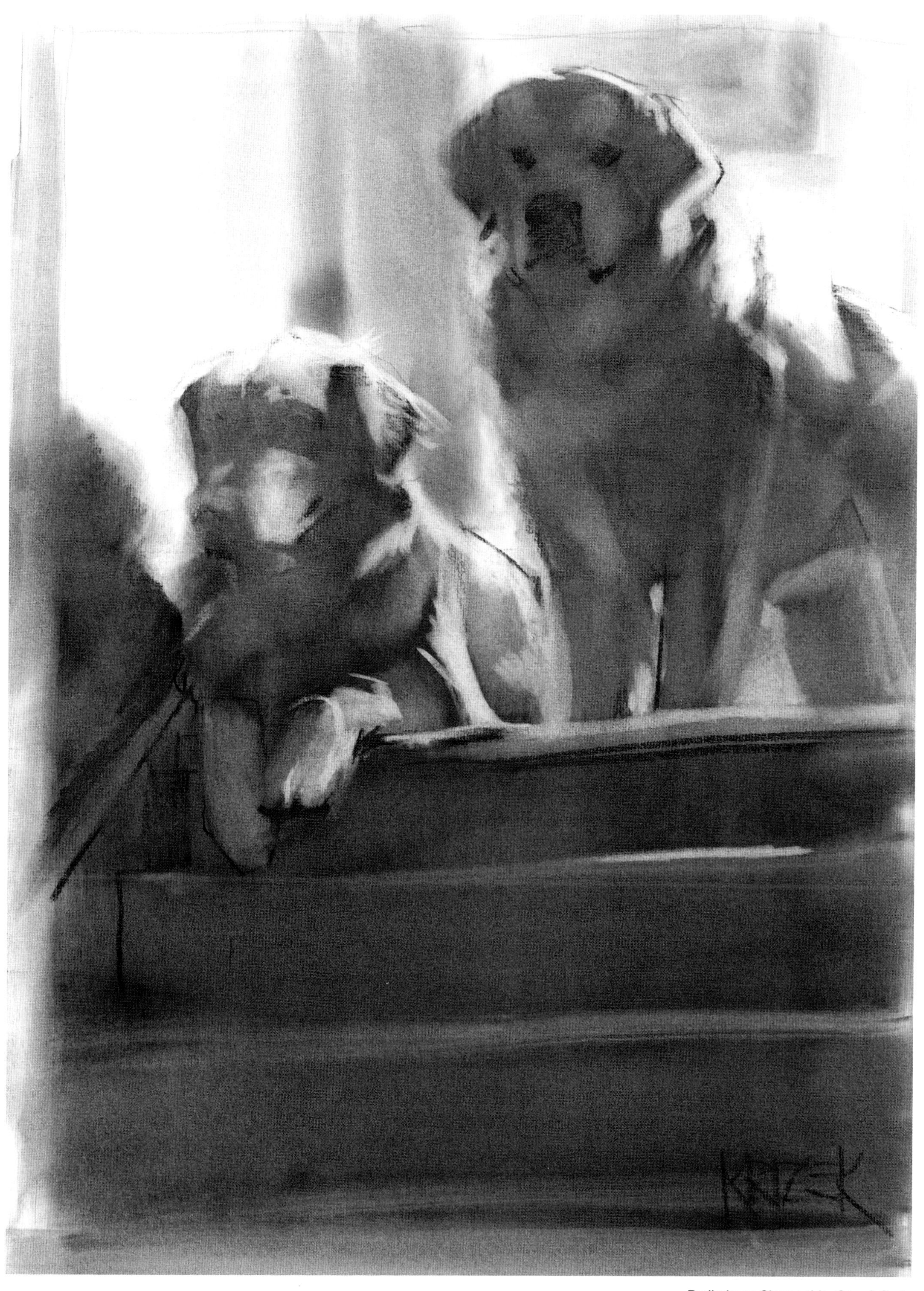

Preliminary Charcoal for Sam & Cody
Donna Krizek · Charcoal on laid paper · 24" × 18" (61cm × 46cm)

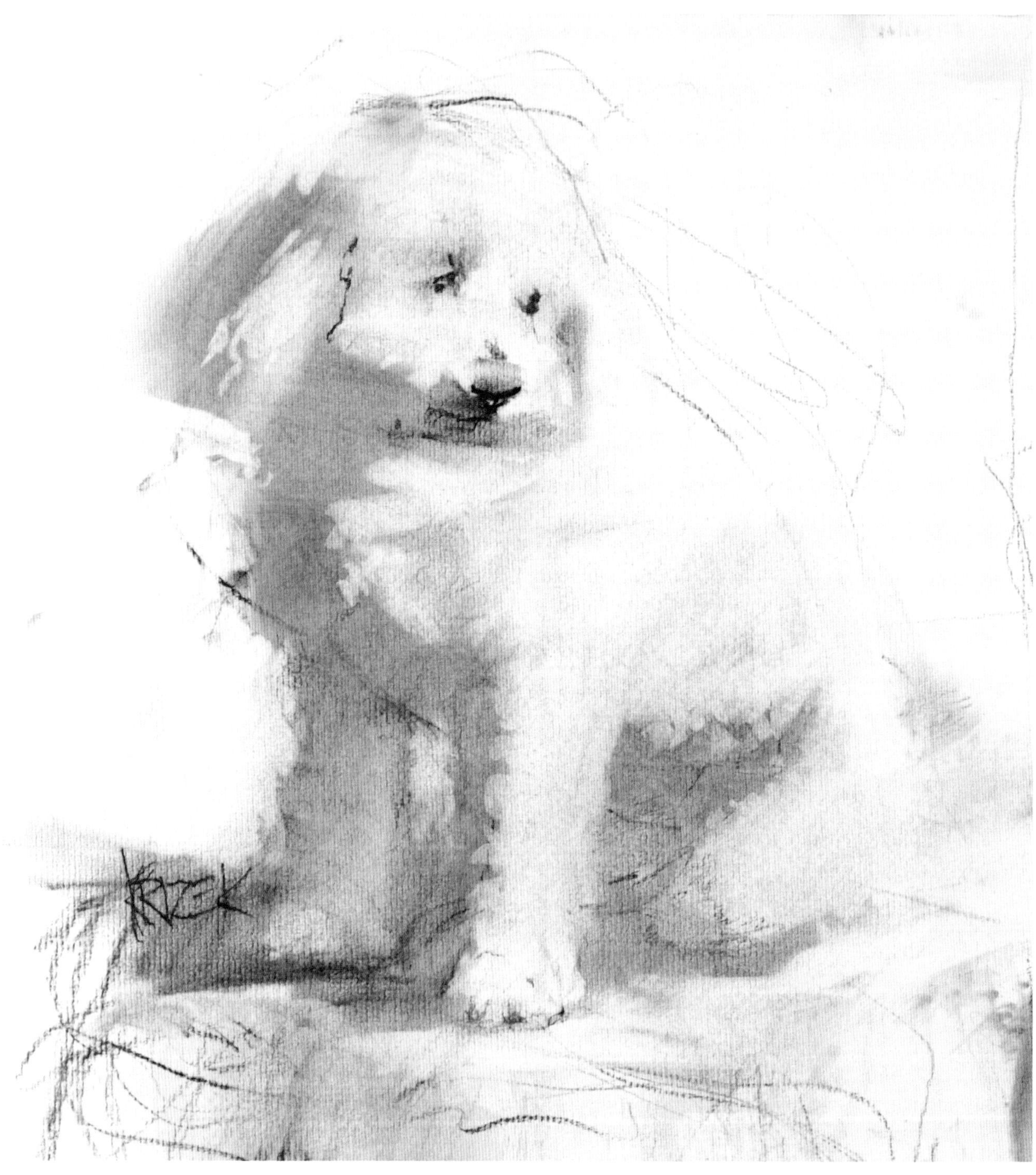

Maggie Pup
Donna Krizek · Charcoal on laid paper · 11" × 11" (28cm × 28cm)

DRAW IN WHATEVER TIME YOU CAN CLAIM

Maggie Pup was done with a similar technique as the drawings on pages 48–49. I laid in a quick gesture sketch in vine charcoal to get the subject on the page. Then I moved a dash of charcoal powder around with a sponge, chamois and kneaded eraser to create the shadow shapes that flesh out the pup and give her form.

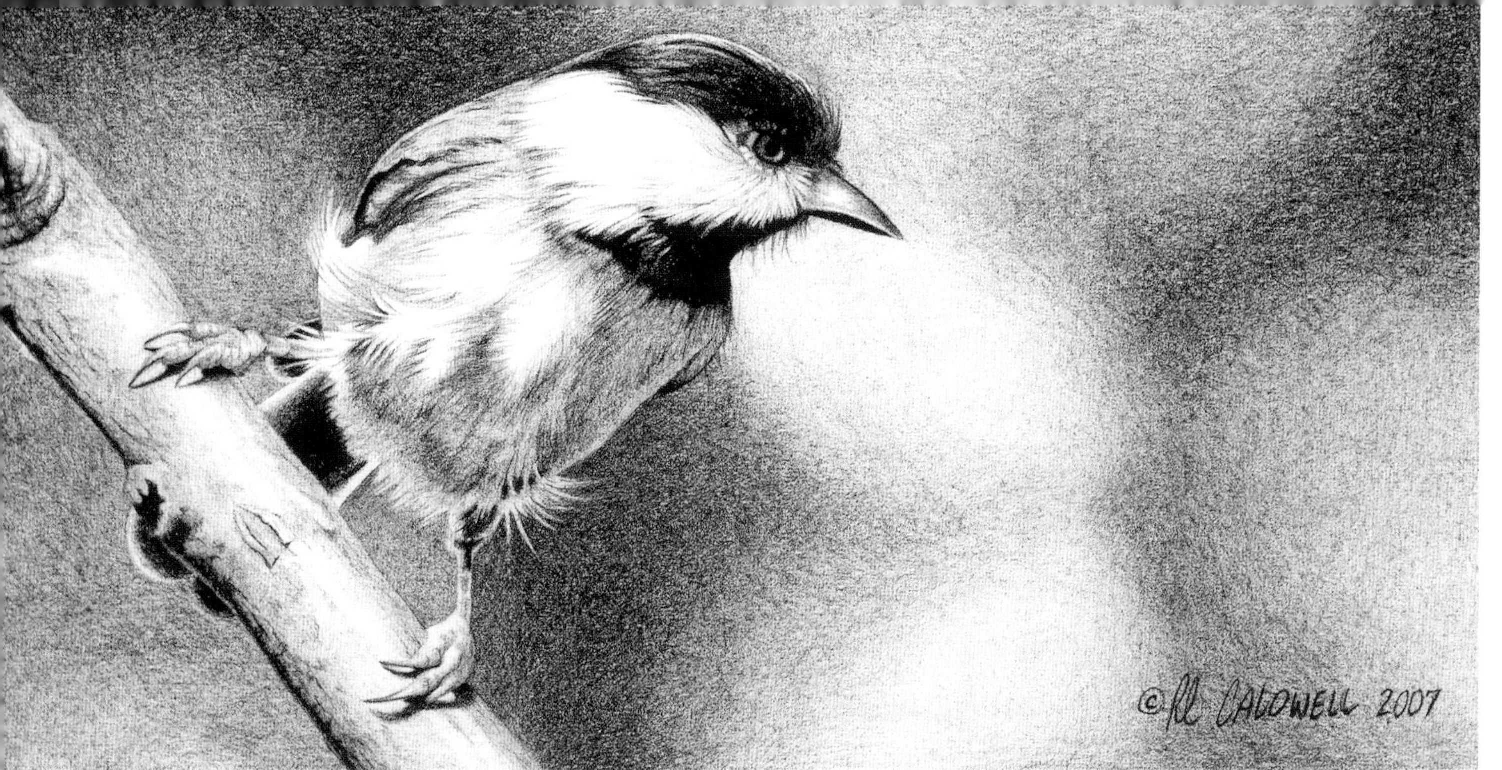

Lookout (Black-Capped Chickadee)
Robert L. Caldwell · Graphite on cold-pressed watercolor paper · 4" × 8" (10cm × 20cm)

COMPOSE YOUR DRAWINGS CAREFULLY

Working from photographic references taken on research trips, each of my drawings is carefully composed and a value sketch completed before the first pencil stroke touches paper. Then I build the drawing, layer by layer, starting with the hardest grade pencil and working through the values to the softest grade pencil. Building on top of each layer fills in the tooth of the paper, giving the drawing solid tonal values. Using this technique allows me to achieve my desired result—a highly detailed, realistic image.

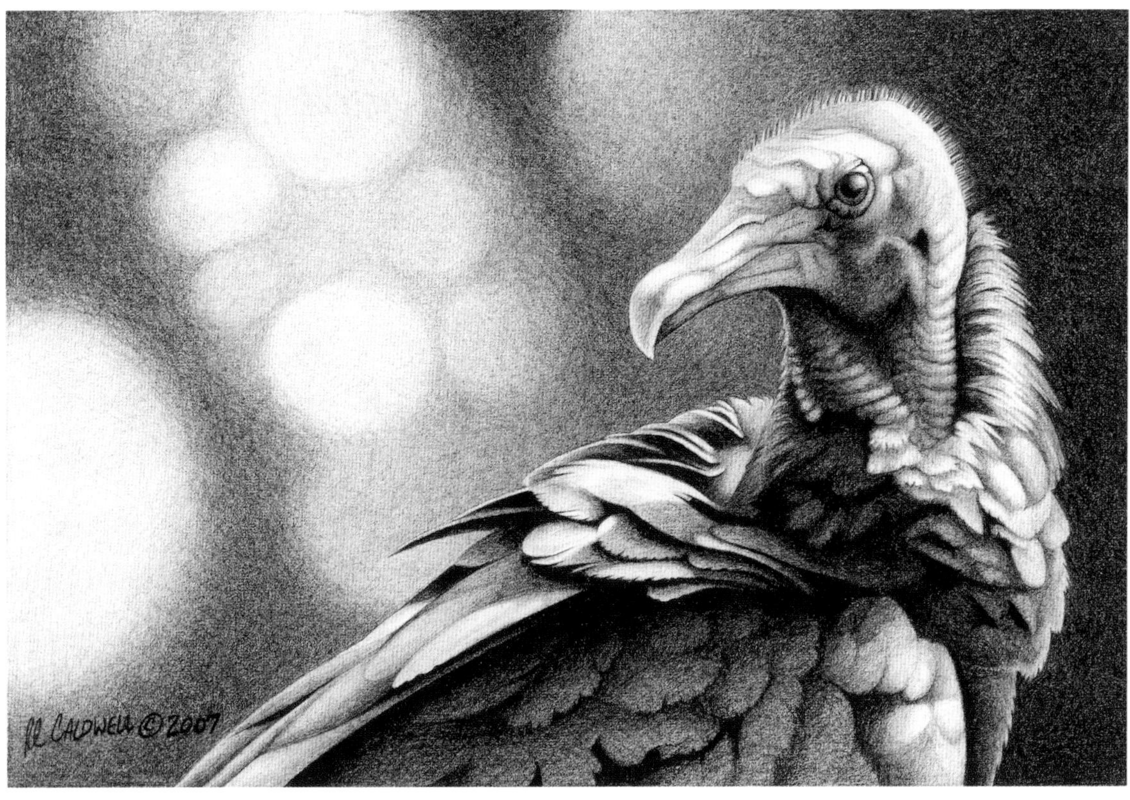

Your Majesty (Black Vulture)
Robert L. Caldwell · Graphite on cold-pressed watercolor paper · 6" × 9" (15cm × 23cm)

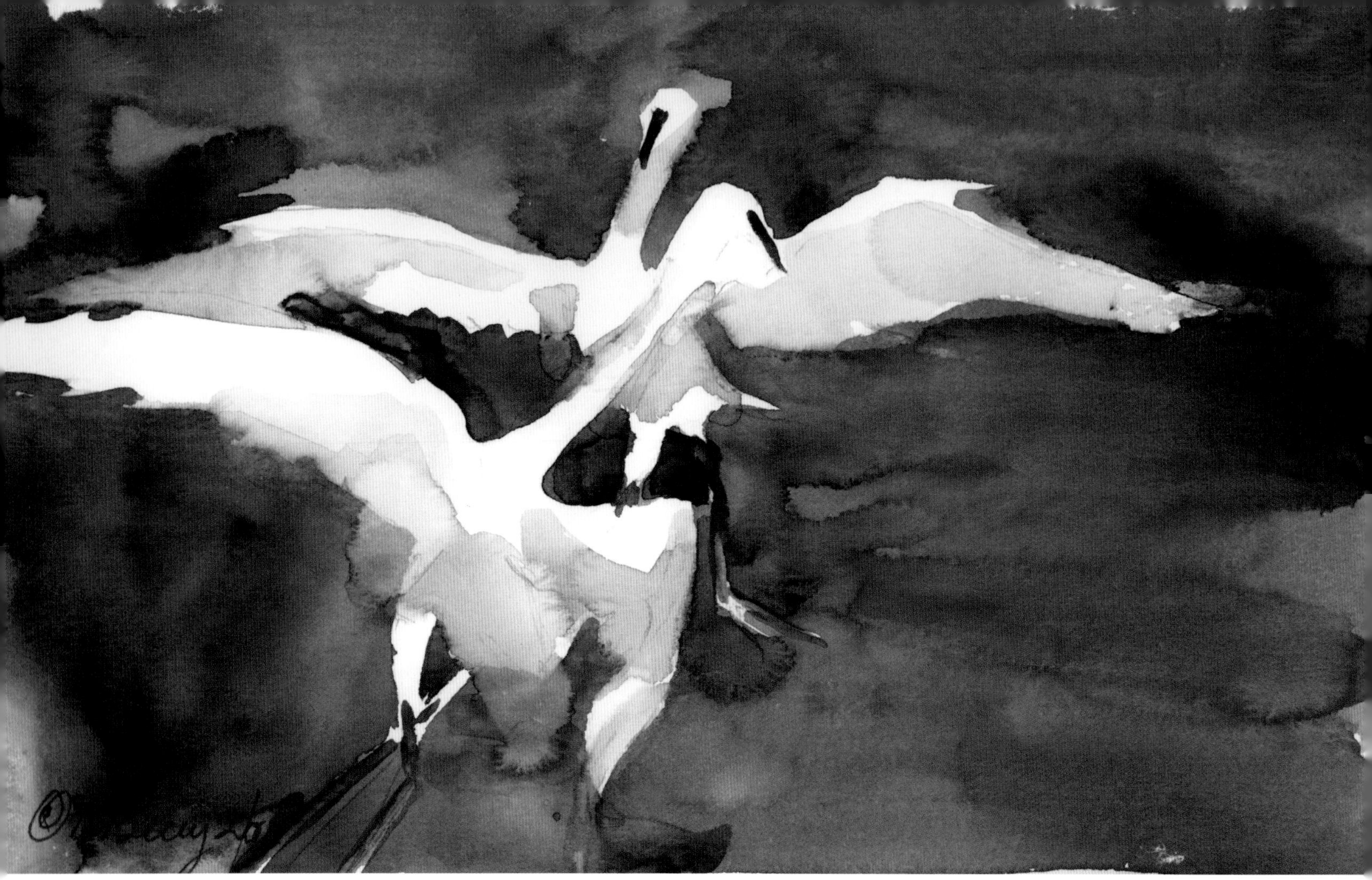

Reddish Egrets Canopy Feeding
Robin Berry · Watercolor · 5½" × 9" (14cm × 23cm)

KEEP YOUR EYE ON THE BIRD

Birds rarely sit still long enough to do a detailed drawing, so mastery of the ten-second gesture sketch is essential. For *Egret on the Move*, I kept my eyes on the bird as I set the felt-tip pen on the paper and, with quick strokes, recorded only what I had time to see. In *Reddish Egrets,* I made a rapid pencil gesture drawing of the birds feeding. Then, using a brush with watercolor, I painted the negative space behind the white birds, up to the gesture lines, finally moving the brush into the bodies of the birds where there were shadows. This sketch took about two minutes. When drawing light and shadow on a person or animal in motion, the faster it is moving, the greater the extremes of light, dark and color. Learning to observe these extremes quickly enhances the visual "snapshot" required to capture light and shadow.

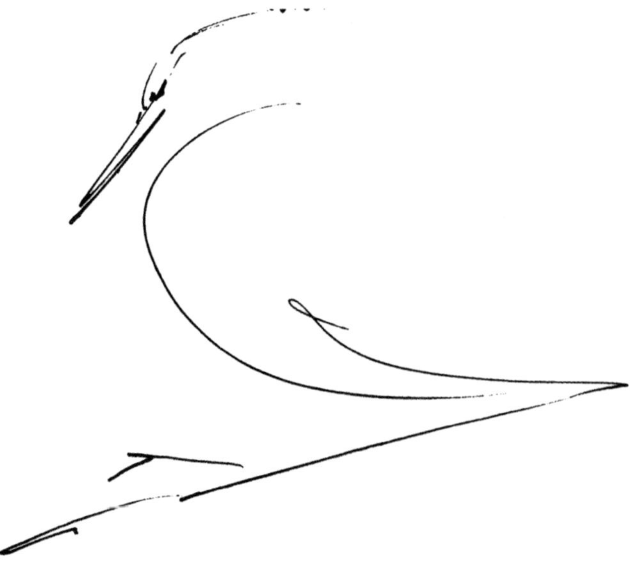

Egret on the Move
Robin Berry · Felt-tip pen on paper · 7" × 9" (18cm × 23cm)

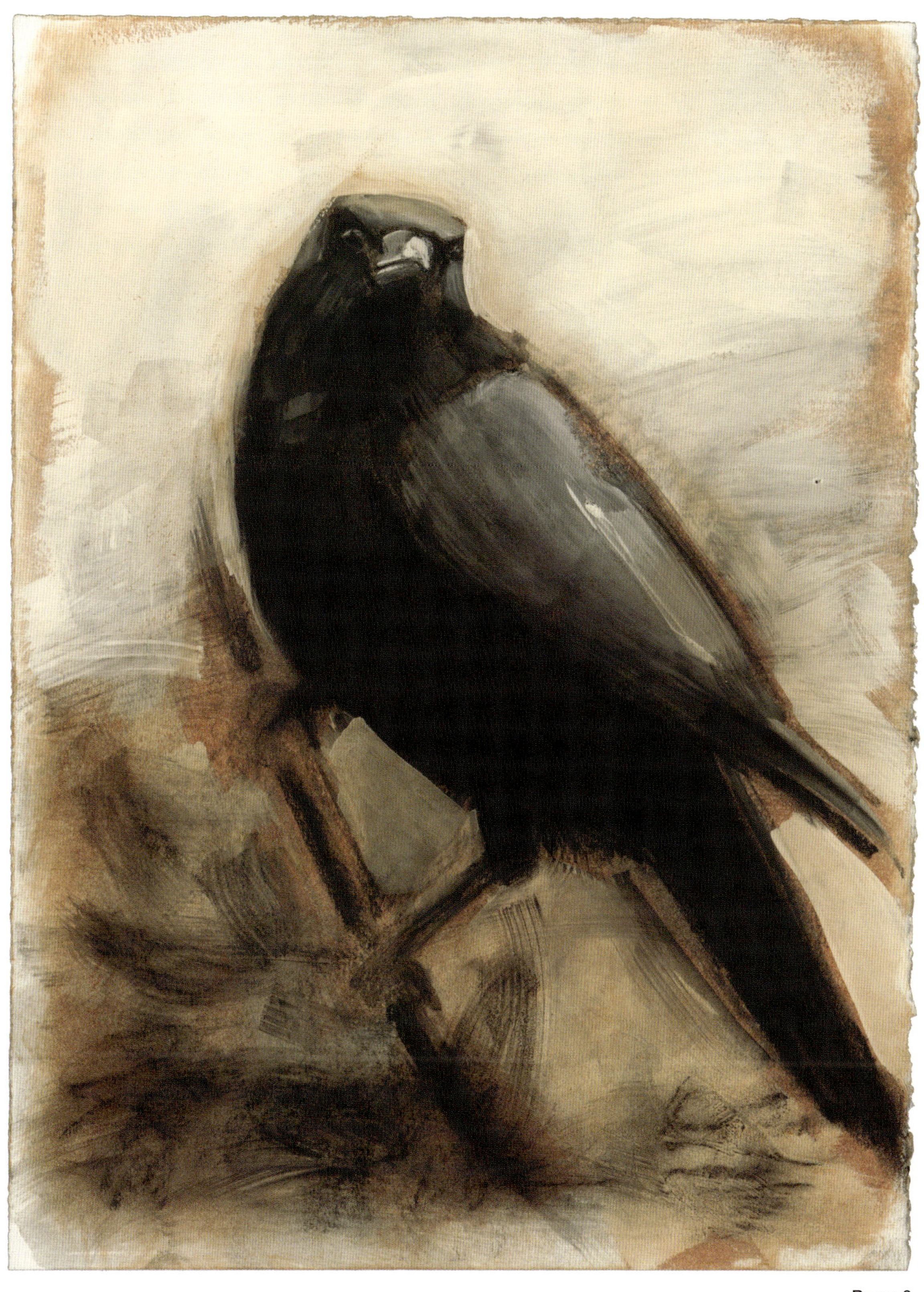

Raven 2
Candace Brancik · Charcoal, gesso and oil glaze on paper · 15" × 11" (38cm × 28cm)

GET TO KNOW A SPECIES WELL

I love the raven because it carries an air of mystery and intelligence, and because it lends itself to wonderful graphic composition. This drawing was part of a series of raven drawings done in the studio from photos. I first sketched out the raven using vine and compressed charcoal. I then painted into and around the charcoal with gesso, creating the midtones and highlights. I went back and forth with the charcoal and gesso until I was happy with the final drawing. I then spray-fixed it thoroughly and covered the entire drawing with a Burnt Sienna-tinted oil glaze.

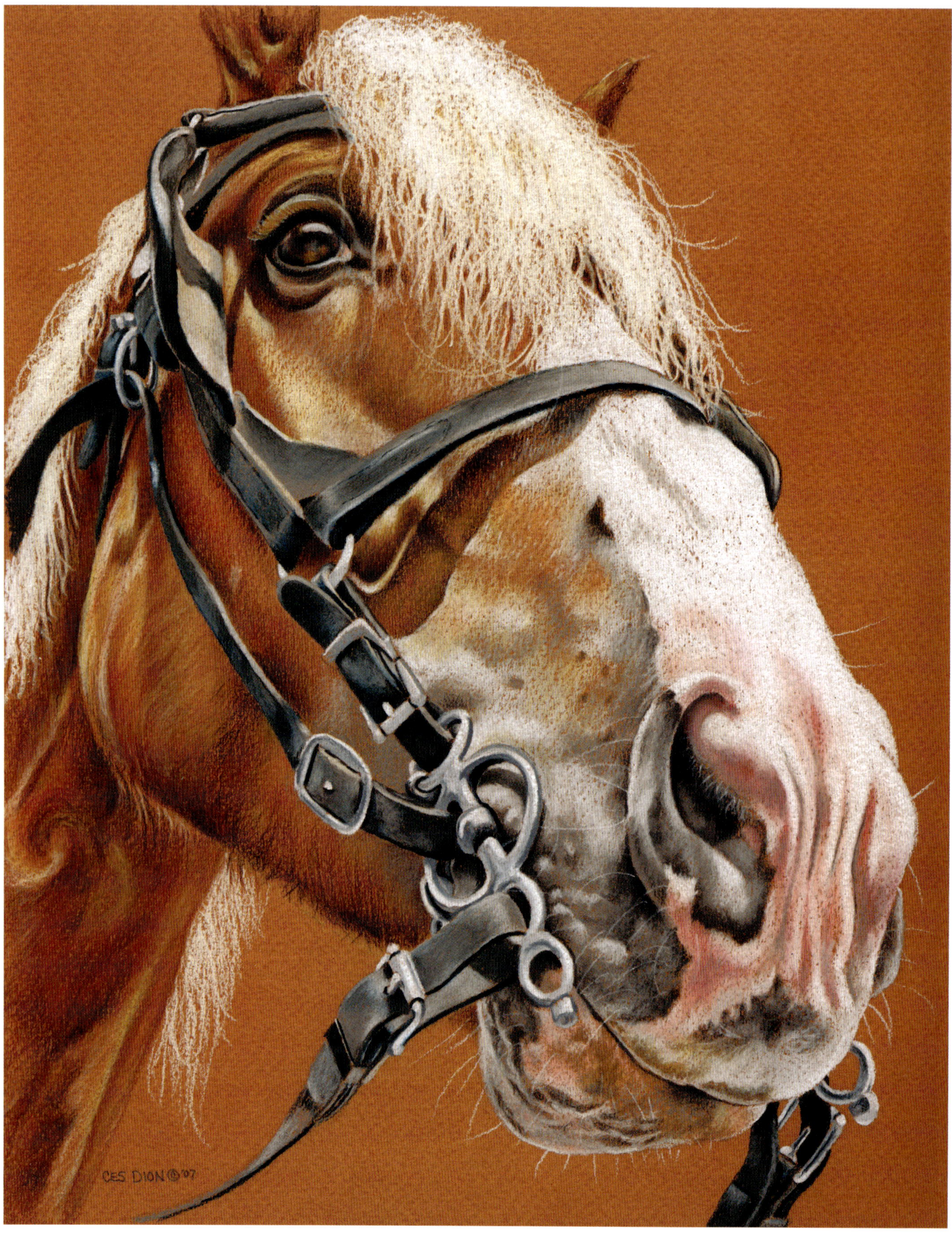

Doc of Dock Square
Christine E. S. Dion · Colored pencil on Fabriano Tiziano pastel paper · 12" × 9" (30cm × 23cm)

INCORPORATE DRAMATIC ANGLES IN A POSE

Doc is a carriage horse in Kennebunkport, Maine. I photographed him on an overcast morning in June. My animal portrait compositions typically incorporate dramatic angles and poses. Doc's headgear provides a wonderful amount of detail, perfect for colored pencil. I use light layers of Prismacolor pencils, and I work on Fabriano Tiziano pastel paper in a variety of colors. The texture of the paper is perfect for accepting many layers of colored pencil. I keep my colored pencils incredibly sharp, thanks to a Dahle mountable pencil sharpener. It doesn't break the tips, which preserves the pencil for a longer time.

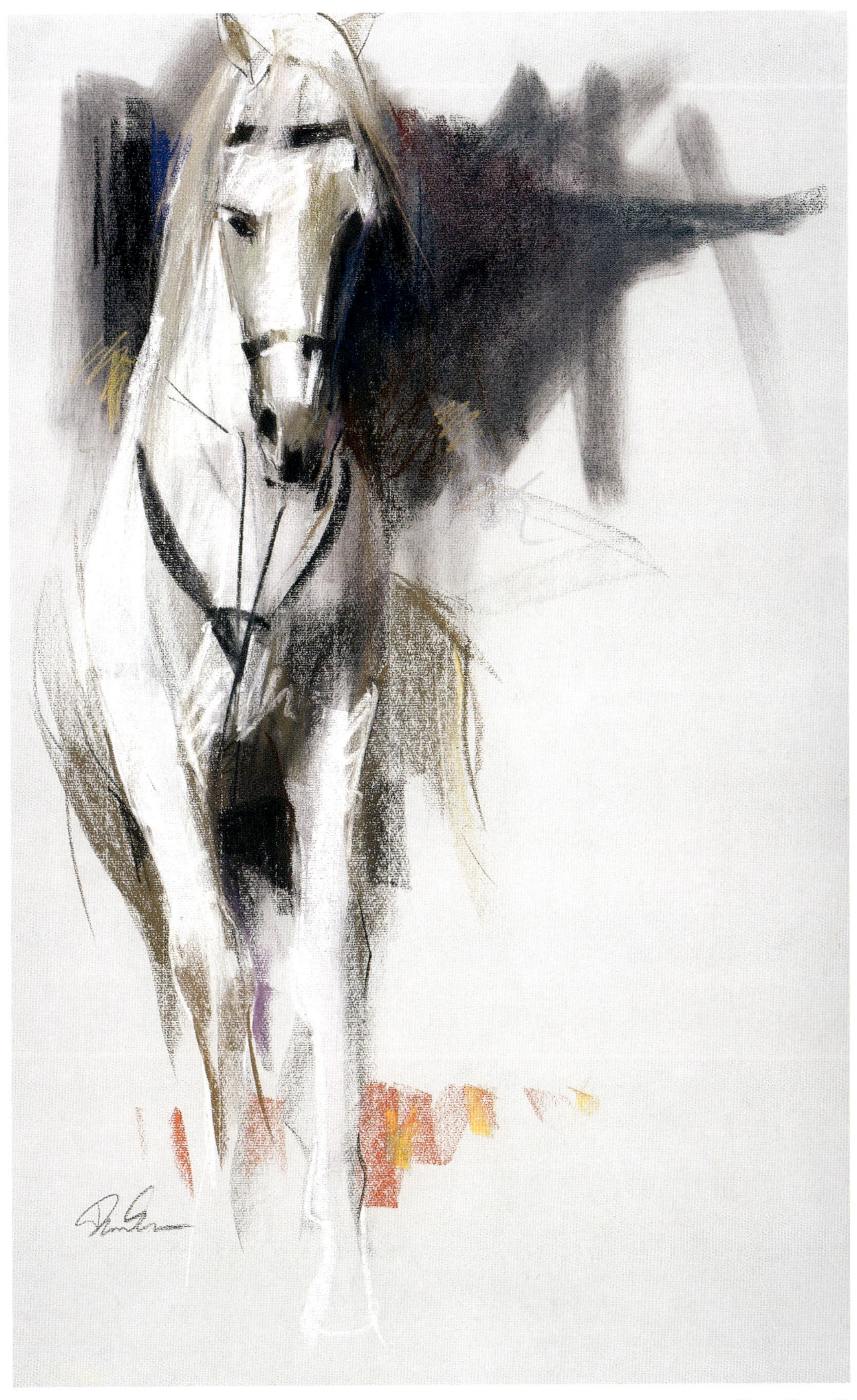

Circus Horse #1

Dawn Emerson · Charcoal and pastel on light gray German handmade paper · 32" × 20" (81cm × 51cm)

A Gesture Sketch May Be All That's Needed

I loved the look in this horse's eye when I saw him performing for this small traveling circus. I consider this a finished "gesture sketch" in the sense that the spontaneity of the lines, the overall graphic design and the simple values carry the piece. No further detail was needed to get the feeling of the horse coming directly at the viewer, and the light gray tone of the paper allowed me to use a pure white pastel to make the value jump off the page once the dark background shape was defined.

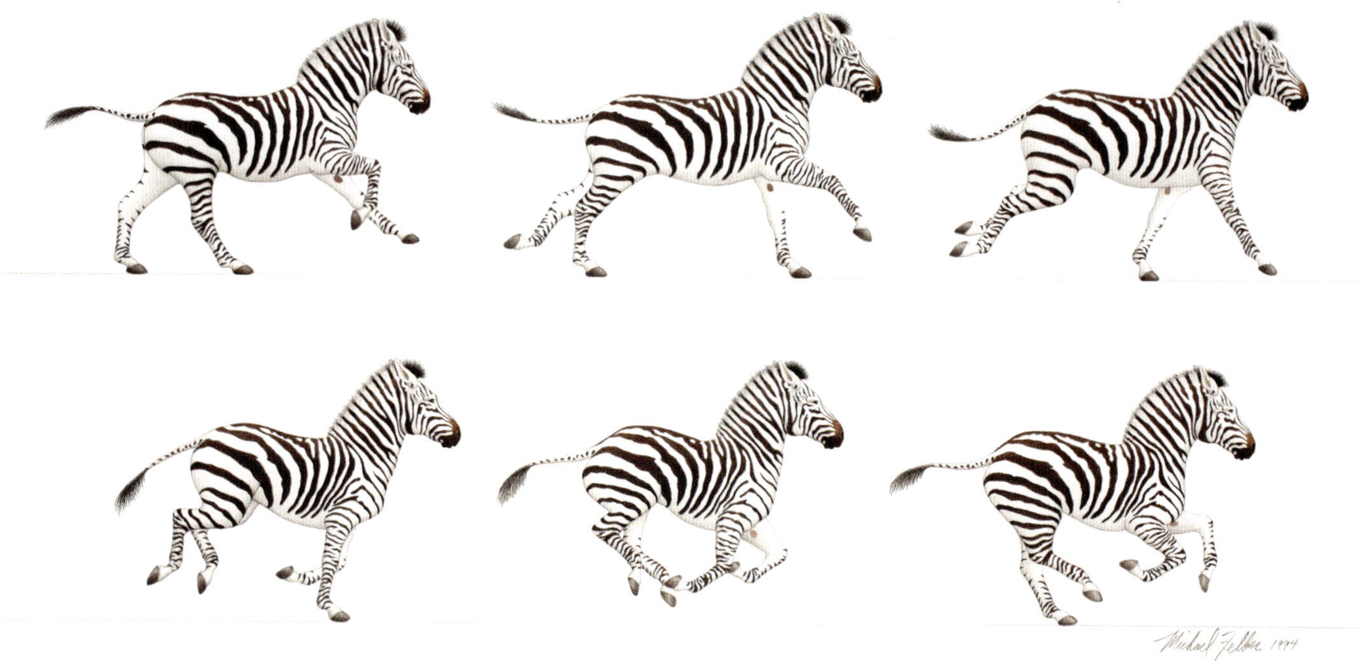

Galloping Burchell's Zebra
Michael J. Felber · Colored pencil over watercolor on coquille paper · 11½" × 23" (29cm × 58cm)

STUDY AN ANIMAL'S MOVEMENTS FOR ACCURACY

While working as an animator, I made thousands of line drawings of dogs and foxes for the animated film *The Plague Dogs*, and I had the idea of making a poster called "Animals in Motion." To get the positions just right, I studied the movement using nature books and videos, tracking books and Eadweard Muybridge's photographs. I used Muybridge's galloping horse photos for the zebra's positions, as well as various zebra photos for other details. I made up some of the movement (as in the tail) using my experience as an animator. Working on an animation disc with registration pegs, I started by creating six line drawings and then made sure that the movement was accurate by flipping the drawings in sequence. Then I transferred the six line drawings to a piece of coquille paper, painted a base of pale watercolor first, and shaded with colored pencil.

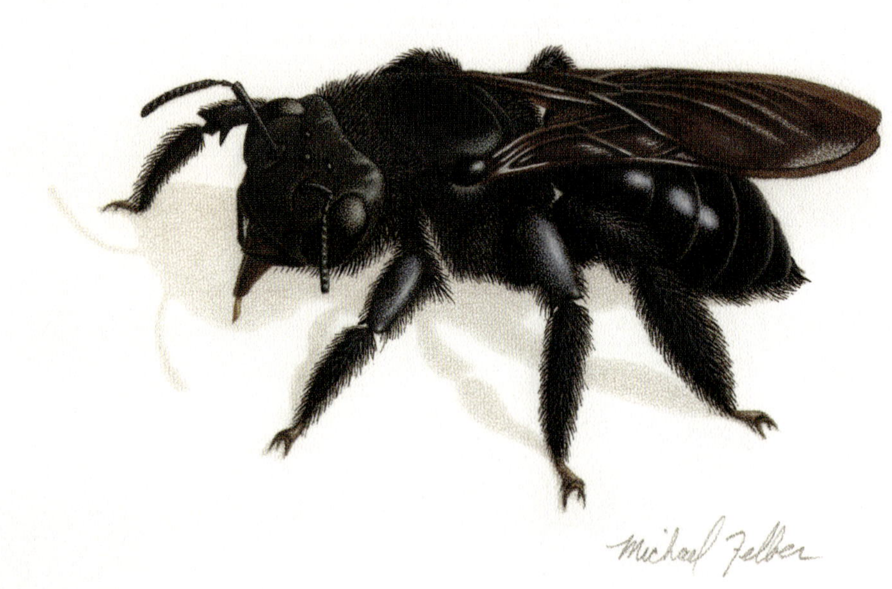

Carpenter Bee
Michael J. Felber · Colored pencil and ink over watercolor on coquille paper · 2¾" × 5" (7cm × 13cm)

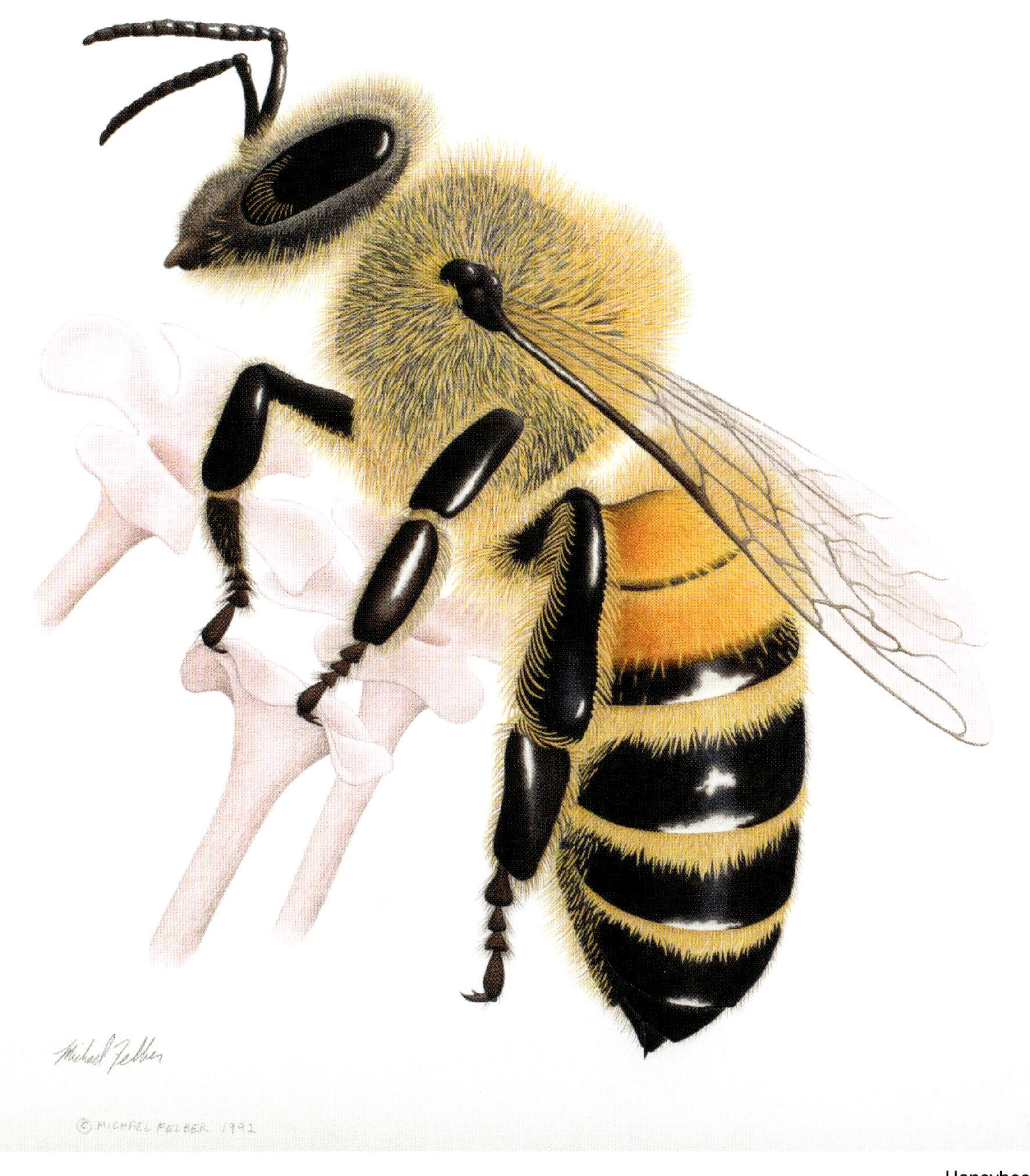

Honeybee
Michael J. Felber · Colored pencil over watercolor on coquille paper · 13" × 12" (33cm × 30cm)

TAKING A BEE'S-EYE VIEW

The process of drawing animals gives me the opportunity to study and observe them very closely. The bees above and at left were drawn from dead insects; one I obtained from an entomologist, and the other I found in a spider's web. The low vantage point that I chose for these drawings helps to bring the viewer into the bee's world. Choosing an angle that shows the spaces between the bee's body parts helps to visualize the forms, especially with black bugs. Using a magnifying glass and a 10-power binocular microscope to see the details, I start with a line drawing and then paint a base of pale watercolor. I then darken and shade the details with Derwent Studio colored pencils. The watercolor base prevents the appearance of white flecks of paper through the colored pencil, which tends to flatten the illusion of depth in a drawing. For the iridescent reflections on the carpenter bee, I first painted a watercolor base of pale violet for the legs and abdomen, and light turquoise for the head and thorax. Then I shaded with a black colored pencil. The translucent effect of the honeybee's diaphanous wings was created with a pale watercolor wash over the drawing of the bee's body.

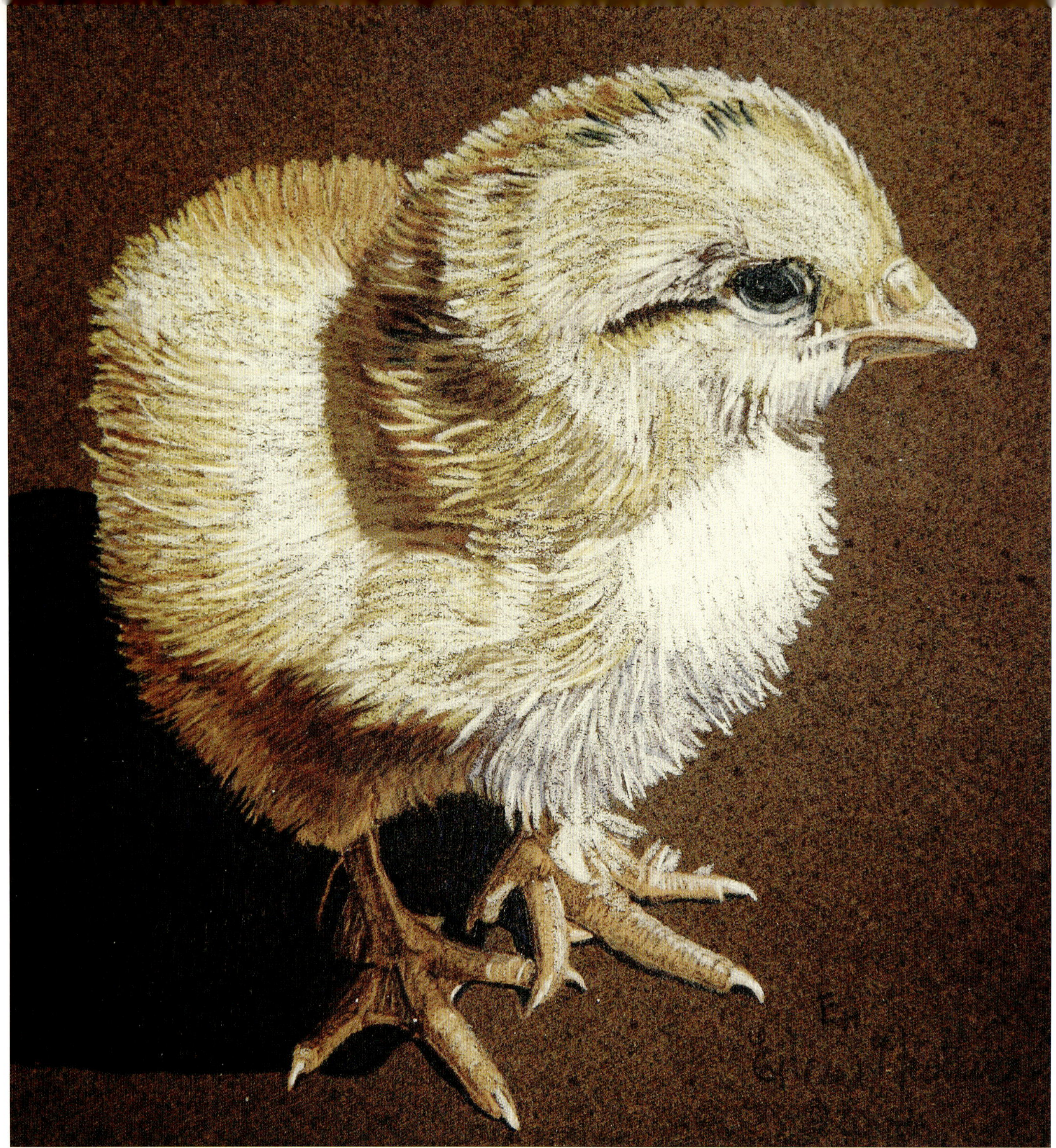

Cute Chick With Hairy Legs
Eileen Nistler · Colored pencil on scrapbook paper · 6½" × 6" (17cm × 15cm)

HUMOR CAN BE A GREAT MOTIVATOR

This drawing was created from photos I took of our baby chickens a few years ago. It was created on archival scrapbook paper that had a little texture. This drawing was drawn as a birthday present for a dear friend (who is also an artist) as an art trading card. The real name of this is *Cute Chick With Hairy Legs for a Cute Chick...?*

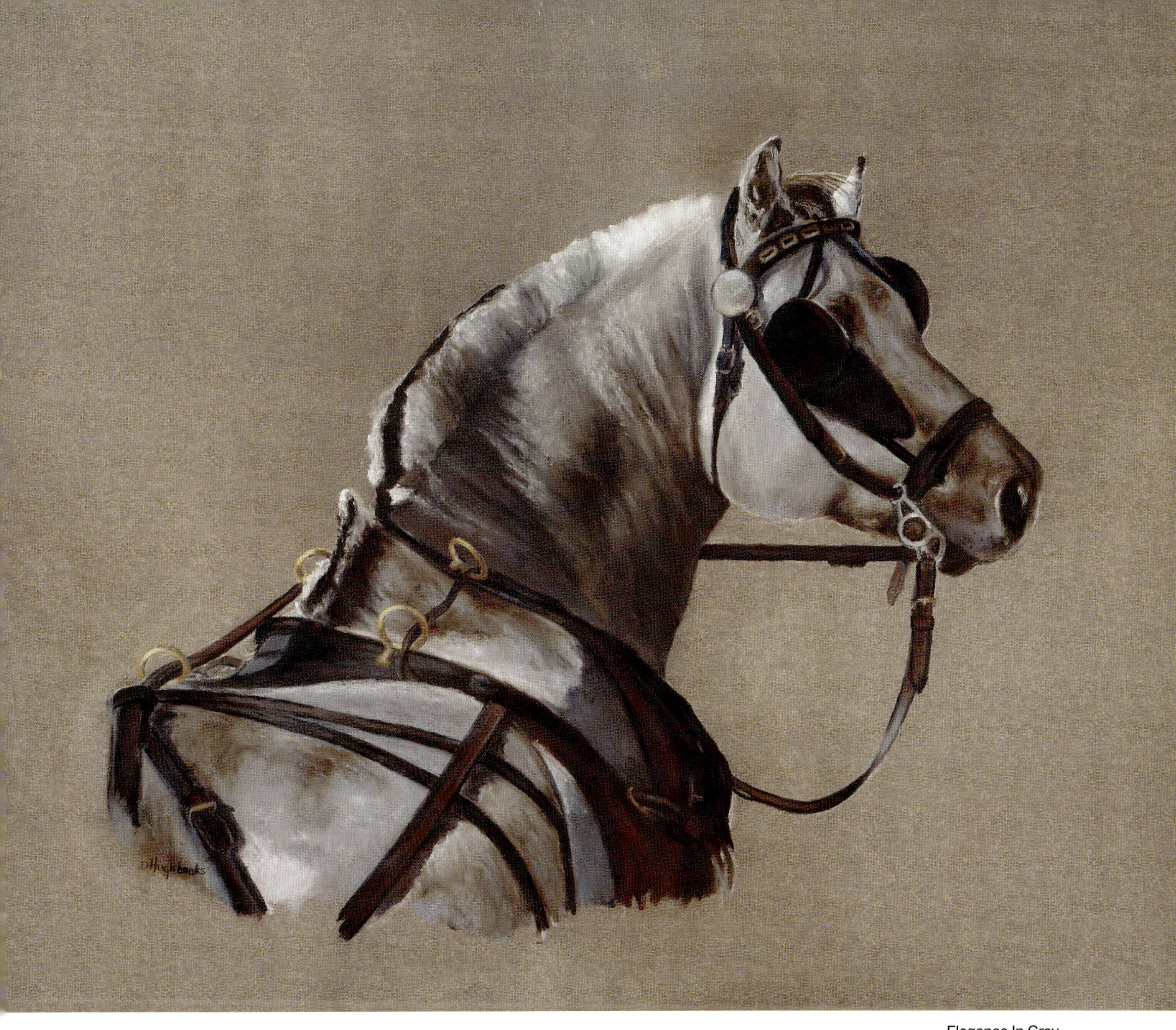

Elegance In Grey
Debbie Hughbanks · Pastel on Wallis Belgian Mist sandpaper · 14" × 18" (36cm × 46cm)

CAPTURE THE NATURAL ELEGANCE OF A BREED

I am passionate about both animals and art, and horses are a frequent subject of mine. I met this stunning
Norwegian Fjord on a visit to a breeder while doing research for a series of paintings. I wanted to capture
both his elegant beauty and spirited nature in pastel. This piece was completed in my studio, working from
reference photos and the firsthand knowledge gained by watching him at work and play. I prefer a surface
with tooth and used a variety of pastels, working from dark to light. The use of lavenders, purples and pinks
enhanced the richness of the horse's gray coat.

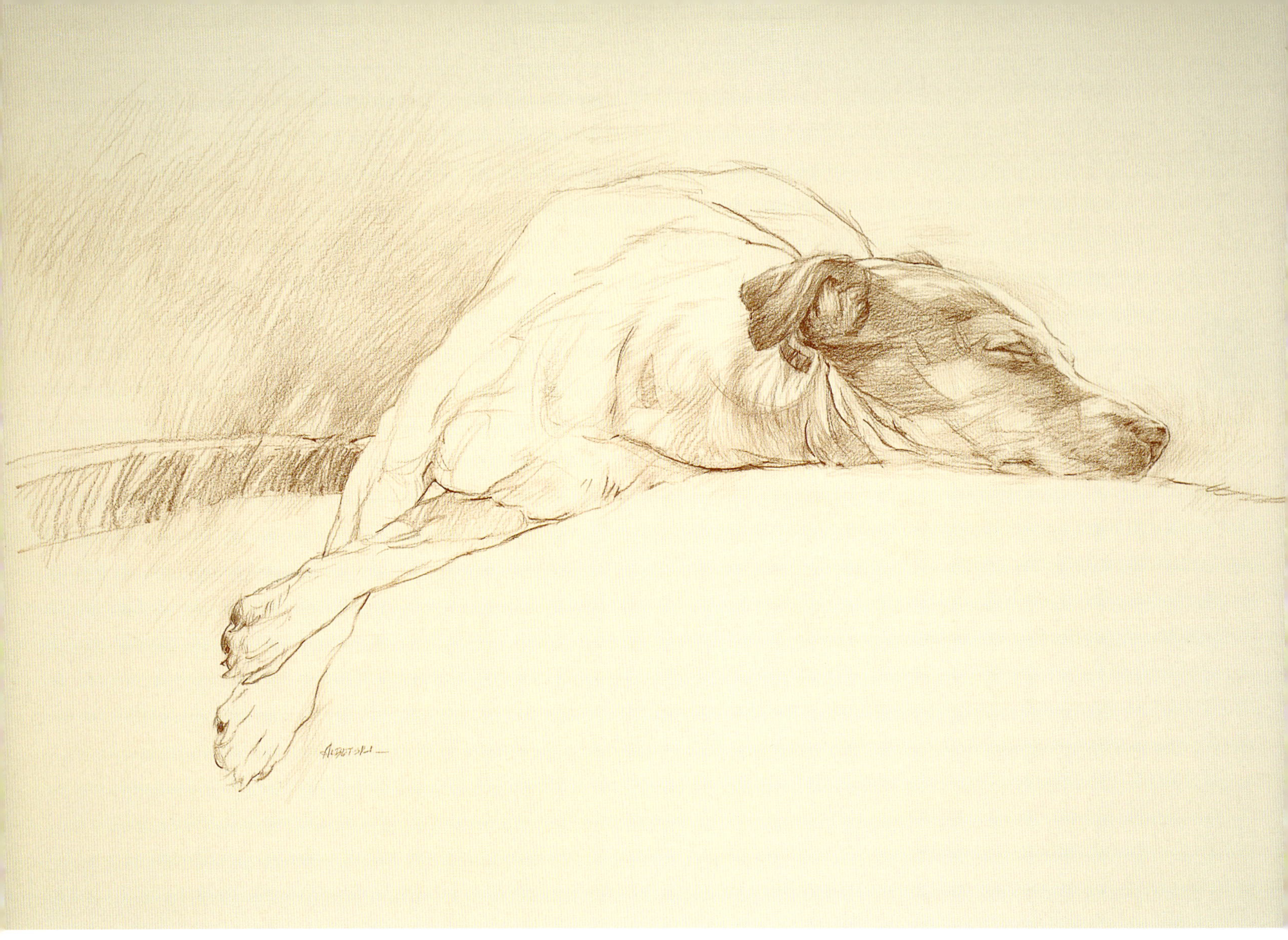

Catnap
Dennis Albetski · Conté crayon · 16" × 23" (41cm × 58cm)

Finding Spontaneity in Conté Crayon

The spontaneity of Conté crayon suited my needs in representing the attitude and energy of Lucy, the pet Jack Russell terrier. Capturing the basic attitude and feeling in the first few lines was imperative to the final outcome of this drawing. I tried not to labor on any one area of the sketch, but moved rapidly about. I wanted to create the effect of an animal that could easily be stirred. Random marks and diagonals helped to create the unusual "catnap" of this energetic dog.

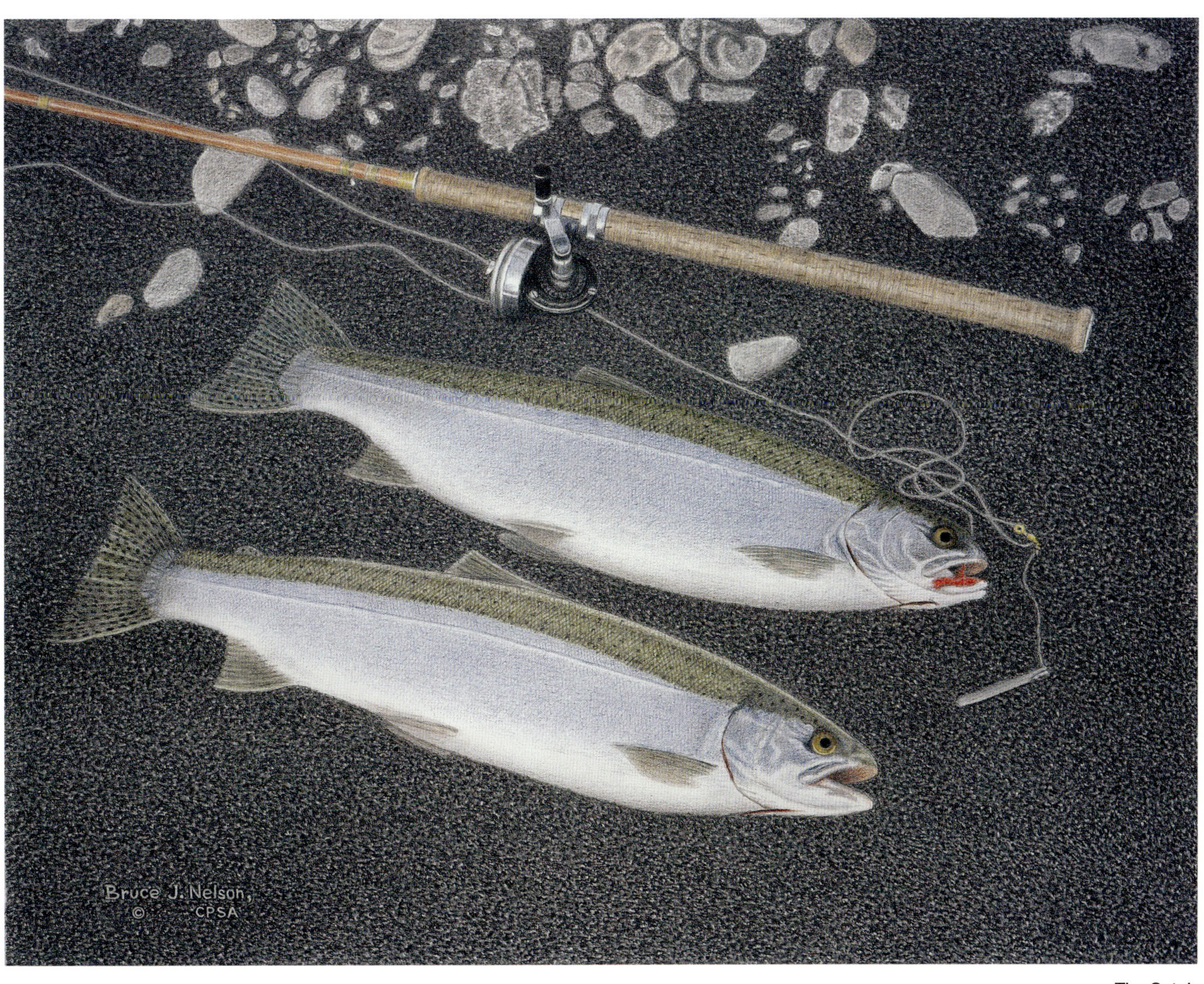

The Catch
Bruce J. Nelson · Colored pencil on hot-pressed paper · 17" × 22" (43cm × 56cm)

CATCH A GOOD PHOTO REFERENCE

It was a late-fall fishing trip on the Dosewallips River, which flows from the Olympic Mountains to Hood
Canal in northwest Washington state. I was the photographer because I don't fish. My friend caught
two nearly matched steelhead that I thought would make a good photo for a later drawing, so we
found a black sand beach along the river and created a setup with the fish and the fishing gear.
It was an overcast day with no shadows, and a good photograph was made. I saved this one for
drawing until I had perfected the Pointillism technique I used to draw the sand.

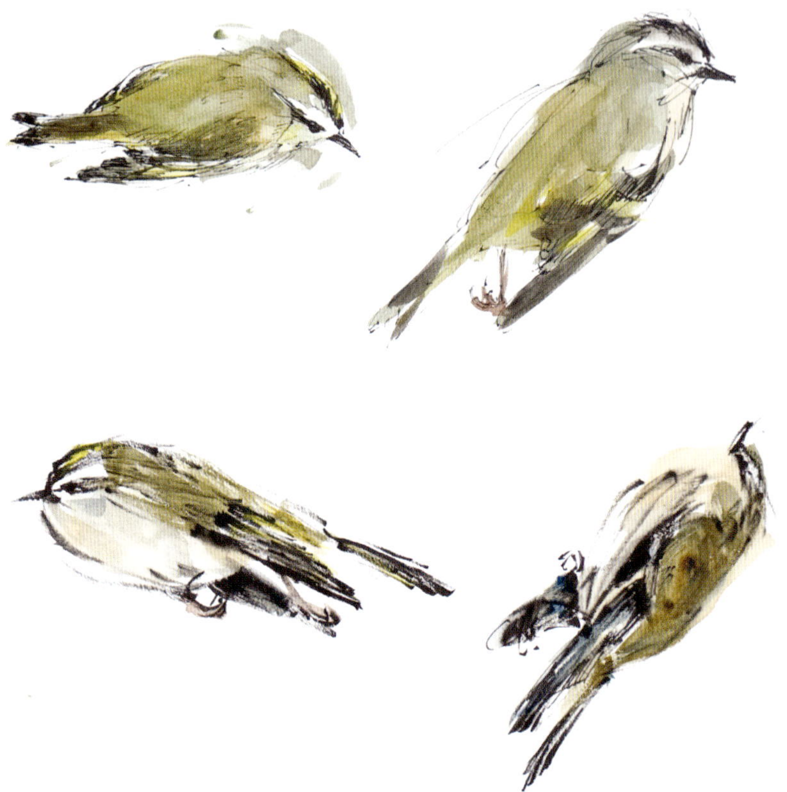

Draw From Life to Learn an Animal

I often work from life, filling sketchbooks with drawings done on the spot, taking advantage of opportunities such as this one, when a golden-crowned kinglet unfortunately died after hitting a window. This is a series of quick drawings done as I placed the bird in different positions on a drafting table to sketch it from various angles. My intent was to convey as much as possible with a minimum of line, color and value. I began the drawings with a Pigma Micron pen while carefully observing the bird. I worked as quickly as possible to give the lines energy, vitality and expression. Finally, I used a light watercolor wash to indicate the kinglet's color markings.

Golden-Crowned Kinglet
Randena B. Walsh · Ink and watercolor on paper · 3" × 4" (8cm × 10cm)

Requiem
Kathleen O'Connell · Graphite on illustration board · 8" × 11" (20cm × 28cm)

Firm, Toothy Paper Holds Up to Layering

This drawing was created in the studio from two of my photographs. It was done on Strathmore 100 percent cotton illustration board, vellum surface, which has a firm, toothy quality that holds up to repeated layering of graphite. I don't want to risk indenting the surface, so I make my initial layout of the drawing on vellum and transfer it to the board. To create crisp detail, I use 2mm mechanical lead holders and a variety of leads (3H–4B). The fine leads allow me to obtain the razor-sharp points that I need. I use very light pressure as I layer my values, harder to softer, leaving the white of the paper for the highlights.

I keep a clean piece of vellum under my hand to avoid smearing, and clean up with white plastic erasers. This drawing was inspired by a bird-watching walk at Eagle Creek Park in Indianapolis. A member of the group had gone downtown to retrieve the bodies of birds that are killed when they strike the tall buildings so we could study them upclose. The catbird resting in my friend's hands came from one of my photographs of these. The background of the fallen oak leaves came from another photo and symbolizes a season of declining vitality. My father provided the title for this drawing and passed away shortly after I finished it.

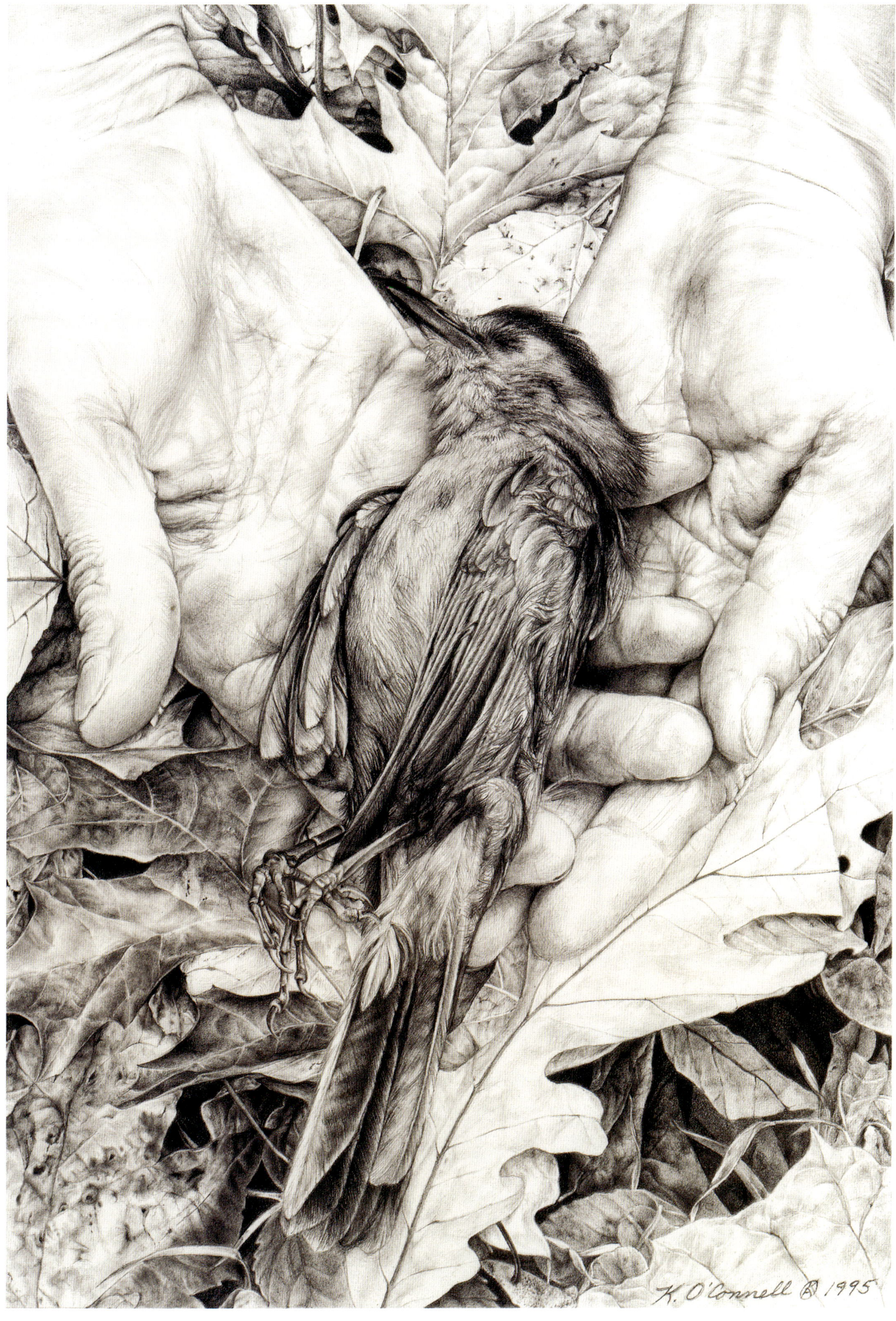

K. O'Connell © 1995

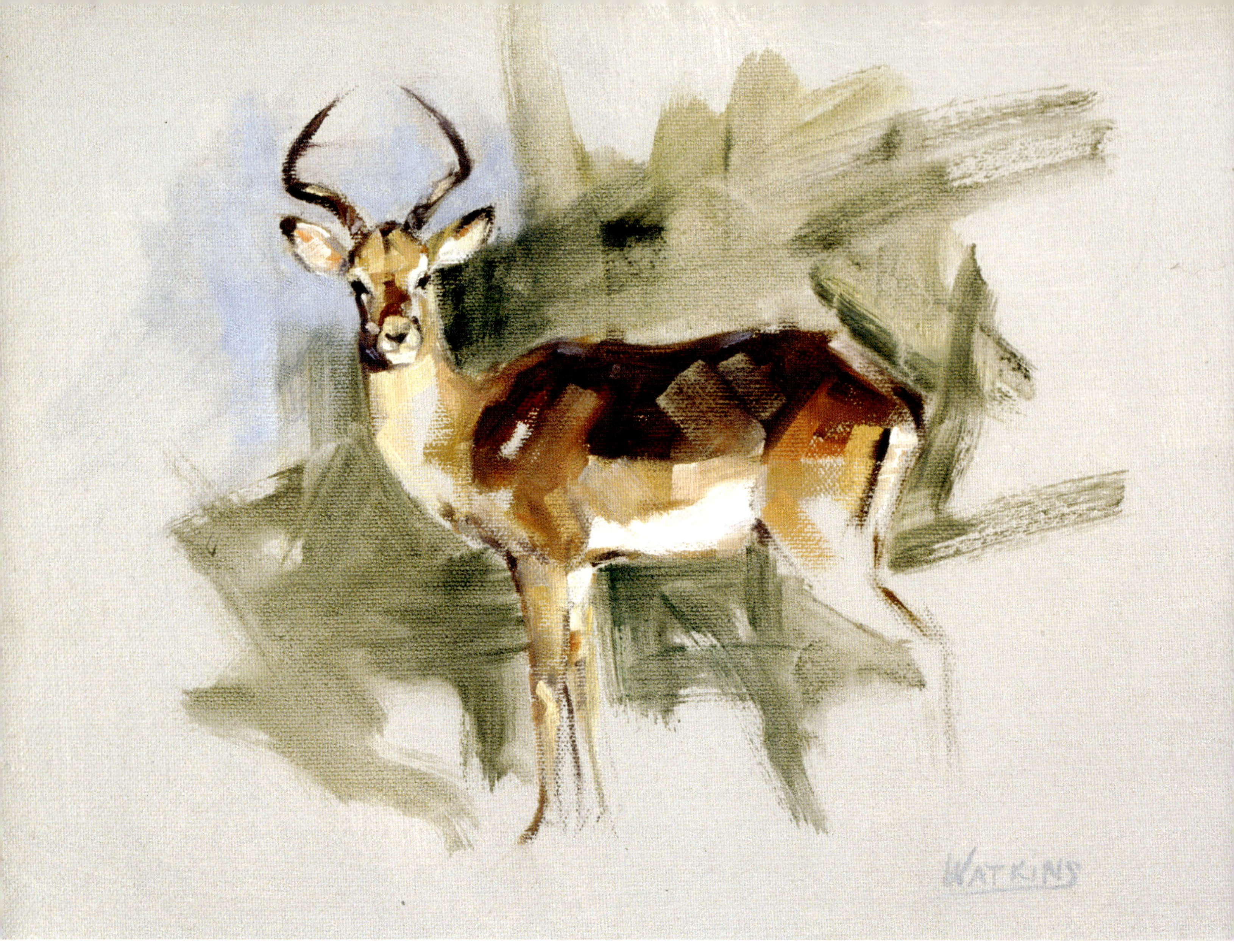

Now You See Me…
Peggy Watkins · Oil on canvas · 9" × 12" (23cm × 30cm)

MAKE EACH STROKE COUNT

This work is an exercise in making each stroke of the brush have meaning in describing my subject. I intentionally limited my total time on this project to one hour. First I toned my canvas with stone gray gesso. Next I lightly sketched the impala on the canvas. I then mixed on my palette the most dominant warm and cool colors. Using as few strokes as possible, I simply applied the paint, not worrying about covering every inch of the animal and background. My reference was a photograph I had taken in South Africa.

I portray **SHADOW AREAS** of a composition with a transparent wash and **LIGHT AREAS** with more opaque paint.

-Peggy Watkins

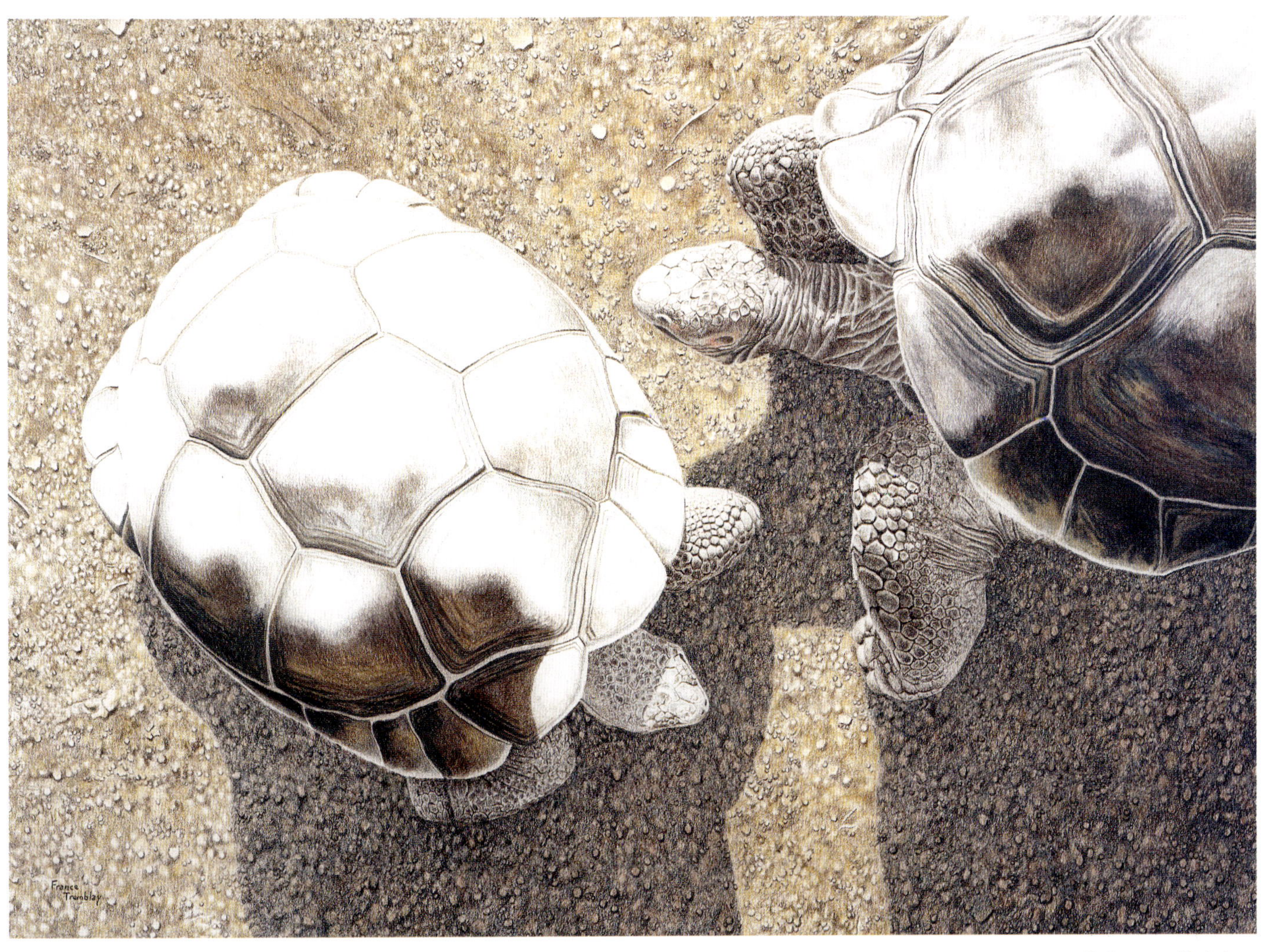

Galapagos Tortoises
France Tremblay · Colored pencil on paper · 13½" × 19" (34cm × 48cm)

OBSERVE UNCOMMON WILDLIFE WHEREVER YOU FIND IT

I travel around the world to observe uncommon landscapes and rare wildlife. My camera, my notebook and I are inseparable on these intense field trips. I visited the Galapagos Islands twice to study its unique wildlife and volcanic landscapes. Soon after, I visited a tiny zoo in Bermuda. Unexpectedly, from the top of a small hill, I saw two Galapagos tortoises. The view from above and the dramatic light offered a unique composition. Combining this concept with previously acquired knowledge of the subject, I created *Galapagos Tortoises*.

Between **LIGHT AND SHADOW**
lies an extraordinary thing: **THE EDGE**.
We live in a world made of edges.

-France Tremblay

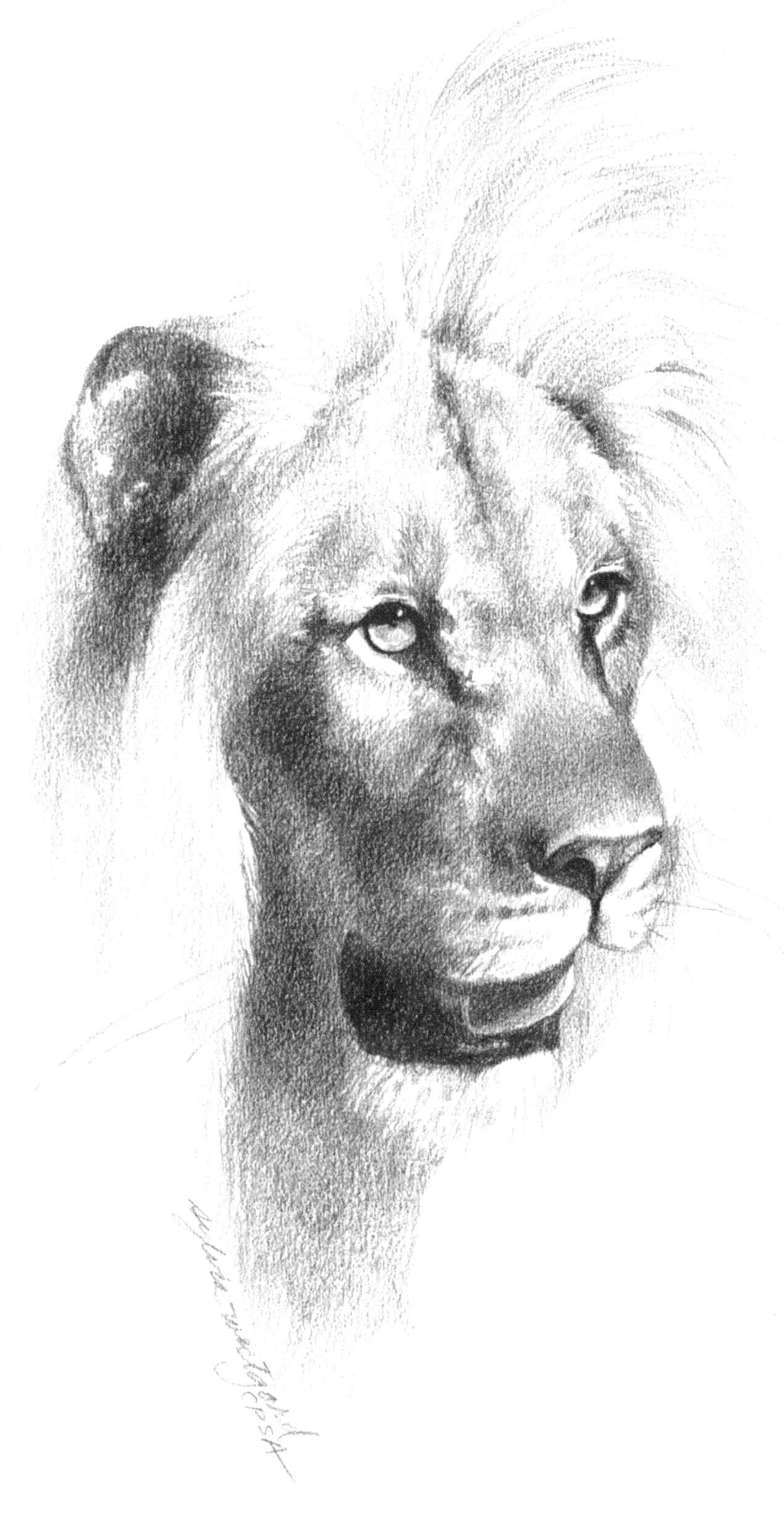

Lion
Sylvia Westgard · Black colored pencil on sketchbook paper · 14" × 11" (36cm × 28cm)

Your Zoo Is a Great Source for Wildlife

The ideas for my drawings come from everywhere. I work from my own photographs, so I travel with several cameras, lenses and my ever-present sketchbook. The zoo has given me some wonderful views of wildlife, including this young lion. He was done as a sketch, using only one colored pencil, the Derwent Coloursoft Black, on acid-free, heavy-weight sketchbook paper. Later I drew this same image on black paper using colored pencils. The lion continues to be one of my favorite subjects at the zoo.

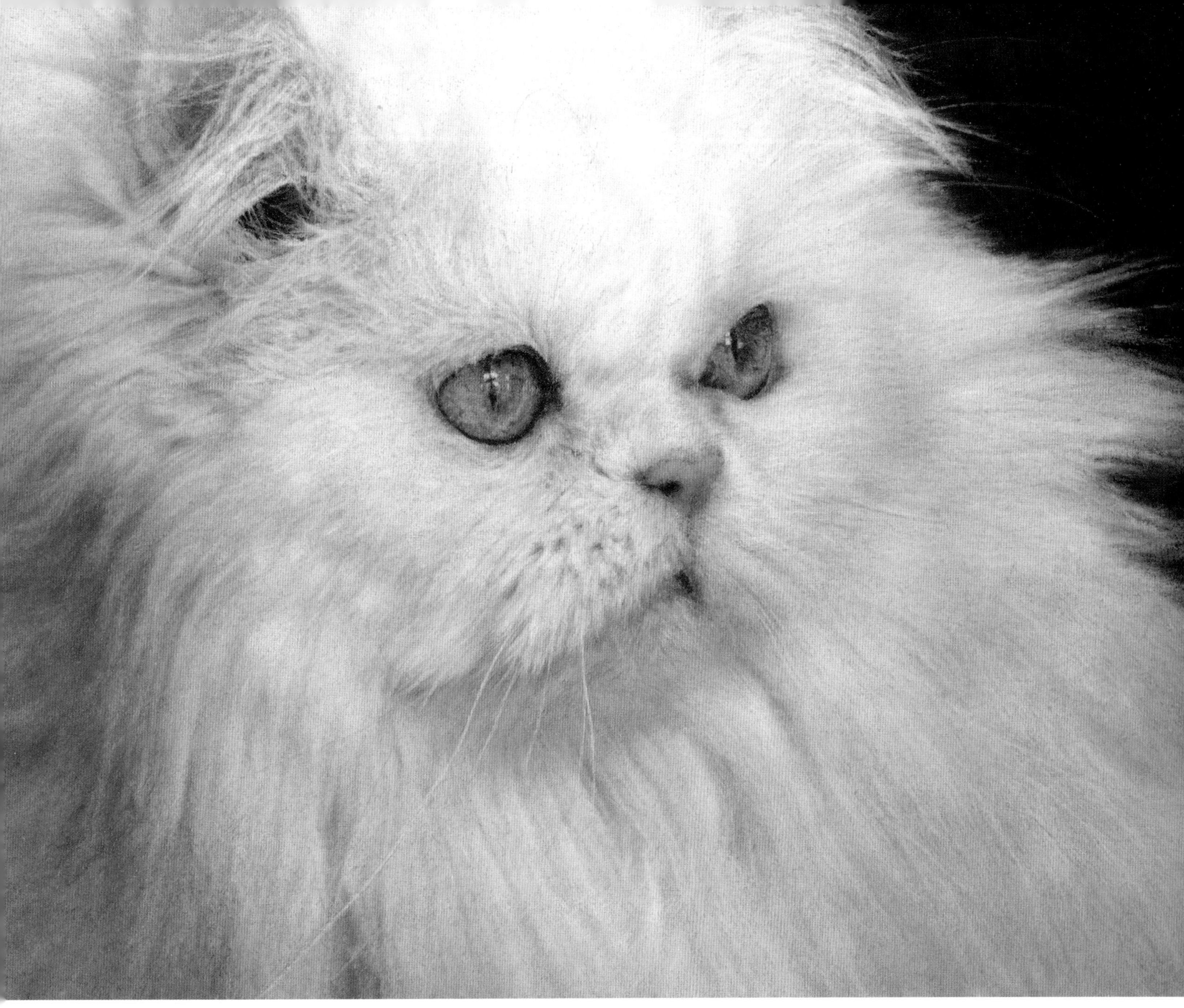

Olivia
Helen Crispino · Charcoal on paper · 6" × 8" (15cm × 20cm)

Layering Dark to Light

This drawing of my little Persian treasure, Olivia, was done
using black and white charcoal pencils. I began with an
extremely light sketch, using the softest grades of charcoal.
I carefully applied values working from dark to light. As the
drawing developed, I began to use harder grades of charcoal
to smooth out the surface. Final details were added, bringing
to life one of my most cherished subjects.

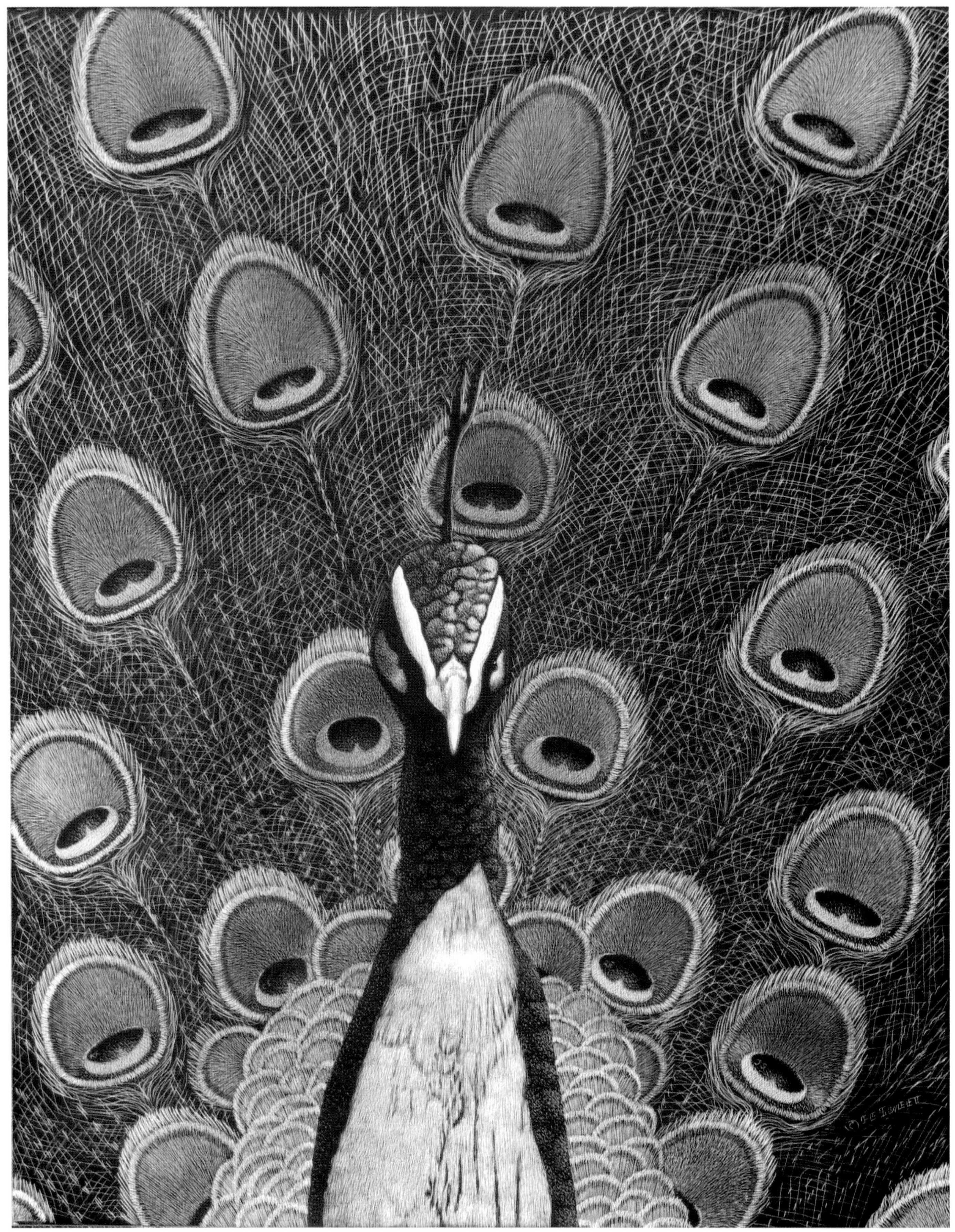

The Eyes Have It
Francis Edward Sweet · Scratchboard · 24" × 18" (61cm × 46cm)

EXPRESS COLOR IN BLACK AND WHITE

The male peacock and its beautiful tail feathers were an ideal subject for the
scratchboard medium. Trying to create all the different hues, as well as all the
barbs of the tail feathers, was quite a challenge for a black-and-white drawing.

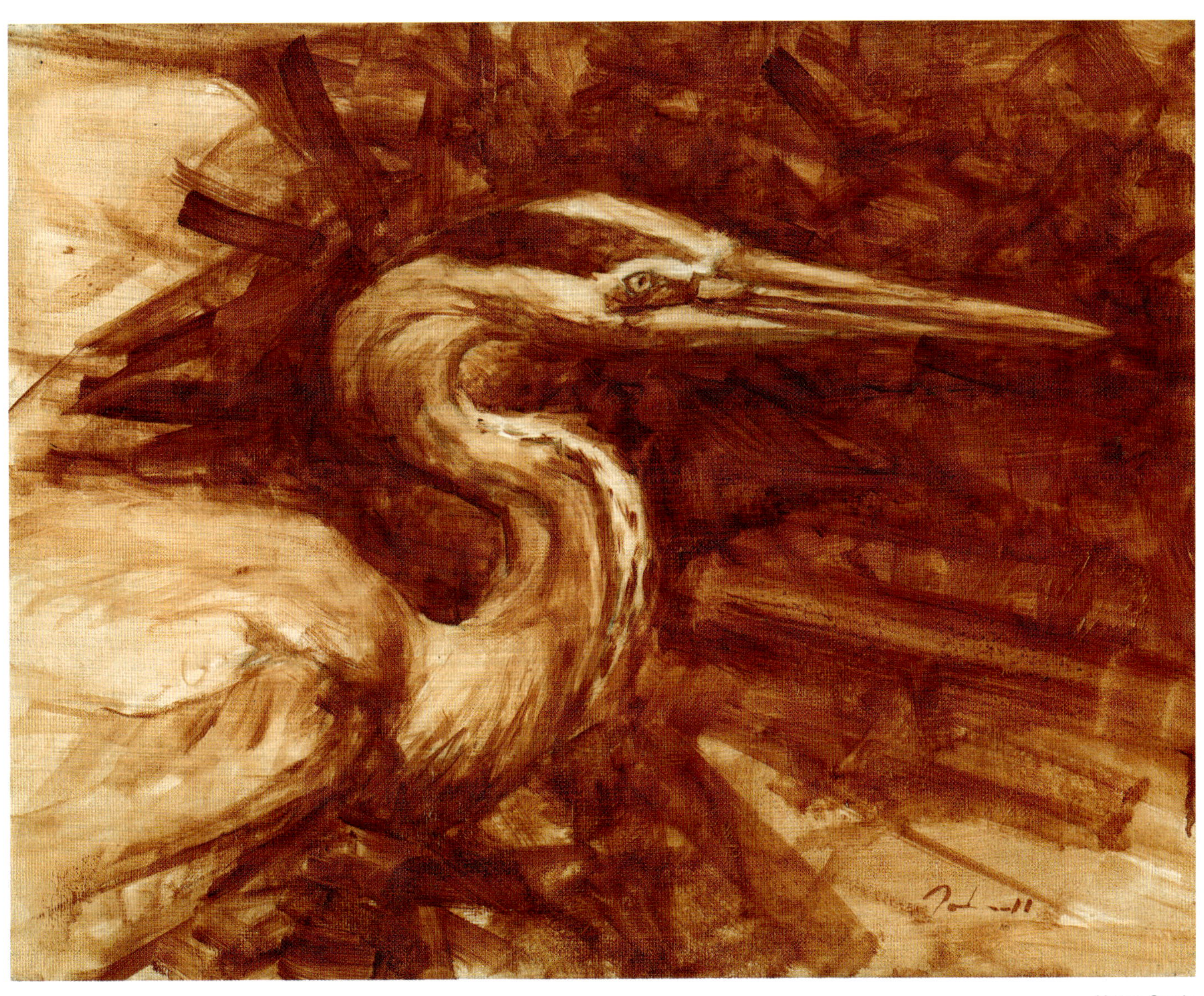

Heron Study
Michael Todoroff · Oil on board · 11" × 14" (28cm × 36cm)

FIND SPECIES THAT SPEND TIME MOTIONLESS

I'm fortunate to live near a nesting colony of great blue herons. This offers me great opportunities to study these birds up close. Herons often stand motionless for extended periods of time in search of prey. This provides me with the time to do several gestural sketches of these beautiful birds.

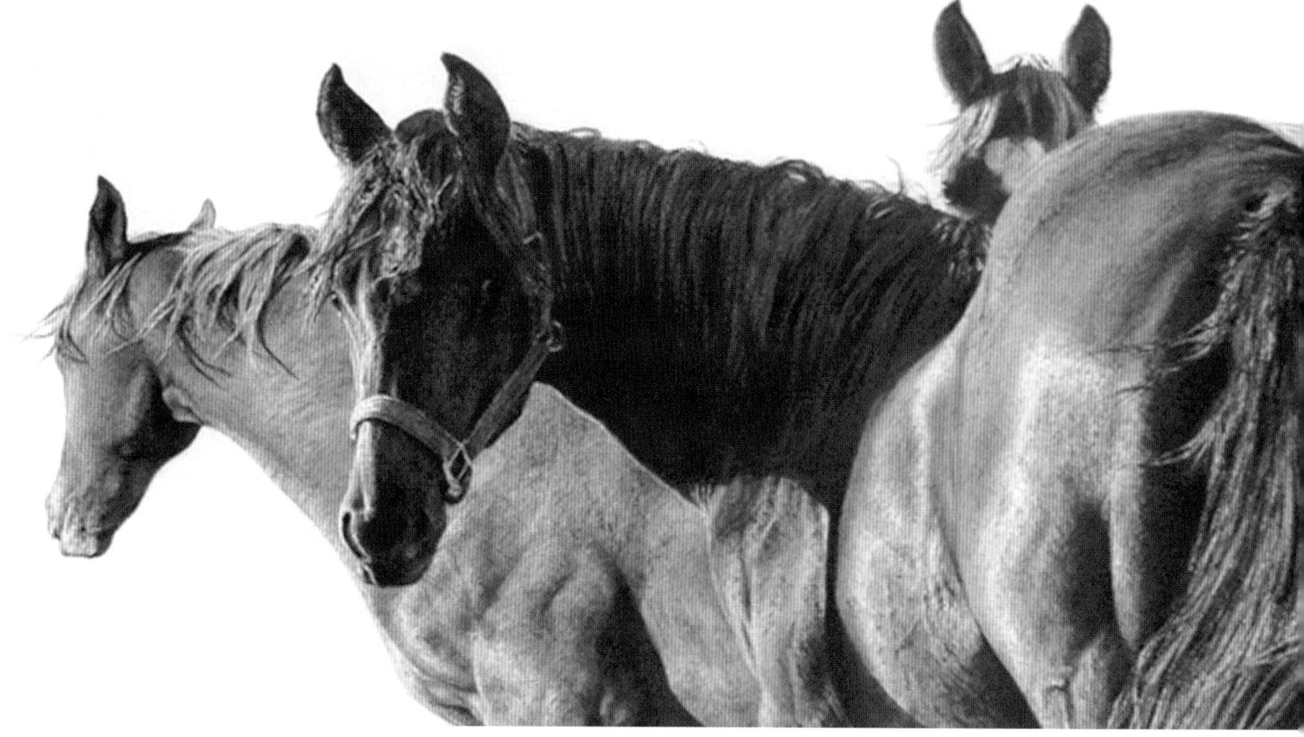

Indian Summer
Terry Miller · Graphite on bristol board · 9" × 21" (23cm × 53cm)

Use Atypical Viewpoints and Humor for Interest

Because animals are my primary subject matter, I am continually looking for interesting ways of portraying them beyond strict portraiture. By using atypical angles or viewpoints, humor, clustering and overlapping, or unusual gestures, always within the context of strong lights and darks, I hope to develop a unique take on the subject. Areas of bright highlight are worked away from, rather than created through erasing; dark shadow is built up slowly in layers so as not to throw off the balance being created across the entire work.

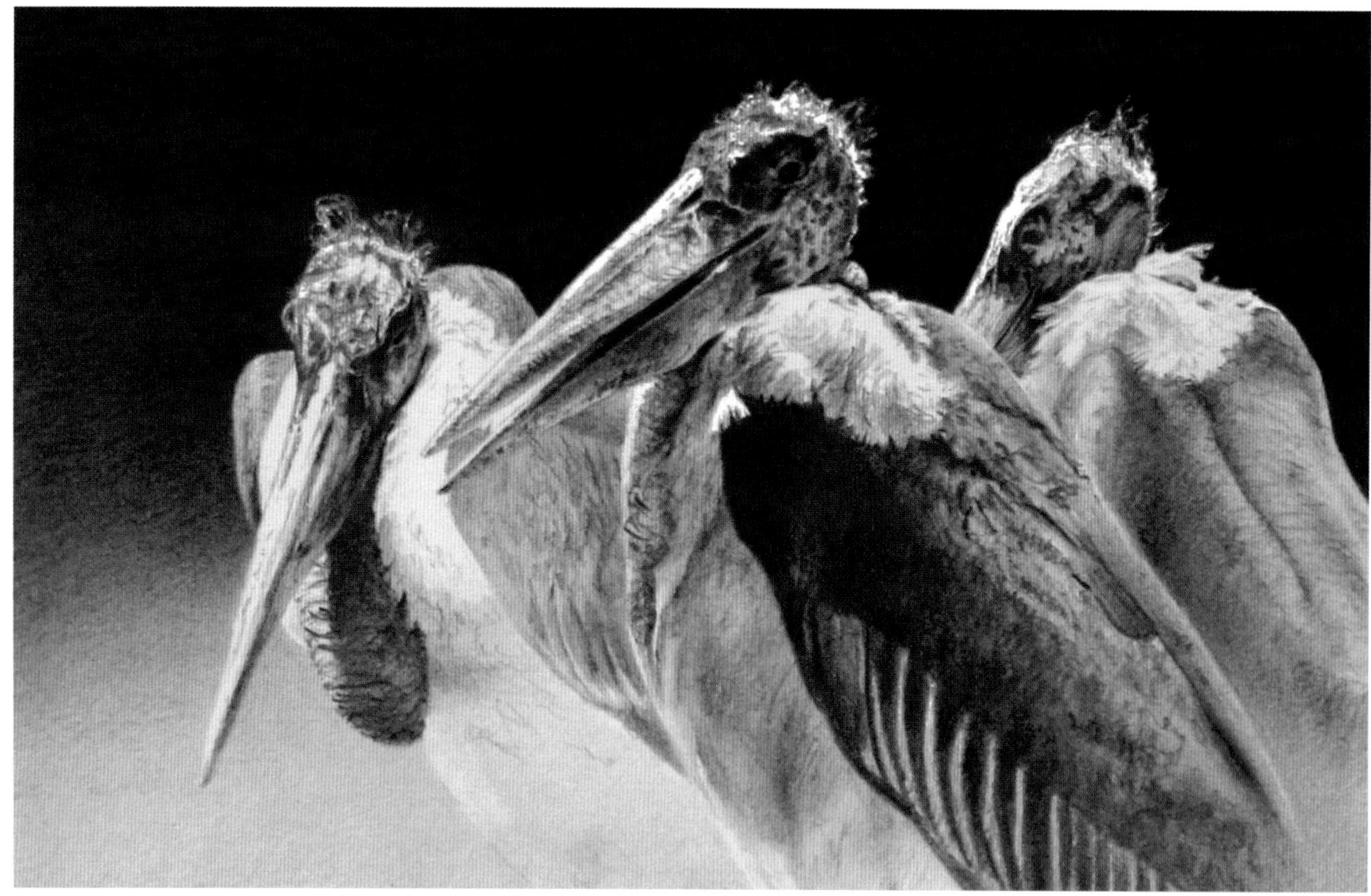

Caucus
Terry Miller · Graphite on bristol board · 5" × 8" (13cm × 20cm)

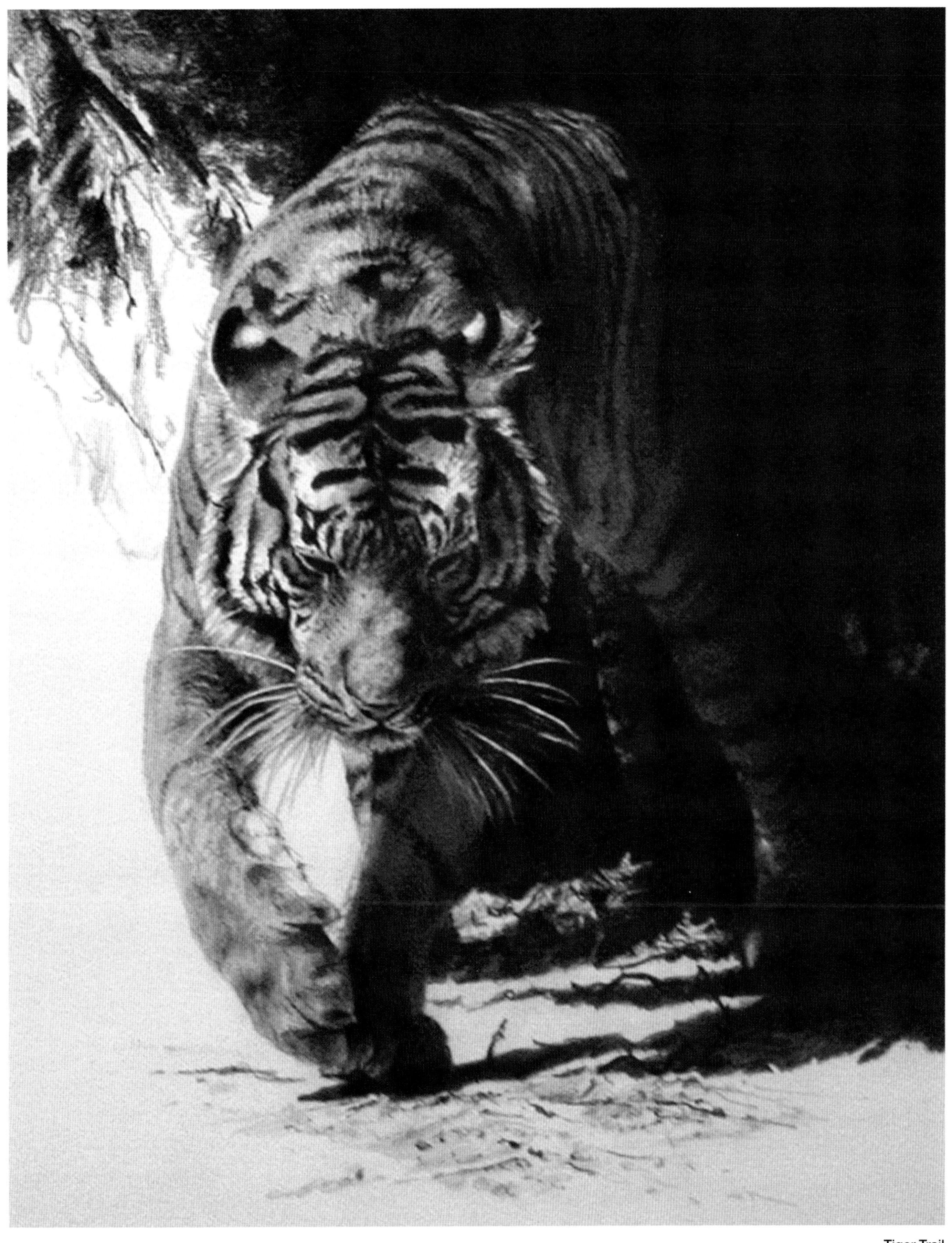

Tiger Trail
Terry Miller · Graphite on bristol board · 9" × 7" (23cm × 18cm)

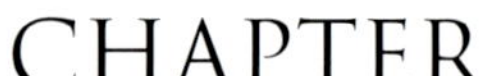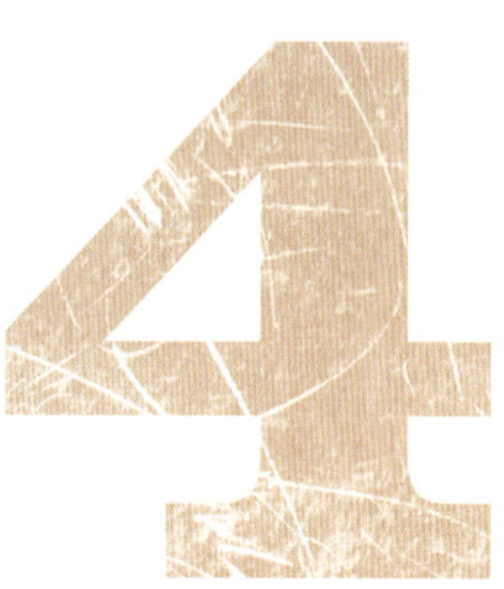

CHAPTER 4   THE HUMAN FIGURE

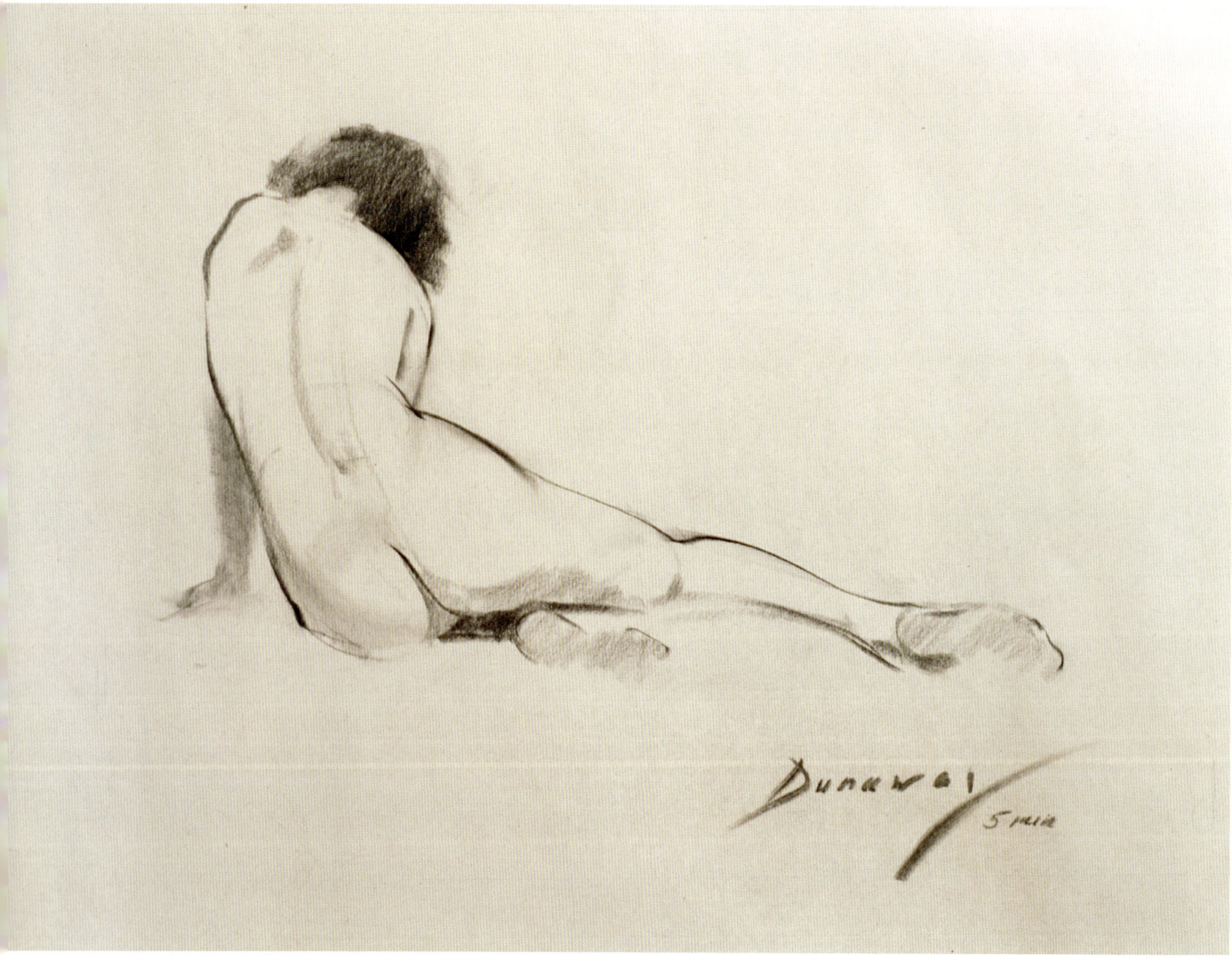

5-Minute Quick Sketch From Life
Michelle Dunaway · Charcoal · 14" × 18" (36cm × 46cm)

GESTURE DRAWING IS HONEST AND EXHILARATING

As much as I love finished drawings, quick figure gestures are one of my favorite things to draw. There is an immediacy of response to the dynamic movement of the model that is exhilarating and honest. Five-minute figure sketches have always reminded me of music: fluid rhythms punctuated with anatomical notes of structure. I use smooth newsprint with vine charcoal and soft (6B) charcoal pencils sharpened with a razor blade. Sharpening the pencil this way enables me to create a variety of edges that help convey the calligraphy of movement and form. It's all about capturing the essence.

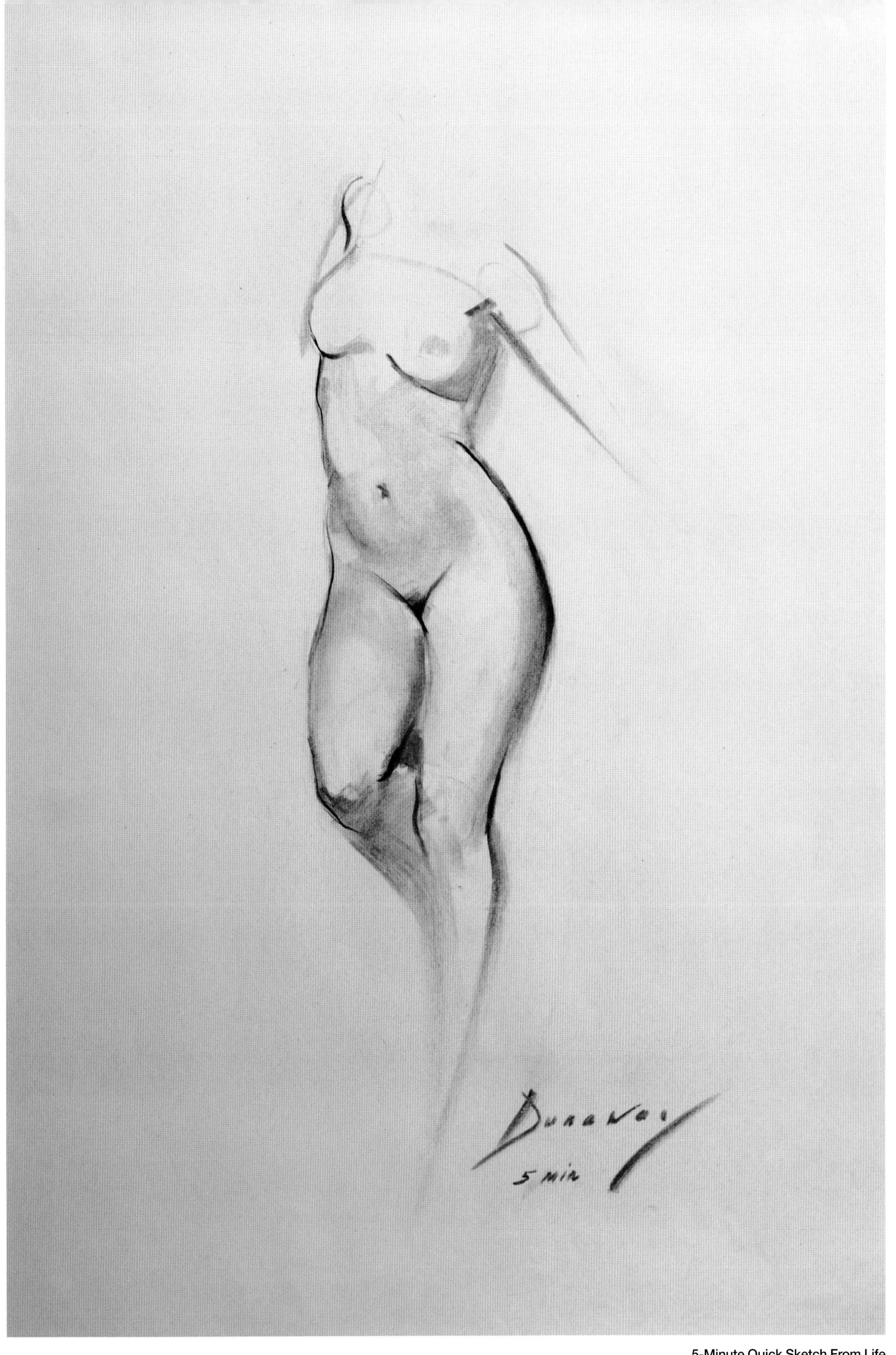

5-Minute Quick Sketch From Life
Michelle Dunaway · Charcoal · 24" × 18" (61cm × 46cm)

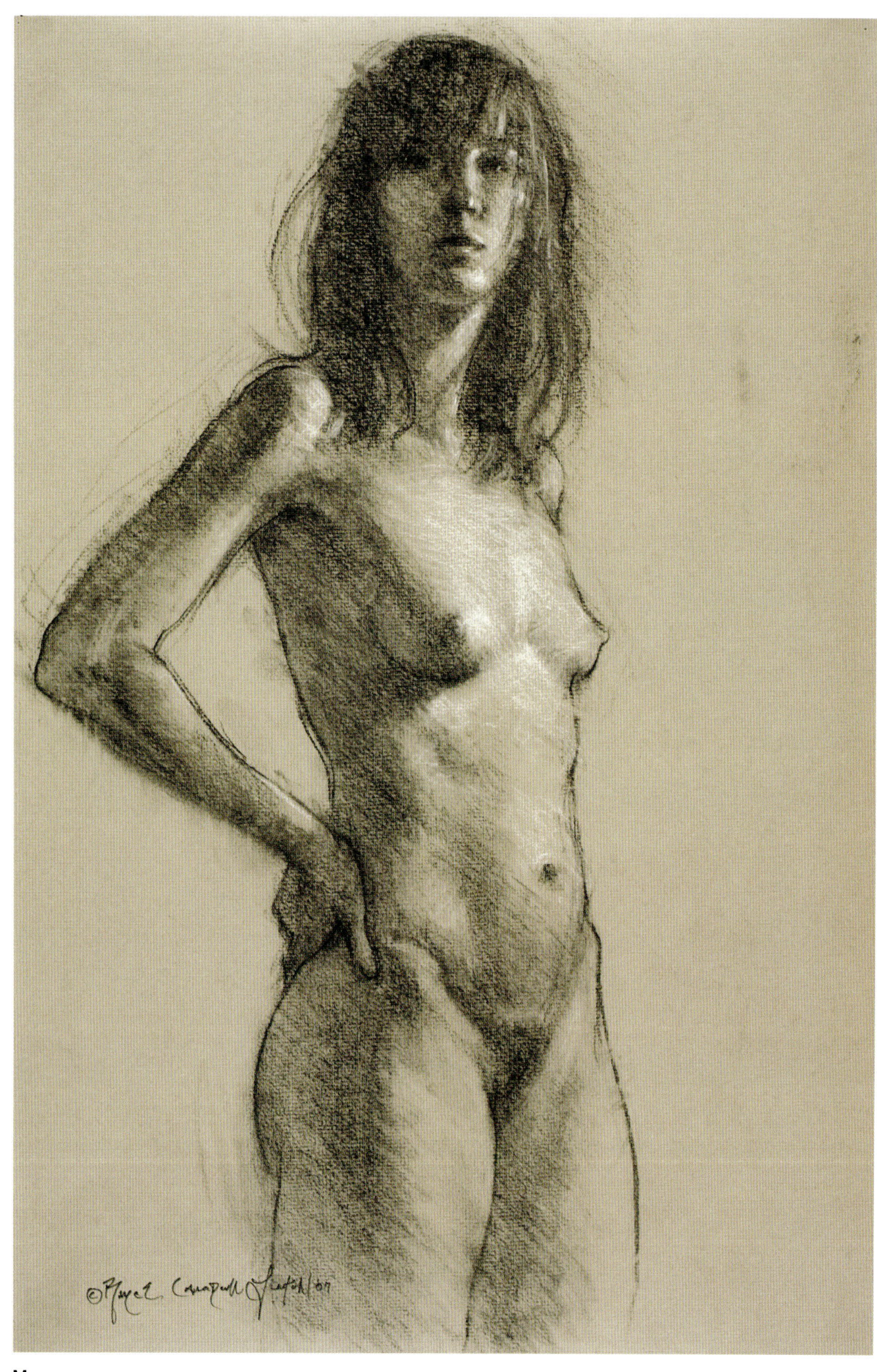

May
Bryce Cameron Liston · Charcoal and chalk on warm gray-toned paper · 18" × 12" (46cm × 30cm)

RESERVE TONED PAPER FOR MIDDLE VALUES

This drawing was done on Hahnemuhle laid paper, which has a medium tooth and accepts charcoal very nicely. Using a soft charcoal pencil, I lightly sketch the basic position and proportions of the figure and establish the overall direction and gesture. Then I start again, pushing the darks and working more closely with line quality, shapes, and shadow patterns, reserving the tone of the paper for the middle tones and light areas. When I have the shadows well established, I then turn to the light areas, using an Off-White Nupastel stick to bring out the highlights.

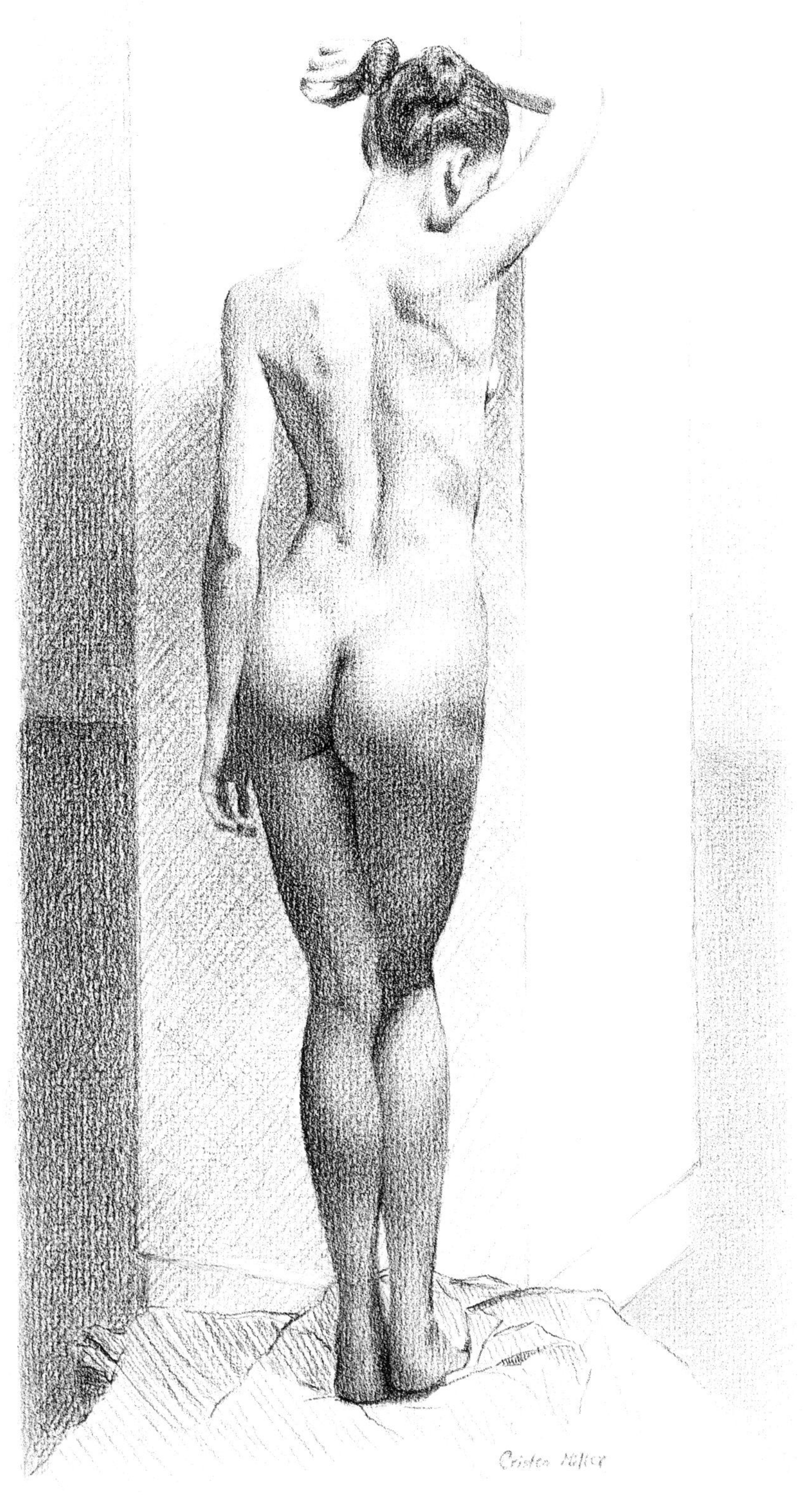

Quiet Rhythm
Cristen Miller · Charcoal on paper · 14" × 7" (36cm × 18cm)

LOST AND FOUND EDGES BRING SUBTLE RHYTHM

My intention was to explore the subtle rhythms that can be created through the repetition of lost and found line. I am greatly inspired by the drawings of Ingres and have done many master copies of his work. I tried to create a visual flow through the piece by the careful placement of a few crisply defined edges. I began with a sketch from life and then executed the final piece from a photograph, using a 6B charcoal pencil. I started with a very light touch and then layered the charcoal where I wished to go darker.

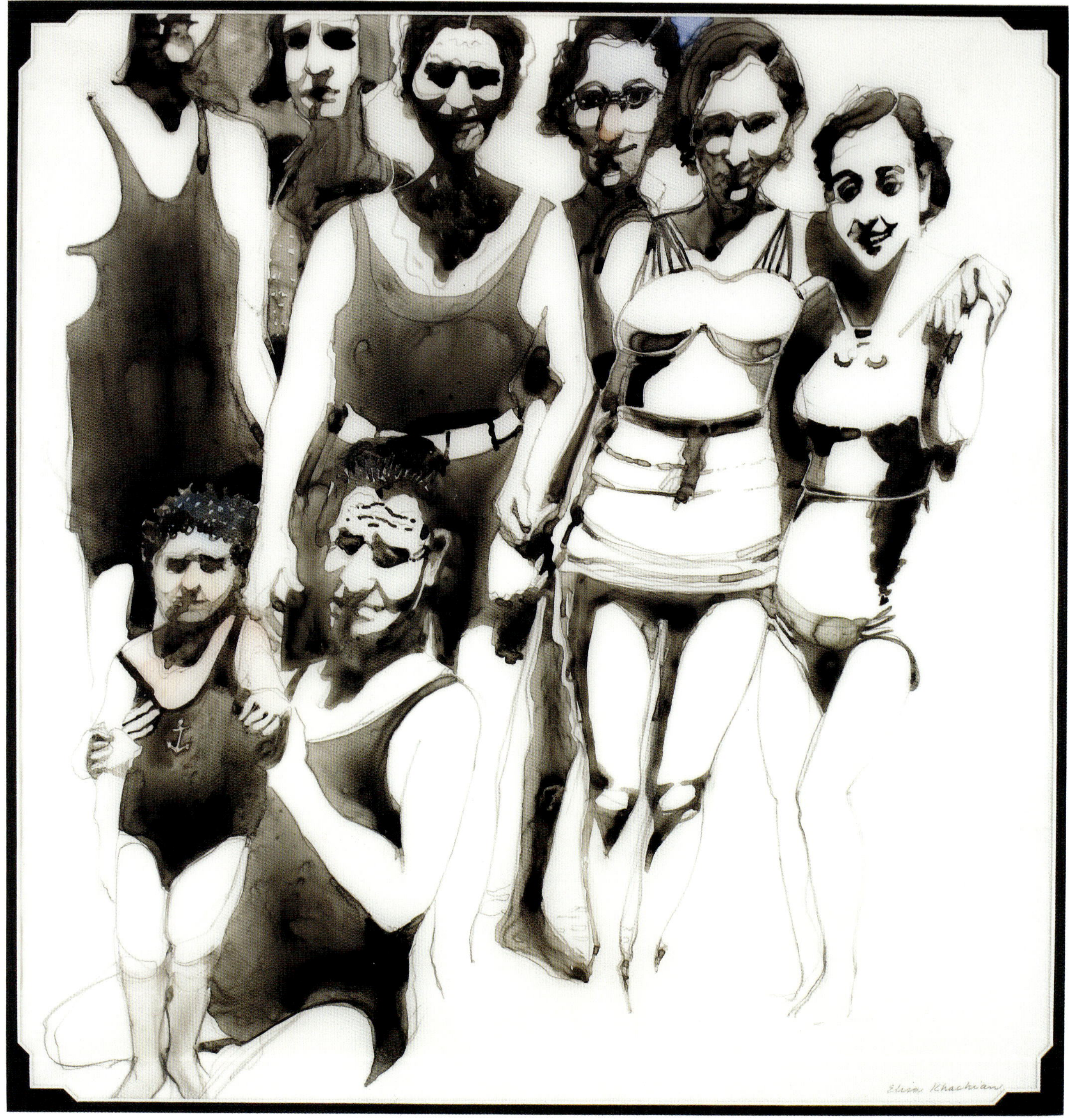

Beauties
Elisa Khachian · Pencil with watercolor on transparent Mylar paper · 16" × 15¾" (41cm × 40cm)

FIND BEAUTIES IN OLD FAMILY PHOTOS

Beauties was drawn freehand using selected lines, shapes and patterns from an old family photo. The sunlit figures are connected through black-and-white patterns, their bathing suits completing the picture.

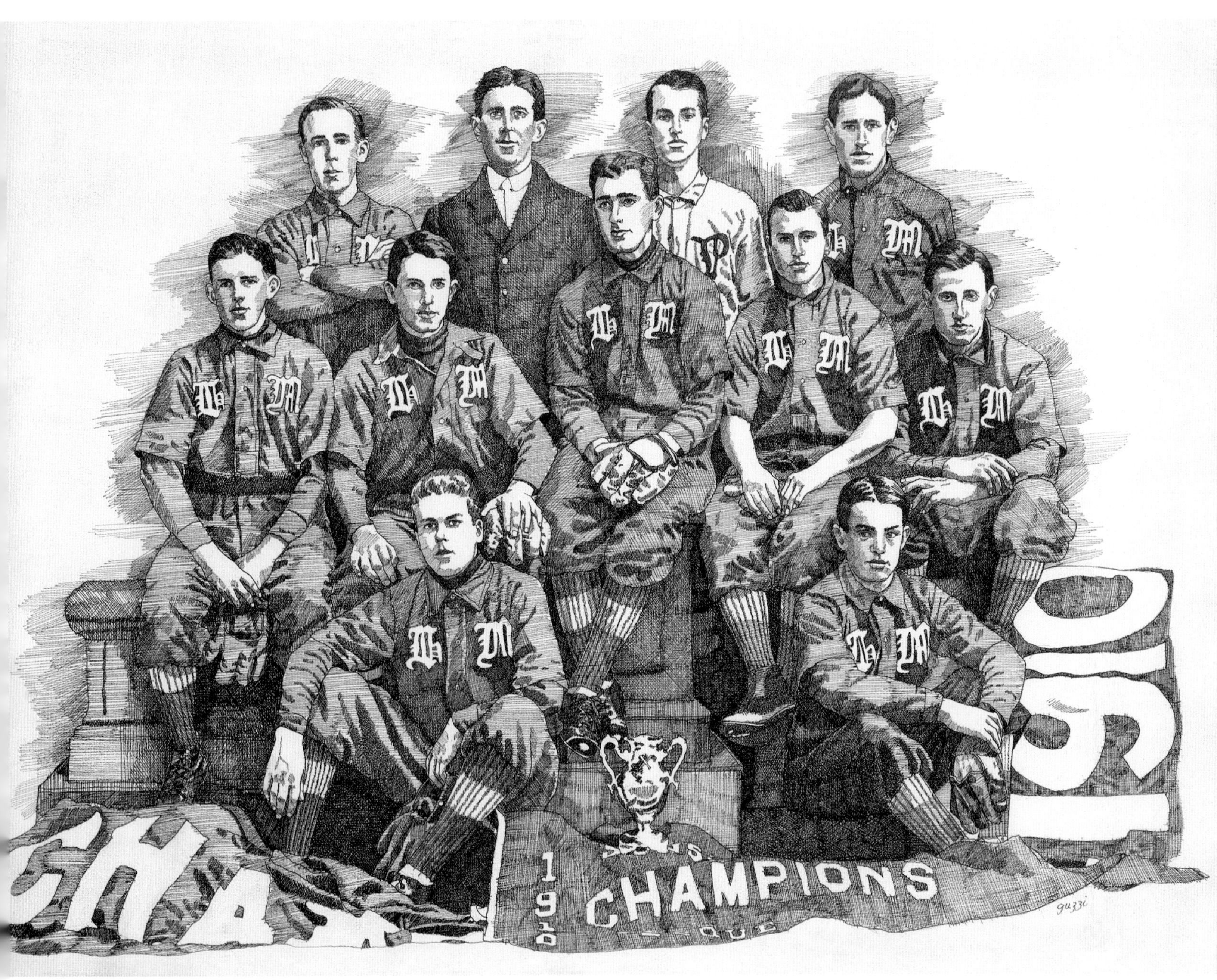

1910 Champions
George Guzzi · Pen and ink on illustration board · 15" × 20" (38cm × 51cm)

DRAWING BRINGS THE PAST TO LIFE

Many of my illustrations are derived from old family photographs or photos from collectible shops. I purchased this reference photo at an antique shop in Scarborough, Maine. As with most of my illustrations, the basic drawing for *1910 Champions* was rendered freehand in pencil on vellum and then transferred to the illustration board. I then used 000 and 0000 Rapidograph pens to layer in crosshatch lines until the darks and lights were properly balanced. The entire process took about thirty-six hours.

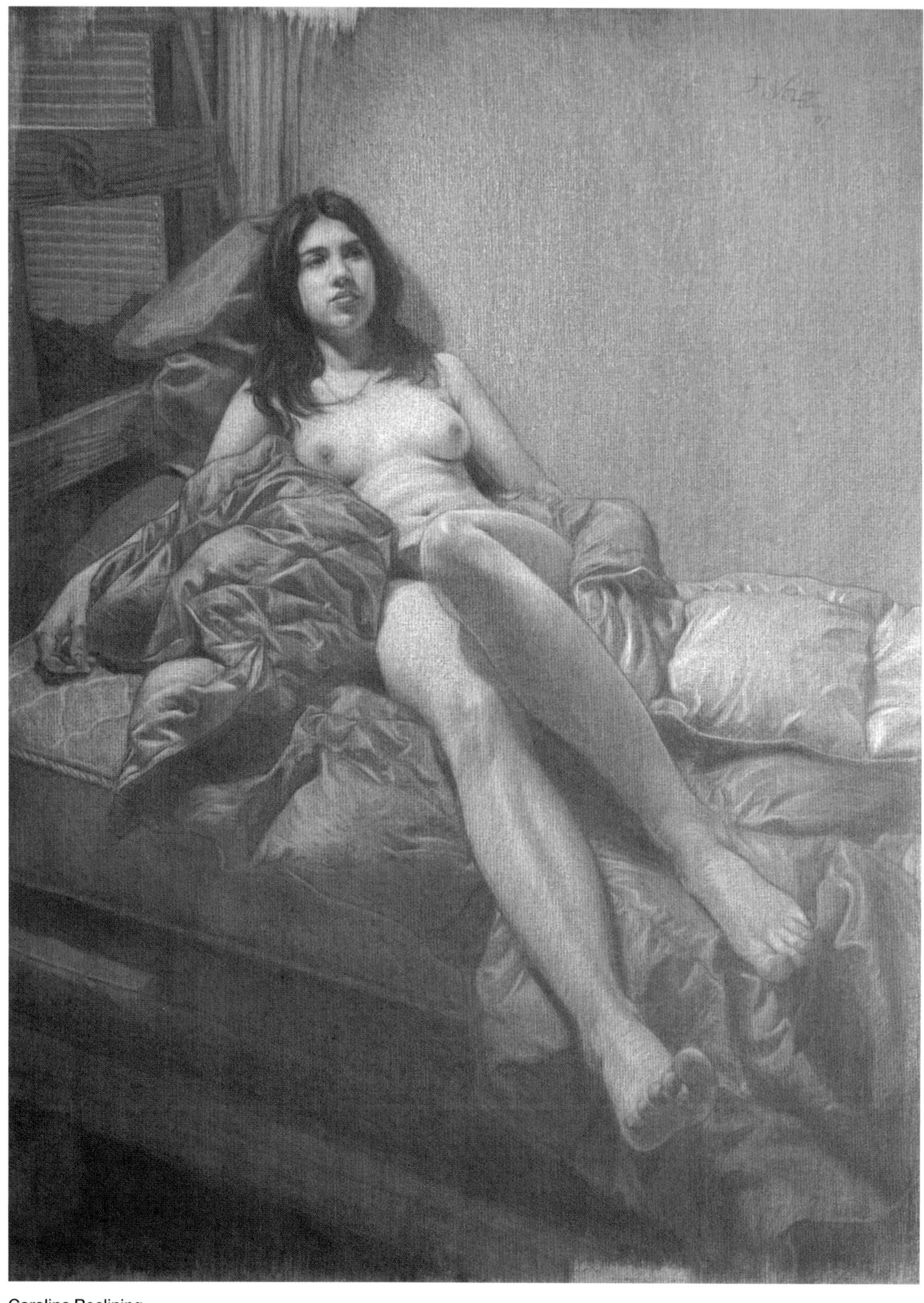

Carolina Reclining
Joe Velez · Graphite and colored pencil on toned canvas · 32" × 24" (81cm × 61cm)

Use Acrylic for a Mid-Gray Ground

I enjoy putting pencil to canvas because of its rough surface and the challenge this presents for varying degrees of detail. In *Carolina Reclining*, I began by toning a canvas with blue-gray acrylic paint. After a few quick compositional sketches, I made some initial marks for proportion. I started with the head, then the body, followed by the fabric and entire background. Only when I was fully satisfied with the graphite drawing did I begin the light areas in colored pencil.

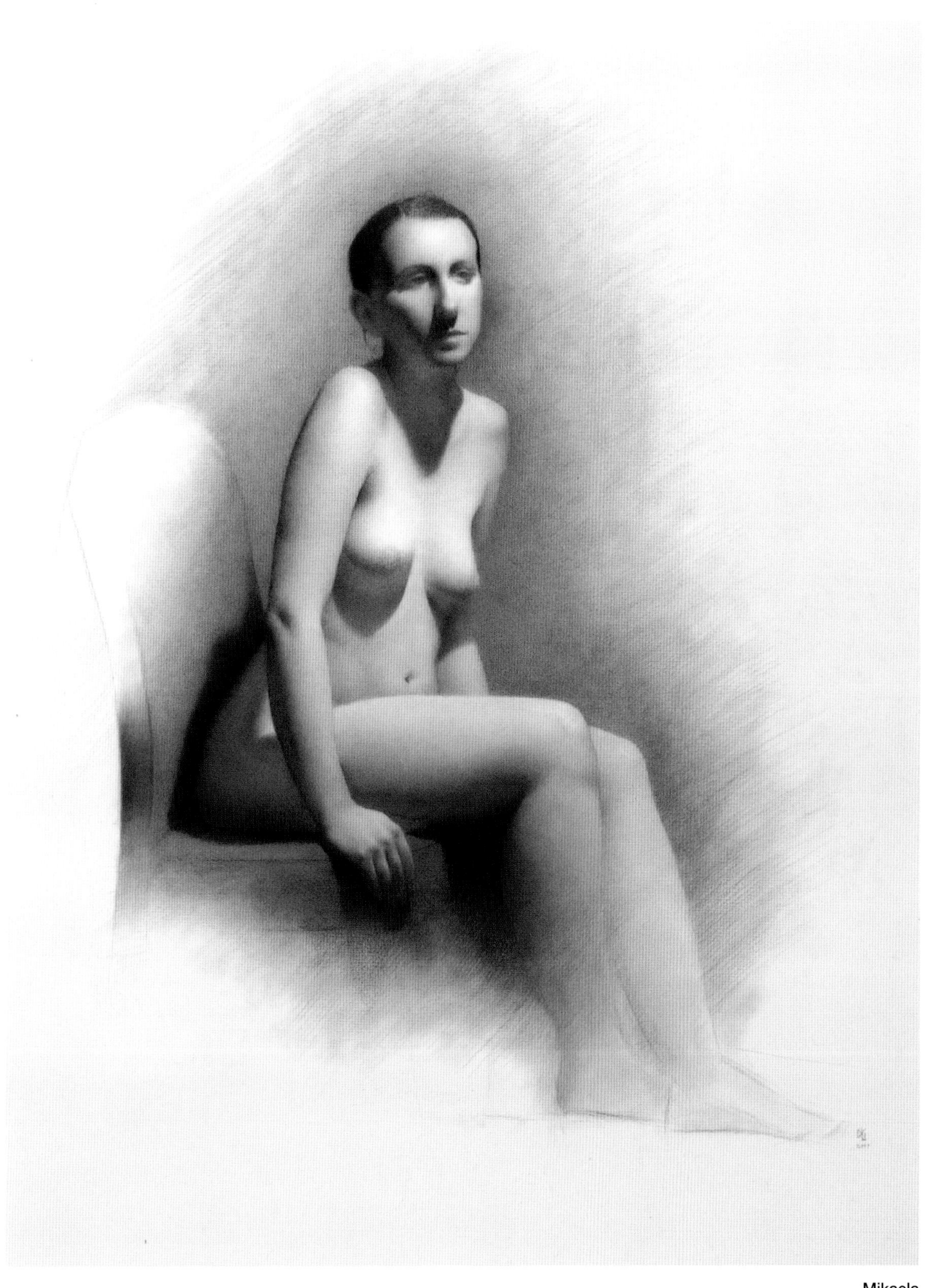

Mikaela
David Gluck · Carbon pencil · 18" × 16" (46cm × 41cm)

TEXTURE CONTRAST DISTINGUISHES DRAWING

Mikaela was created directly from the live model in an atelier environment where I am also an instructor. The pose ran the course of twelve weeks, twice a week, for three hours. I made a stylistic choice to vignette the figure so as to juxtapose areas of tight rendering with loose hatching. Apart from the aesthetic quality of contrast in textures, this device tells the viewer instantly that the work is a drawing and not a photograph—a distinction that realist artists often have difficulty communicating.

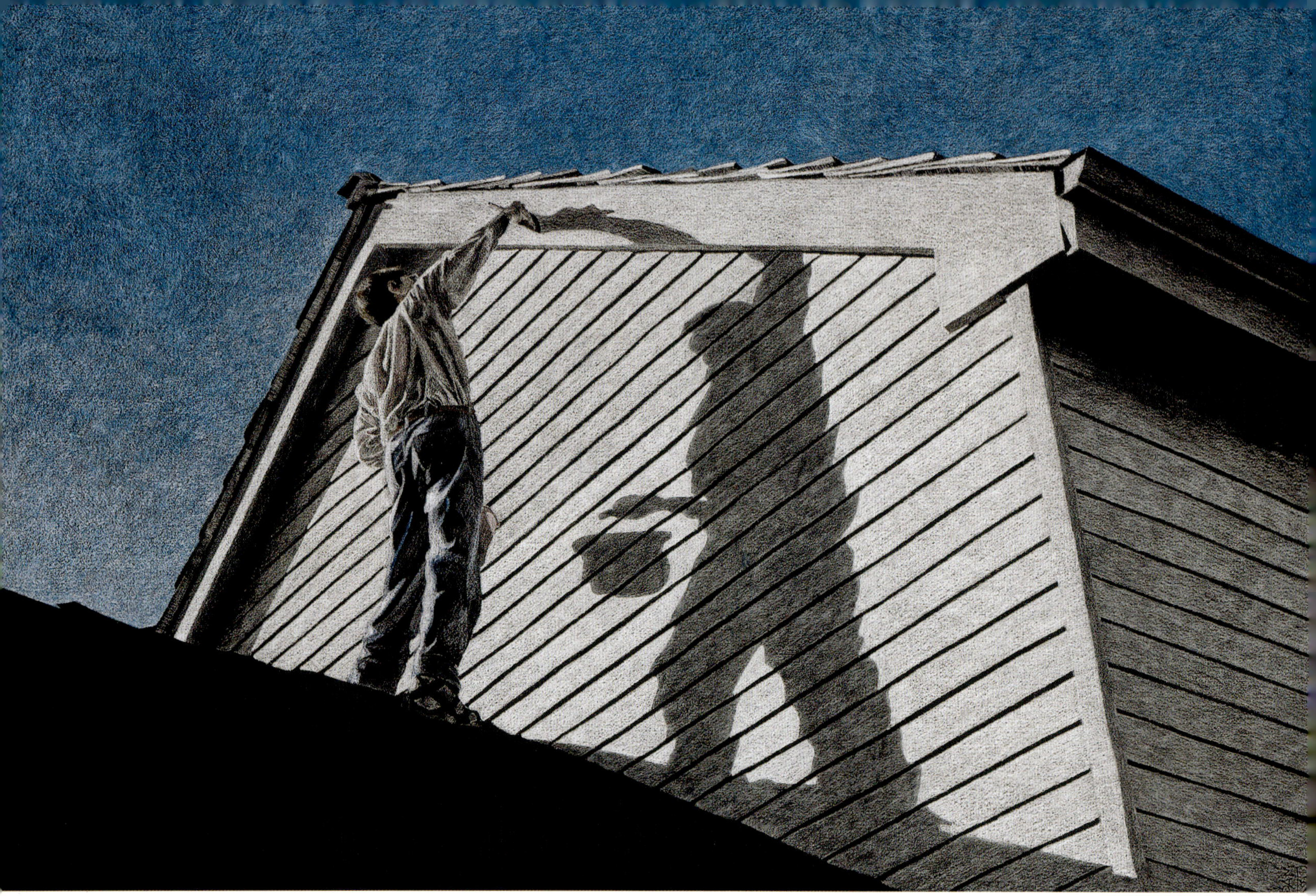

Painting Partner
Pamela Belcher · Colored pencil on black paper · 10¾" × 16¾" (27cm × 43cm)

Capture a Dramatic Gesture

My husband was perched on our steeply sloped roof, painting. I was standing guard, making sure he didn't fall, when I noticed the spectacular lighting of the late summer afternoon. I told him to freeze, and I ran in to get the camera and then snapped several reference photos. I executed the drawing on black paper to help capture the drama. Just a few pencils were needed, and most were applied as a single layer. Black paper does not work for many subjects, but when it does, it speeds up the process and creates a lot of pop.

Sunday Morning Breakfast
Wanda Kemper · Oil on board · 11" × 14" (28cm × 36cm)

Capture a Fleeting Moment of Light

Early one December morning, the sun cast a charming glow on my husband as he was having breakfast. I captured this fleeting moment with my camera and then made several quick pencil sketches. Using hardboard prepared with a warm white acrylic gesso, I sketched the image with asphaltum oil paint. I started with the darks, then the middle values, and left the board surface for the lightest lights. I finished by picking out the highlights with a dry brush. I spent about three hours re-creating this magic moment.

YOU CAN SKETCH FROM YOUR TV

I love sketching in pen and ink, and often keep a watercolor palette nearby. I was heavily into watching sumo on the Japanese channel (NGN) when I decided to see if I could capture the action of the tournament and bulk of the wrestlers in my sketchbook. I started drawing but soon switched to a watercolor sketchbook. Nonerasable pen and ink records the drawing process and the search for forms, adding interest and excitement.

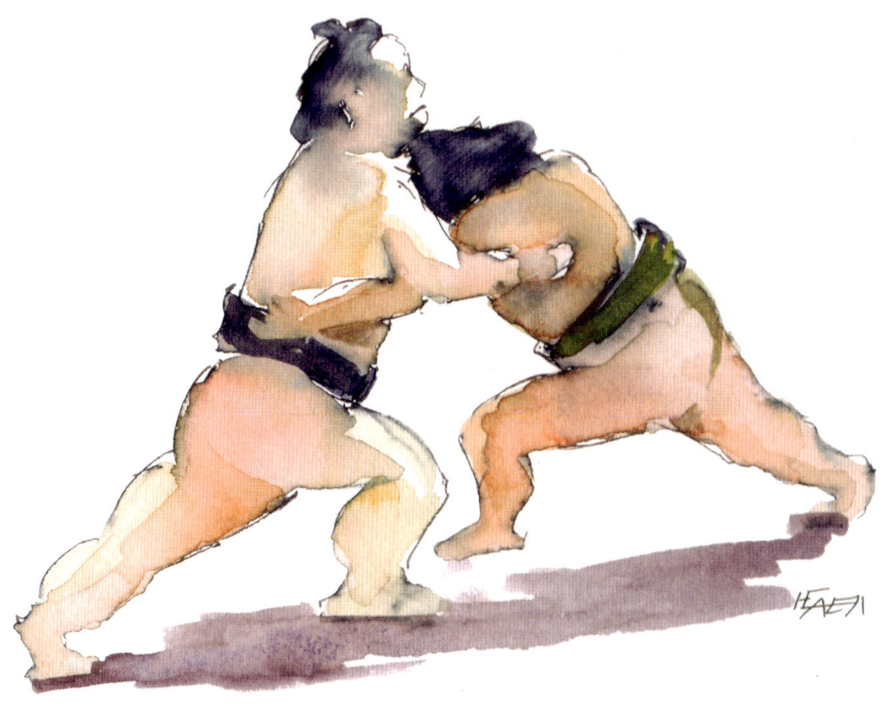

Sumo Series #9
Helen C. Iaea · Pen and ink with watercolor washes on watercolor paper · 6½" × 8½" (17cm × 22cm)

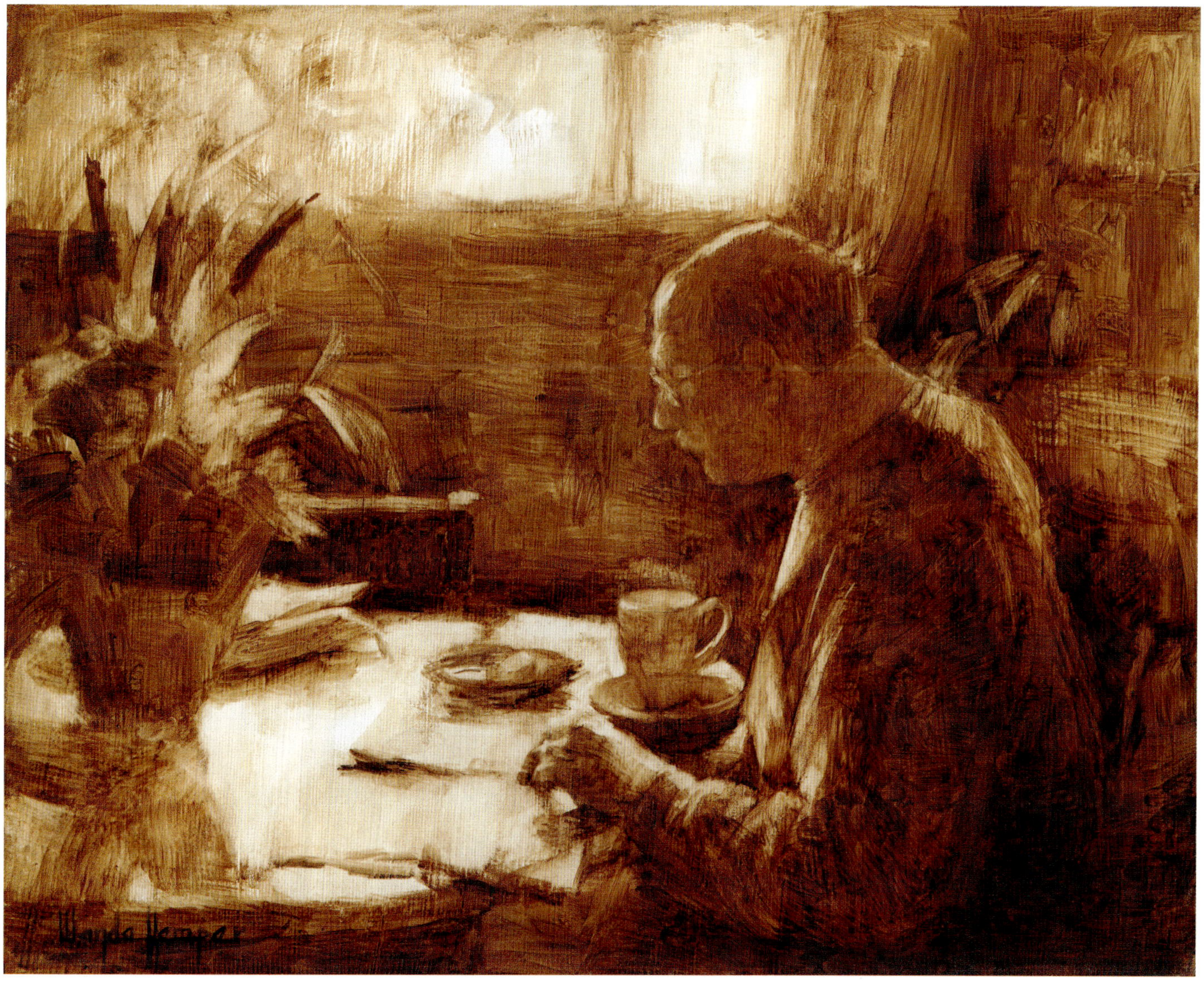

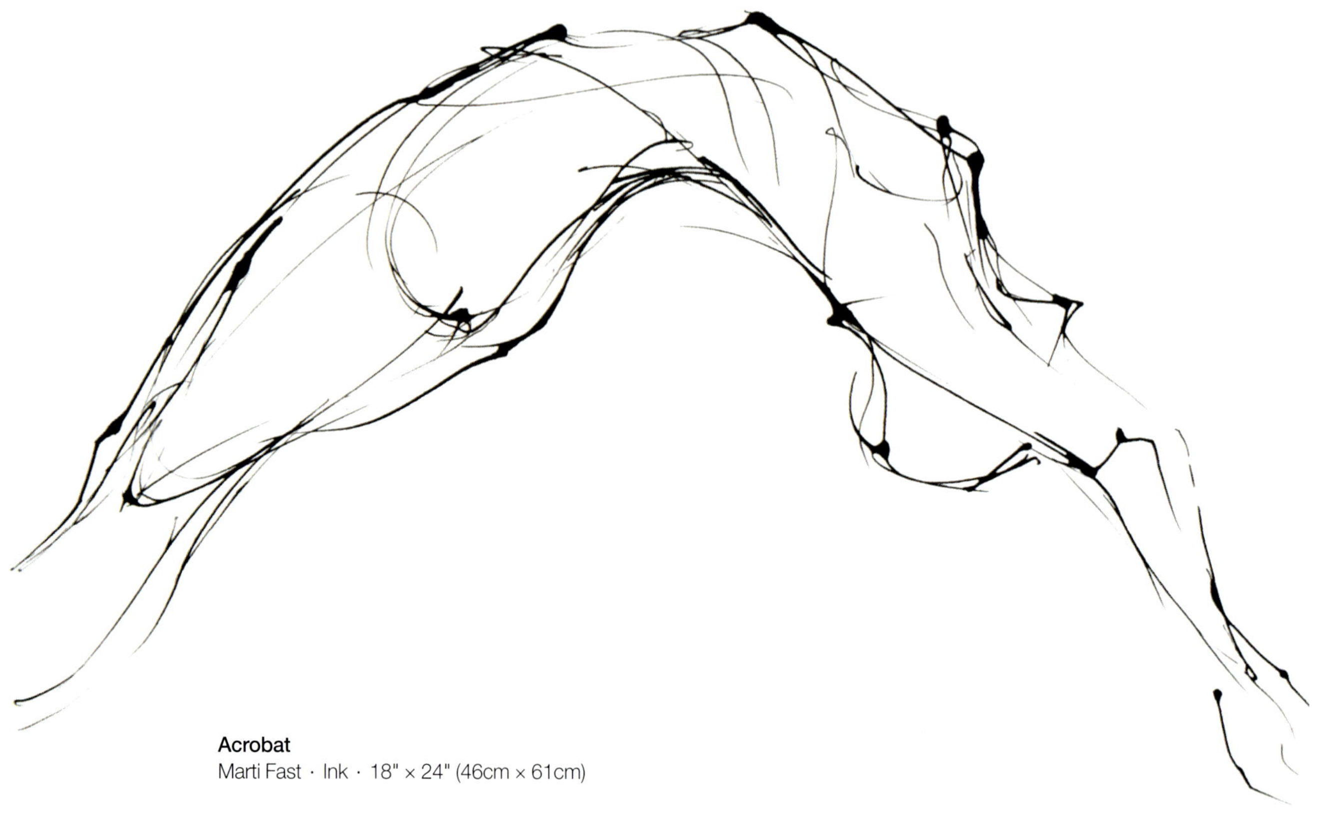

Acrobat
Marti Fast · Ink · 18" × 24" (46cm × 61cm)

DRAW FROM THE SHOULDER

Acrobat was from a pose held by a wonderful Pilates practitioner. We cushioned a short stool with some foam, she held this backbend for five minutes, and I worked very quickly with a stick and ink. I worked with my entire arm moving from the shoulder to capture the arcs of the form, and was pleased that the little blobs at the start of some strokes seemed to record the location of bones very effectively.

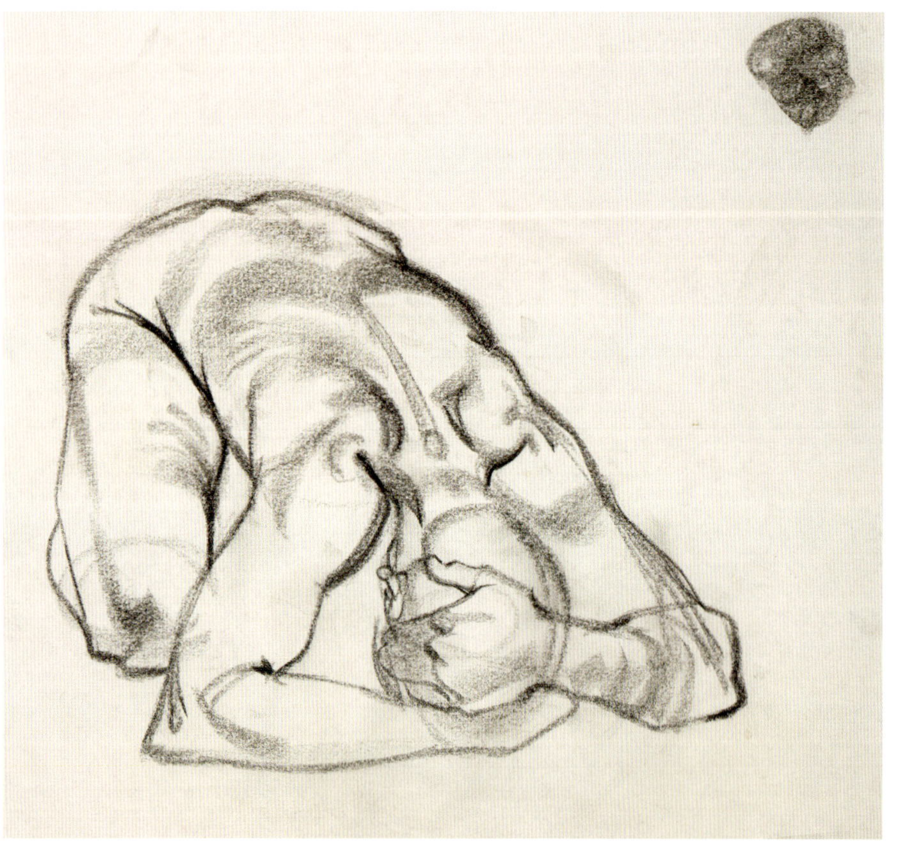

DRAW DIRECT WITH NO ERASURES

This was the result of a twenty-five-minute pose with a live model in a studio drawing group. It was drawn in a direct manner with no erasures. After beginning with a light block in, all form development and corrections were achieved by overdrawing with progressively heavier lines.

Kneeling Male Figure
Paul R. Alexander · Conté crayon on paper · 7" × 8½" (18cm × 22cm)

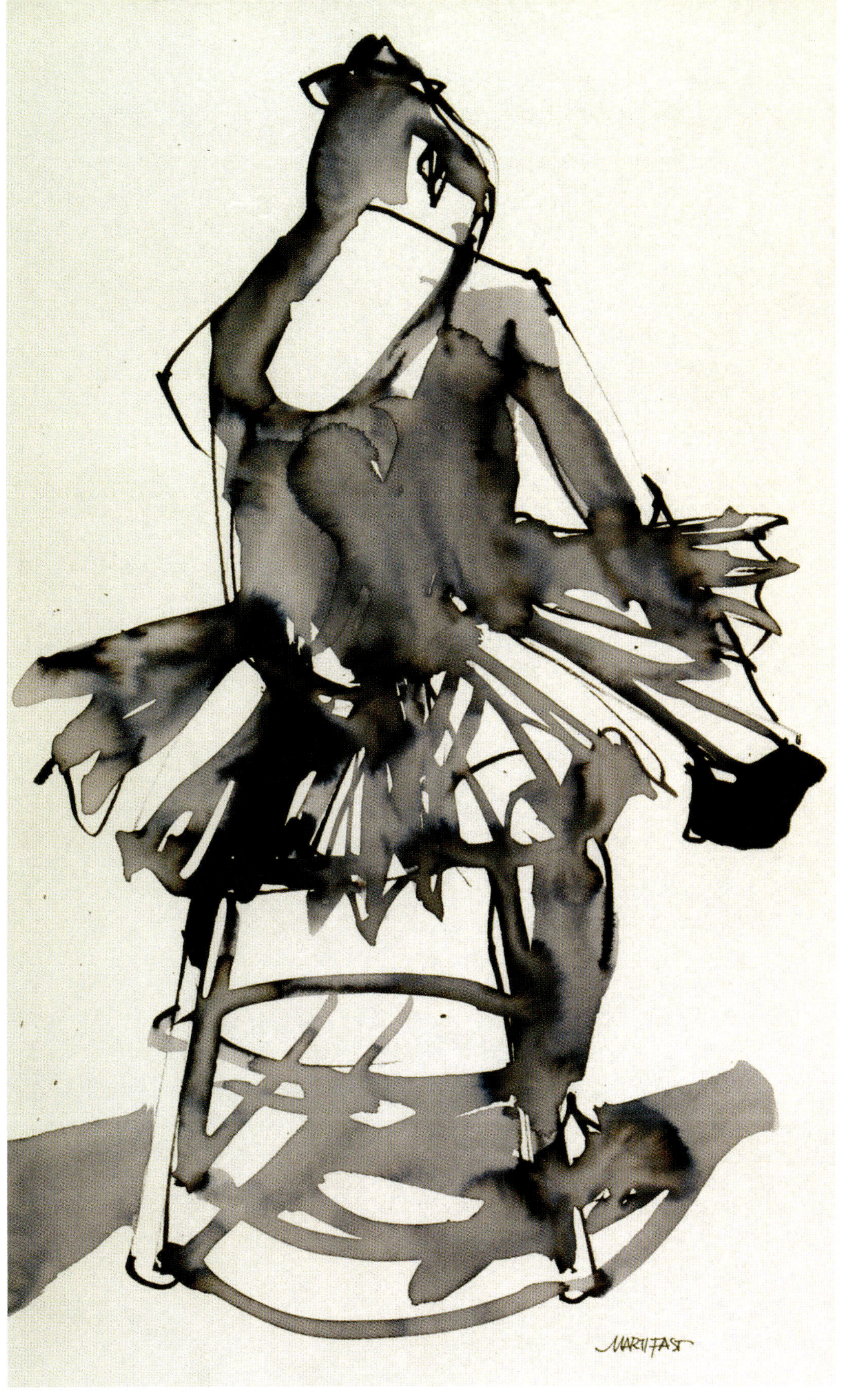

Dancer I: Tired Feet
Marti Fast · Ink and ink wash · 17" × 11" (43cm × 28cm)

A Difficult Tool Proves Useful

One of my passions is gestural work. In *Dancer I*, the model had worked very hard, and then took this five-minute pose, in which her need to rest was compelling. The shadow patterns were made with a handmade brush that is limp and hard to control, which I love because it forces me to pay close attention to what is happening on the page.

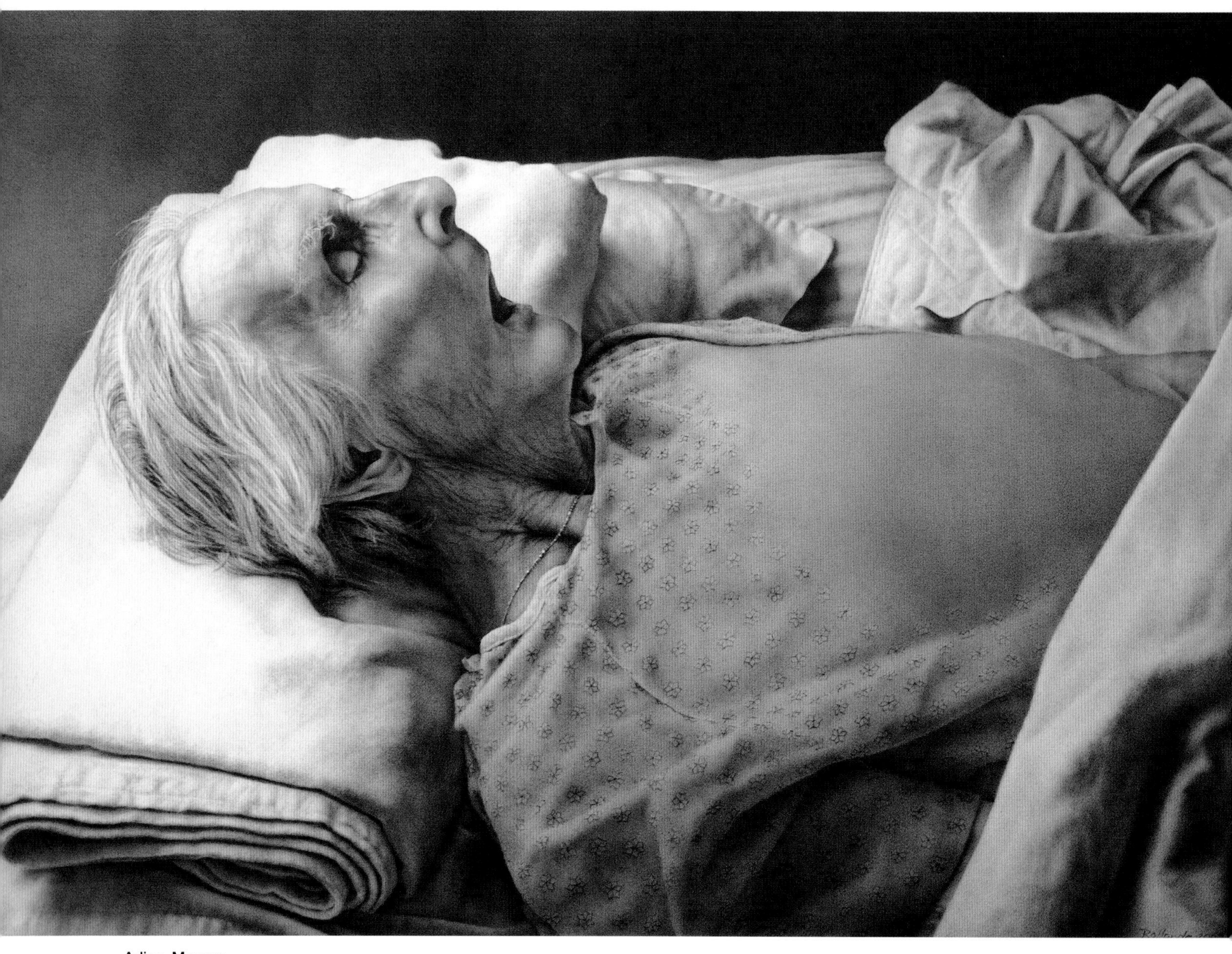

Adieu, Maman
Janvier Rollande · Graphite on paper · 10¼" × 14¼" (26cm × 36cm)

Understand Your Feelings Through Drawing

For *Adieu, Maman*, the lengthy process of my technique (described on page 17) helped me to process and come to terms with my mother's impending death. Drawing has always been a way for me to deeply know and understand, not only my subject, but my feelings about it as well.

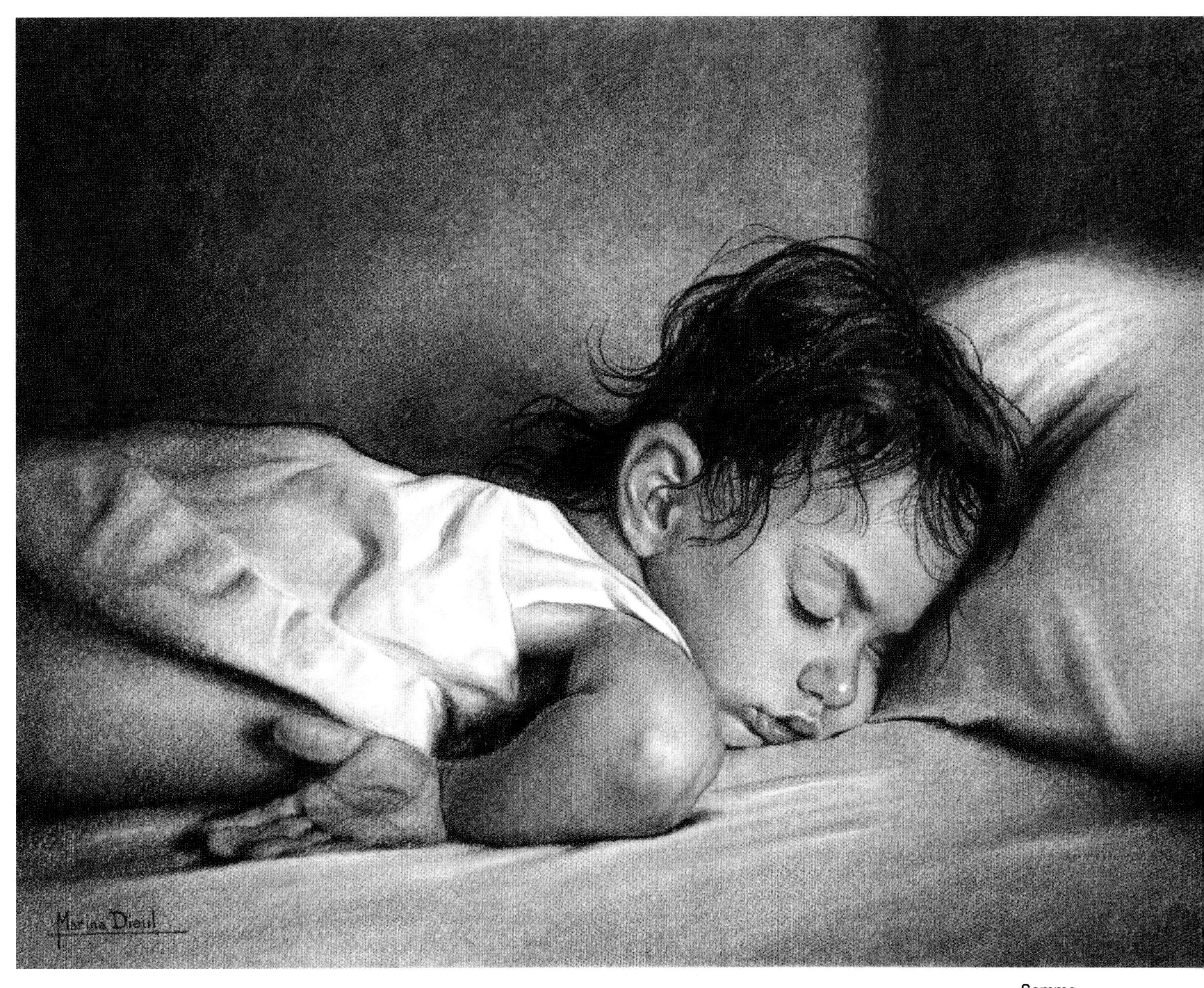

Somme
Marina Dieul · Charcoal on paper · 12" × 16" (30cm × 41cm)

KEEP HIGHEST CONTRASTS NEAR YOUR FOCAL POINT

This artwork is about the fascination of watching a child sleeping, totally vulnerable and confident.
I decided to keep the drawing in low key, although I wanted to have a few spots of perfect white.
I massed the values to obtain a balanced composition, keeping the highest contrasts near my focal
point, the baby's face. Then I worked mostly by big masses, refining more and more the small shapes,
using a lot of stomp, chamois and kneaded eraser. During the process, it became clear which edges
needed to be very soft and where to keep some line works.

I used a soft **LIGHT,** almost frontal, but with a fast fall-off
to enhance the idea of **WHITE ACCENTS GLOWING**
in the warm atmosphere of a **DARK** room.

-Marina Dieul

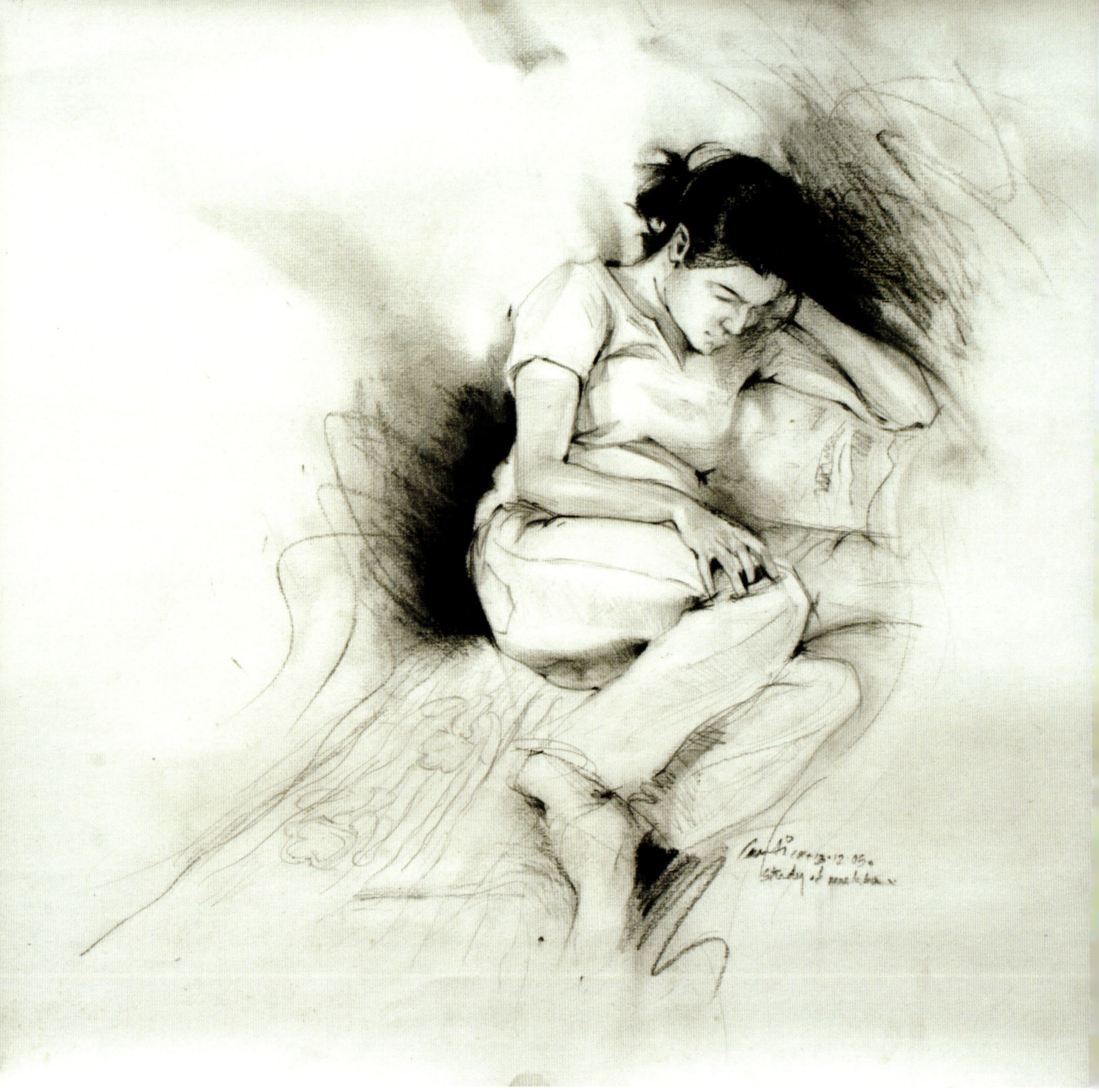

Mukta Reading
Aditya Shirké · Charcoal on cartridge paper · 14" × 15" (36cm × 38cm)

Establish Proportions First

I did this drawing from life in my studio. First I carefully established
the overall proportions of the figure with a 2B pencil. I then rendered the
figure using a charcoal stick and a charcoal pencil for finer details.
The model, Mukta Avachat, is also an artist.

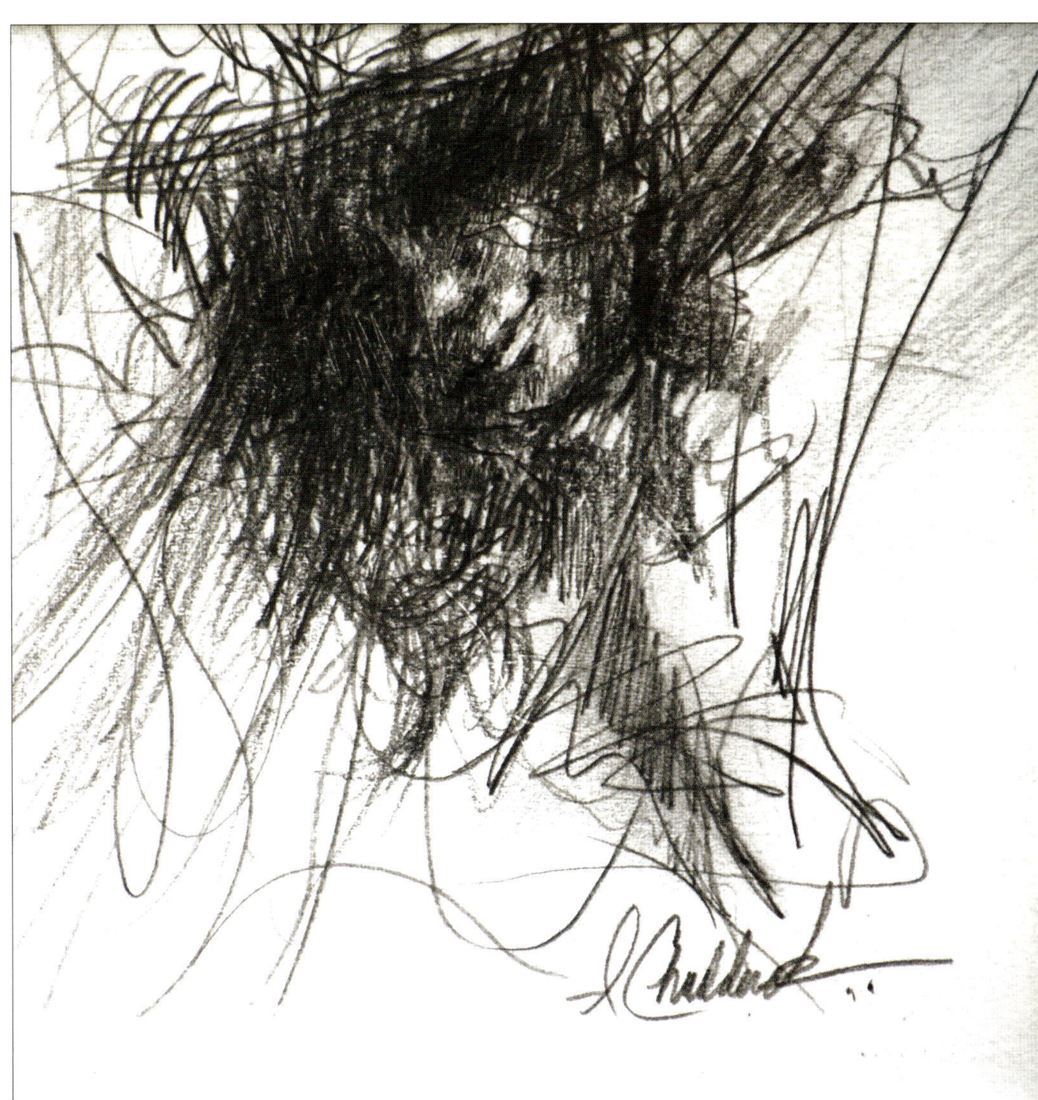

She Loves
Anne Chaddock · Pencil · 4" × 4" (10cm × 10cm)

LET YOUR IMAGINATION TAKE OVER

This drawing was created in my studio from my imagination. I used a 4B pencil and began gesturing this feeling, and the subject formed on its own. I wanted the subject to move outside of the image area so the viewer can move beyond what is there. In deep areas, the paper is covered and becomes very dark. In lighter places, I used fewer lines and lifted the highlights with an eraser. The process was highly intuitive.

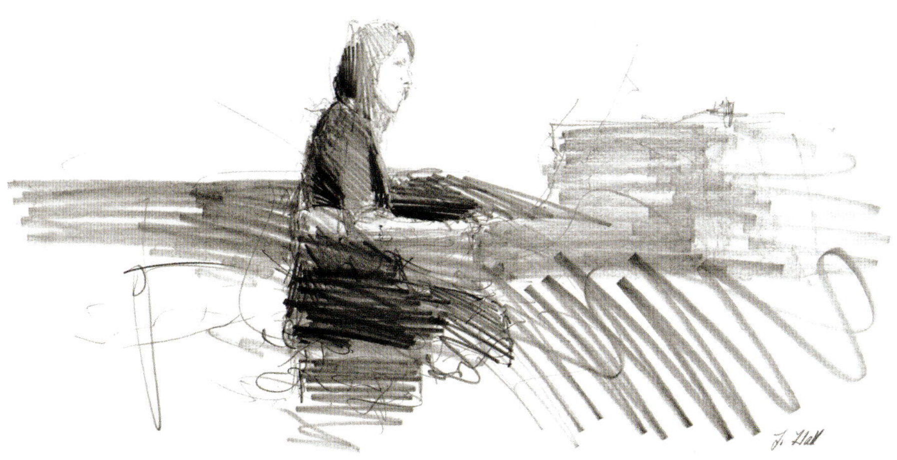

Emily at Piano
Lane Hall · Pencil on paper · 8" × 11" (20cm × 28cm)

DON'T FORGET THE SIDE OF YOUR PENCIL POINT

Emily was playing piano at her church while I did this five-minute drawing in my sketchbook. The majority of the lines were made using the side of the pencil point, while the few fine lines were created using the end of the point.

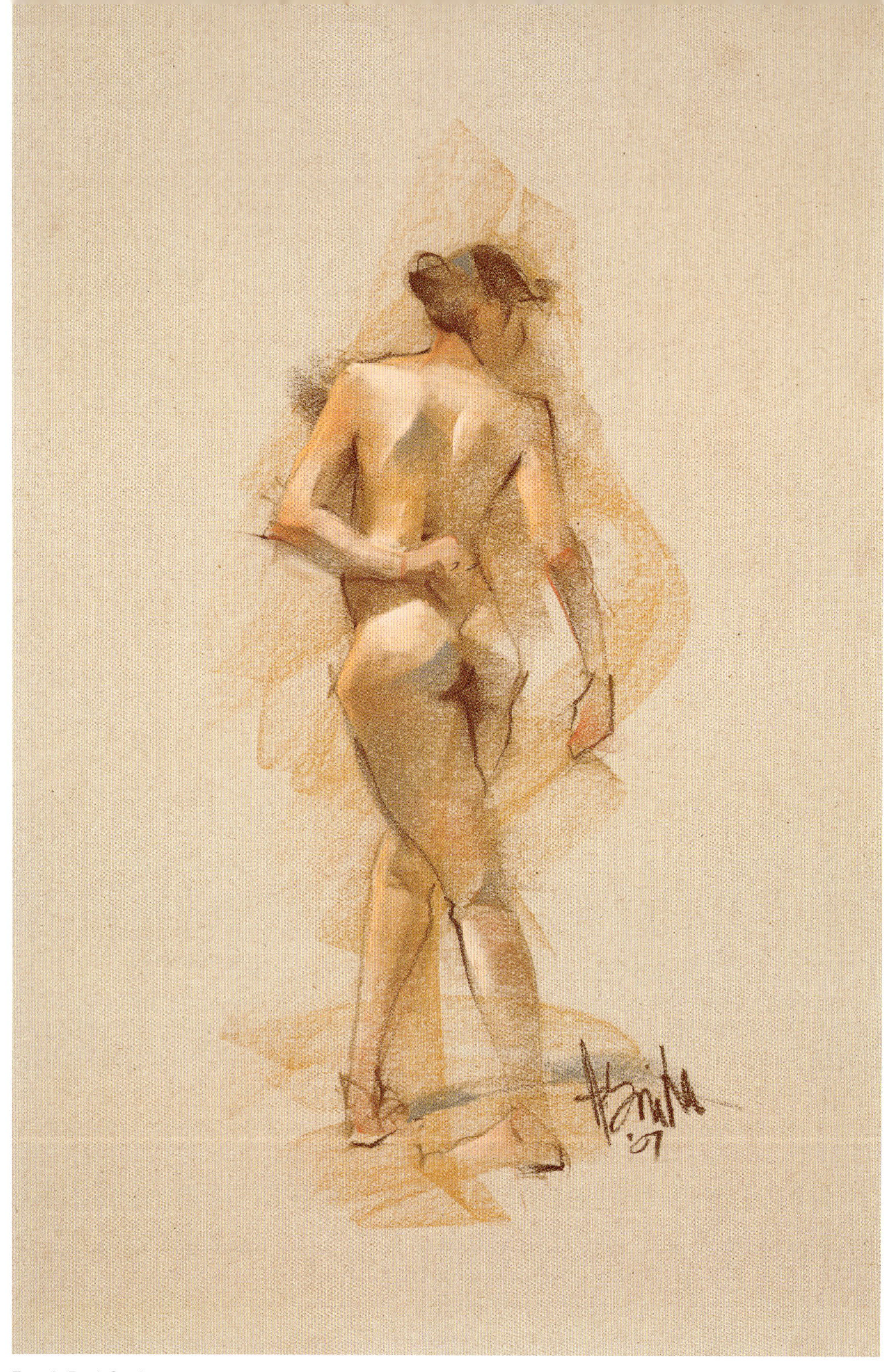

Female Back Study
Annette Smith · Pastel and Conté on toned paper · 17" × 10½" (43cm × 27cm)

LIGHT AND FORM EMERGE FROM SPACE

My goal in figure drawing is to convey a sense of light and form emerging from space. I begin by swiping a few quick strokes of pastel on toned paper to express movement and establish a simple background. Switching to a sepia drawing lead, I sketch the figure's general structure and lightly indicate its shadow pattern. Using the side of a pastel, I mass in the darks and then quickly move to the light areas, slowly building them up and saving the highlights for last. If time permits, I may restate some of the drawing and add halftones and reflected light where I see fit.

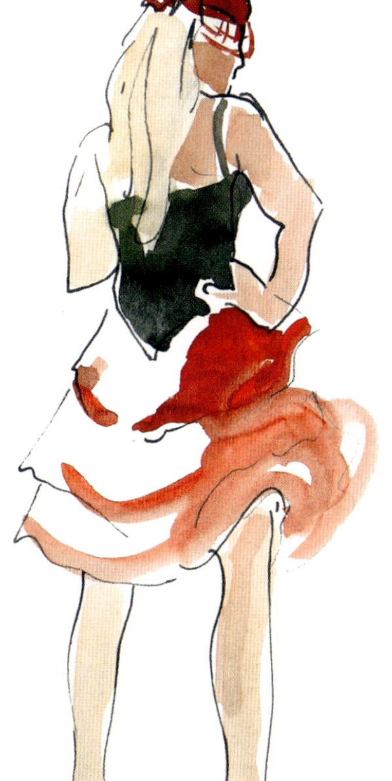

DRAWING IS LIKE FLUID DANCING

Drawing is dancing—fluid and passionate—a moment of action. The flick of the brush reflects both the dancer's movement and my reaction to that movement.

This sketch was drawn from life in a studio, with a series of quick gestures in one or two minutes with a felt-tip pen and a splash of watercolor to accent the movement.

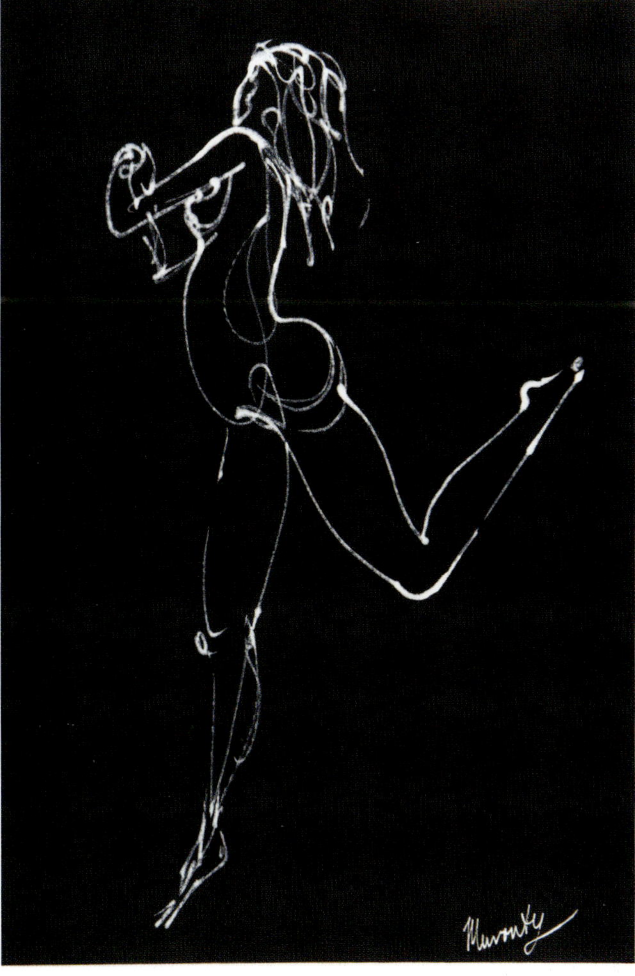

PRACTICE BLIND CONTOUR DRAWING

Practicing blind contours (drawing in one rapid fluid line without looking at the paper) is a great way to make sketches more spontaneous. Armed with a series of photographs and life sketches, I followed the form of the model using a white correction fluid pen on black paper, treating every risky mark as a gleam of light on a dark body dancing and leaping through space. It's an exacting method, and the irony is that correction fluid drawings cannot be corrected! The light on the figure represents the electricity I feel when I'm drawing.

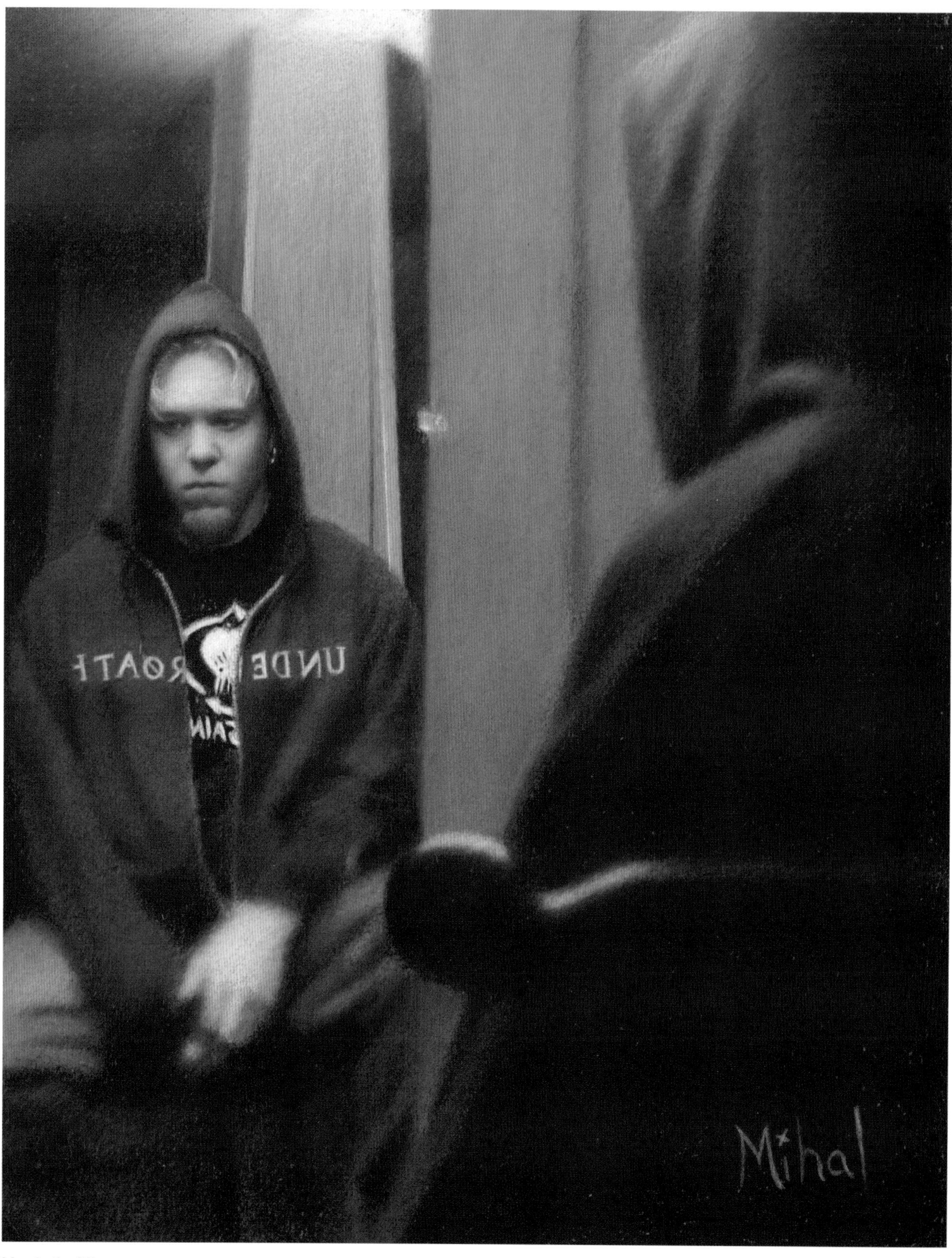

Man in the Mirror
Steve Mihal · Charcoal on paper · 10" × 8" (25cm × 20cm)

LOOK INSIDE AS WELL AS OUTSIDE

I started with a very light line drawing and then began to add values to the entire drawing. Next I finished the face and worked my way out to the rest of the drawing. Switching direction with the charcoal, I was able to give the drawing a polished look. To me the mirror was a metaphor, expressing my need to look inside, to capture more than just the values in the mirror's reflection. That thought helped me show more emotion in the drawing. I left some of the drawing out of focus to bring more attention to the face reflected in the mirror. I wanted to give the viewer a bit of insight into who I am.

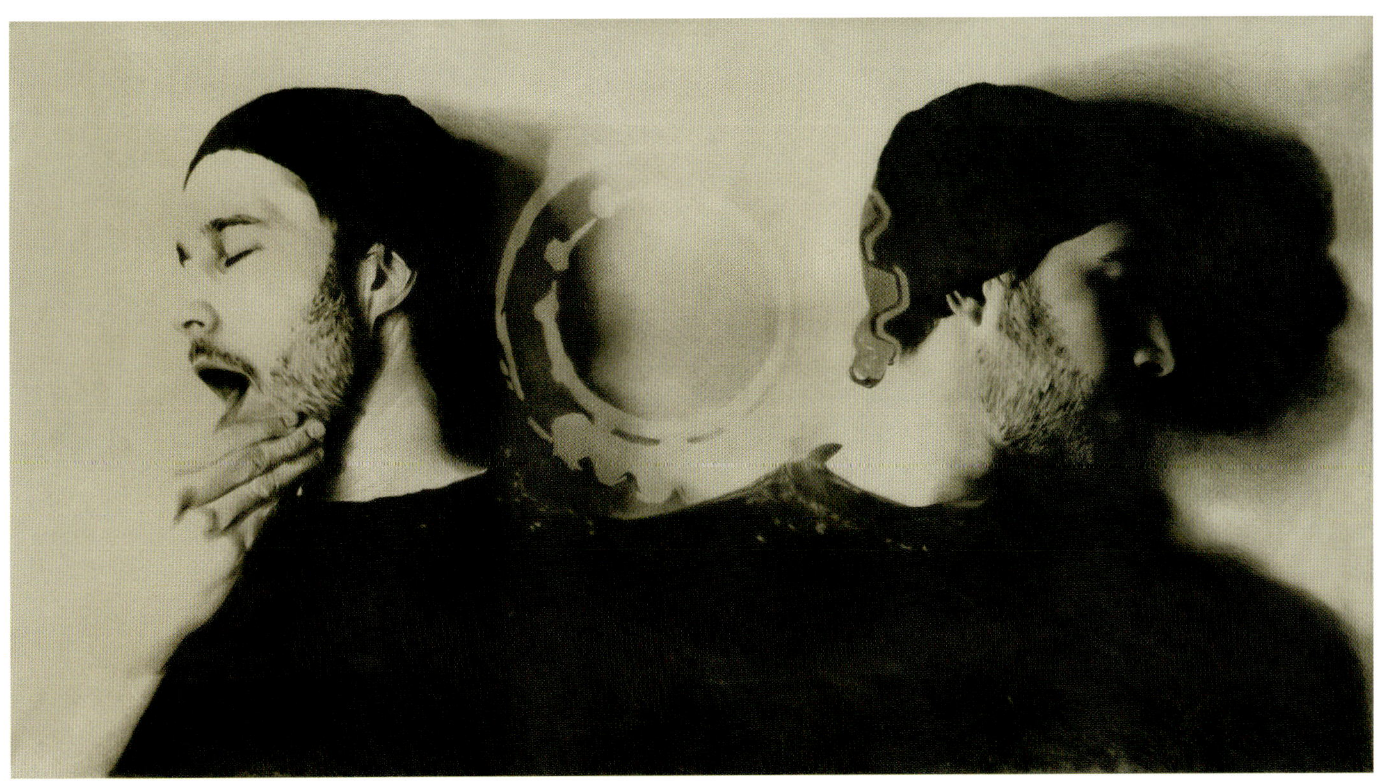

Lower Your Eyelids
Joseph Crone · Colored pencil on frosted acetate with toned paper backing · 11" × 21" (28cm × 53cm)

EXPLORE THE GRITTY SIDE OF EMOTIONS

My intent is to explore, through photorealistic drawing techniques, the gritty and uncomfortable aspects of human emotion. To accomplish this, I use Prismacolor Verithin colored pencils on layers of one-sided frosted acetate. This layering technique creates unusual depth. I use my perfectionist methods of pressure-based drawing to re-create photos that I have previously staged. I strive to capture a single, thought-provoking moment.

FIGURE SANS HEAD BECOMES GENERALIZED

Emily Reading is from a photograph I took of my daughter. Because the main focus is the atmosphere created by the light falling on the figure, I chose not to include the head. I wanted an iconic pose, suggesting the general experience of relaxing with a book, rather than a particular person. I built up the tones very gradually using charcoal pencil, reinforcing the blacks with carbon pencil and using hard graphite for the very lightest areas.

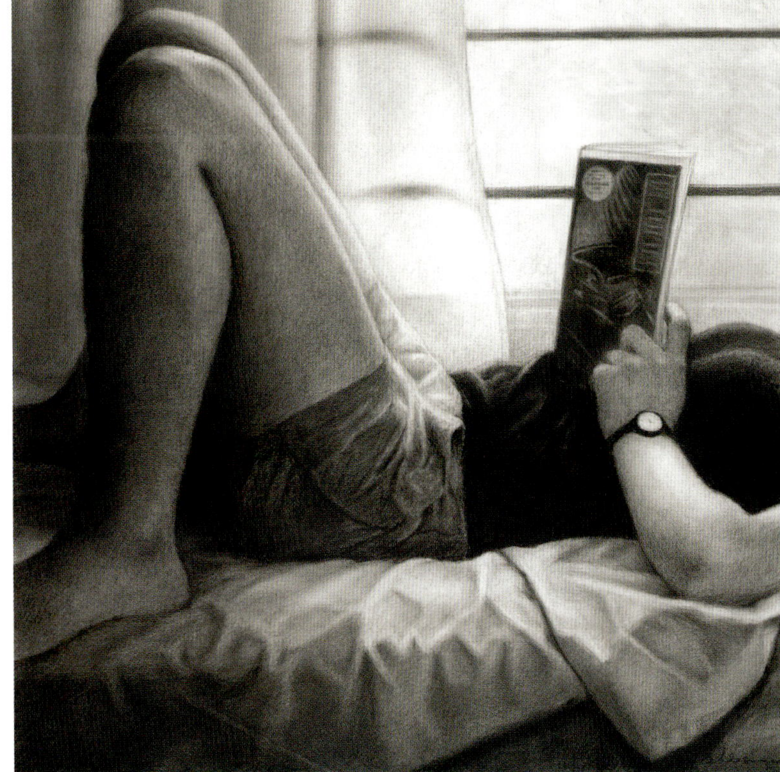

Emily Reading
Jaye Schlesinger · Charcoal, graphite and carbon pencil · 12" × 12" (30cm × 30cm)

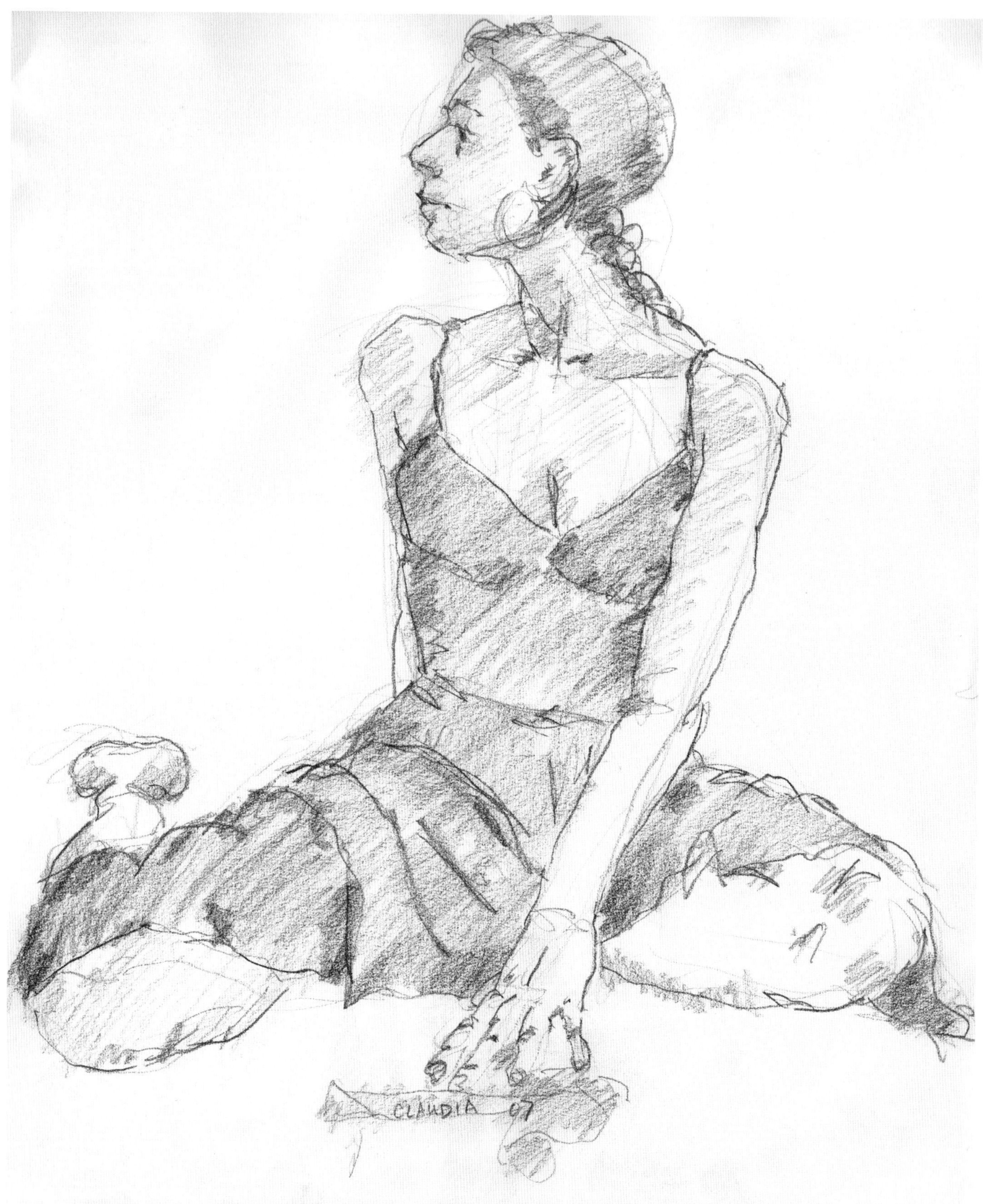

Claudia #1
James G. Meeks · Graphite on paper · 17" × 14" (43cm × 36cm)

Quick Gesture; Few Measurements

This drawing was done from life in the studio in about twenty minutes.

The initial gesture was done very quickly with minimal measurements.

I strive for expressive qualities over exact likeness and proportions.

Combine Gesture and Finished Drawing

Tsana was done at a weekly life-drawing session. It was a twenty-minute pose that started with a quick gesture drawing. After the gesture was completed, I started to model some of the form over it. I like the incorporation of gesture with finished areas. Working regularly from short poses that range from one to twenty minutes keeps my drawing skills lively.

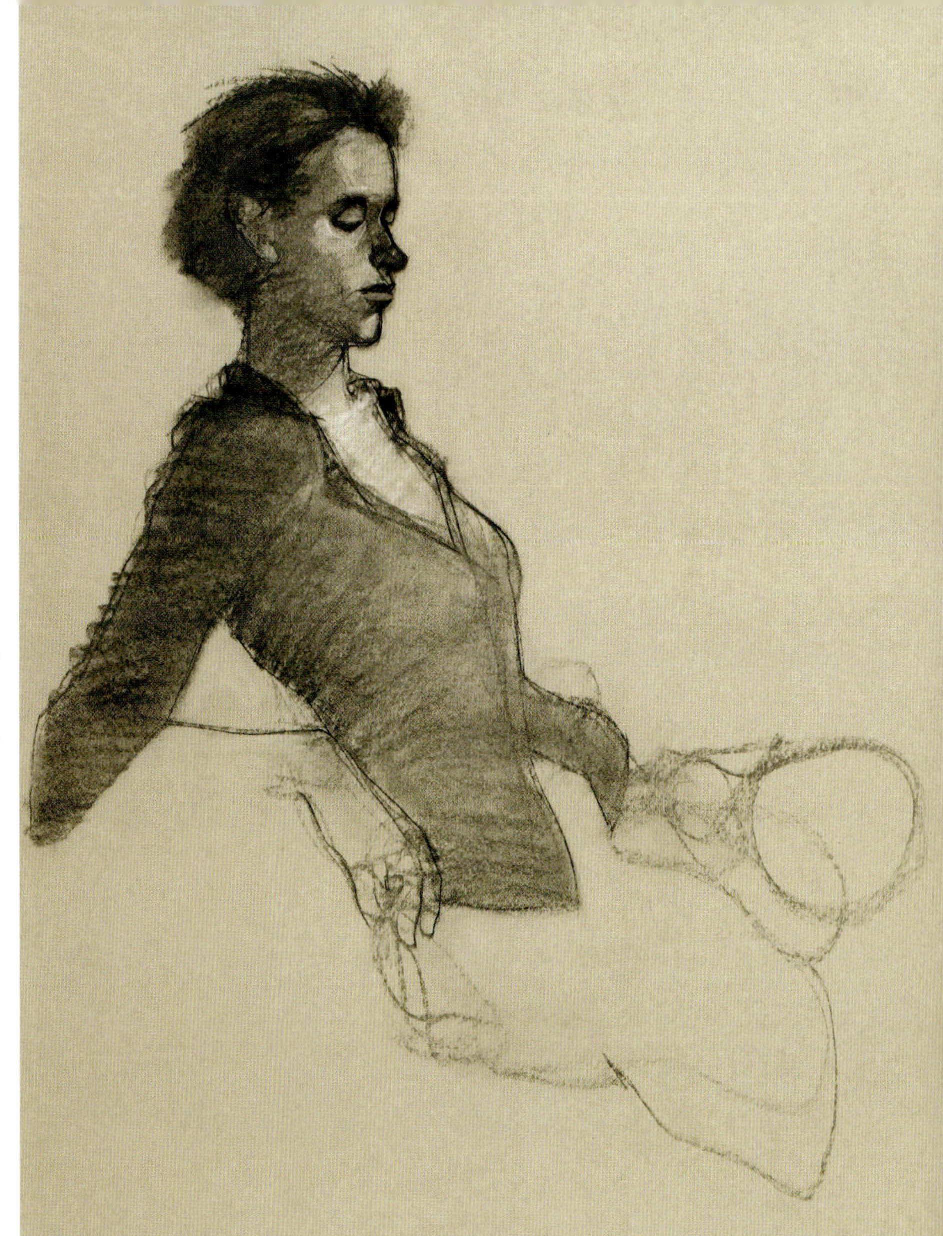

Tsana
George Thompson · Charcoal on toned paper · 24" × 18" (61cm × 46cm)

Materials for Quick Life Drawing

This was a fifteen-minute drawing done from life on Domtar 60-lb. (130gsm) acid-free paper with Conté. I frequently use these materials for quick, life-drawing exercises because they deliver great effects. Both the side and an edge of the Conté is used to accomplish shading and finer lines.

Inanna
Connie Herberg · Conté on paper · 14" × 14" (36cm × 36cm)

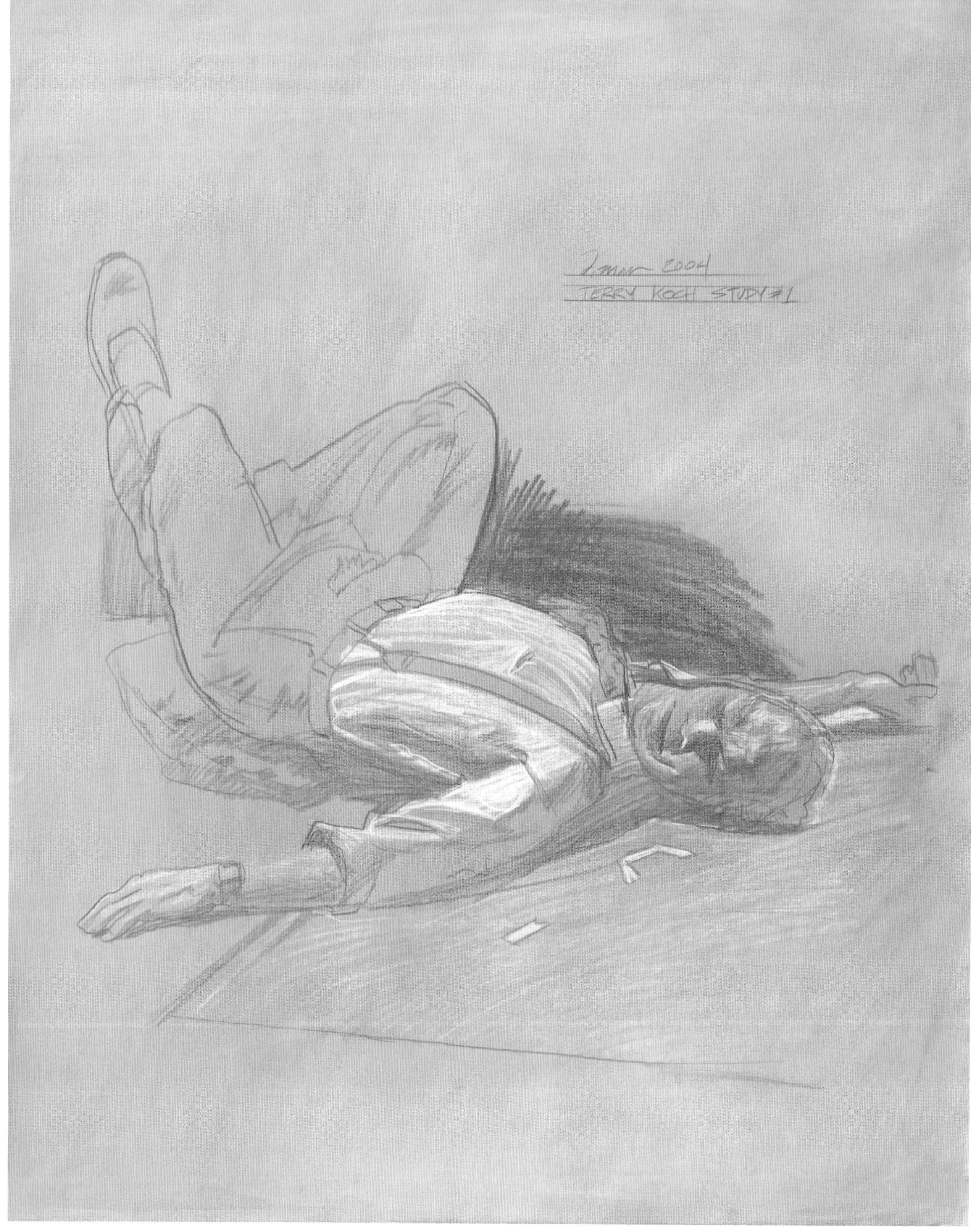

Terry Koch Study #1
David Mar · Graphite and white colored pencil on tan paper · 23¾" × 19" (60cm × 48cm)

Start With the Head

This was drawn from life at a workshop I ran at the San Francisco Academy of Art. It was drawn more vigorously than I normally might for this technique, but the pose was initially only twenty minutes. I start with the head to get a sense of the model's attitude and likeness, and to measure proportions of the body from the head height. The model kindly gave an extra eight or ten minutes, which I spent switching to white colored pencil and adding some of the environment.

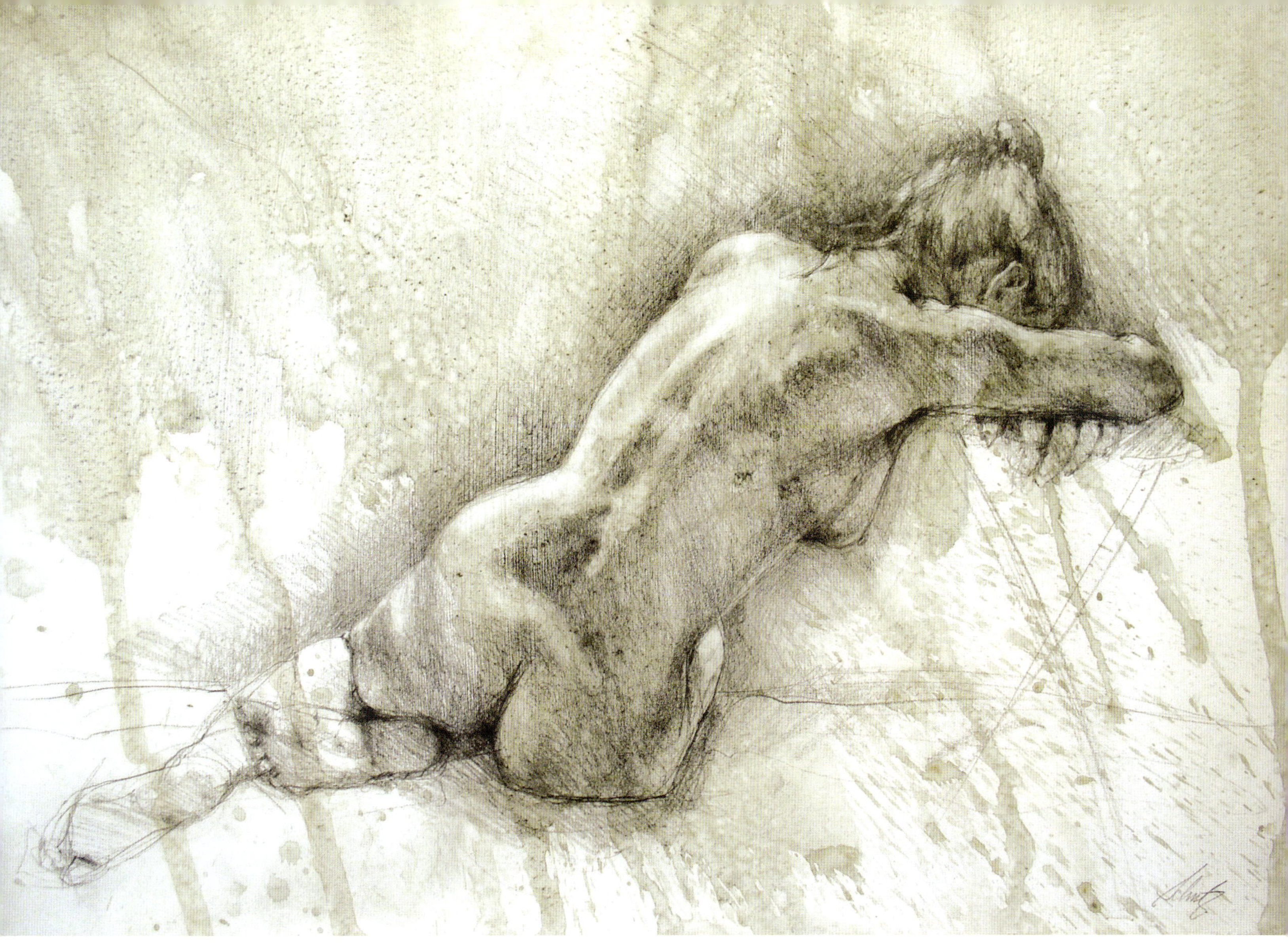

Leaning Figure
Suzy Schultz · Watercolor and graphite on watercolor paper · 15" × 20" (38cm × 51cm)

TIME LIMITATIONS CAN PROVE USEFUL

I stretched a piece of watercolor paper, put on a layer of gesso and then splattered watercolor on top. I took that into a life-drawing open studio where I did the drawing. I liked the pose of the model and wanted to capture something of its contemplative mood. I like to leave some parts of the drawing unfinished to contrast with parts that are more fully rendered. Working from life encourages this because of the time limitation—when the model's done posing, I'm done with the drawing.

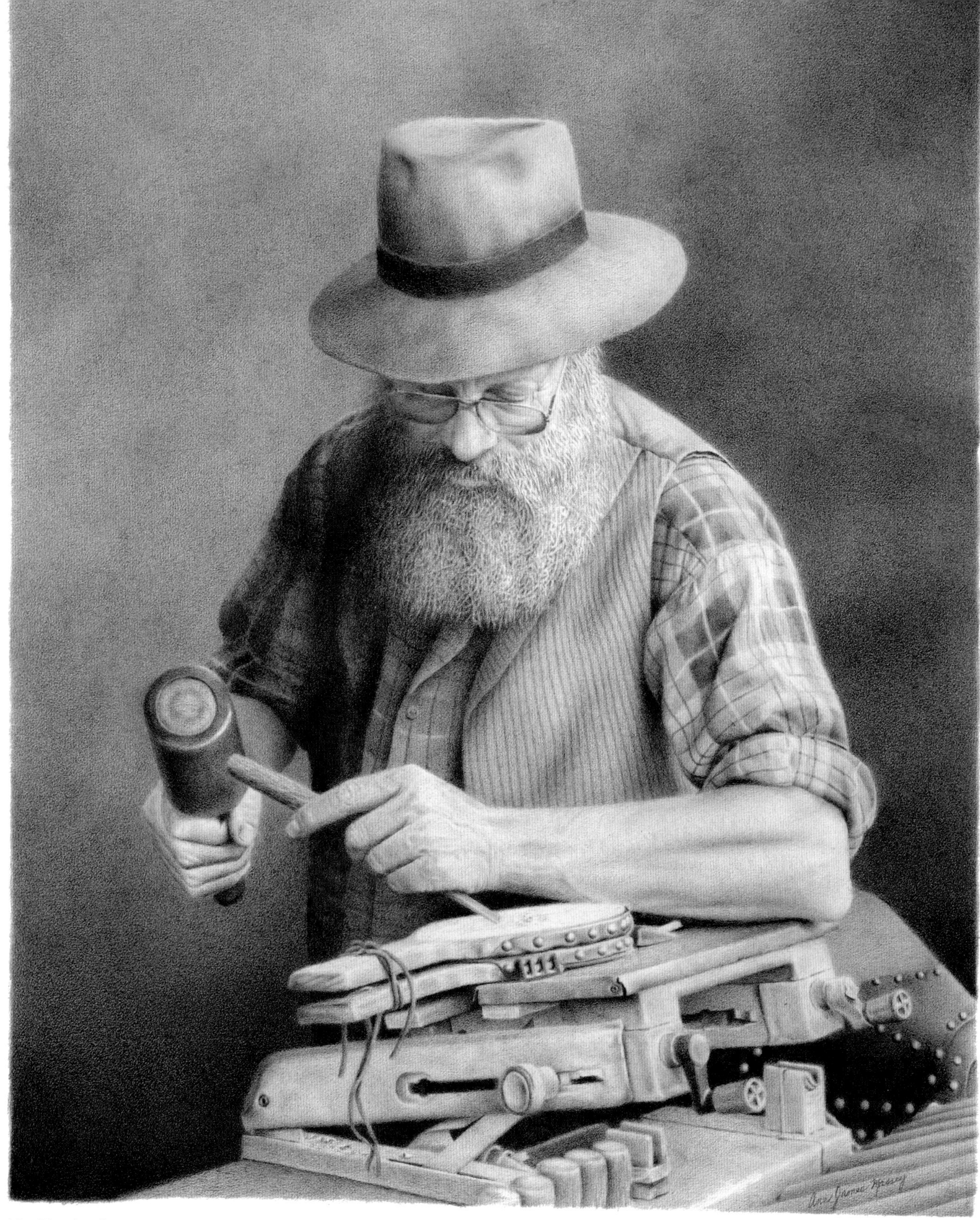

The Woodworker
Ann James Massey · Black colored pencil on bristol paper with plate finish · 12" × 9½" (30cm × 24cm)

FIFTY LAYERS BUILT WITHOUT ERASING

The inspiration for *The Woodworker* is loosely based on a photo I took of a Silver Dollar City artisan. First, a quick gestural sketch on tracing paper to decide composition, size and basic proportions; then a second tracing paper placed on top to create a clean line drawing; then a last tracing paper to add all the important details. After transferring my final line drawing to the bristol paper, I gently built up fifty-plus layers, without erasing or smearing, using needle-sharp black colored pencils. The darks were drawn in between the lights to create the beard.

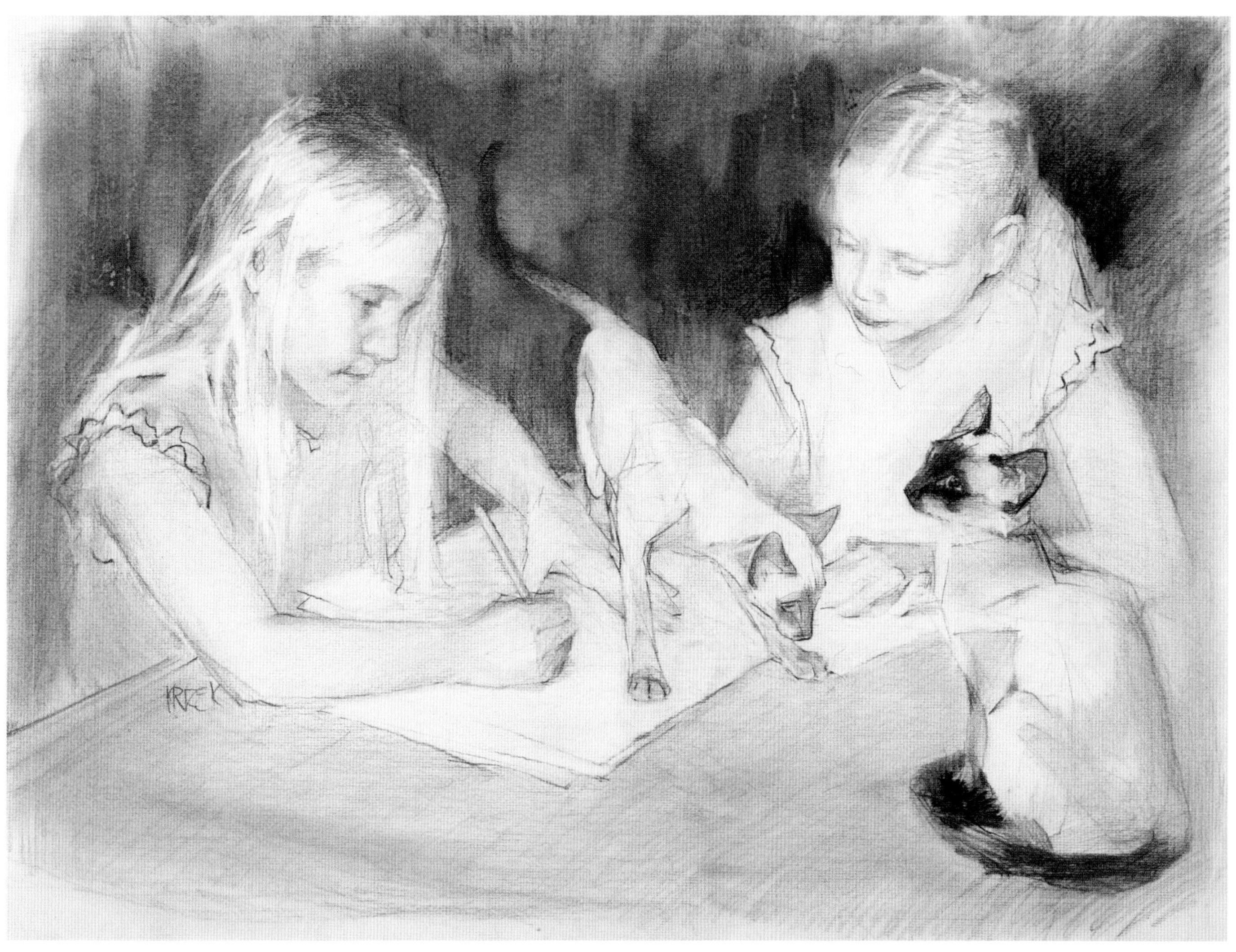

Emilee Mae & MacCayla
Donna Krizek · Charcoal on laid paper · 18" × 24" (46cm × 61cm)

AN AFTER-SCHOOL PORTRAIT SITTING

Drawn from life, this commissioned piece captures the spirit of after-school time. I spent time Tuesdays and Thursdays for several weeks drawing these two little girls and their cats. The cats always came running when we started drawing, attracted by the scratchy sounds of pencil and charcoal on rustling papers. The girls and I did homework and drawings, shared stories and laughter. It made me feel like I was twelve years old again.

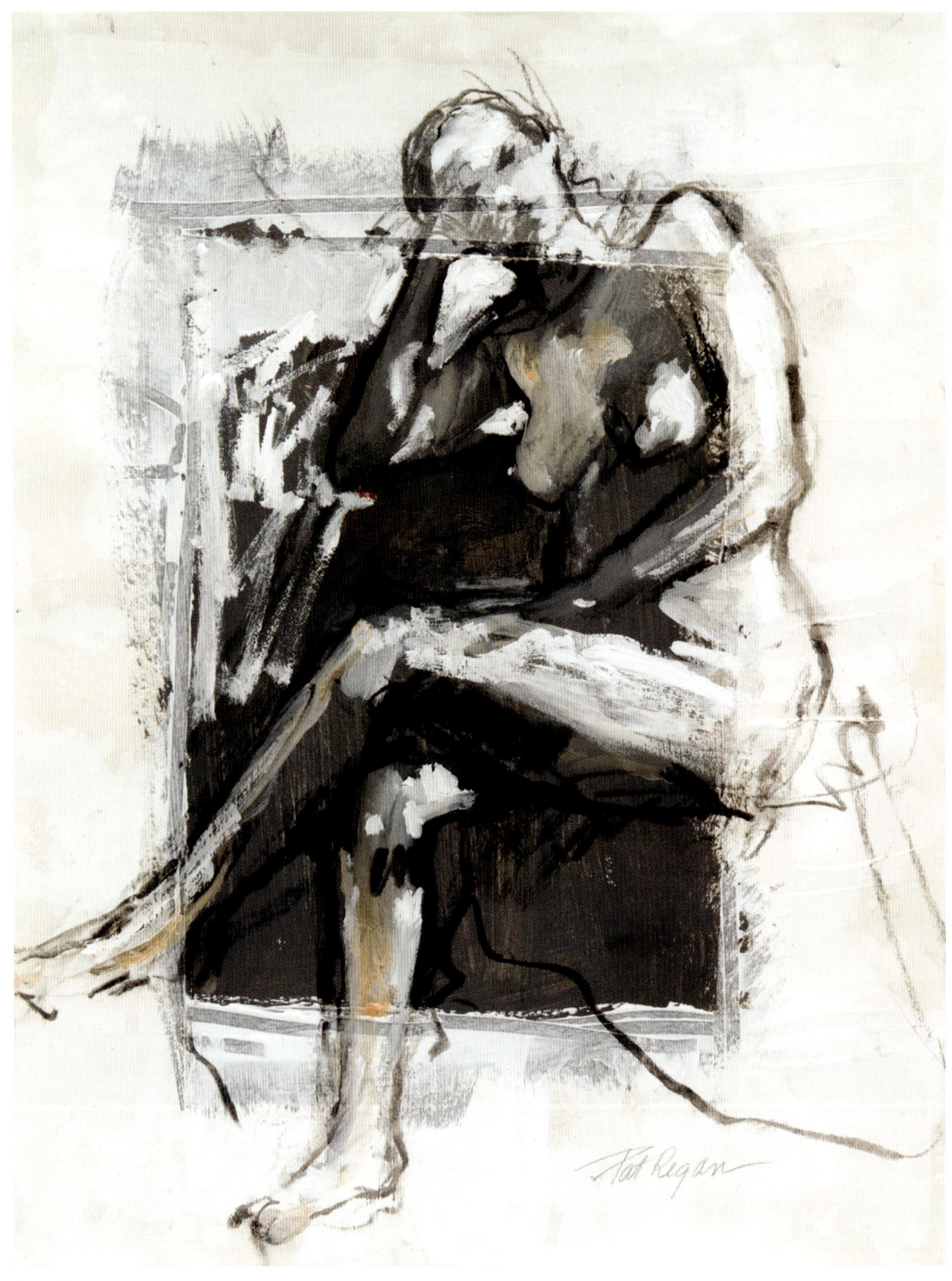

Boxed In
Pat Regan · Gouache and charcoal on toned paper · 11" × 8½" (28cm × 22cm)

PLAY WITH YOUR SURFACE TO ADD DESIGN ELEMENTS

Drawing from life enables me to see the nuances and gestures inherent in the human form. *Testing the Waters* began as a watercolor underpainting. The central figure was drawn with Caran D'Ache, using multiple lines that literally show my search for the gesture and movement. For *Boxed In*, I used résumé paper that was toned by pulling acrylic across the surface with a credit card. After toning the paper with acrylic, any wet or dry medium can be used to render the figure. In *Boxed In,* I used charcoal and gouache. Keeping the work loose and gestural is always my objective.

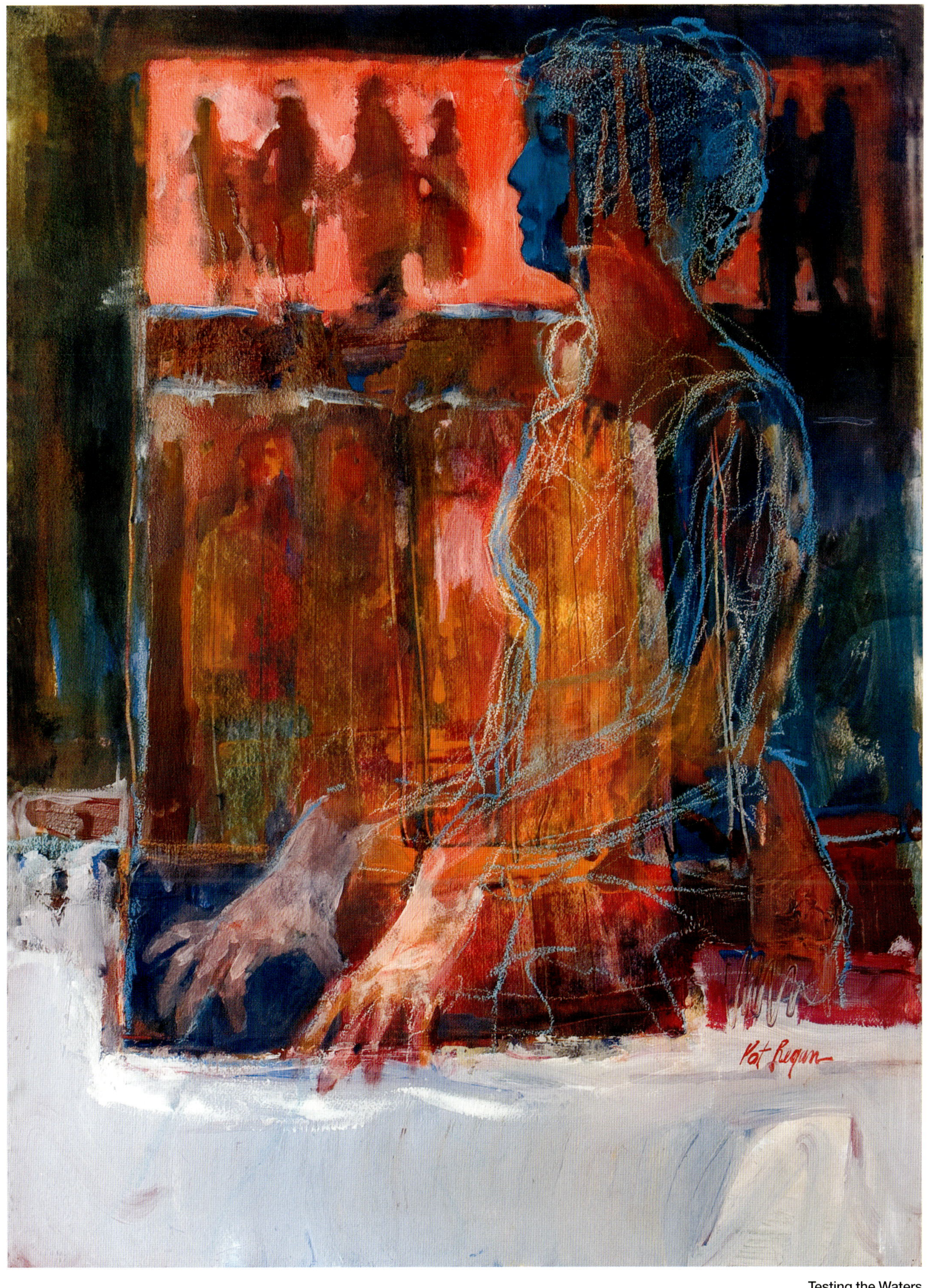

Testing the Waters
Pat Regan · Caran D'Ache, acrylic and watercolor on watercolor paper · 30" × 20" (76cm × 51cm)

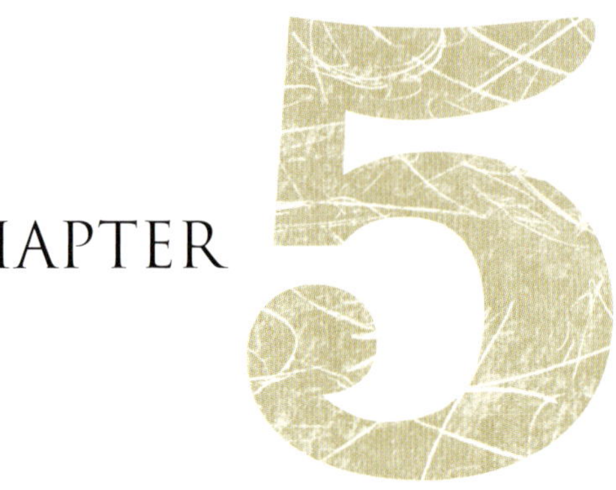

CHAPTER 5 LANDSCAPES

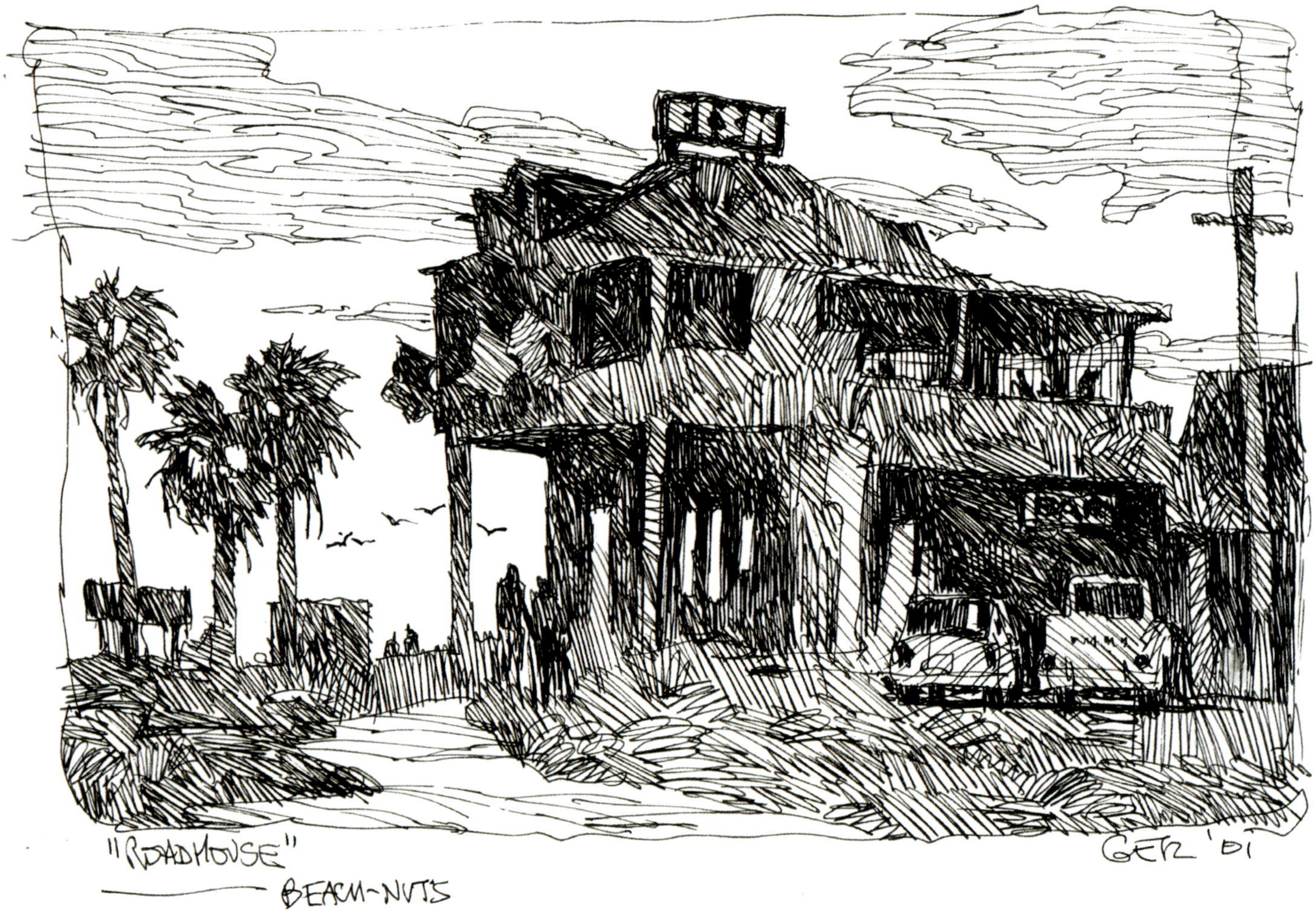

Roadhouse
Don Getz · Fiber-tipped black marker · 5" × 7" (13cm × 18cm)

TRY A FABRIC MARKER

These sketches were created with a double fiber-tipped black Identi-Pen by Sakura. A fabric marker, it is a very permanent ink. I primarily use the small tip of the marker, varying the line weight by the pressure applied to the paper. I generally use a 70-lb. (150gsm) rag drawing paper with a toothy surface. These sketches were done on location in about ten to fifteen minutes. I only include the shapes that convey the story. I work patterns of lines in different directions to create a look of action in certain areas. Always draw shapes, not things.

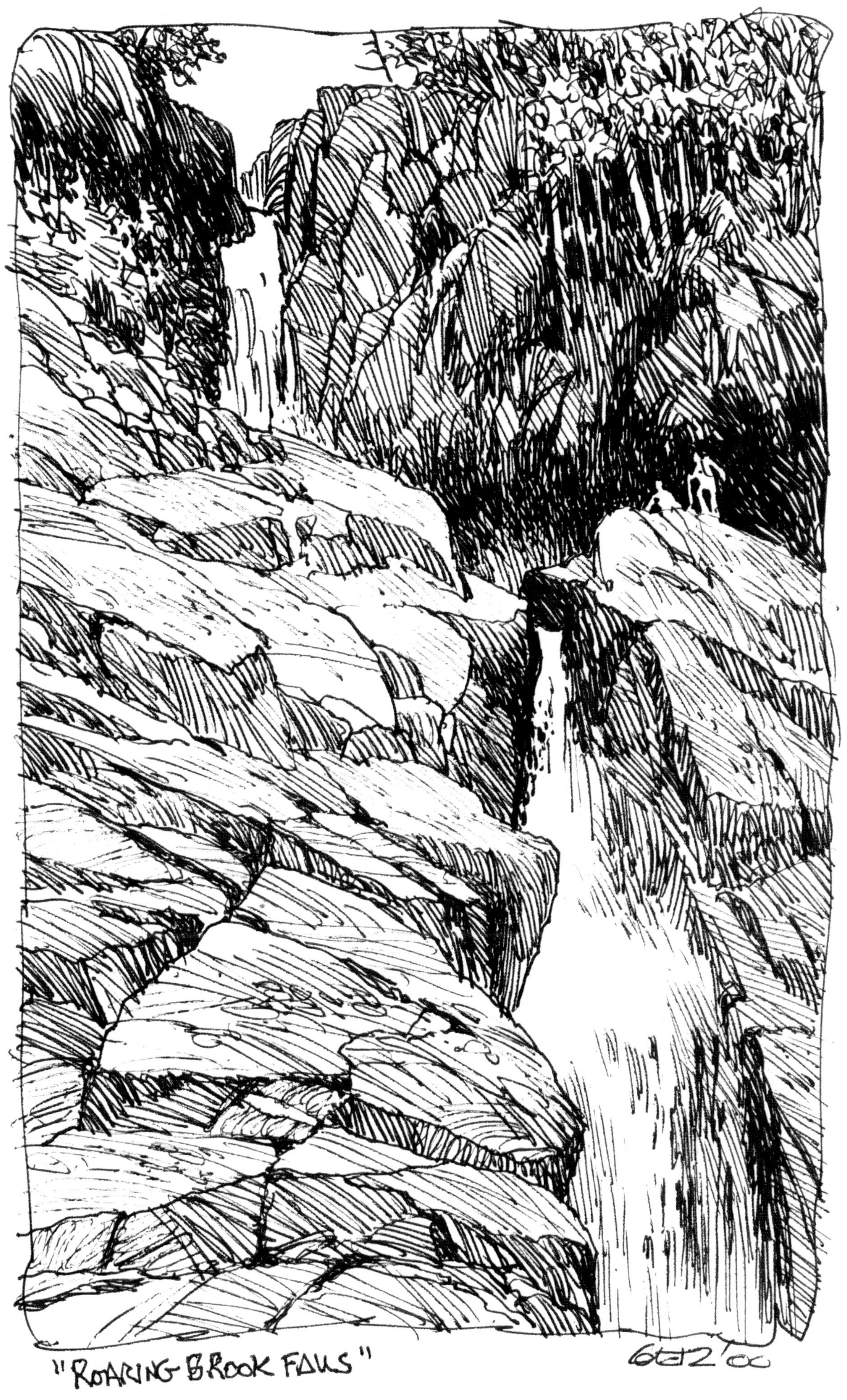

Roaring Brook Falls
Don Getz · Fiber-tipped black pen · 10" × 7" (25cm × 18cm)

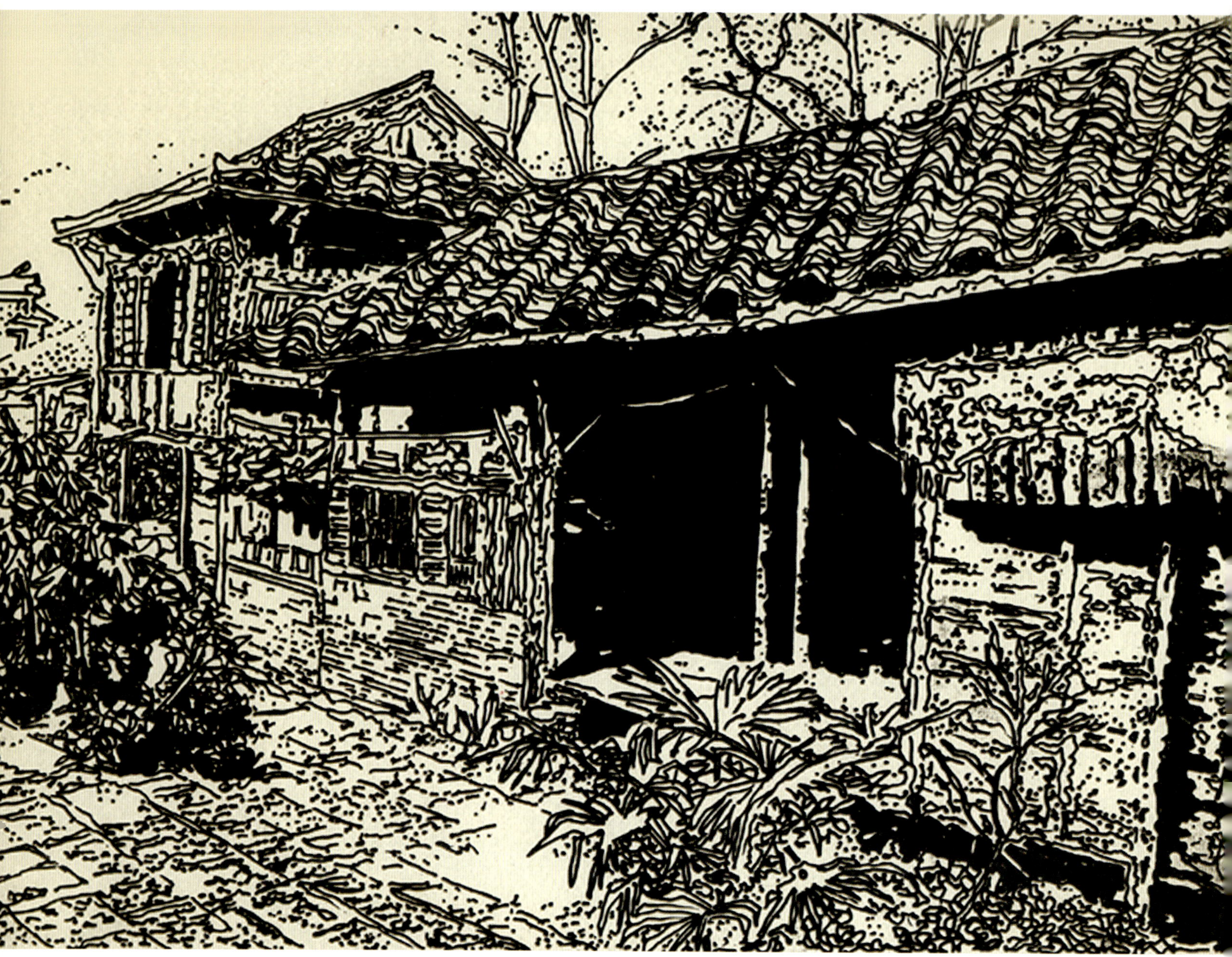

Fenghuang Ruin—Hunan, P. R. China
D. Matzen · Thin film polymer plate lithograph · 9" × 12" (23cm × 30cm) plate · 7½" × 10" (19cm × 25cm) image

TURN YOUR SKETCHES INTO PRINTS

I did a preliminary sketch on paper from a photo taken when I lived in China. I then placed the sketch under a thin film polymer plate by SmartPlate (Hurst Graphics). The plate is semitransparent, allowing me to see my sketch through it. I proceeded to draw directly onto the plate with a Sharpie medium-tipped felt marker, adding details not included in the sketch. The plate is then treated with gum arabic, wiped with a damp sponge, inked and run through the press. I used Rives BFK heavyweight print paper. The ink adheres only to the carbon-based (Sharpie pen) drawing.

Since it was pouring rain when I was at this location, there was not a lot of **VALUE CONTRAST.** This scene is about **TEXTURE;** using pure line to capture that texture was the real challenge.

-D. Matzen

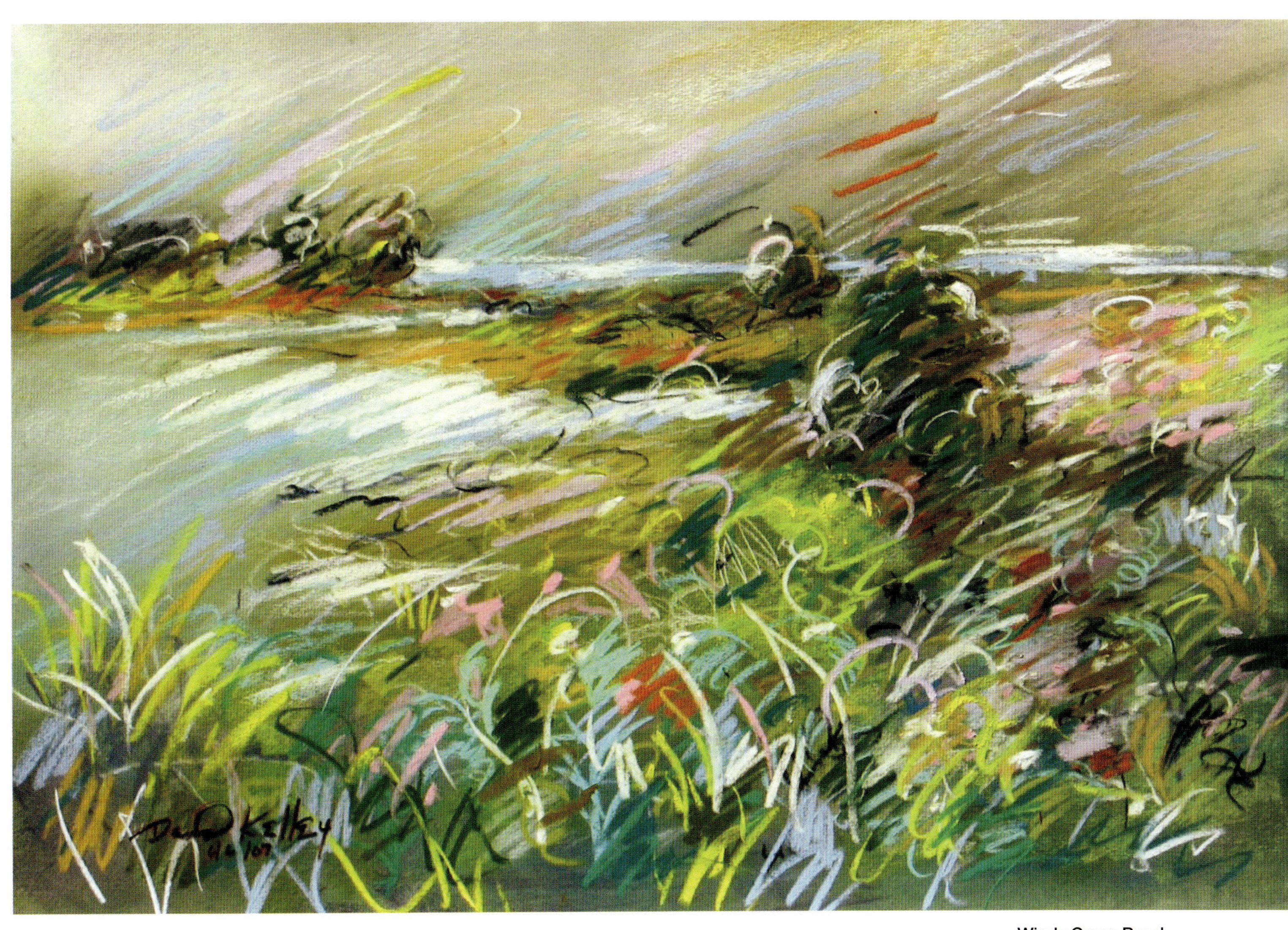

Windy Green Pond
David F. Kelley · Pastel on sanded paper · 11" × 17" · (28cm × 43cm)

CHANGING CONDITIONS FORCE YOU TO WORK QUICKLY

My reference drawing for this piece was done late in the day using pastels on Canson paper with the wind blowing, the clouds and light quickly changing, and only a little time to get it done. I enjoy working quickly under such changing conditions to meet the challenge of capturing the dynamics of the situation. I often use these live, on-site drawings as the basis for further drawings, as I did here. In the studio, working soon after doing the original sketch, I find that the drawing and ideas have an opportunity to evolve and develop in even more interesting ways.

Just as **LIGHT AND SHADOW**
define what we see, strokes and shapes of
LIGHT in varying shades define art.
-David F. Kelley

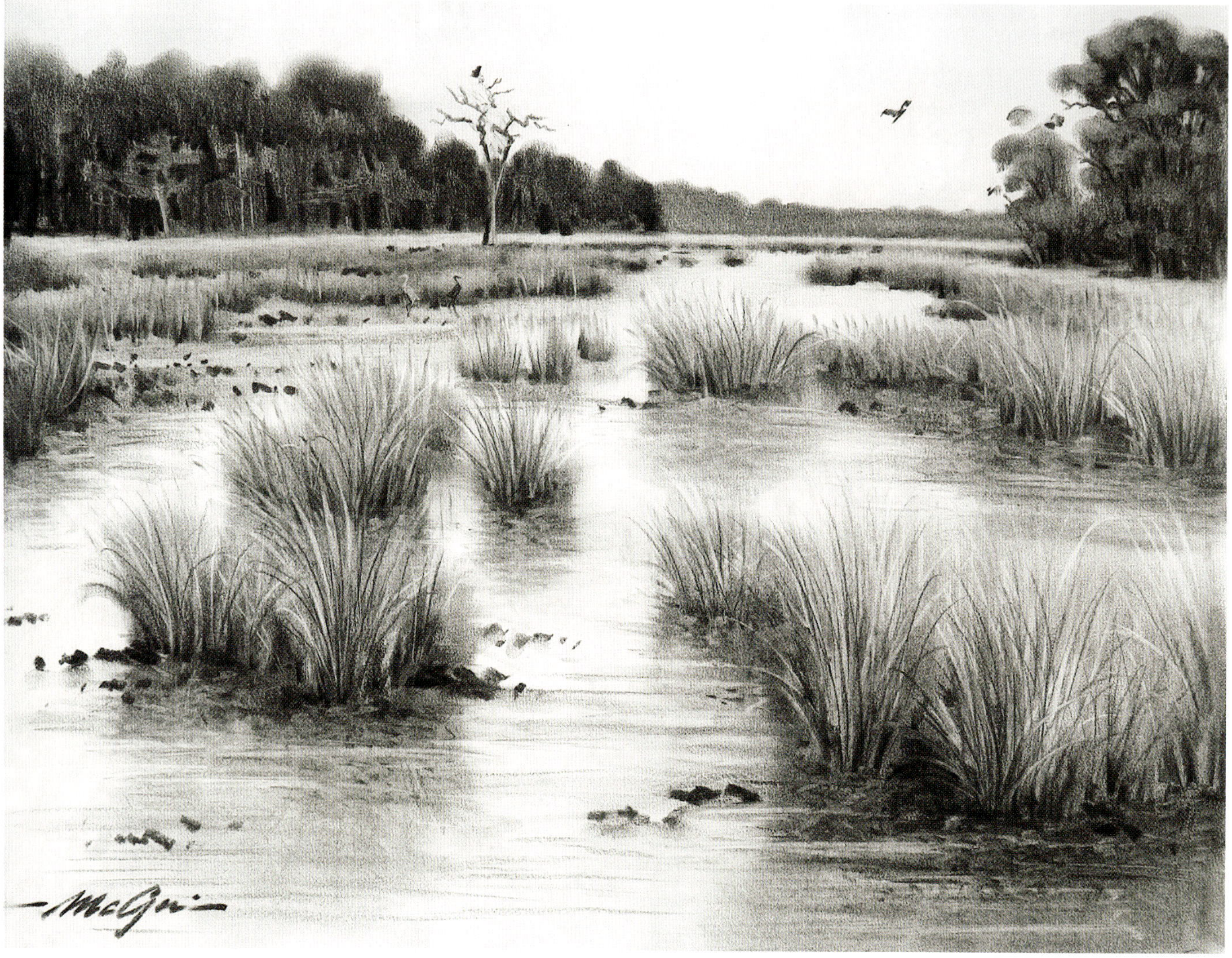

Swamp Marsh—Gulfport, Mississippi
Michael Allen McGuire · Vine charcoal on paper · 18" × 24" (46cm × 61cm)

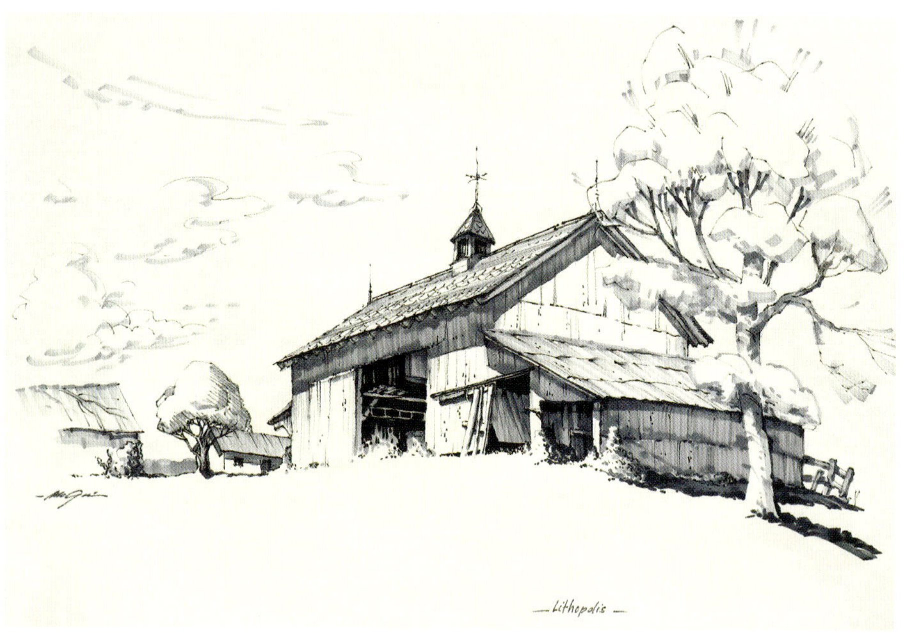

Barn at Lithopolis, Ohio
Michael Allen McGuire · Designer felt pens on paper · 18" × 24" (46cm × 61cm)

HAVE EASEL, WILL TRAVEL

Driving the backcountry roads of America, I often stop, set up my French easel and sketch with a fury. With designer felt pens on small gray pads, I first investigate quick compositional options. For the drawing, I use vine charcoal or graphite sticks on 18" × 24" (46cm × 61cm) rag paper. Because my drawings are developed with paintings in mind, the goal is to capture the essence of the scene by remaining true to the shapes, while designing strong value masses and patterns of interest. The barn drawing was designed for watercolor, while the swamp sketch was conceived for oils.

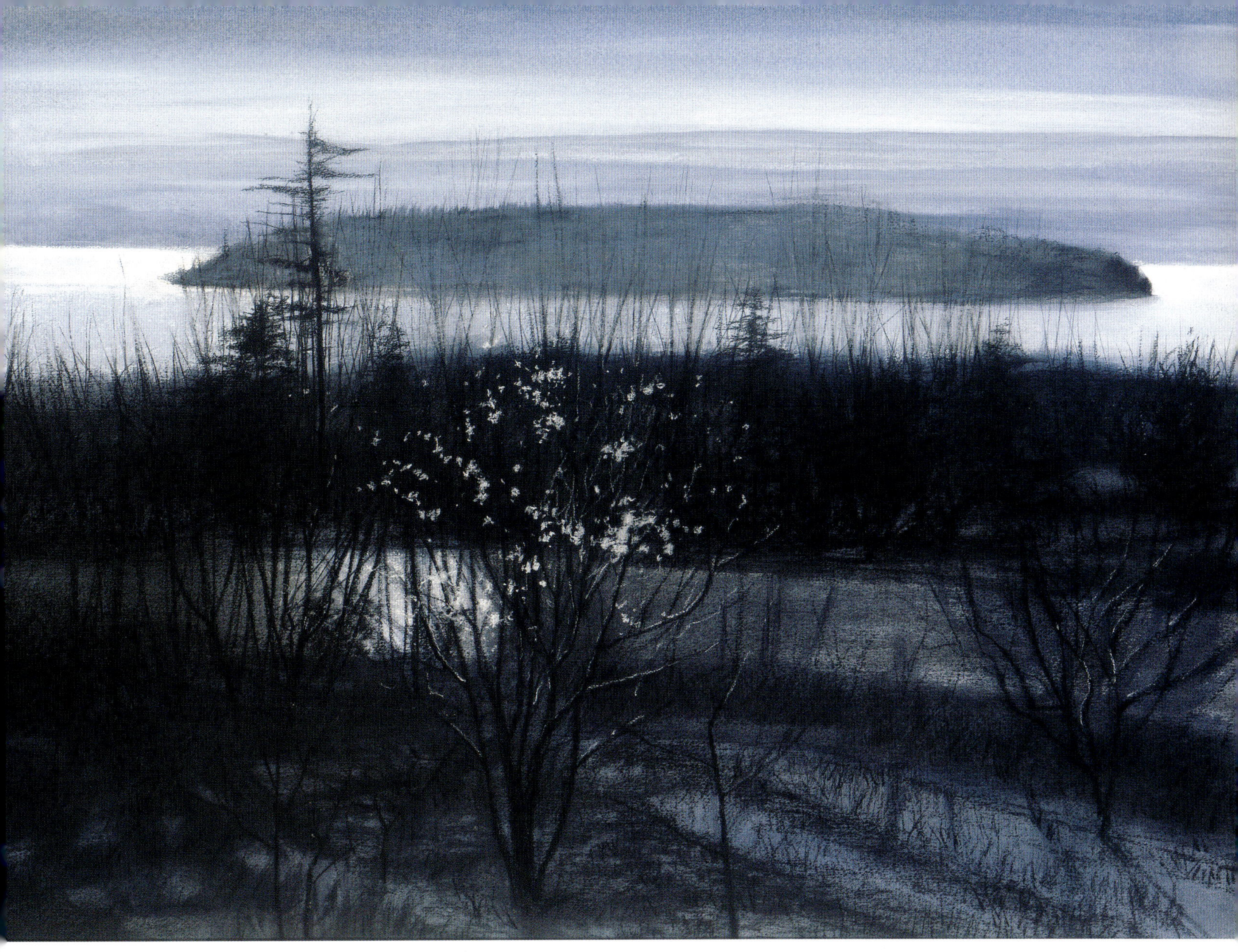

February Landscape

Elaine L. Bassett · Compressed charcoal and black and white pastel over gouache-toned Arches cover paper · 21" × 28¾" (53cm × 73cm)

GRAY, WHITE AND BLUE GOUACHE FOR WINTER LIGHT

In *February Landscape*, the background is derived from my Pacific Northwest memories and imagination. Trees were developed from sketches and photos. To capture the mood of winter light, I stroked washes of various shades of gray, white and blue gouache—my Pacific Northwest triad. When this step was dry, compressed charcoal and pastel were added to create the almost black middle ground, followed by the foreground trees. Last, the dramatic burst of light was added with heavily applied pastel.

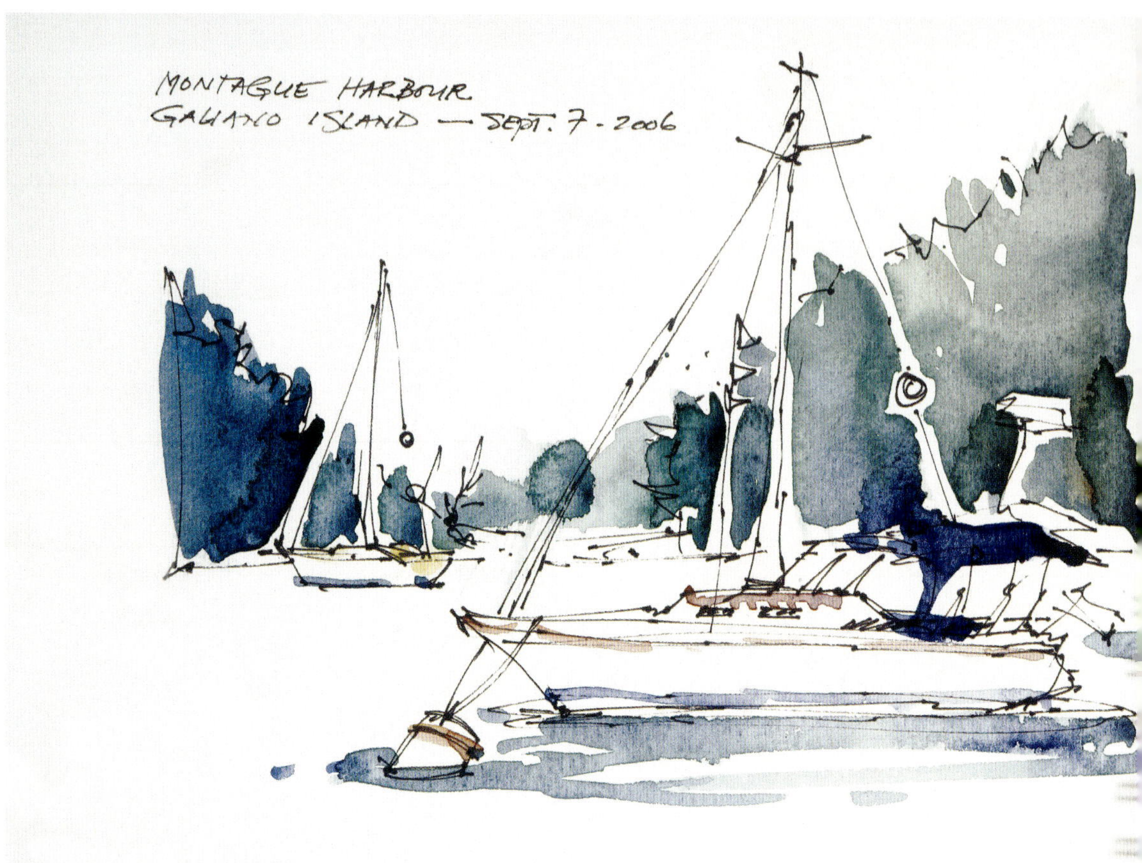

Montague Harbour
Mary Ann Henderson · Ink with watercolor on paper · 7" × 20" (18cm × 51cm)

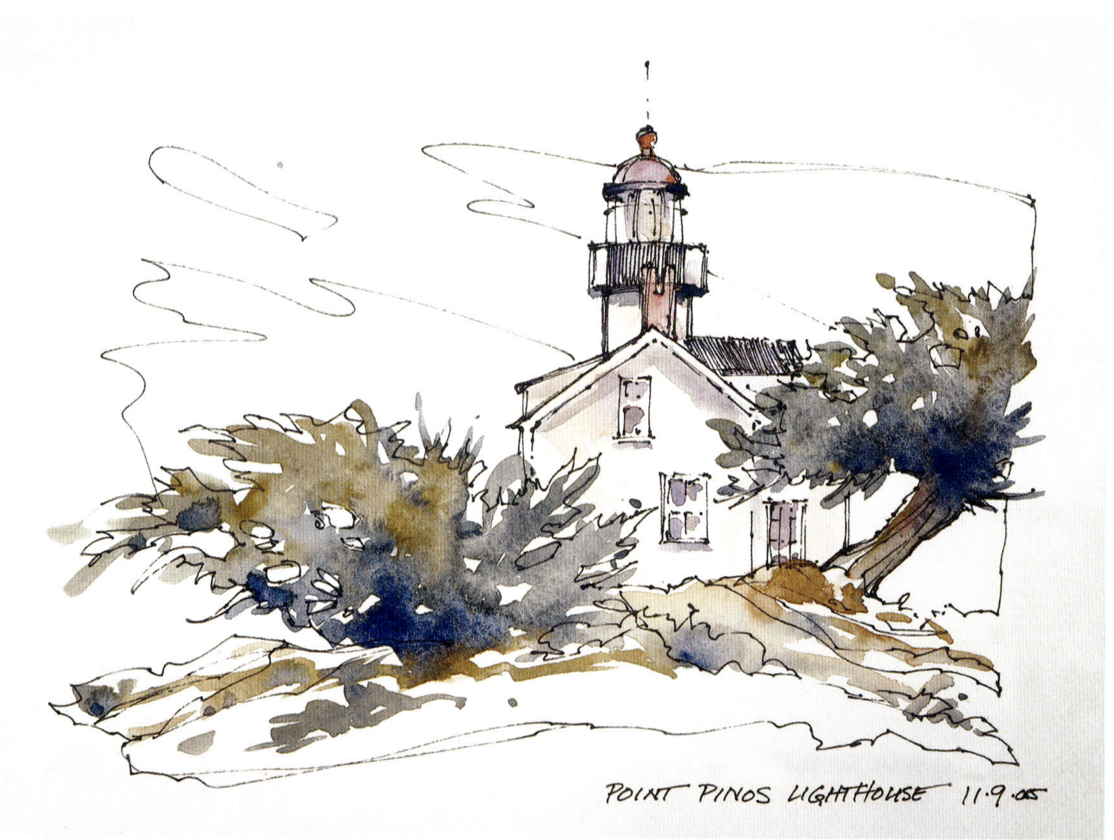

Point Pinos Lighthouse
Mary Ann Henderson · Ink with watercolor on paper · 9" × 12" (23cm × 30cm)

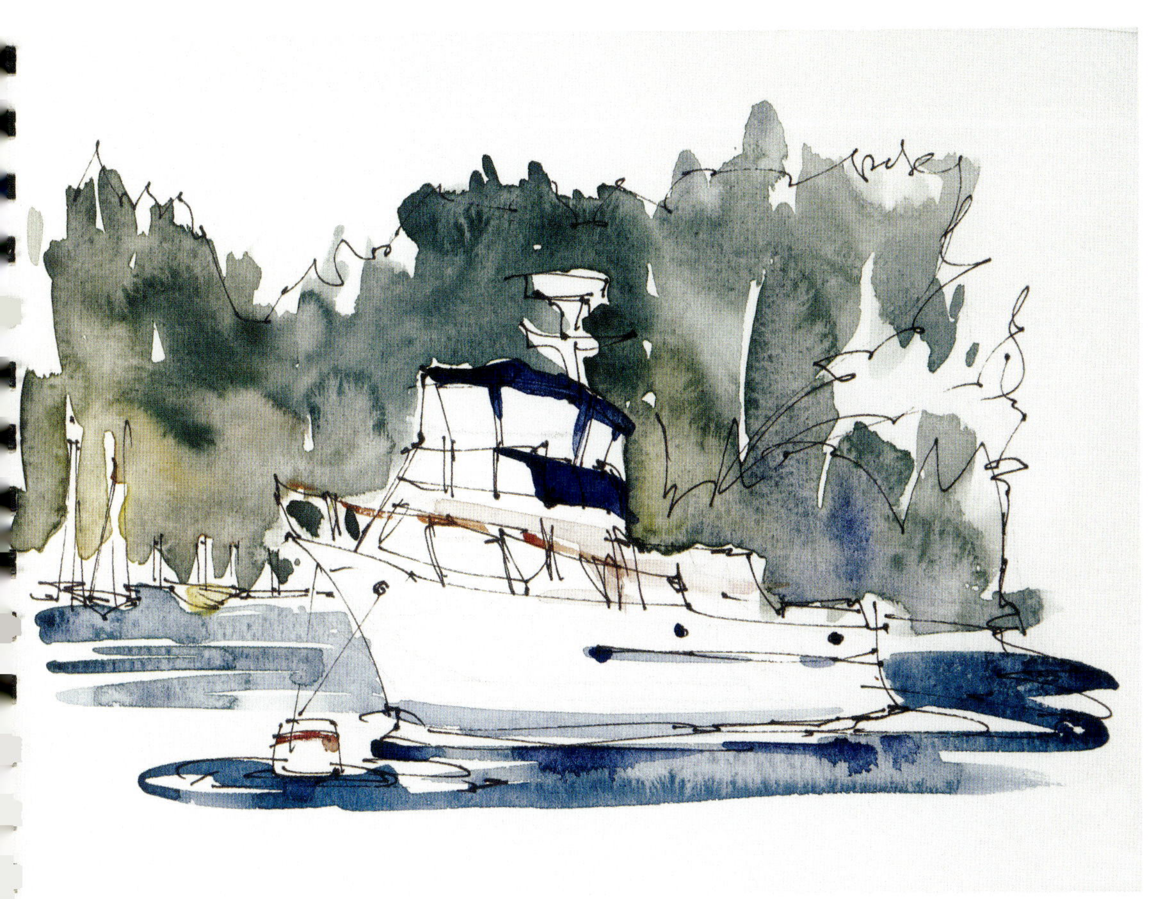

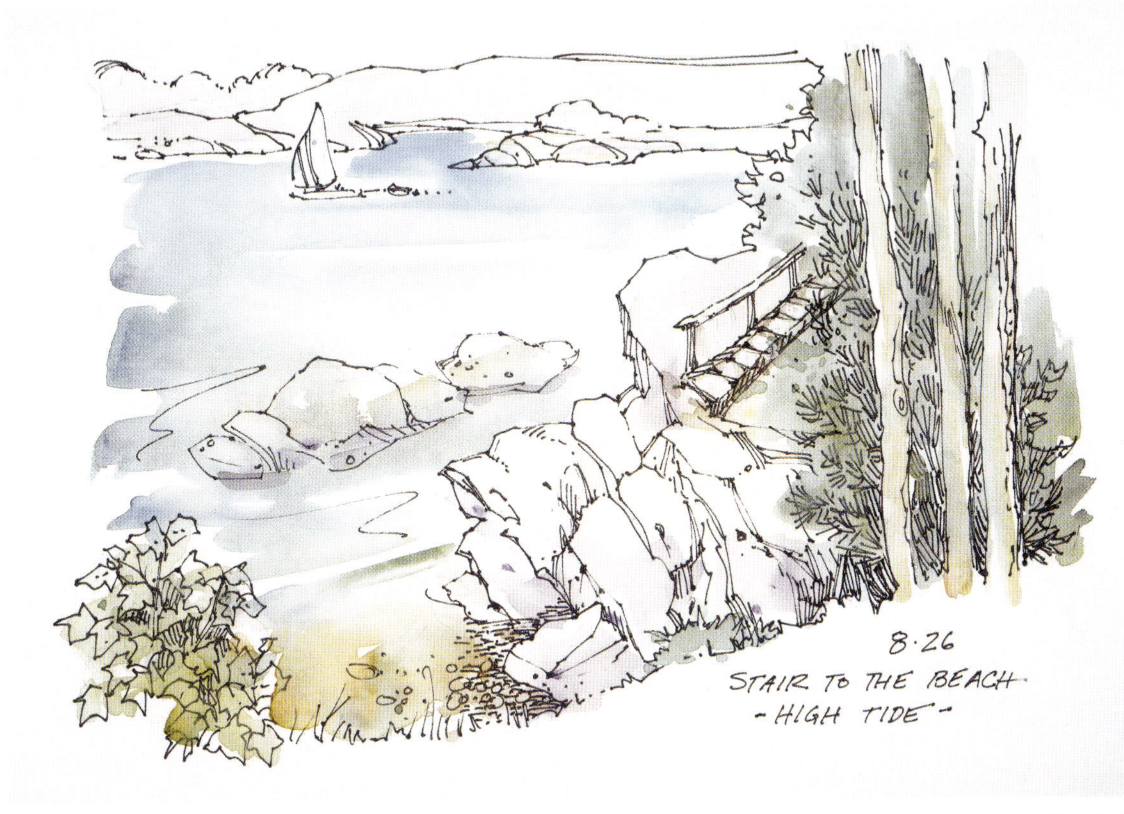

High Tide
Mary Ann Henderson · Ink with watercolor on paper · 9" × 12" (23cm × 30cm)

SKETCHBOOK JOURNALING WITHOUT A SAFETY NET

Sketchbook journaling lets me jump into a scene and out again in fifteen or twenty minutes, well before the light shifts and other interesting views call for the next drawing. To speed up the process, I try not to use a preliminary pencil lay-in. Working in ink without that erasable safety net can be pretty scary at first, but once the pen hits the paper, taking risks can produce lots of interesting surprises. A few simple watercolor washes are useful color references for future paintings.

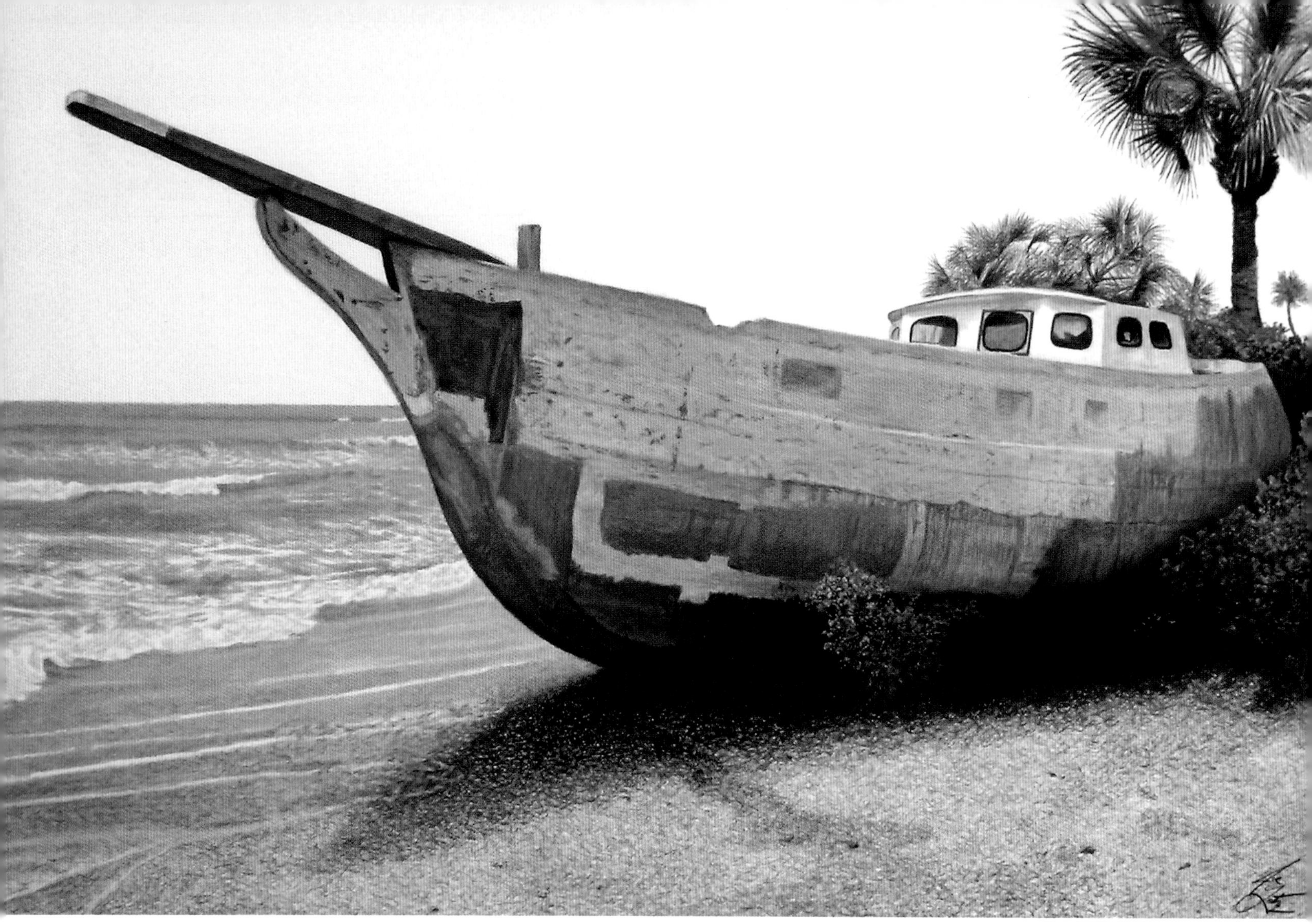

Away From the Things of Man
Joseph Lotz · Colored pencil on bristol board · 15" × 22" (38cm × 56cm)

DEVELOP A COMPOSITION FROM SEPARATE ELEMENTS

I am drawn to the coastline on my research trips, and take hundreds of photos of any elements that catch my eye. In my studio, I mentally develop a new composition while sifting through these photos, putting separate elements together, as in *Away From the Things of Man*. The boat stood in disrepair in a boatyard near Savannah; the coastline was from a beach in northeast Florida; the palms came from other shots. I begin by lightly sketching outlines with a no. 2 pencil, focusing on proportion and overall composition. I then fully develop the piece in colored pencil by working in vertical columns from right to left (being a southpaw). I apply different drawing techniques based on the results desired. In *Away*, the sand was drawn with successive layers of darkening grays, worked quickly, in random swirling but controlled figure-eight motions. The dark background in *Wanderer* was achieved by covering the area with a black colored pencil stick and blending with a bit of odorless paint thinner and a paintbrush. I strive to encompass a full range of values in my work.

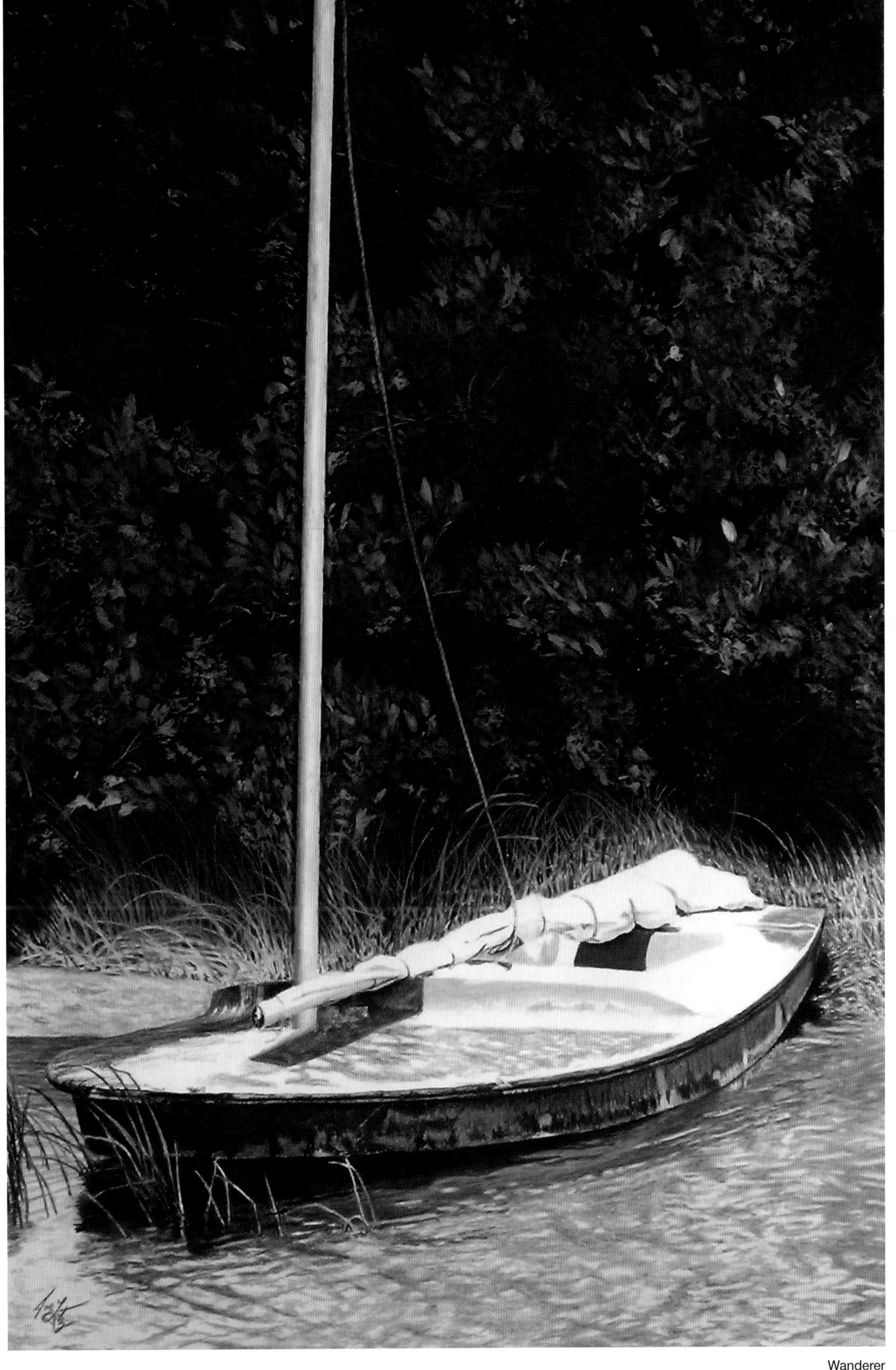

Wanderer
Joseph Lotz · Colored pencil on bristol board · 22" × 15" (56cm × 38cm)

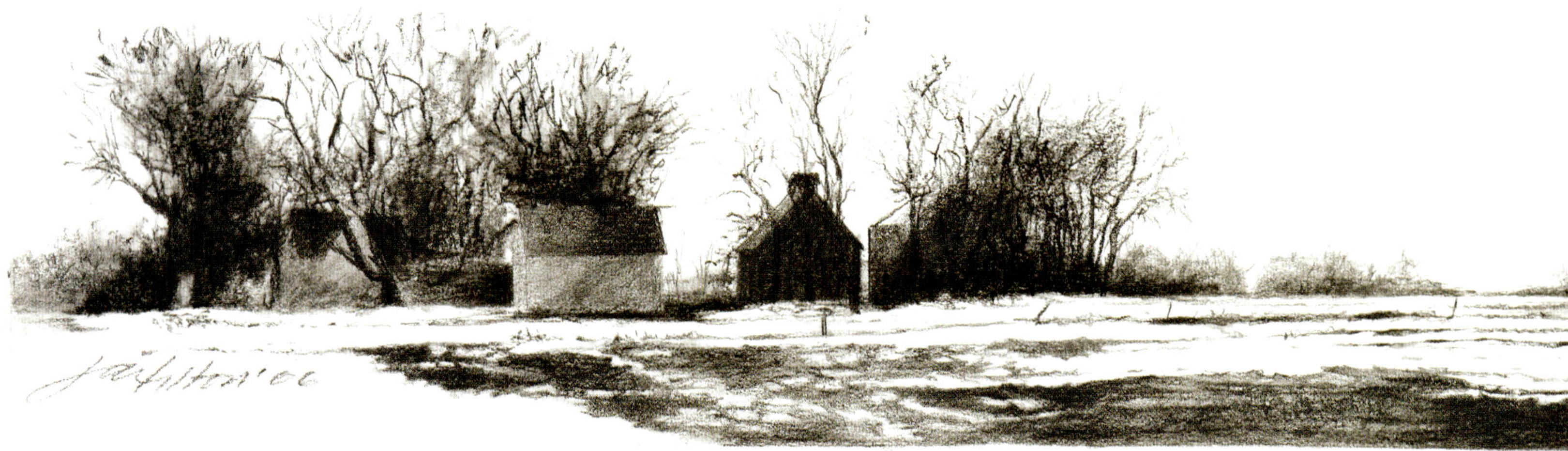

Calender, IA
Jac Tilton · Carbon, charcoal and graphite on paper · 3½" × 10" (9cm × 25cm)

FINDING THE RIGHT TONAL RANGE IN GRAY

I came across this winter scene while driving in rural Iowa. Two things struck me: the dramatic contrast between the near white snow and sky, and the black earth, trees and buildings; and the way in which the trees and buildings seemed to morph into one another. Graphite alone is too gray to achieve the tonal range and contrast required, so I incorporated charcoal and carbon as well. One of the significant challenges was getting the three to work together because charcoal and carbon do not like to lay down well over the oily graphite.

Sunset, Town Center, Napflion, Greece
Laurin McCracken · Sepia ink on paper · 9" × 6" (23cm × 15cm)

IF YOU WANT TO REMEMBER IT, DRAW IT

During a week of traveling around Greece with a group of watercolorists, I settled into a chair in the center of Napflion, a small Italianate town on the peninsula of the Peloponnesus, and ordered an espresso. I pulled out my sketchbook and, using a fine-point calligraphy fountain pen, recorded the setting sun streaming into the square between the two buildings opposite me. The deep shadows, the juxtaposition of the buildings and the fortified hill behind held my attention through the waning light of the afternoon. The best way to remember something is to draw it.

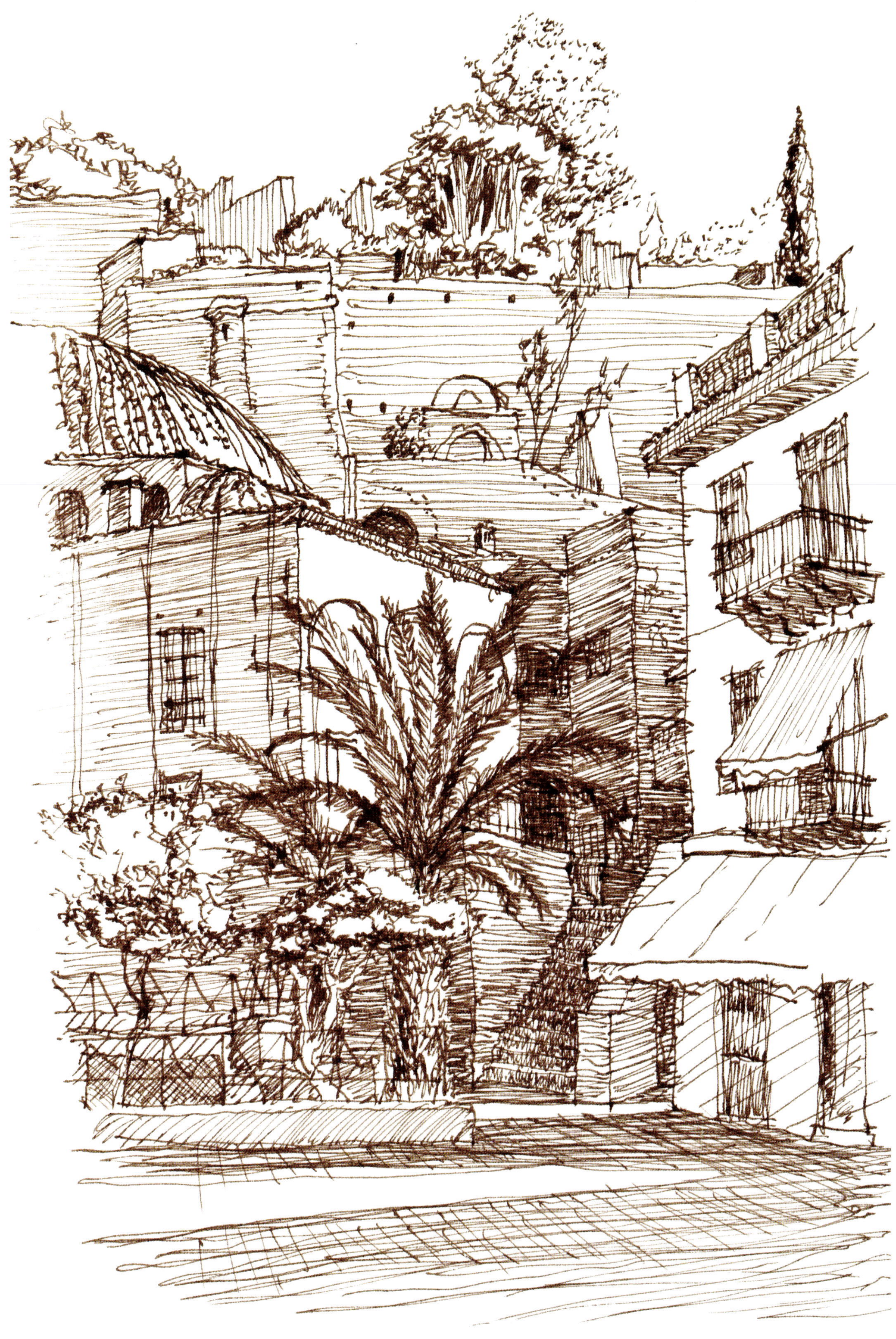

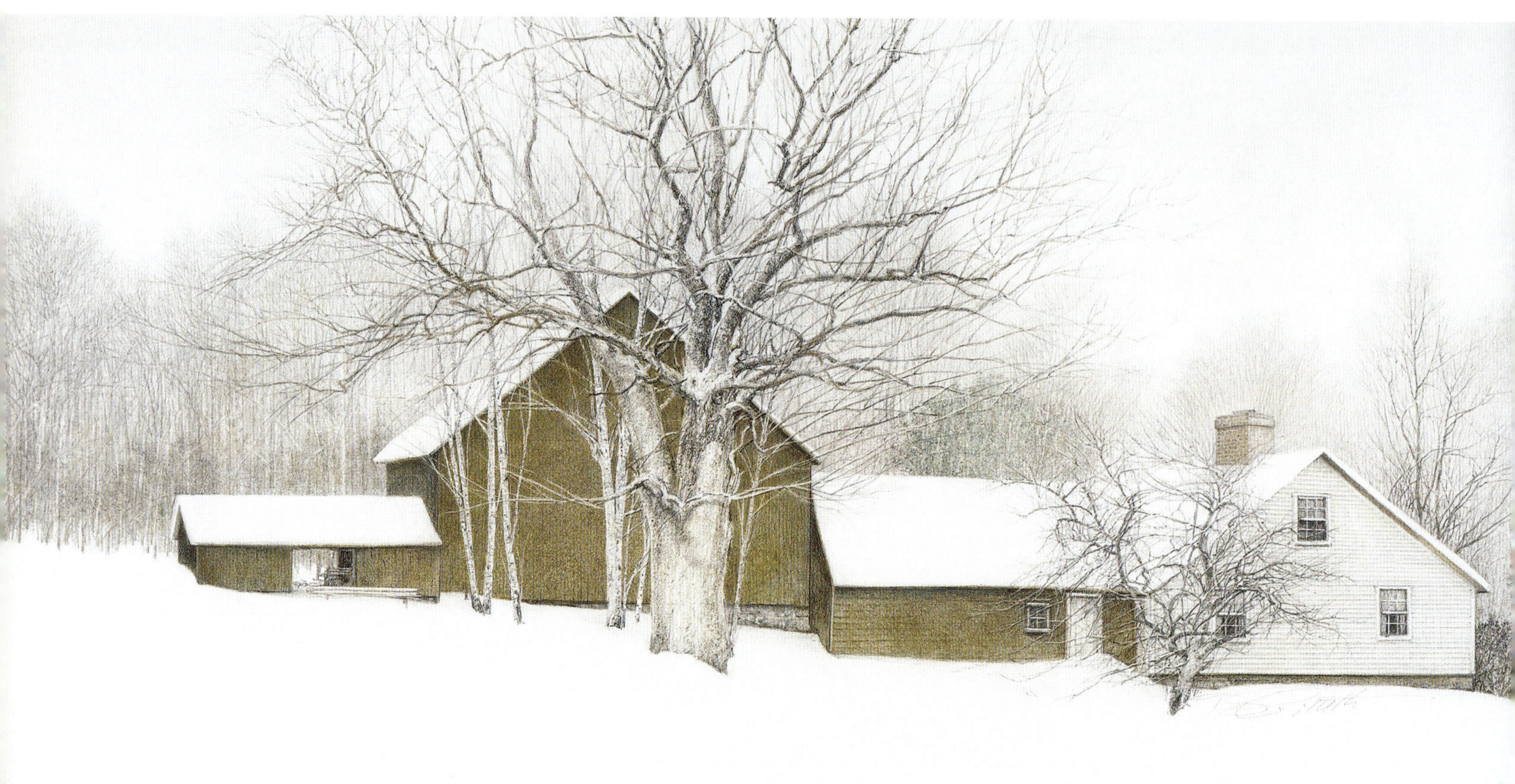

Winter Passage
Douglas Gillette · Silverpoint with colored pencil on gessoed panel · 12" × 18" (30cm × 46cm)

REGIONAL BUILDING STYLE INSPIRES DRAWING STUDIES

The rural architecture of New England is often seen as a series of connected buildings, referred to by the locals as "big house, little house, back house, barn." My fascination with this building style prompted many photographs, numerous drawings, and ultimately, this invented farmhouse rendered in both silverpoint and colored pencil. Careful to capture the connective unity of each building, the image was laid out in line and tonal values using a sharpened 2mm rod of sterling silver in a mechanical pencil on gessoed panel. Blending varying shades of colored pencils into the silverpoint drawing and softening the overall tone with copper point finalized the soft green and sepia tint of the overall image.

As I worked on *Winter Passage*, I spent considerable time reflecting on what nature would tell me about **LIGHT,** such as how **SHADOWS** are diffused over long distances. This kind of **REFLECTIVE ANALYSIS** brings the subject alive to me.

-Douglas Gillette

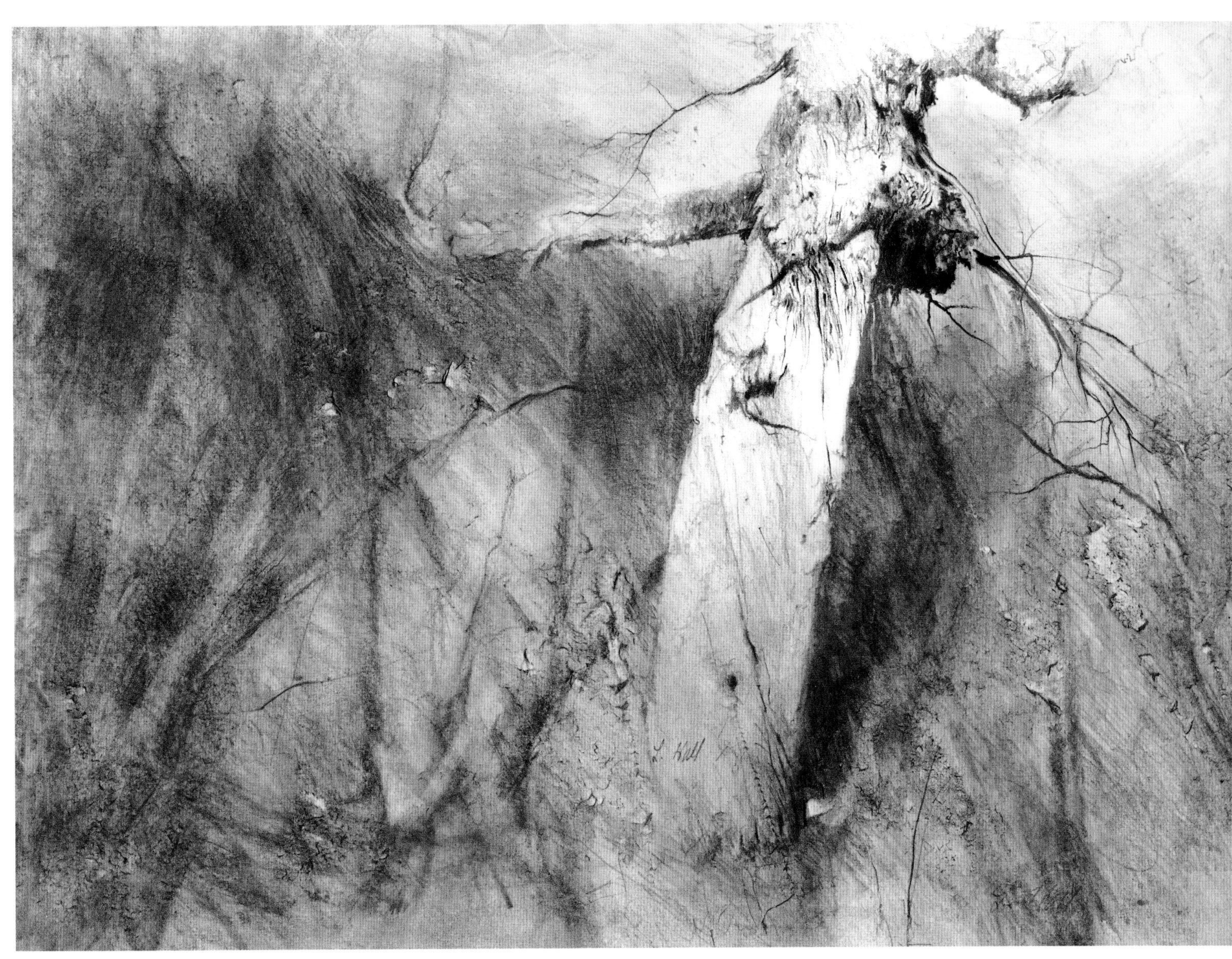

Torn
Lane Hall · Pencil on paper · 7¾" × 11" (20cm × 28cm)

USE AN ERASER FOR WHITE AREAS

I did this drawing from my sketchbook on site where I often hike. I used the point of my pencil to create a line drawing for the focal point and much of the detail within it. The larger, dark values were made using the side of my pencil point and a wet, pencil-smudged eraser. The eraser also caused white areas to appear, which added interesting shapes and textures conducive to forms found in nature. I try to produce at least one quick drawing every day, so I take my sketchbook on most of my travels.

The strongest contrasts of **LIGHT AND SHADOW** are almost always at my focal point; the midvalues support and add **CONVICTION.**
-Lane Hall

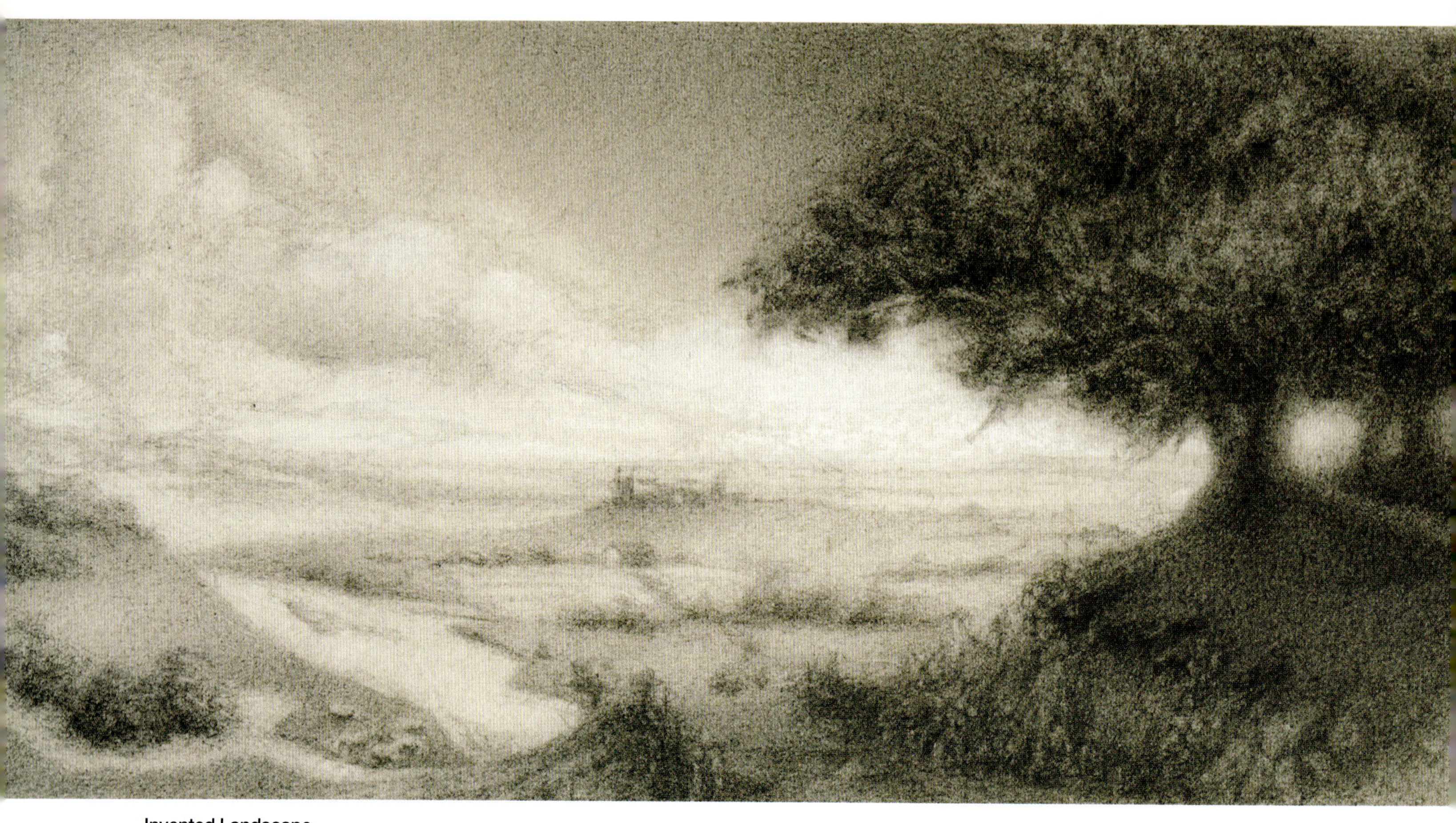

Invented Landscape
David Gluck · Graphite and white chalk on hand-toned paper · 4" × 8" (10cm × 20cm)

START A LANDSCAPE WITH AN ABSTRACT DESIGN

Invented Landscape, as the title indicates, was created directly from my imagination. I started by designing a complex compositional web based on intersecting verticals, all tied together with a series of curving elements. It was, essentially, a work of abstract art upon which a realist work was draped. Based upon the abstract web, I slowly built a landscape on top of it. It took a lot of experimenting and fiddling to get the right ratio of variation to pattern, the correct values, and so on. The piece is meant to lead the eye throughout the entire composition, never stalling on any given area too long. I feel that too often the design potential of a drawing, or even a quick study, is not fully tapped.

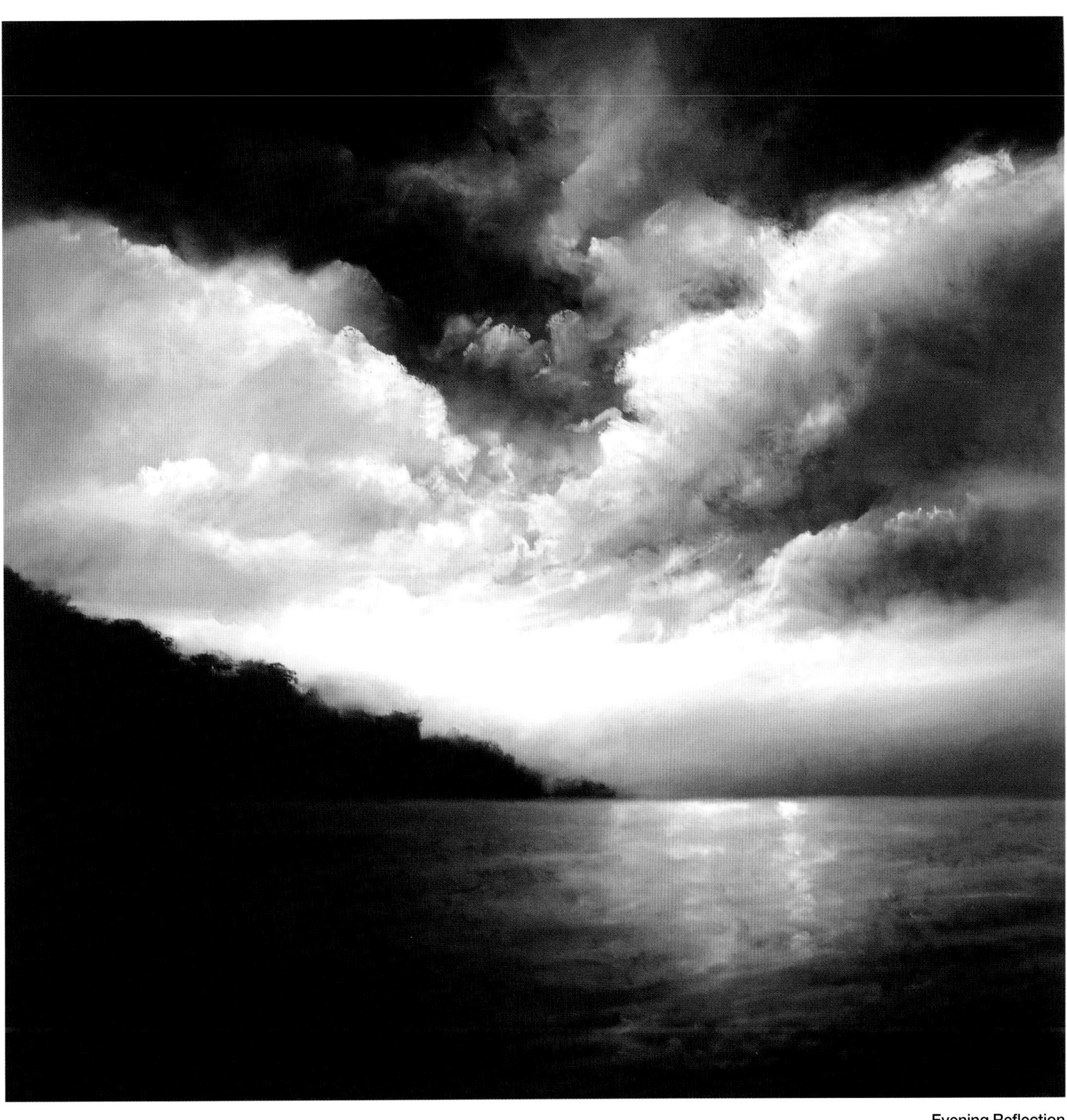

Evening Reflection
Donna Levinstone · Black and white pastel on paper · 30" × 30" (76cm × 76cm)

TRY USING ONE BLACK PASTEL AND ONE WHITE PASTEL

My pastel drawings are created mainly from imagination. I use 3M 811 tape to mask my drawing area, leaving a 3" (76mm) border. For *Evening Reflection*, I used one black pastel and one white pastel. I like extra-large homemade pastels by Diane Townsend; I protect my hands with Winsor & Newton Art Guard. I start by drawing the sky using my darkest black and then add the clouds and foreground using my white pastel. I like to wipe down the drawing with tissue paper. This allows me to layer and bring out the whitest whites. It is similar to using turpentine with oil paints. The rest was created by blending black and white pastels, concentrating on the use of light and shadow to create atmosphere.

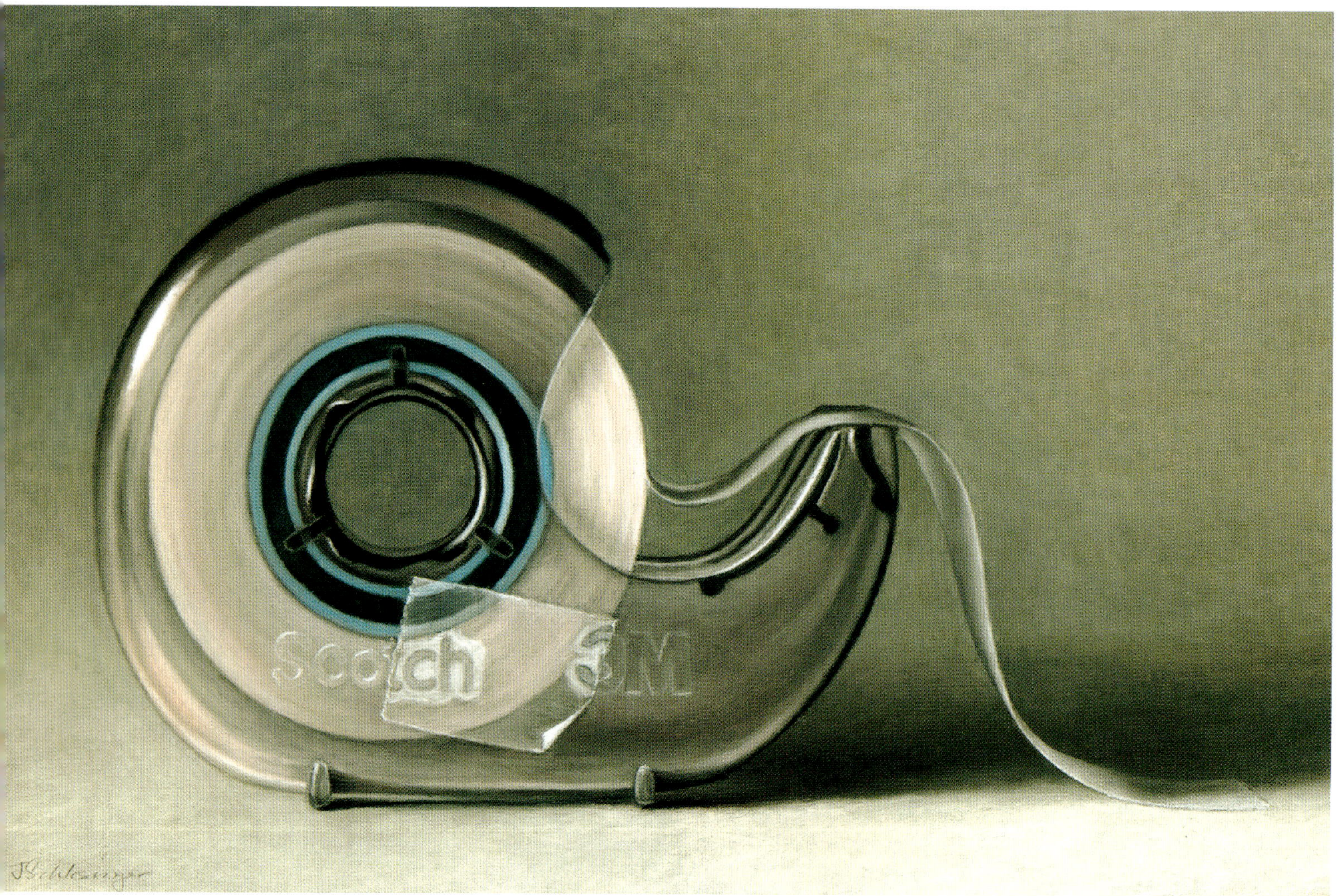

Tape Dispenser
Jaye Schlesinger · Pastel on sanded pastel paper · 7" × 11" (18cm × 28cm)

TAKE ANOTHER LOOK AT EVERYDAY OBJECTS

In creating these works, I was exploring my fascination with translucent and transparent objects. I worked from direct observation, using a single light source to define the form and to create a somewhat ethereal mood. I built up the values of the object and the background simultaneously. Using CarbOthello and Derwent pastel pencils allowed me to produce subtle color variations. I applied the bright white highlights as I went along because they provided a reference point for the middle grays. I enjoy compelling the viewer to look at commonly overlooked objects.

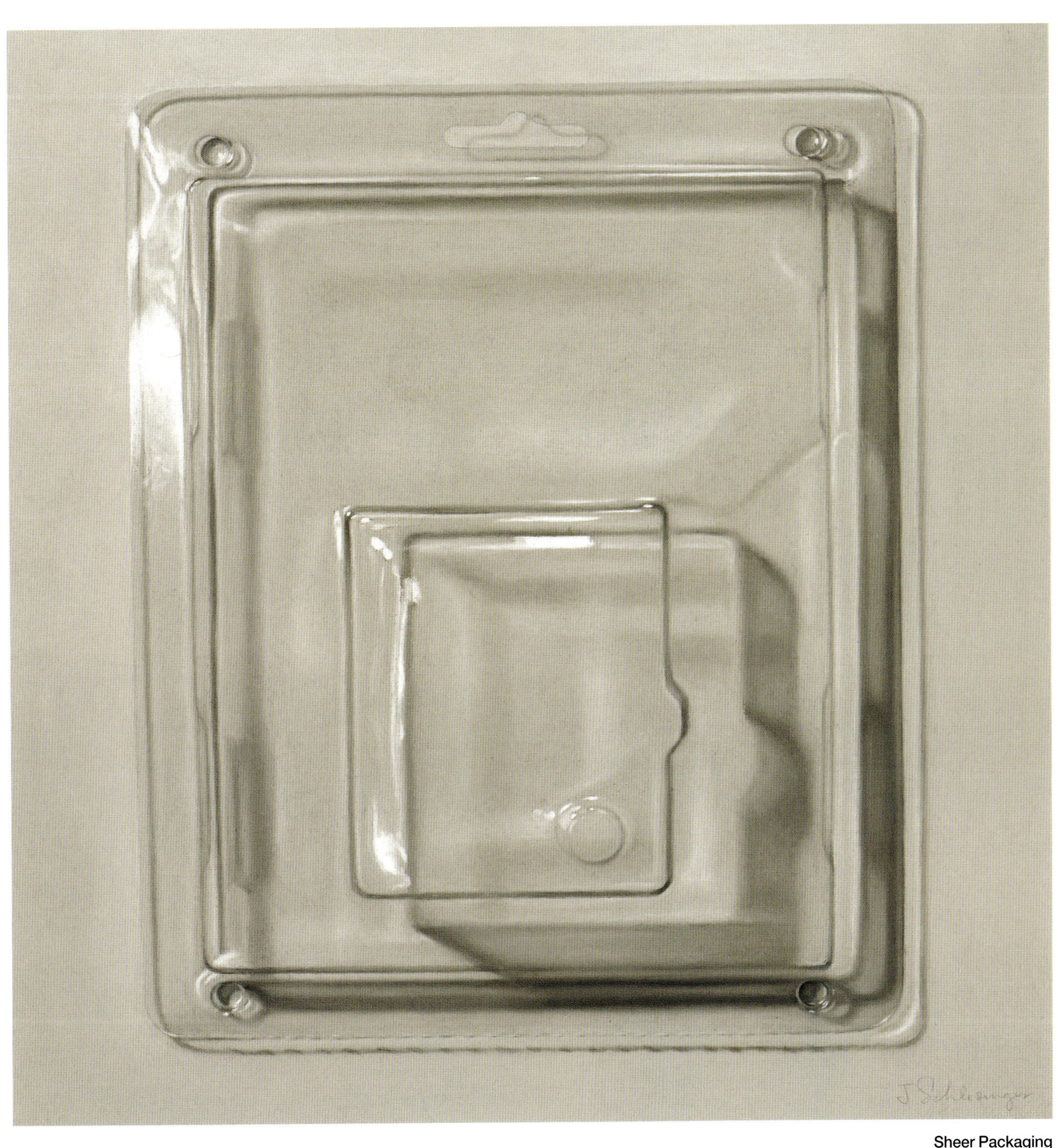

Sheer Packaging
Jaye Schlesinger · Pastel on sanded pastel paper · 12" × 11" (30cm × 28cm)

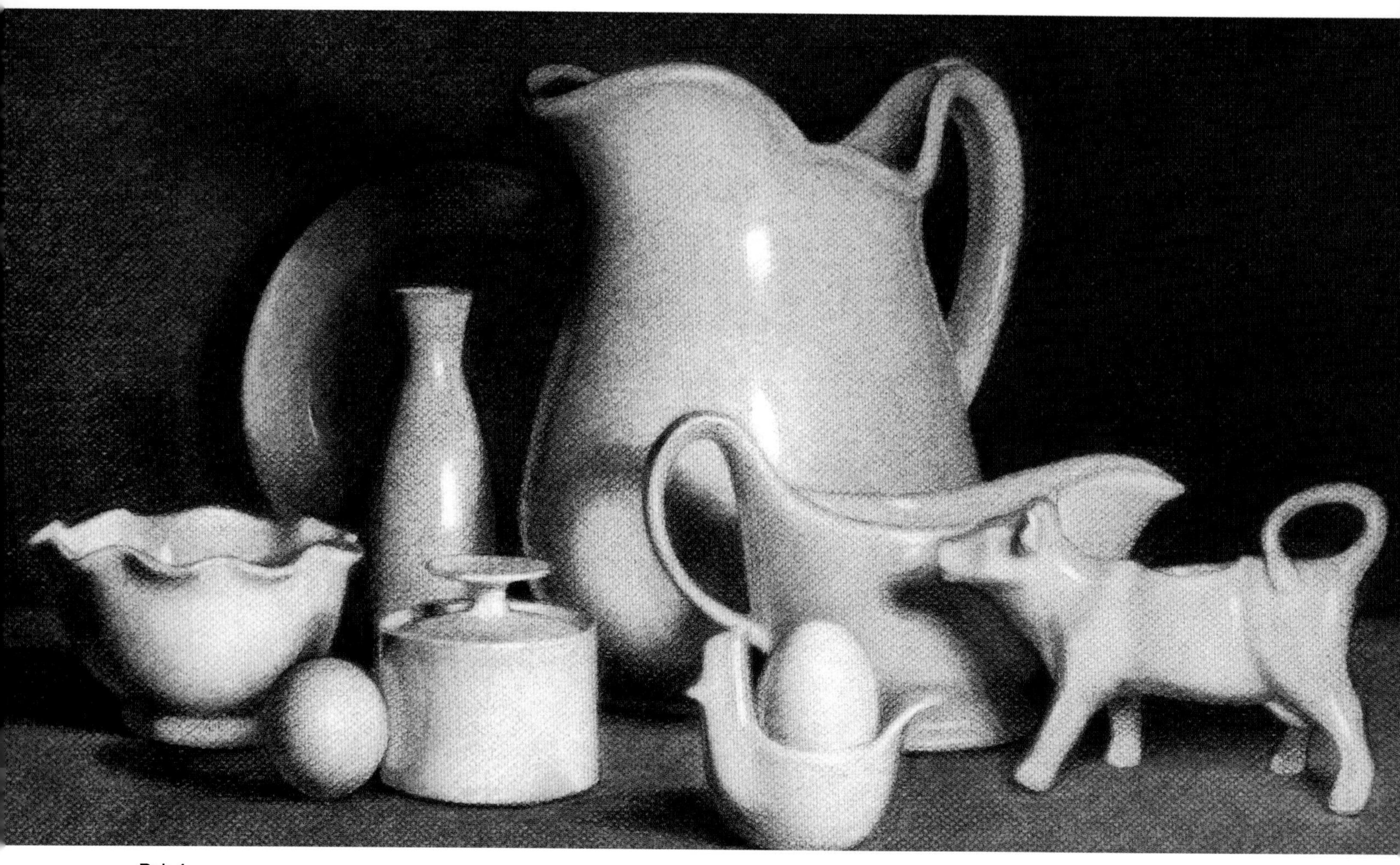

Rob 4
Carol Kummer · Fusain nitram charcoal on Canson Mi-Teintes paper · 12" × 22" (30cm × 56cm)

SIGHT-SIZE METHOD FOR CLASSICAL RESULTS

This drawing was done using the sight-size method. For this method, the still-life subject
and the drawing surface are set up side by side. I positioned myself at a view spot six feet
(183cm) away from and centered exactly between the still-life setup and the parallel drawing
surface. This drawing method requires a process of measuring and comparing the objects
in the still life, always from that view spot, and then rendering those measurements onto
the drawing surface. I first created a very accurate line drawing of each object in the still life
using fusain nitram soft charcoal on Canson Mi-Teintes paper. Then I slowly built up the
values until I achieved as full a value range as possible using that same media. This still
life took about 250 hours. Familiar objects take on an air of mystery and poetry rendered
in shadowy black and white; this one suggests a miniature fantasy landscape. *Rob 4* is
named for Rob Anderson, who taught me the sight-size method at the Atelier School of
Classical Realism in Oakland, California.

First Dress
Jacqueline Hoats Shields · Graphite pencil on paper · 12½" × 8" (32cm × 20cm)

A TEXTURE STUDY IN HIGH KEY

First Dress began as a study in my sketchbook; as it developed, I saw it could be a finished piece.
The dress itself is one my youngest daughter had worn as an infant. One challenge was to render the
textural differences between the fabric and the wood and twine used for display. Much of the work
involved establishing and refining the range of values to produce the illusion of three-dimensionality
within a very shallow space. The shallow picture plane gives the effect of a shadow box where a
treasured item such as this dress might be kept.

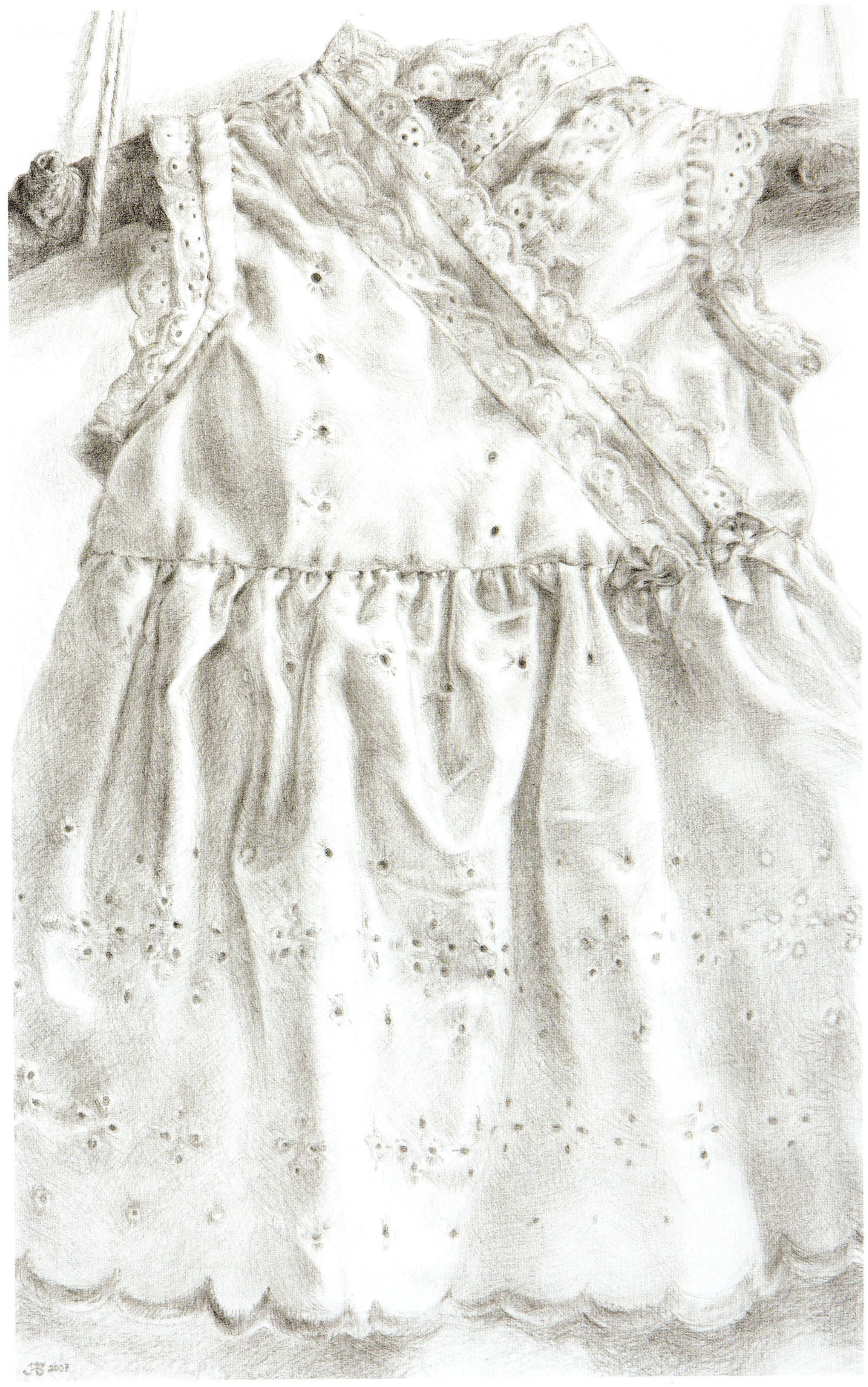

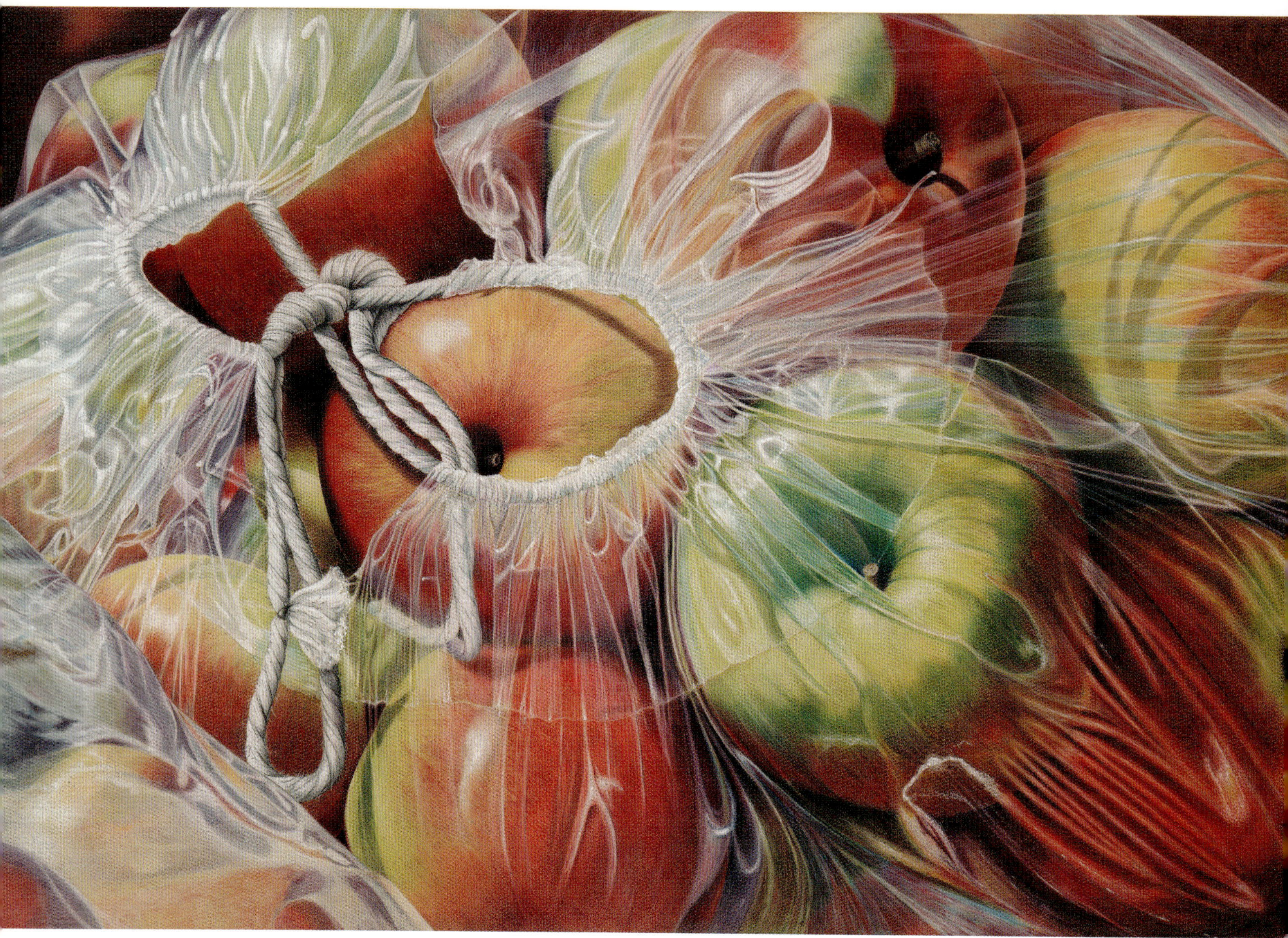

Undercover Spies
Cynthia C. Morris · Colored pencil on pale green mat board · 16" × 24" (41cm × 61cm)

USE A TINTED MAT BOARD FOR UNIFYING COLOR

Working from photos I had taken at a farmers market, I sketched the apples directly onto mat board. I like working on a tinted mat board that has a dominant color within my subject matter—in this case, pale green. I then began building up layers of "color on color" (no burnishing), working mostly light to dark. The folds of plastic gathered by the drawstring were created by drawing numerous sections of small abstract shapes and colors, while the larger, stretched areas of plastic were created with streaks of color blended over already finished apples. I like the contrast between the geometric shapes created by the plastic and the colors of the apples coming through.

A strong pattern of **LIGHT** AND **SHADOW**
is what gives a drawing or painting **SUBSTANCE,**
DEPTH AND **DIMENSION.**
-Cynthia C. Morris

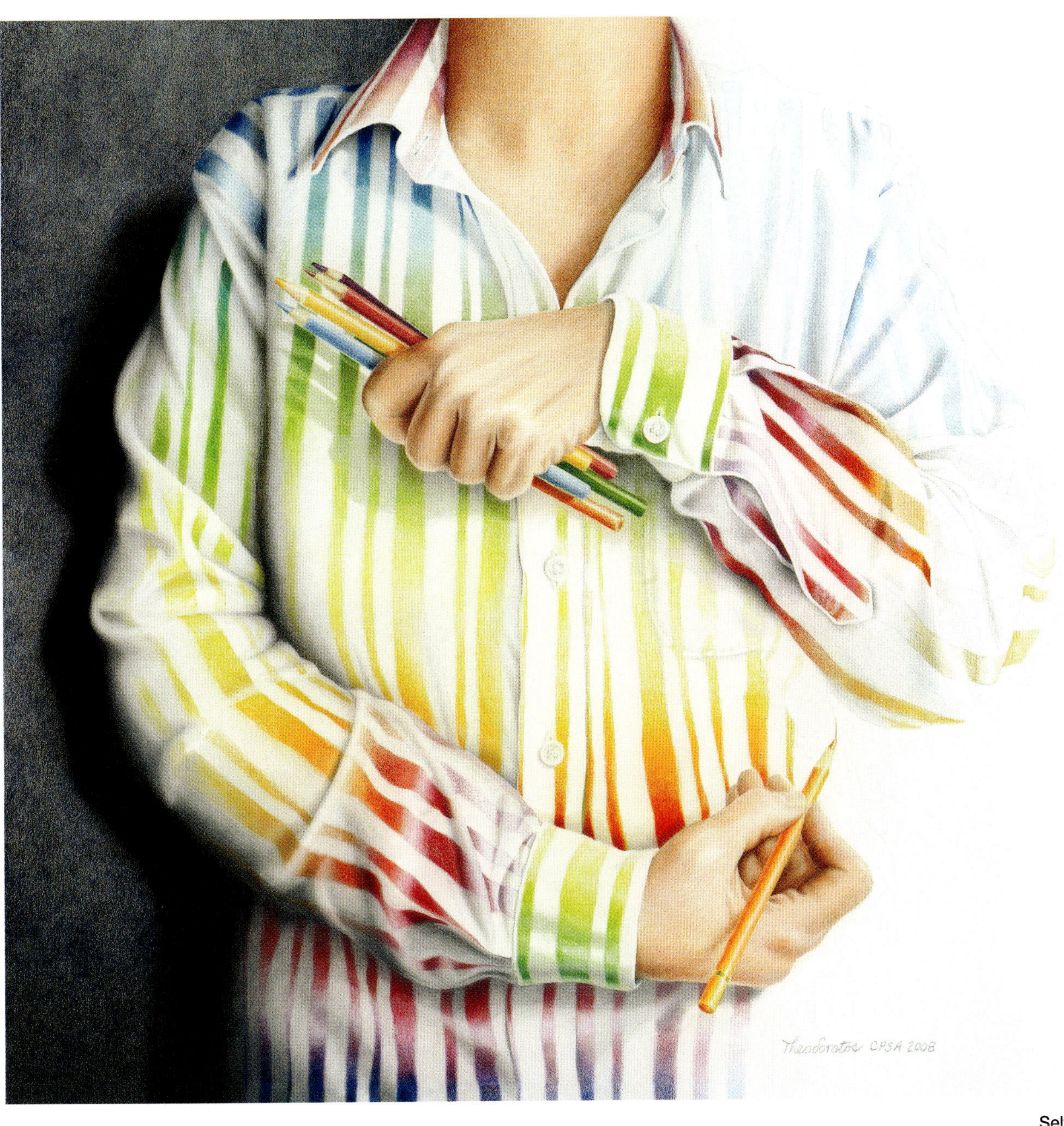

Self: In Progress
Sheila Theodoratos · Colored pencil on paper · 18¼" × 20¼" (46cm × 51cm)

TEMPER SYMBOLISM WITH WHIMSY

After capturing an "idea flash" for this self-portrait in a quick sketch, I recorded color notes and brain-stormed titles. Staged reference photos helped me refine my composition and concepts. Throughout the entire drawing process, I carefully preserved the light and open areas of pristine paper to symbolize possibilities of the future. Stripes represent memories that have helped shape who I am and may become. Some are vivid and continuous. Others, partial or dim. My torso fades into the darkness, giving this seemingly whimsical composition a *vanitas* effect. We are all works in progress.

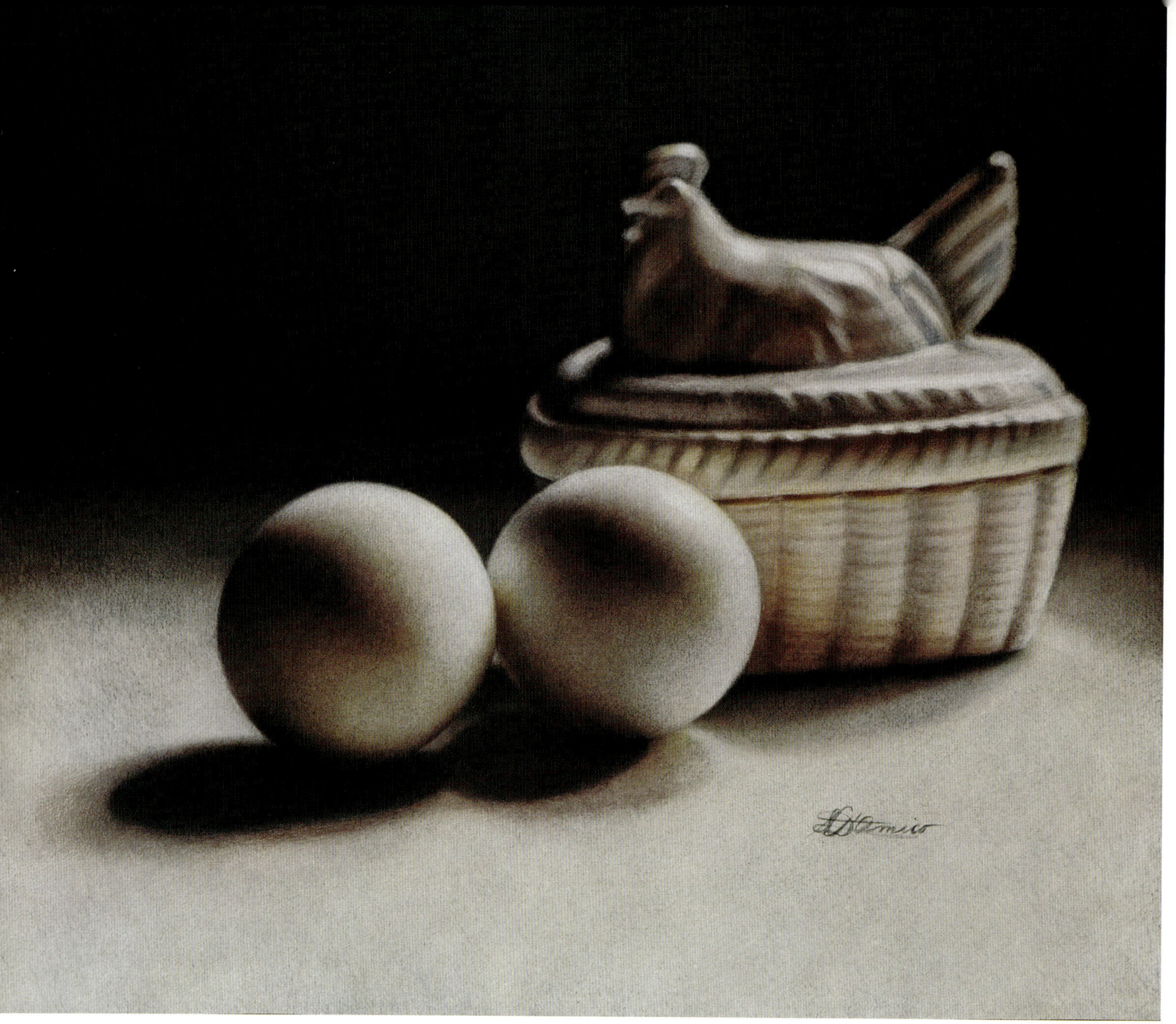

French Greys
Susan C. D'Amico · Colored Pencil on black paper · 11" × 15" (28cm × 38cm)

BLACK PAPER SETS THE MOOD

This still life was staged in front of a north-lit window and photographed. I loved the image but couldn't find the medium to give me the moody ambiance I wanted to portray. Several years later, after finishing a portrait in Prismacolor pencils on Black Stonehenge paper, I was finally inspired to do the still life. After doing a detailed drawing, I transferred it to the paper with White Saral. Because the paper was black, I started by layering the background and shadows. There are many layers of pencil to give a rich, blended effect. The same layering technique was used on the light areas, with more layers. The value changes were carefully modulated for realism, but because the painting is done on a black surface, the lightest values are subtle, creating the mood I had originally envisioned.

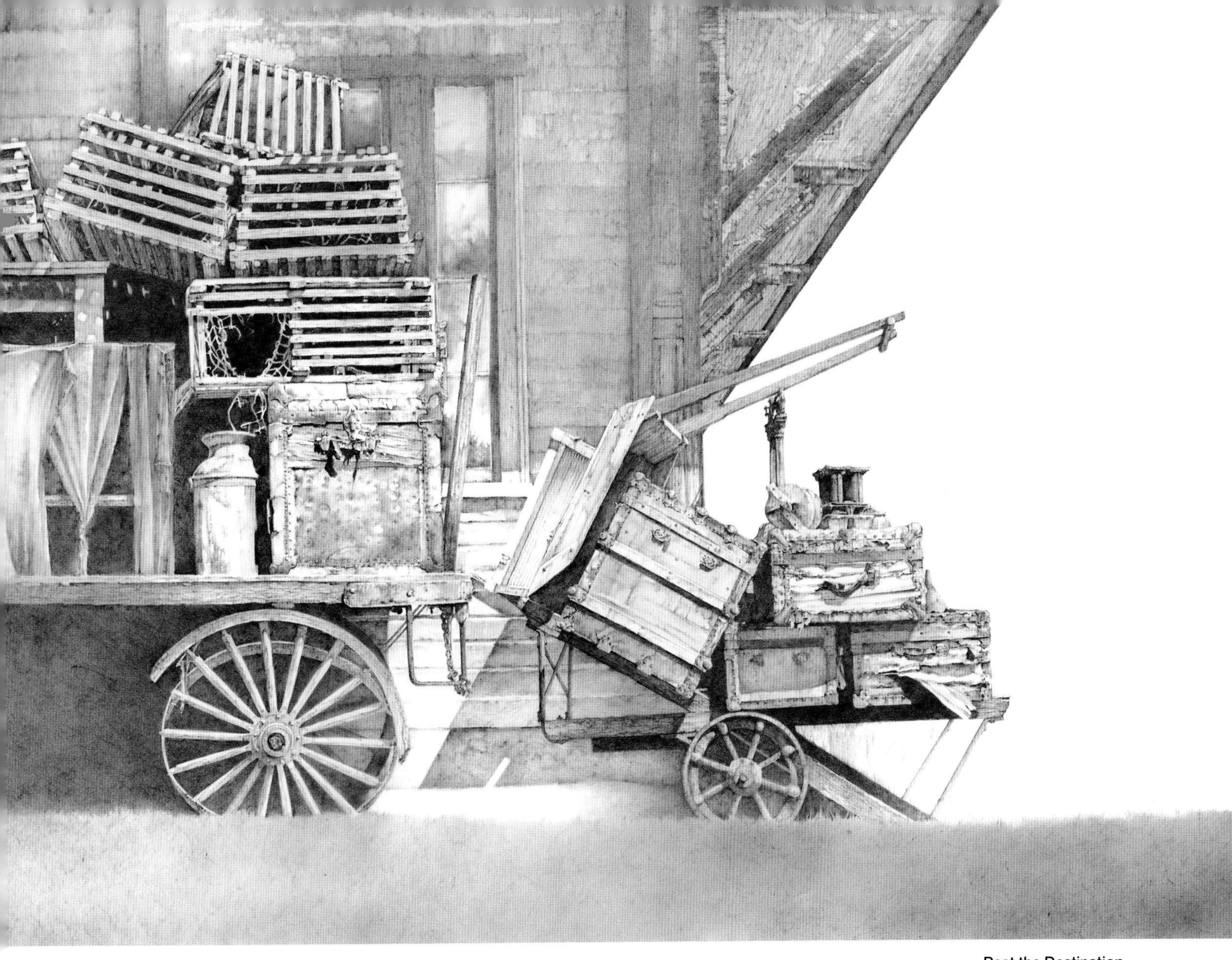

Past the Destination
Steve Wilda · Pencil on illustration board · 17" × 23½" (43cm × 60cm)

USE A VARIETY OF PENCIL LEADS, LAYERING AND BLENDING

My artwork often contains weathered elements from the past. Objects with character and in textural ruin motivate me to create art. This work took many months to complete in the studio. I used a variety of pencil leads, in addition to layering and blending techniques. Each area was drawn to its finished value and detail; I rarely return to make any adjustments. The scene was drawn as it appeared in the environment, although I took the liberty to replace a few objects.

Values of **LIGHT AND DARK** are created along the roofline, dividing the image into **POSITIVE** AND **NEGATIVE SHAPES.**
-Steve Wilda

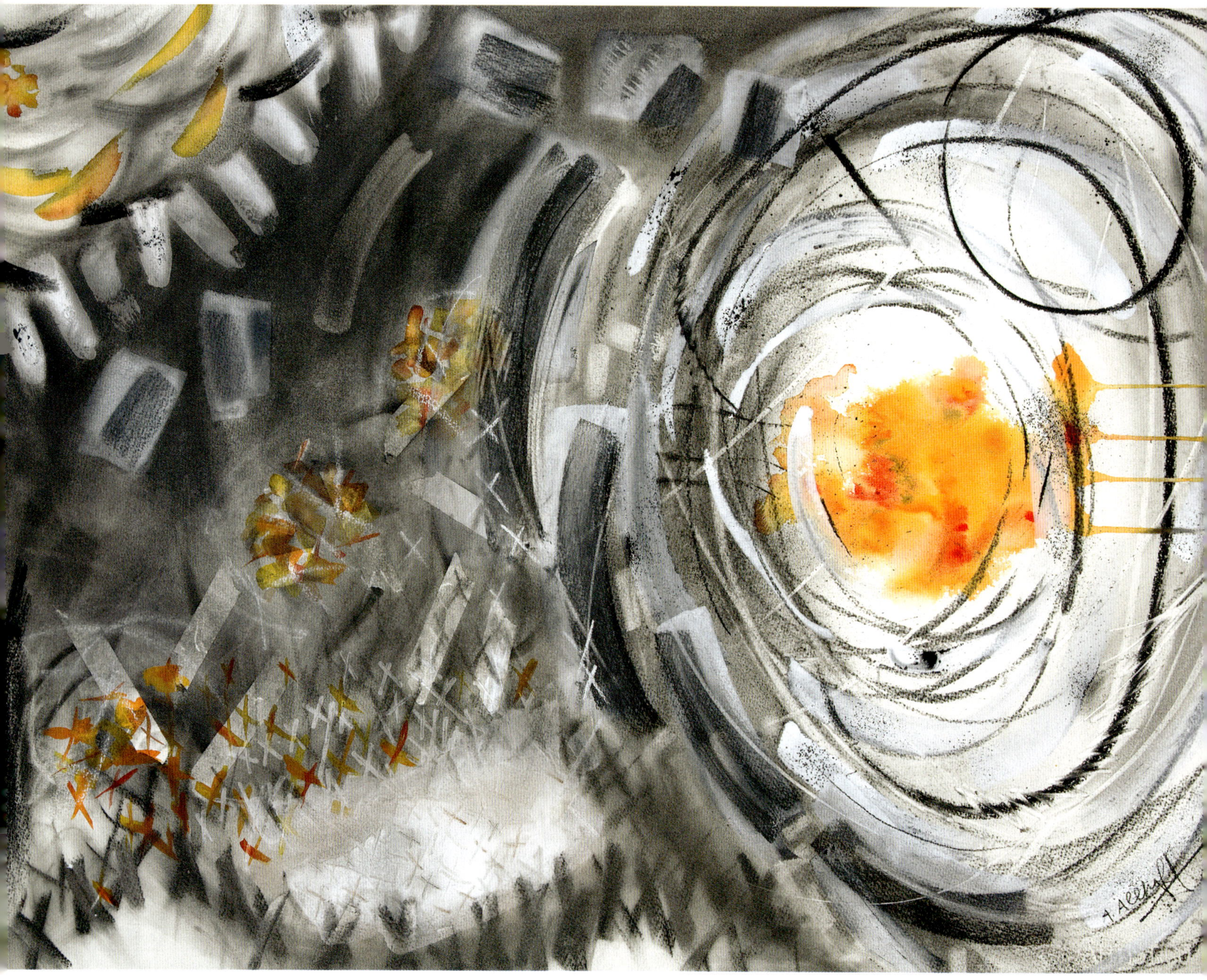

Stroke Play
Alice Allhoff · Charcoal with gesso and watercolor · 22" × 30" (56cm × 76cm)

LARGE MOVEMENTS MOVE YOUR VIEWER

Stroke Play began as a simple pencil sketch indicating the major movement and size of the strokes
and where the color or lighter areas would occur. Soft, rubbed charcoal tones support the broad
strokes of charcoal, eraser, tape and watercolor. The final thin/thick circular movements on the right
cast the viewer off into the composition and back again across a field of lighter areas and all those
xxXxXX's! I want to compel the viewer to visually walk around my work—to explore all the layers,
enjoy all the nuances.

Macho Machine
Clay McGaughy · Charcoal on watercolor paper · 15" × 19" (38cm × 48cm)

LET THE SUBJECT SUGGEST A TECHNIQUE

Sometimes the subject dictates the style. During a painting outing, this
parked road machine seemed a seething brute. I thought it deserved to
be treated as such, so I got out my vine charcoal and rough watercolor
paper and flailed away at it. Simple, small shots of raw color as a final
touch seemed indelicately appropriate for this resting roughneck.

Joan Lok · Ink on rice paper · 18" × 14" (46cm × 36cm)

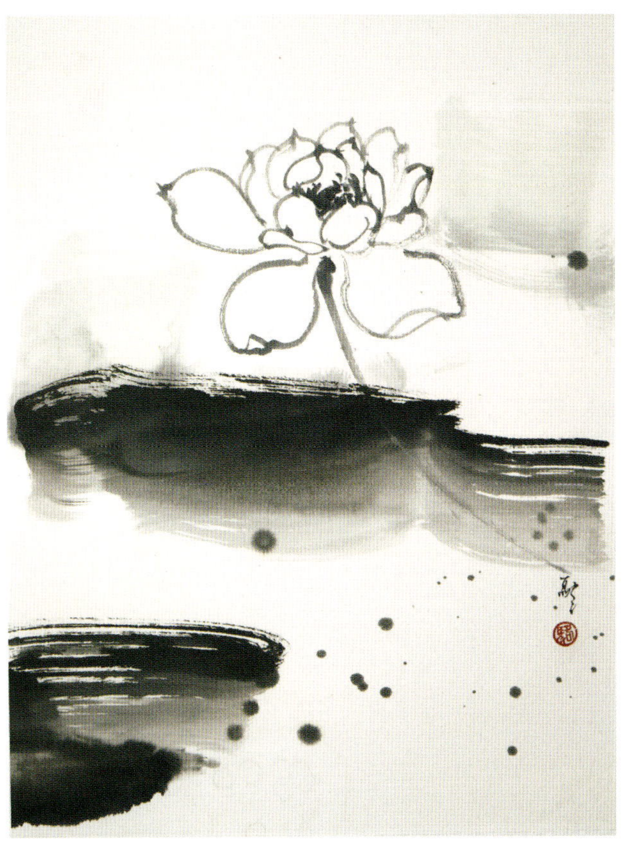

CONTROLLED CHINESE TECHNIQUES PRODUCE ELEGANCE

The lotus symbolizes purity and integrity. I try to capture the beauty and the "chi" (spirit) of the flower with a mixture of elegant and bold brushstrokes. To draw the soft petals, I held a round brush perpendicular to the paper, as if writing Chinese calligraphy. This technique, called "center stroke," allows maximum control to produce dance-like brush movement. For the lotus leaves, I changed to a 3" (76mm) hake brush and loaded it with dark and diluted ink. Quick brushwork produced "flying white," textured lines of surface untouched by the ink. Finally I splattered drops of ink to add visual interest to my minimal design.

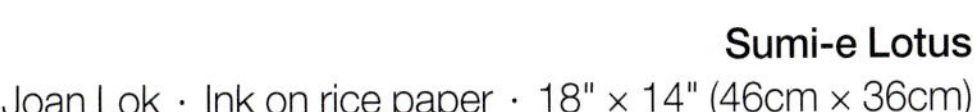

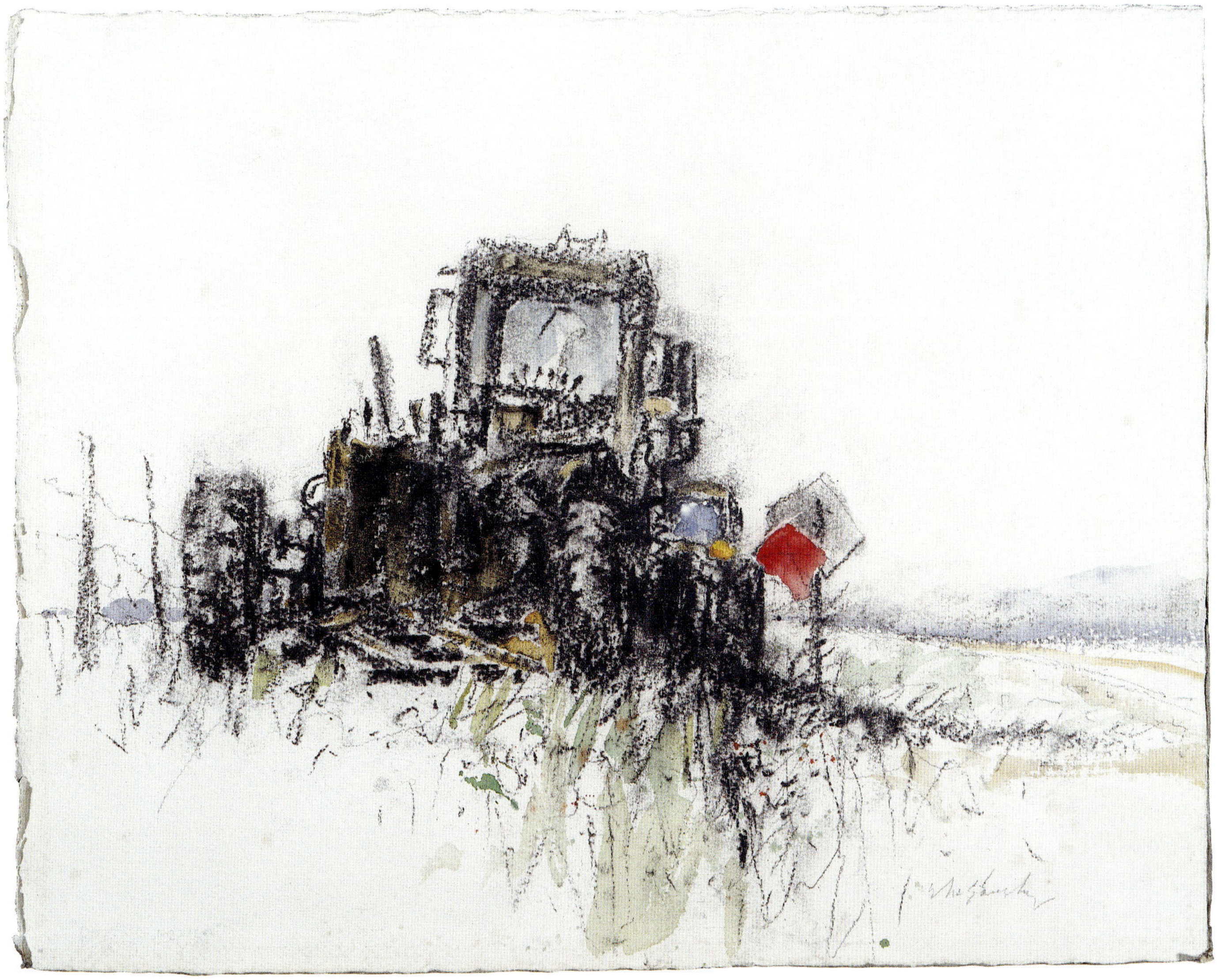

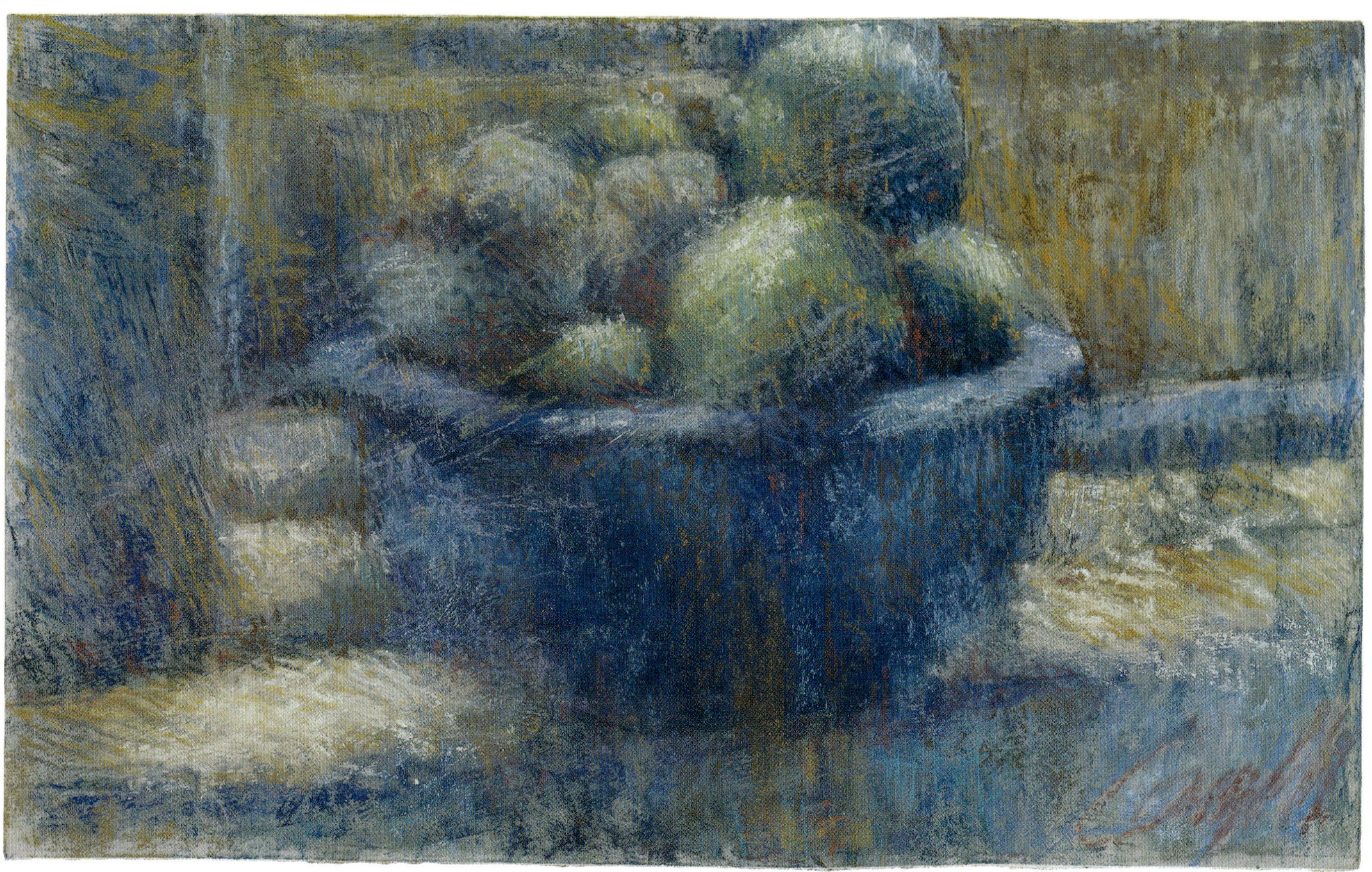

Blue Morning
Naomi Campbell · Soft pastel on hand-prepared board · 10" × 16" (25cm × 41cm)

Fluid, Organic Pastels Reflect Life

This was one of those spontaneous responses to a moment in time. The rush of early-morning light invaded my kitchen and my senses, and found me balancing my board and pastels delicately over a sink full of dirty dishes as everyone slept. The in-depth exploration of surface is influenced by my work with sculpture and printmaking. I have done years of color study, and I choose pastels because their mark-making process encourages expressions of light over form and treatment of space. The fluid, organic nature of the work reflects my understanding of life.

My work reflects the **CYCLICAL NATURE** of life on our planet. *Blue Morning* suggests how the **SPARKLING LIGHT** of early morning promises a hopeful future.

-Naomi Campbell

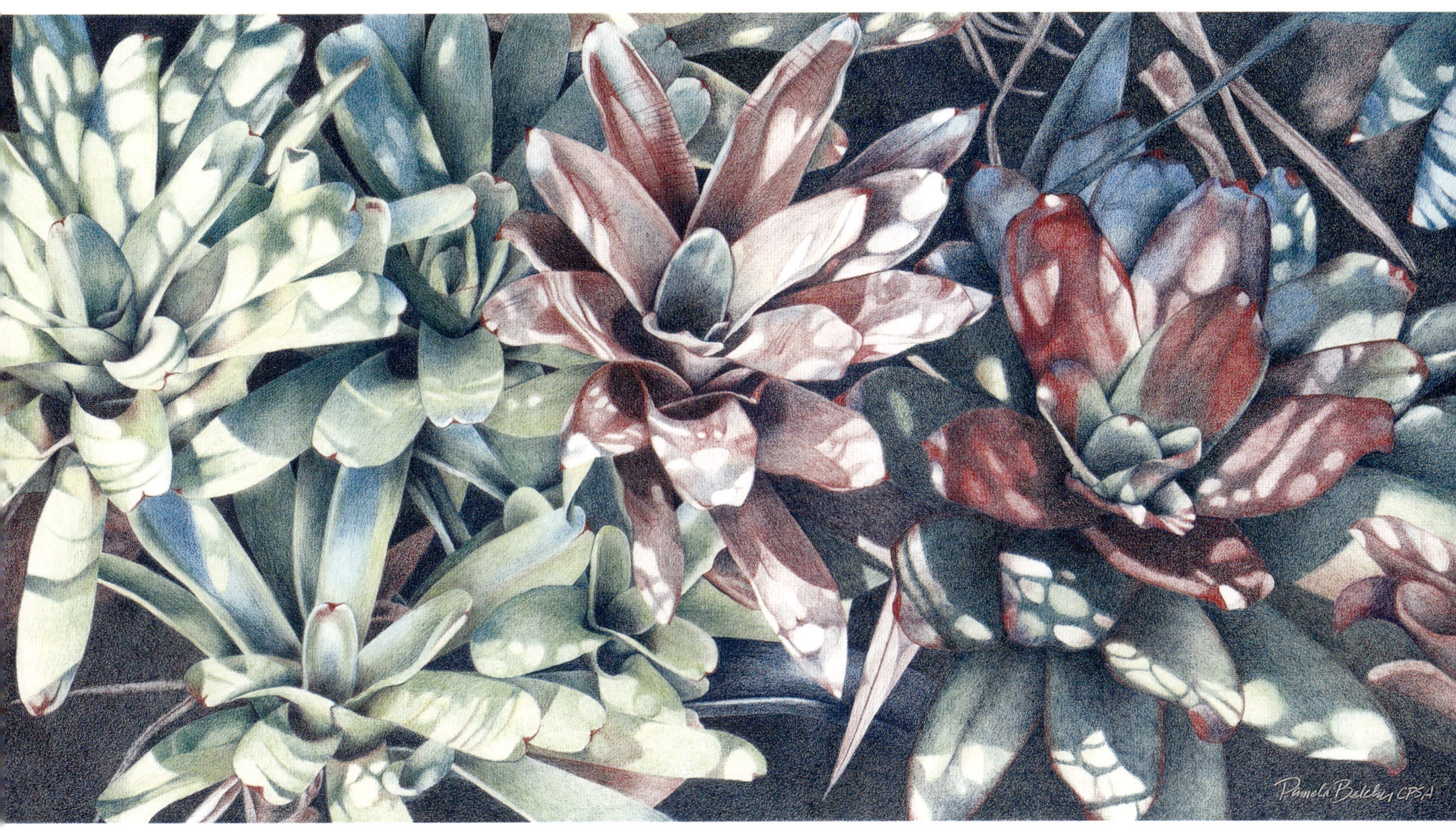

Sunspots
Pamela Belcher · Colored pencil on white paper · 13" × 25" (33cm × 64cm)

TROPICAL PLANTS CALL FOR DEEP DARKS TO WHITE

Seeing Hawaii's abundant plant life for the first time was an astounding experience. The National Tropical Botanical Garden on Kauai held a plethora of spectacular, colorful specimens. These bromeliads were made more beautiful by the dappled sunlight playing on their already varied, native color. I worked from several photographs and rearranged some values. Even though the darks were deep, I used white paper for this piece to make sure the light areas sparkled.

As the sun falls through foliage, additional patterns of **LIGHT AND SHADOW, AND COLORS,** are thrown onto the already complex leaf shapes.

-Pamela Belcher

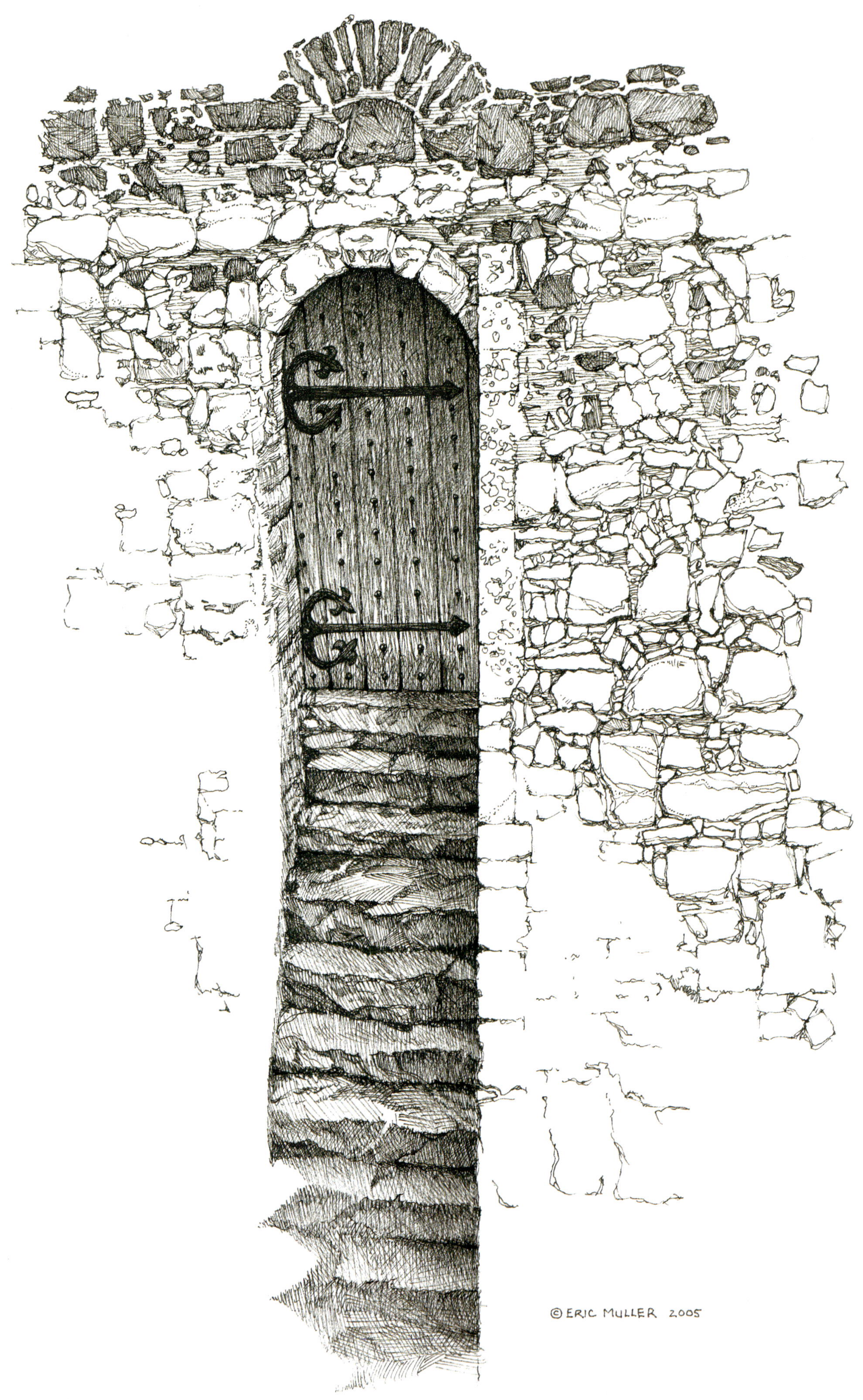

©ERIC MULLER 2005

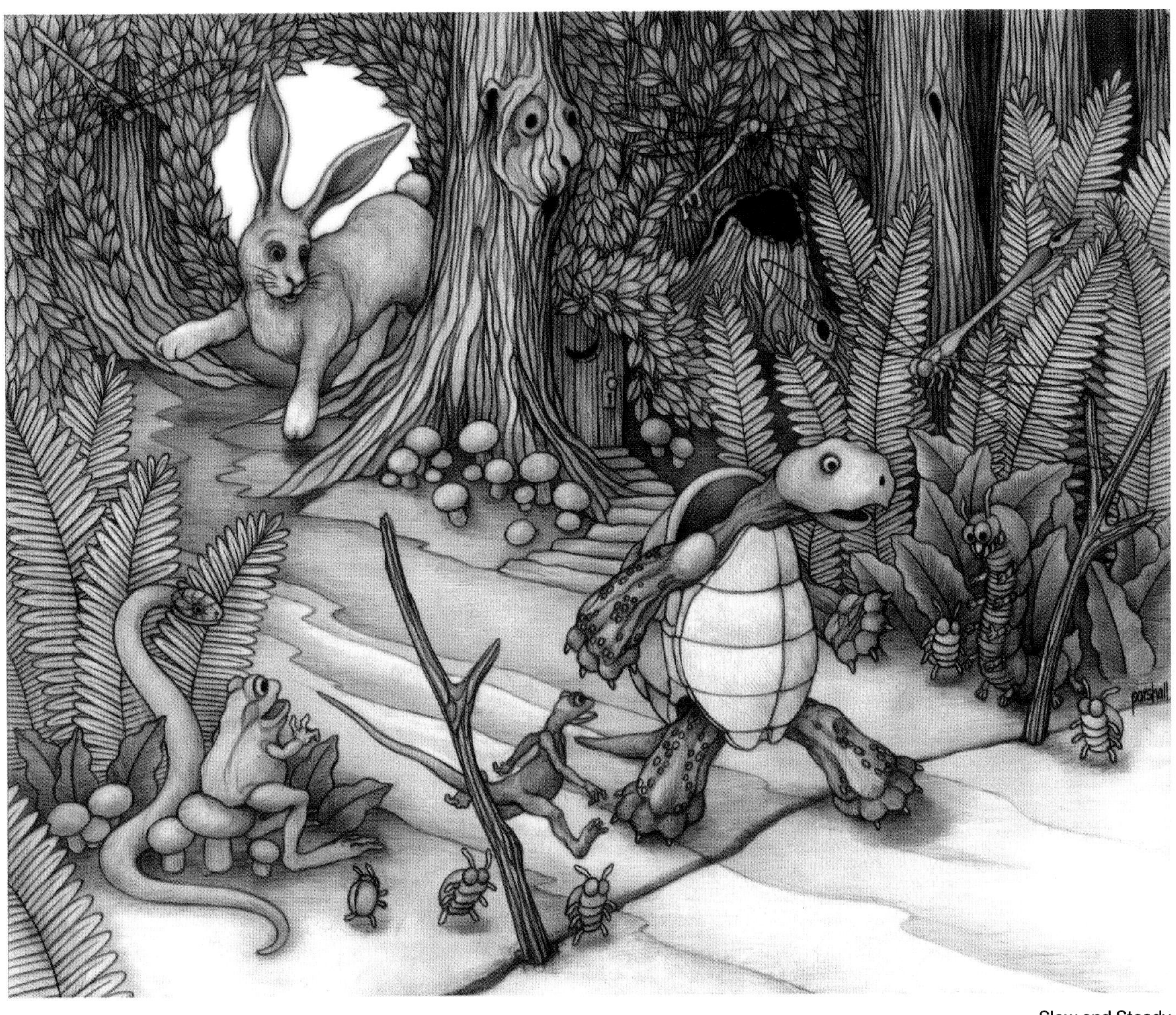

Slow and Steady
Glenn Parshall · Pencil · 14" × 17" (36cm × 43cm)

CHALLENGE YOURSELF TO COMPOSE AN IMAGINARY SCENE

To win a race.... The moral to this story was the inspiration behind my vision for *Slow and Steady*. I wanted to portray an imaginary scene; after the initial concept was developed, the overall composition took shape as work progressed. I applied several layers of line and crosshatch to refine details and shaded with softer leads to define contrast. I finished the drawing by carefully using an eraser to enhance highlights.

The Back Stair
Eric R. Muller · Pen and ink on bristol with smooth finish · 14" × 11" (36cm × 28cm)

IMAGINATION ADDS A STORIED QUALITY

This piece was done from a photograph of an old castle taken by a friend in Ireland. I was at once attracted to the rich textures of the aged materials on this ancient structure. They lent themselves to crosshatching and varied weight line work to give the structure an aging organic character.

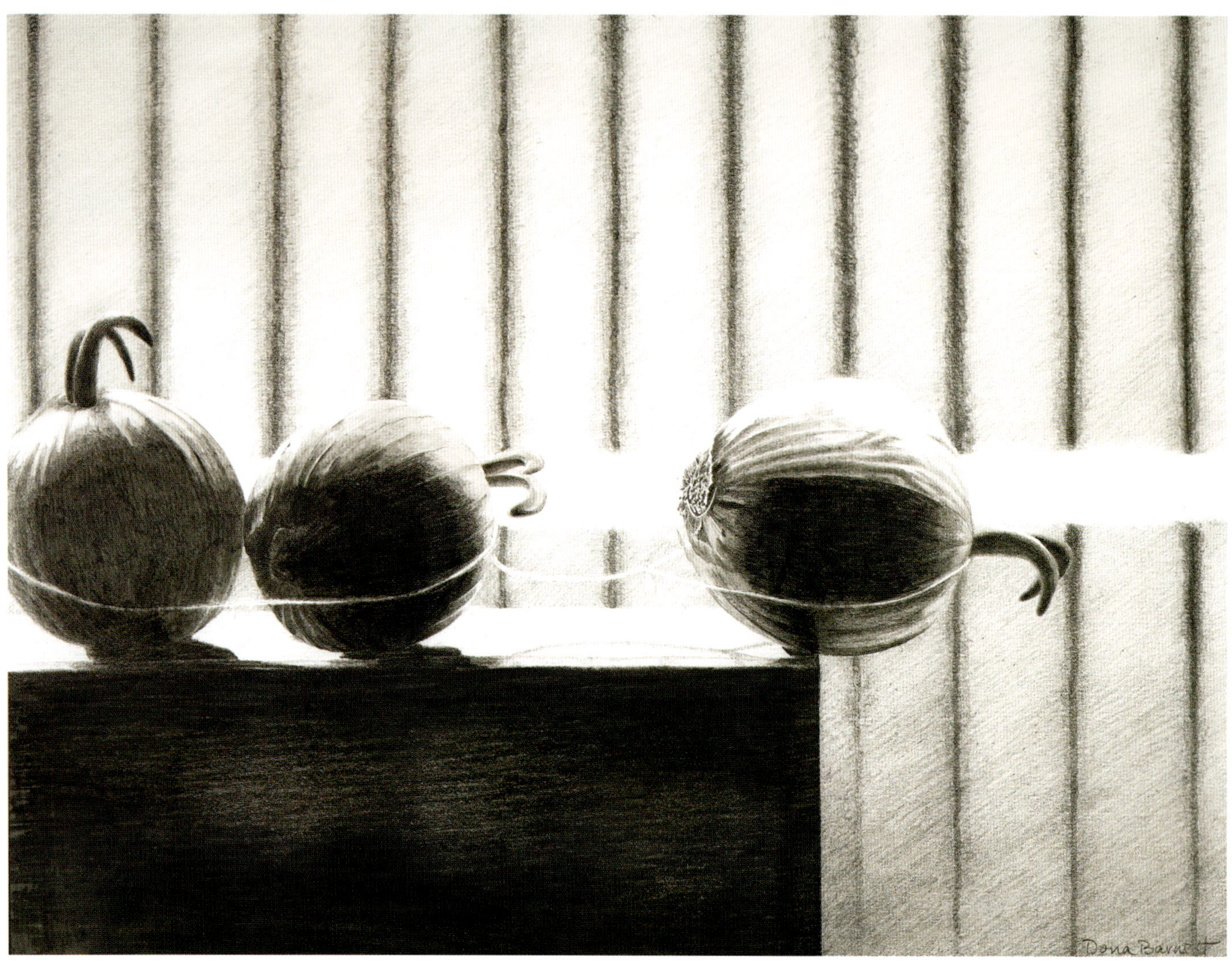

Wait
Dona D. Barnett · Graphite pencil on paper · 12" × 16" (30cm × 41cm)

Symbolism Adds Meaning to Still Life

Sadly, this drawing is about an acquaintance who struggled with depression. The onions, representing the many layers of human struggle, are all the same one, drawn from both life and photographs. Tension is created by positioning one onion on a block the moment before it tips over the edge. The downward pull is emphasized by several elements, including vertical lines, varying values and subtle reflections. The direction of the sprouts in each drawing, as well as the downward tilt, emphasize movement away from the band of white light, a symbol of hope in the true and living God.

By keeping the whites pure and clean of any graphite, the **LIGHT** looks all the brighter. Conversely, varying the values from **MIDTONES** to the **DEEPEST BLACK** serves to enrich the **SHADOW.**

-Dona D. Barnett

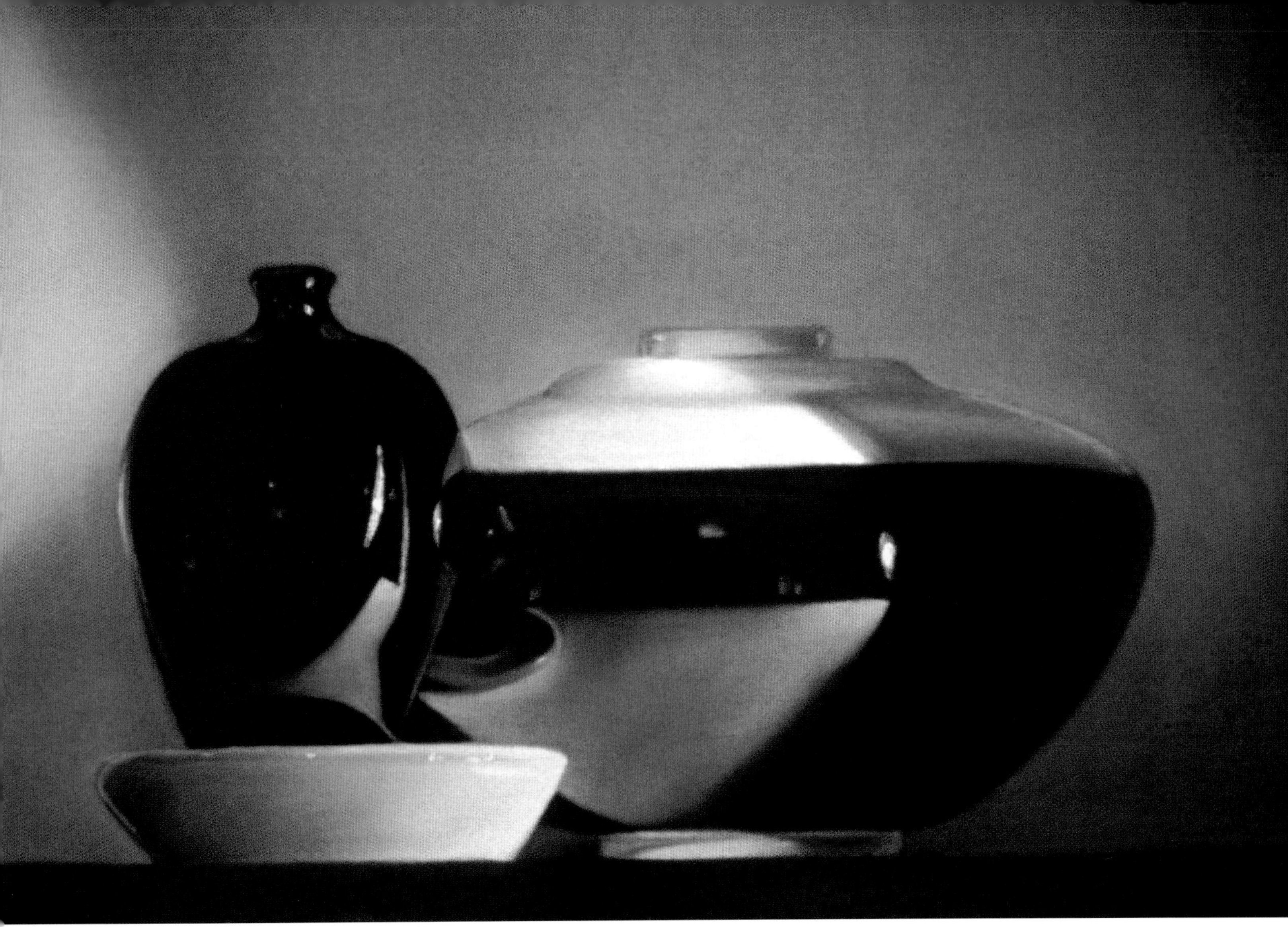

Light Washed
Nicora Gangi · Black and White Conté on antique white paper · 14" × 17" (36cm × 43cm)

RENEW YOUR VALUES WITH STRONG LIGHTS AND DARKS

The drawing was executed from life in my studio. An initial outline of the forms was done with vine charcoal. Afterward, I applied the Conté, first the whites and then the darks. These two values were blended to achieve the middle tones. I was motivated at this point in my career to return to a very limited palette, to reorient my eye to the lusty and spirited character of value. These types of exercises contribute to my works in color that expresses a strong spiritual light for the viewer's deeper contemplation.

Underlying all of my work is a
TRANSCENDENT LIGHT,
A TONAL SYSTEM, which compels
the viewer to look deeper.
-Nicora Gangi

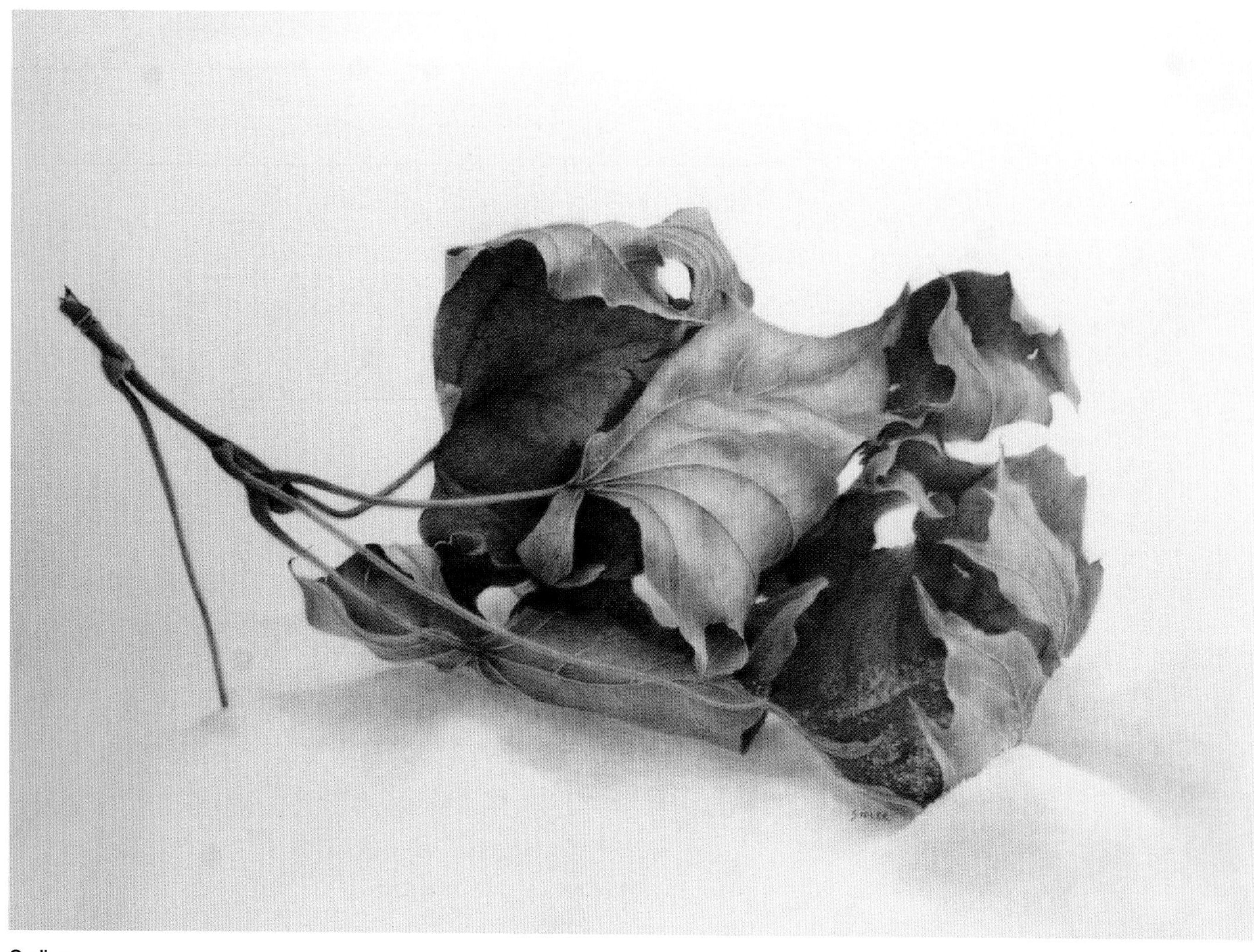

Curling
Nan Sidler · Graphite on paper · 12" × 18" (30cm × 46cm)

RENDER TONES WITH A RANGE OF PENCILS

Simple objects in nature provide unlimited beauty and inspiration. Working from the actual leaves that I brought into my studio, as well as a digital photo taken on location, I began *Curling* by drawing a cartoon of the image. I transferred this to Stonehenge using tracing paper. After redefining all the edges, including those in the shadows, I rendered the tones using a series of pencils from 2H to 8B. Pencils were kept needle sharp, especially in the final stages, which were done with a 2H pencil. Soft, lost edges were developed throughout the image by using a small stomp and a soft cat-tongue brush. A kneadable eraser was useful in lifting out, while a mol stick kept my hand from smudging the image as I worked.

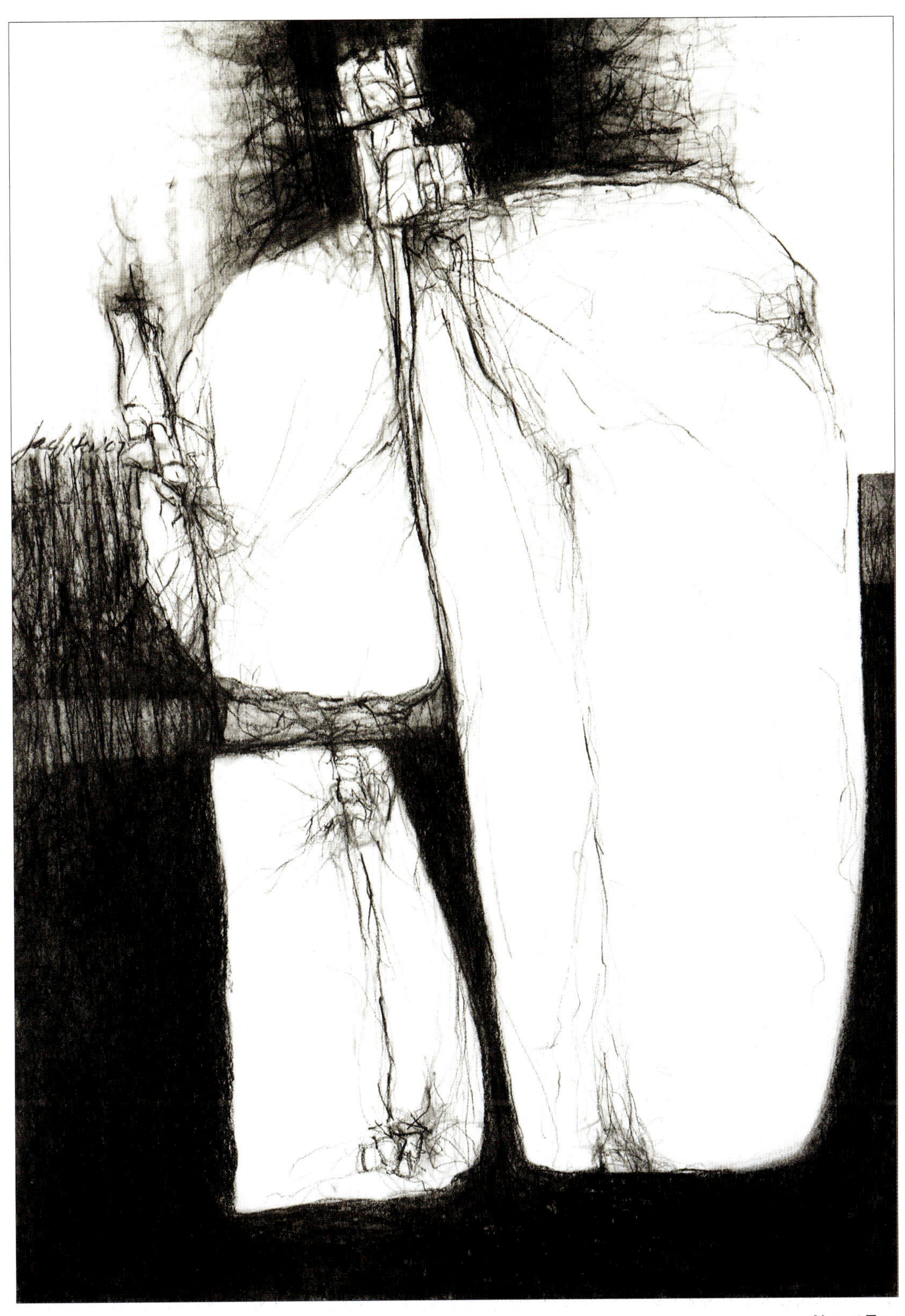

Ajax at Troy
Jac Tilton · Carbon, charcoal and graphite on paper · 13" x 9¼" (33cm × 23cm)

SMEAR, SMUDGE AND ERASE YOUR WAY TO TEXTURES

My nonobjective works begin as a continuous line doodle. Finishing the work
is strictly process driven. It involves smearing, smudging, erasing and adding
additional line/value until an interesting combination of values, textures and
shapes is achieved. A variety of materials—cotton balls, paper towels, paper
stomps and cotton swabs—are used to create smears and blends. A similar
variety of erasers, hard and soft, is used to create and restore highlights and
develop textures. Some of the most interesting areas result from partially
erasing an area and then adding and erasing line/value again, creating a kind
of veil or layers of texture and value.

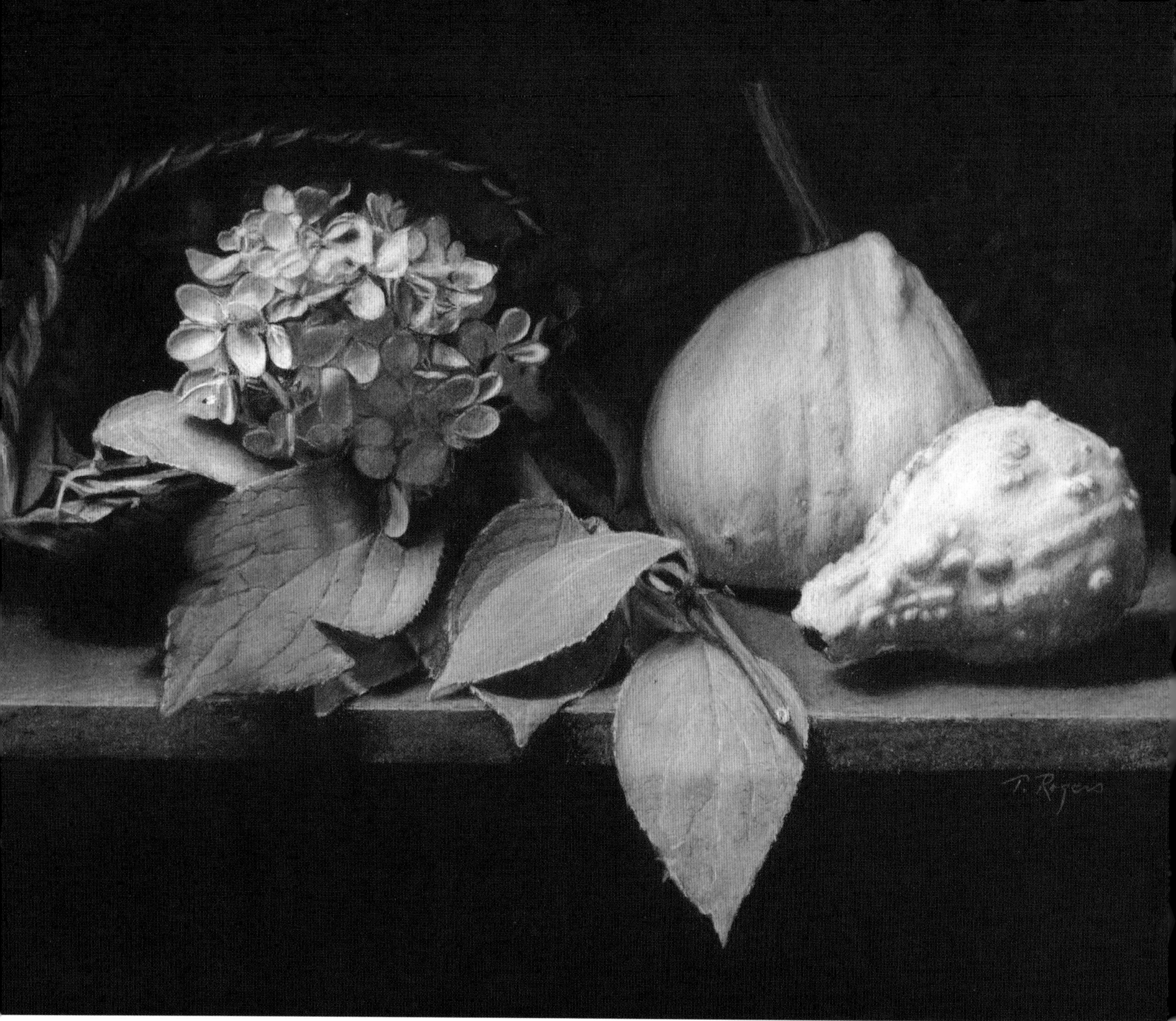

Hydrangea
Terese Rogers · Charcoal on paper · 8" × 10" (20cm × 25cm)

CONTRASTING TEXTURE AND SHAPE ADDS INTEREST

Knowing that I wanted to portray hydrangeas from my garden, my husband and I visited a local farm, looking for something of interest to complete the composition. The gourds that we found added contrasting texture and shape. I worked from life and photographs in a studio setting. I began with a simple charcoal sketch of the composition and then concentrated on small areas to capture the varying values in a realistic manner.

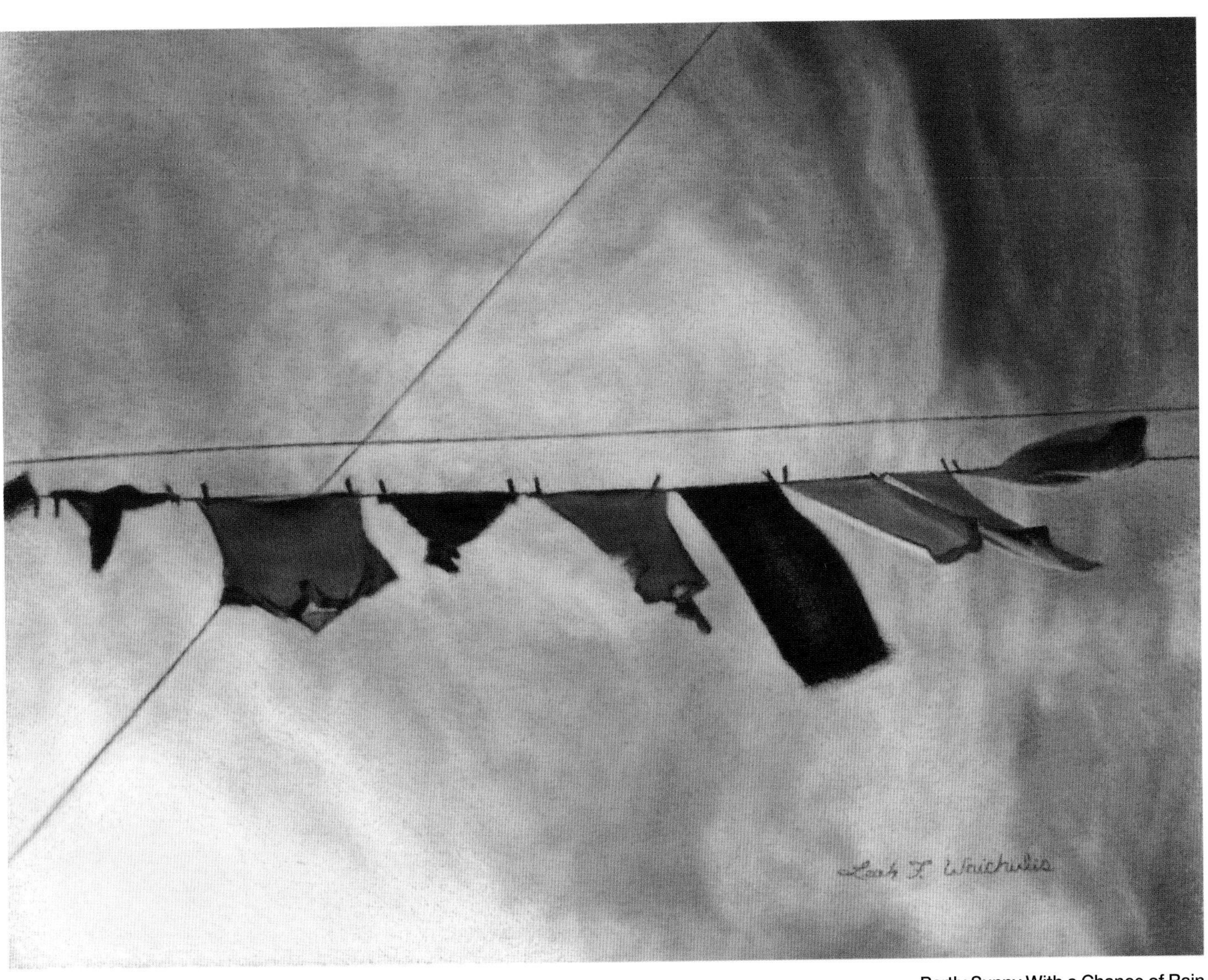

Partly Sunny With a Chance of Rain
Leah F. Waichulis · Charcoal on paper · 6" × 7¼" (15cm × 18cm)

A New Viewpoint on Laundry Day

Partly Sunny With a Chance of Rain is a charcoal drawing based on a photograph I took while lying
on the ground looking up at the sky. I began with a simple line drawing and slowly blocked in the
values of the laundry and then the clouds. I began to refine the shapes and add subtle detail. When
I was satisfied with the amount of detail, I went over the entire artwork and softened certain areas,
like the sky, to make sure the picture worked well as a whole and conveyed an interesting mood.
I enjoyed trying to capture the contrast between things man-made and nature, and the movement of
the swirling sky and billowing laundry.

Emphasizing **CONTRASTS,** whether in
theory or technique, can provide added
INTEREST AND DRAMA.
-Leah F. Waichulis

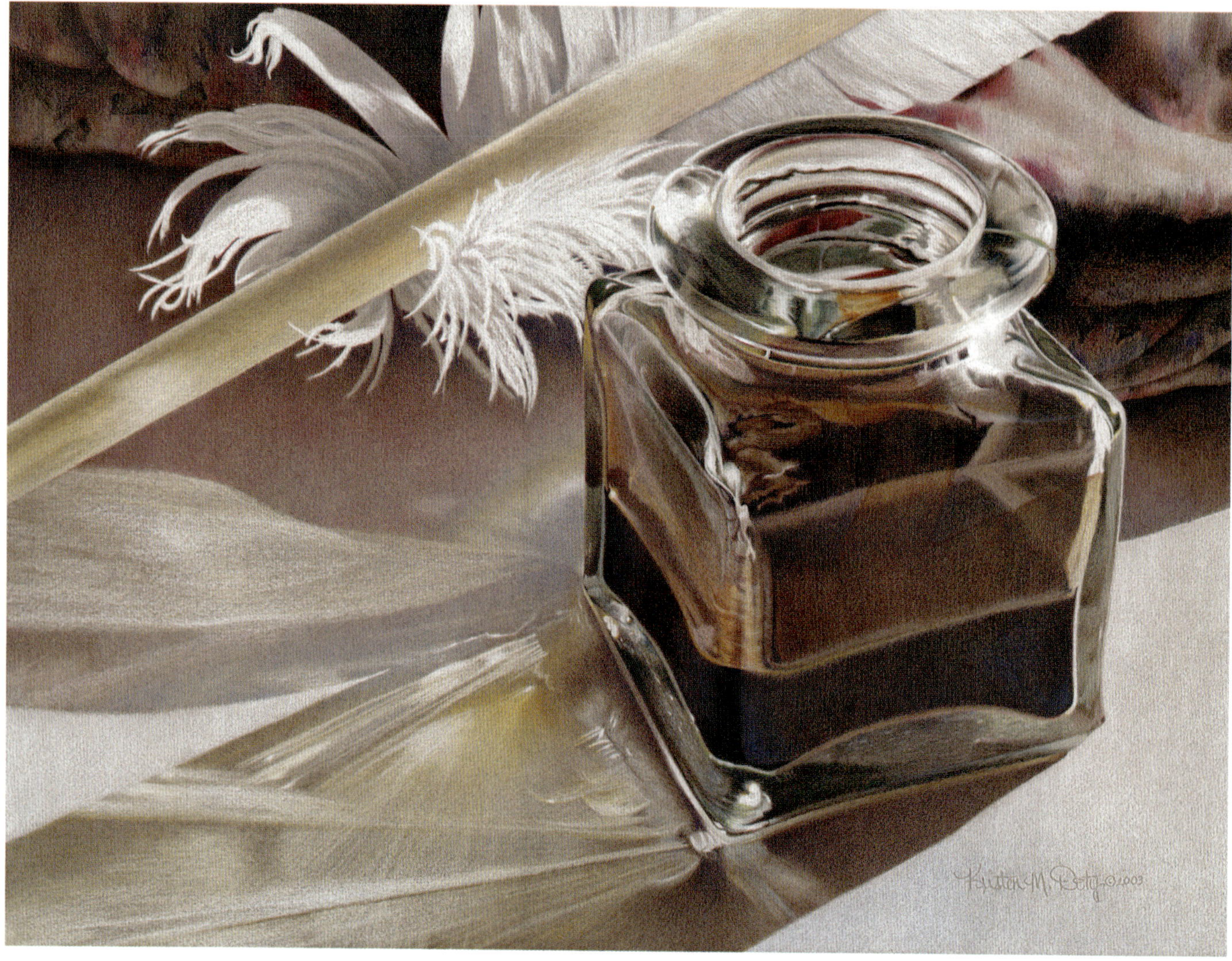

Half Full
Kristen M. Doty · Colored pencil and white charcoal on gray-colored paper · 14¼" × 19" (36cm × 48cm)

White Charcoal Enhances White Colored Pencil

Calligraphy is a passion of mine, so I found this inspiration in my studio. Working from photographs and the actual objects, I made a detailed drawing on tracing paper and transferred it to Canson Mi-Teintes paper (felt gray) with Saral white transfer paper. Because the white, wax-based colored pencil lacked the intensity I was trying to achieve for the highlights, I first applied a layer of white charcoal pencil in those areas and then used the wax-based white colored pencil on top, effectively sealing the charcoal. Then I gradually built up layers of colors and value using colored pencils with a sharp point.

Do a Drawing on a Washed-Off Watercolor

Working from life, I painted a pot of blooming bulbs on 300-lb. (640gsm) watercolor paper. This painting sat in my studio until one day I decided to wash the paint off in the kitchen sink. The remaining ghost of the image inspired me to apply charcoal, Conté crayon, ink and gouache to redefine both the negative and positive shapes of the flowers, stems and bowl. I used black gouache textured with charcoal to create deep space and gold gesso to unify the remainder of the background. There is a wonderful sense of freedom when you allow yourself to choose whatever tool seems right at the moment—including the kitchen sink.

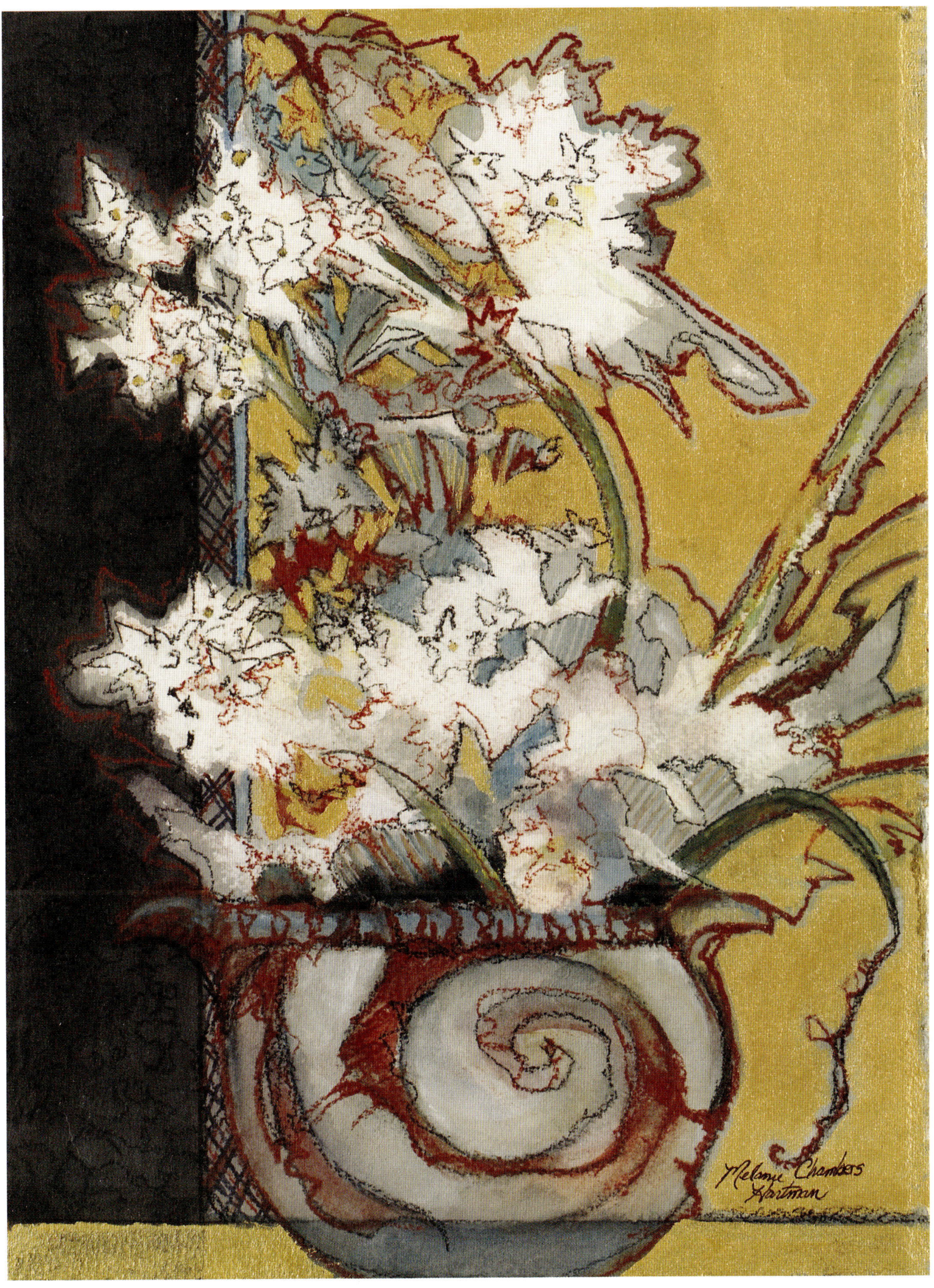

Paperwhites

Melanie Chambers Hartman · Charcoal, Conté crayon, ink and mixed watermedia (gold gesso and gouache) on watercolor paper · 15¼" × 11½" (39cm × 29cm)

CONTRIBUTORS

Dennis Albetski
P.O. Box 166
Rochdale, MA 01542
dalbetskiart@yahoo.com
www.DennisAlbetski.com
p. 13 *Bethany*
p. 60 *Catnap*

Paul R. Alexander
Greenville, Ohio
p. 82 *Kneeling Male Figure*

Alice Allhoff
25312 Ursuline
St. Clair Shores, MI 48081
(586) 772-9623
aliceallhoff@aol.com
p. 124 *Stroke Play*

Justin Balliet
202 Hughes St.
Berwick, PA 18603
justbarts@yahoo.com
www.thewaichulisstudio.net
p. 16 *Paulina*

Dona D. Barnett
Fairview, North Carolina
dona@donabarnett.com
www.donabarnett.com
p. 130 *Wait*

Elaine L. Bassett
Stanwood, Washington 98292-9729
elaine@courtingfrogs.com
p. 105 *February Landscape*

Pamela Belcher
Kenmore, Washington
pam@pamelabelcher.com
www.pamelabelcher.com
p. 80 *Painting Partner*
p. 127 *Sunspots*

Robin Berry
(612) 824-5488
tabetberrystudio@comcast.net
www.natureartists.com/robin_berry.asp
p. 52 *Reddish Egrets Canopy Feeding*
p. 52 *Egret on the Move*

Candace Brancik
980 Hickory Ridge Circle
Milford, MI 48380
(248) 685-3032
cbrancik@yahoo.com
www.thepixelcollective.com/cbrancik
p. 53 *Raven 2*

Robert L. Caldwell
5816 Laurel Trail Court
Midlothian, VA 23112
(804) 639-7604
robert@rlcaldwell.com
www.rlcaldwell.com
p. 51 *Lookout (Black-Capped Chickadee)*
p. 51 *Your Majesty (Black Vulture)*

Naomi Campbell
177 7th Ave. #3L
Brooklyn, NY 11215
(917) 754-7349
campbellnao@aol.com
www.naomicampbelltheartist.com
p. 126 *Blue Morning*

Nicole Caulfield
17 Roxbury St. #7
(603) 852-0040
nicolecaulfield@gmail.com
www.nicolecaulfield.com
p. 10 *Katie: Defiance*

Devin Cecil-Wishing
(415) 290-8953
d@devincecil-wishing.com
www.devincecil-wishing.com
p. 15 *Preliminary Drawing for Self-Portrait
With Django*

Stephen Cefalo
(501) 888-5075
stephencefalo@sbcglobal.net
www.stephencefalo.com
p. 14 *Self-Portrait With Paintbrush*

Anne Chaddock
5 Hunting Ridge Rd.
Manakin-Sabot, VA 23103
(804) 740-1400
forartssakegallery@comcast.net
www.forartssakegallery.com
p. 87 *She Loves*

Helen Crispino
P.O. Box 224
Dalton, PA 18414
(570) 563-1254
hcrispinoart@gmail.com
www.thewaichulisstudio.net
p. 67 *Olivia*

Joseph Crone
40 N. Shamrock Rd.
Hartford City, IN 47348
(317) 353-4014
josephcrone@hotmail.com
www.josephcroneart.com
p. 91 *Lower Your Eyelids*

Alina Dabrowska
822 - 3130 - 66 Ave. SW
Calgary, AB T3E 5K8
Canada
(403) 249-7008
eva4265@shaw.ca
p. 45 *Louvre Museum, Paris*

Susan C. D'Amico
2994 Spinnaker Dr.
Bandon, OR 97411
(541) 347-4482
hollywoodsmiles@mindspring.com
bellalunaportraits.com
p. 122 *French Greys*

Mina dela Cruz
minad1@sympatico.ca
www.minadelacruz.com
p. 11 *Spencer*

Marina Dieul
(514) 561-2098
marinadieul@yahoo.ca
www.marinadieul.blogspot.com
p. 85 *Somme*

Christine E. S. Dion
174 Long Pond Brook Way
Manchester, NH 03109
(603) 494-1904
christine@christinedion.com
www.christinedion.com
p. 54 *Doc of Dock Square*

Kristen M. Doty
P.O. Box 302
Chehalis, WA 98532
contactkd@kristendoty.com
www.kristendoty.com
p. 136 *Half Full*

Michelle Dunaway
P.O. Box 91436
Albuquerque, NM 87199
(818) 269-7482
mdunawaystudio@aol.com
www.dunawayfineart.com
p. 72 *5-Minute Quick Sketch From Life*
p. 73 *5-Minute Quick Sketch From Life*

Dawn Emerson
3259 N.E. Wilcox Ave.
Terrebonne, OR 97760
(541) 504-8905
emerson@ykwc.net
www.dawnemerson.com
p. 55 *Circus Horse #1*

Marti Fast
P.O. Box 7157
Halcyon, CA 93421-7157
(805) 489-2665
martifast@sbcglobal.net
p. 82 *Acrobat*
p. 83 *Dancer I: Tired Feet*

Michael J. Felber
670 Adelma Beach Rd.
Port Townsend, WA 98368
(360) 385-0202
wetdog@cablespeed.com
www.michaeljfelber.com
p. 56 *Galloping Burchell's Zebra*
p. 56 *Carpenter Bee*
p. 57 *Honeybee*

Susan Gallacher
2233 South 700 East
Salt Lake City, UT 84106
(801) 486-5019
sgallaart@yahoo.com
www.susangallacher.com
p. 21 *Cassandra's Ponytail*

Nicora Gangi
218 Buckingham Ave.
Syracuse, NY 13210
(315) 289-3413
nmanwari@twcny.rr.com
www.machairastudio.com
p. 131 *Light Washed*

Bob Gerbracht
1301 Blue Oak Court
Pinole, CA 94564
(510) 741-8518
bgerbracht@sbcglobal.net
www.bobgerbracht.com
p. 23 *Jennings*

Don Getz
1239 W. Hines Hill
Peninsula, OH 44264
(330) 657-2807
digetzbgolly@hotmail.com
www.watercolor-online.com/DonGetz
p. 100 *Roadhouse*
p. 101 *Roaring Brook Falls*

Douglas Gillette
Enfield, Connecticut
(860) 763-3766
dougbeth@cox.net
www.douggillette.com
p. 112 *Winter Passage*

David Gluck
(416) 767-3183
david.gluck@gmail.com
www.davidgluckart.com
p. 79 *Mikaela*
p. 114 *Invented Landscape*

George Guzzi
11 Randlett Park
West Newton, MA 02465
(617) 244-2932
guzzifamily@verizon.net
p. 77 1910 *Champions*

Lane Hall
4608 Eagle Trace Dr.
Medford, OR 97504
(541) 261-7986
lanehallart@gmail.com
www.lanehall.com
p. 87 *Emily at Piano*
p. 113 *Torn*

David Hardy
Founder & Director, the Atelier School of
 Classical Realism, Oakland
dnshardy@yahoo.com
www.davidhardy.net
www.atelierschoolofclassicalrealism.net
p. 12 *Classical Bust*
p. 13 *Head of Arturo*

Melanie Chambers Hartman
110 Winders Lane
Yorktown, VA 23692
(757) 898-3706
melanie_hartman@cox.net
www.melaniehartman.com
p. 137 *Paperwhites*

Mary Ann Henderson
19880 Lark Way
Saratoga, CA 95070
(408) 354-4622
p. 106 *Montague Harbour*
p. 106 *Point Pinos Lighthouse*
p. 107 *High Tide*

Connie Herberg
8556 Razor Creek Rd.
Shepherd, MT 59079
(406) 373-5513
c_raedesign@yahoo.com
p. 93 *Inanna*

Debbie Hughbanks
3734-F N. Deer Lake Rd.
Loon Lake, WA 99148
(509) 233-9352
debbie@hughbanksart.com
www.hughbanksart.com
p. 59 *Elegance In Grey*

Helen C. Iaea
95-319 Waianuhea Pl.
Mililani, HI 96789
(808) 225-0711
artinparadise4u@aol.com
www.brushstrokeshawaii.com
p. 81 *Sumo Series #9*

Bill James
509 N.W. 35th St.
Ocala, FL 34475
(352) 694-8080
artistbilljames@earthlink.net
www.artistbilljames.com
p. 27 *Jupiter Cowboy*

David F. Kelley
22 Amherst Ave.
Falmouth, MA 02540
(508) 457-1183
dfkelley@pair.com
www.davidkelleydesign.com
p. 103 *Windy Green Pond*

Wanda Kemper
(925) 691-5030
kwkemper@msn.com
www.portraitartist.com/kemper
p. 81 *Sunday Morning Breakfast*

Elisa Khachian
artistelisa@optonline.net
p. 76 *Beauties*

Yvonne Kozlina
1922 Wharton St.
Pittsburgh, PA 15203
(412) 780-0727
ykozlina@comcast.net
yvonne@yvonnekozlina.com
www.yvonnekozlina.com
p. 24 *All Dressed Up*

Donna Krizek
www.artistsregister.com/artists/co1159
p. 5 *Bonnie*
p. 48 *Spirit Guide*
p. 49 *Preliminary Charcoal for Sam & Cody*
p. 50 *Maggie Pup*
p. 97 *Emilee Mae & MacCayla*

Carol Kummer
33 Mandana Circle
Oakland, CA 94610
(510) 268-9429
cakummer@comcast.net
p. 118 *Rob 4*

Donna Levinstone
1623 3rd Ave., Apt. 22F
New York, NY 10128
(212) 348-9664
(917) 459-3617
levinstone@hotmail.com
www.donnalevinstone.com
p. 115 *Evening Reflection*

Bryce Cameron Liston
4391 Wander Lane
Salt Lake City, UT 84124
(810) 277-7679
bcameron@listonart.com
www.listonart.com
p. 74 *May*

Sandra Lo
sandra.lo@comcast.net
www.sandralo.com
p. 30 *Thinking*

Joan Lok
P.O. Box 6271
Columbia, MD 21045
(410) 730-7597
joan@radiantbrush.com
www.radiantbrush.com
p. 125 *Sumi-e Lotus*

Joseph Lotz
Loganville, Georgia
www.joelotz.com
p. 108 *Away From the Things of Man*
p. 109 *Wanderer*

Wei Lu
9728 Kingsbridge Dr., #104
Fairfax, VA 22031
luweixx@hotmail.com
p. 31 *Self-Portrait*

Larry R. Mallory
686 Fire Tower Rd.
Glen Campbell, PA 15742
(814) 845-7854
p. 46 *Times Past*

David Mar
www.david-mar.blogspot.com
p. 44 *Clay St. and Waverly*
p. 94 *Terry Koch Study #1*

Ann James Massey
4, rue Auguste Chabrières
Paris, France 75015
(33) 1-75-51-72-45
ajmassey@annjamesmassey.com
www.annjamesmassey.com
p. 96 *The Woodworker*

D. Matzen
P.O. Box 13
Clinton, WA 98236
debobon2001@yahoo.com
www.womenpainters.com/BIO/BioSet.html
p. 102 *Fenghuang Ruin—Hunan, P. R. China*

Candy Mayer
1317 Tierra Roja
El Paso, TX 79912
(915) 581-4971
cc2ccmayer@aol.com
www.candymayer.com
p. 34 *Downtown Architecture*
p. 35 *Guadalajara Cathedral*

Paul W. McCormack
P.O. Box 537
Glenham, NY 12527
pwmccormack@aol.com
www.paulwmccormack.com
www.mccormackstudios.com
p. 33 *Julianna & Charlotte*

Laurin McCracken
777 Main St.
Fort Worth, TX 76102
(817) 773-2163
laurinmc@aol.com
www.lauringallery.com
p. 111 *Sunset, Town Center, Napflion, Greece*

Clay McGaughy
215 Morse
San Antonio, TX 78209
patsyclay@sbcglobal.net
p. 125 *Macho Machine*

Michael Allen McGuire
1007 Calle Margarita
Santa Fe, NM 87507
(505) 471-5733
vistaman@earthlink.net
www.home.earthlink.net/~vistaman/
p. 104 *Swamp Marsh—Gulfport, Mississippi*
p. 104 *Barn at Lithopolis, Ohio*

James G. Meeks
Oklahoma City, Oklahoma
(405) 521-8135
meeks-j@sbcglobal.net
p. 92 *Claudia #1*

Mark Meichelbock
5220 Medina Rd.
Woodland Hills, CA 91364
markmeichelbock@aol.com
www.markmeichelbock.com
p. 20 *Window Light*

Steve Mihal
mihalart@yahoo.com
p. 90 *Man in the Mirror*

Cristen Miller
San Francisco, California
cristenstarmiller@yahoo.com
www.cristenmiller.com
p. 75 *Quiet Rhythm*

Terry Miller
Maryland, USA
www.terrymillerstudio.com
p. 36 *Bones*
p. 37 *The Road Home*
p. 70 *Indian Summer*
p. 70 *Caucus*
p. 71 *Tiger Trail*

Cynthia C. Morris
19431 Eckles Rd.
Sedalia, MO 65301
(660) 826-0312
www.cynthiacmorris.com
p. 120 *Undercover Spies*

Eric R. Muller
5919 Michaels Crossing
Orefield, PA 18069
e.p.muller@att.net
p. 128 *The Back Stair*

Susan Muranty
10 Monash Rd.
Gladesville
NSW 2111
Australia
011-61-2-9879-6910
susan@murantysculptor.com.au
www.murantysculptor.com.au
p. 18 *Jack*
p. 89 *Freedom (How I Feel When I Draw)*

Bruce J. Nelson
2823 Van Dyke Dr.
Centralia, WA 98531
(360) 736-0544
brucejnelson@sipnsearch.com
art-exchange.com
p. 61 *The Catch*

Eileen Nistler
P.O. Box 321
Upton, WY 82730
(307) 468-9270
eileenistler@netscape.net
Galleries: ArtForms Gallery (Hill City, SD),
Western Wings (Newcastle, WY)
p. 58 *Cute Chick With Hairy Legs*

Susan Obaza
408 E. Ridge St.
Nanticoke, PA 18634
(570) 735-8109
obazart@hotmail.com
www.obazart.net
p. 25 *Sara, Smile*

Kathleen O'Connell
5360 Singleton St.
Indianapolis, IN 46227
(317) 791-9628
koconne@iupui.edu
p. 63 *Requiem*

Edmond S. Oliveros
President, Oliveros & Friends —
   Design & Illustration
2112 Bishopsgate Dr.
Toledo, OH 43614
ofriends@aol.com
www.edmondoliveros.com
p. 38 *Self Promotion*
p. 39 *Reflections (Grand Central
   Terminal, NYC)*

Glenn Parshall
Monroe, Connecticut
jgparsh@charter.net
p. 129 *Slow and Steady*

Elizabeth Patterson
North Hollywood, California
patterson900@gmail.com
www.eapatterson.com
p. 40 *Victory Boulevard, 11pm*
p. 41 *Benedict Canyon, 5pm*

Tom Potocki
4377 Cloudmont Dr.
Hollywood, SC 29449
(843) 763-2481
potocki@bellsouth.net
p. 2, 26 *Face With Graffiti*

Pat Regan
120 W. Brainerd St.
Pensacola, FL 32501
patreganart@aol.com
www.patreganfineart.com
p. 7 *The Boxer*
p. 98 *Boxed In*
p. 99 *Testing the Waters*

John Reidy
1320 Whitworth Court
Kernersville, NC 27284
(336) 996-7966
jreidy@triad.rr.com
www.johnreidy.us
p. 19 *Karen*

Lucille Rella
PO Box 845
Sonoma, CA 95476
(707) 938-1809
lurella@sbcglobal.net
www.absolutearts.com/lurella
p. 42 *Playland*

Terese Rogers
DTMKD@aol.com
p. 134 *Hydrangea*

William Rogers
4 Carter Crescent
Antigonish, NS B2G 2S8
Canada
(902) 863-6797
billrogers@eastlink.ca
www.gapacc.ns.ca/williamrogers
p. 22 *Damon*

Janvier Rollande
jrollande@gmail.com
p. 17 *Portrait of Sage*
p. 84 *Adieu, Maman*

Lois I. Ryder
195 Main Rd.
Monterey, MA 01245
(413) 528-2548
p. 43 *Old Ironsides*

Kate Sammons
ks@katesammons.com
www.katesammons.com
p. 8 *My Mother*
p. 9 *American Winter*

Chris Saper
6622 N. 31 Place
Phoenix, AZ 85016
(602) 957-8107
chris@chrissaper.com
www.chrissaper.com
p. 28 *Spencer*

Kristine Sarsons
Sundre, AB
Canada
(403) 638-8136
info@kristinesarsons.com
www.kristinesarsons.com
p. 29 *What I See*

Donald Sayers
(303) 652-8052
donsayersart@q.com
p. 18 *Cirque*

Jaye Schlesinger
jayes@umich.edu
www.jayeschlesinger.com
p. 91 *Emily Reading*
p. 116 *Tape Dispenser*
p. 117 *Sheer Packaging*

Suzy Schultz
Atlanta, Georgia
(404) 687-0488
suzyschultz@mindspring.com
www.suzyschultz.net
p. 95 *Leaning Figure*

Jacqueline Hoats Shields
Detroit, Michigan
jackiehoats@yahoo.com
p. 119 *First Dress*

Aditya Shirké
22/7 Sakal Nagar, Baner Rd.
Pune, Maharashtra 411007
India
09120-25654587
adityashirke@gmail.com
p. 86 *Mukta Reading*

Nan Sidler
593 Homewood Ave.
Peterborough, ON K9H 2N4
Canada
(705) 743-6637
nansidler@hotmail.com
www.sidlerart.com
p. 132 *Curling*

Annette Smith
1942 E. Huber St.
Mesa, AZ 85203
smithers8734@yahoo.com
p. 88 *Female Back Study*

Katherine Stone
Toronto, Ontario
Canada
kate@katestoneart.com
www.katestoneart.com
p. 32 *Maddy*

Francis Edward Sweet
1402 Port Echo Lane
Bowie, MD 20716
(301) 249-6572
fesweet@comcast.net
www.francissweet.com
Agent: Patty Stewart, Bowie, MD
  (301) 805-9355
p. 68 *The Eyes Have It*

Sheila Theodoratos
1215 N.E. 168th St.
Shoreline, WA 98155
(206) 362-6442
sheilatheo@earthlink.net
www.womenpainters.com/bio/theodora-
  tos/theodoratos.htm
p. 121 *Self: In Progress*

George Thompson
5440 Old Easton Rd.
Doylestown, PA 18902
(215) 766-3892
thompsonstudio@comcast.net
www.georgethompsongallery.com
p. 93 *Tsana*

Jac Tilton
260 York St.
Dubuque, IA 52003
(563) 556-8053
jac@jactilton.com
p. 110 *Calender, IA*
p. 133 *Ajax at Troy*

Michael Todoroff
87 Margaret
Whitmore Lake, MI 48189
(734) 449-5413
todoroffmichael@hotmail.com
p. 69 *Heron Study*

France Tremblay
44 Langford Crescent
Kanata, ON K2K 2N5
Canada
(613) 271-9689
francetremblay900@yahoo.ca
www.francetremblay.com
p. 65 *Galapagos Tortoises*

Melissa B. Tubbs
327 Rose Lane
Montgomery, AL 36104-5638
(334) 538-7800
inkartist@knology.net
www.melissabtubbs.blogspot.com
p. 47 *Carnegie Hall, NYC*

Joe Velez
New Jersey
vqtlz@att.net
www.joevelezart.com
p. 78 *Carolina Reclining*

Myrna Wacknov
675 Matsonia Dr.
Foster City, CA 94404
(650) 574-3192
myrnawack@prodigy.net
www.myrnawacknov.com
www.myrnawacknov.blogspot.com
p. 29 *Self-Portrait With Dialogue*

Leah F. Waichulis
LeahFW@gmail.com
www.thewaichulisstudio.net
p. 135 *Partly Sunny With a Chance of Rain*

Randena B. Walsh
29027 Gamble Pl. N.E.
Kingston, WA 98346
(360) 297-7083
randena@yahoo.com
p. 62 *Golden-Crowned Kinglet*

Peggy Watkins
Atlanta, Georgia
art@peggywatkins.net
www.peggywatkins.net
p. 64 *Now You See Me…*

Sylvia Westgard
484 Forestway Dr.
Buffalo Grove, IL 60089
westgard484@comcast.net
p. 66 *Lion*

Steve Wilda
53 Rocky Hill Rd.
Hadley, MA 01035
(413) 584-8482
www.SteveWilda.com
p. 123 *Past the Destination*

Nancy J. Wulff
22780 Mercedes Rd.
Cupertino, CA 95014
(408) 255-0752
njwulff@att.net
www.gallery9losaltos.com
p. 89 *Dancer #1*

INDEX